Praise for *Dr*

"Throughout *Dream Town*, it's clea huge commitment to Shaker Height own biases. . . . Hers is a microappro equity by looking at how it's been handled over decades in one specific place—but it feels like she spoke with everyone and asked them everything." —***Star Tribune***

"[A] charming cast of characters who have tried very hard to solve the city's racial inequalities." —***The New Yorker***

"Reported with compassion, thoroughness and a keen sense of fairness and balance, Meckler's book explores the heroic and sometimes successful effort of one American community to move beyond the hatred and division that has led to racial segregation across most of the country. . . . It would be hard to add up all the ways in which Meckler's book is relevant to the current political and cultural moment." —***The Plain Dealer***

"Anyone interested in race in America will find Laura Meckler's brilliant book *Dream Town* impossible to put down." —**Andy Borowitz, *New York Times* bestselling author of *Profiles in Ignorance***

"Laura Meckler brilliantly explores the racial history of Shaker Heights, the Cleveland suburb where she grew up, to illuminate the troubled dynamics of integration in American life. *Dream Town* is at once a vividly drawn portrait and a significant sociological revelation." —**David Maraniss, Pulitzer Prize–winning author of *Once in a Great City***

"Through detailed research and interviews, Meckler tells a remarkable story about a town that continuously strives to achieve the ideals it long ago set for itself." —***Booklist* (starred review)**

"This is the story of one Ohio town—but also the much bigger story of America. Meckler brings great insight, depth, and wonderful humanity to this important chronicle of one city's grappling with race and the meaning of community. It is eminently readable and genuinely inspiring."   **—Susan Orlean, *New York Times* bestselling author of *The Orchid Thief* and *The Library Book***

"The work of diversity, integration, and equity is hard, messy, and divisive, and Shaker Heights has certainly gotten as much wrong over the years as it's gotten right. But it's only by learning the lessons of those victories and failures that we can construct the schools, communities, and society that we all hope to live in. This book, through rigorous reporting and stunning historical sweep, provides a vital step toward finding our path forward."

—Wesley Lowery, Pulitzer Prize–winning author of *American Whitelash*

"This is the complicated story of racial integration in Shaker Heights as it has never been told, deeply reported by one of its own. Laura Meckler brings a former resident's open heart and a journalist's laser focus to dreams realized and those too often deferred. As a journalist, I marvel at the depth of her reporting. As a former Shaker mom, I am grateful for the mirror that forces us to see the work that remains."

—Connie Schultz, Pulitzer Prize–winning author of *The Daughters of Erietown*

"Whether exploring the intricacies of race relations or delving into the complexities of modern-day identity politics, Meckler's ability to captivate and inform is unparalleled. This is a book for anyone who seeks to understand the past, engage with the present, and envision a better future for us all. An engrossing narrative."

—Jesse J. Holland, author of *Black Men Built the Capitol* and *The Invisibles*

"Laura Meckler's *Dream Town* is a brave and provocative book, breaking new ground in exploring difficulties facing Americans, Black and white, in reaching the goal of integrated schools and communities. Meckler has taken on one of the most important and vexing issues facing the nation, and she does not flinch. *Dream Town* is critical reading not only for those dealing with the politics of race but for everyone struggling to maintain a commitment to fairness, equality, and the achievement of the American dream at one of the most divisive moments in our history."

—**Thomas B. Edsall,** *New York Times* **political columnist**

"A riveting exploration of the long-running quest for racial equality in the public schools of Shaker Heights, Ohio. In the 1960s, as white flight was upending urban America, Shaker was that rare white community that opened its hearts and neighborhood schools to Black people, embracing integration as an ideal. In her clear-eyed account, Meckler makes clear we all have a stake in this community's ongoing quest to do right by its school children."

—**Dale Russakoff,** *New York Times* **bestselling author of** *The Prize*

"A glorious book about people with good intentions. Meckler tells a complicated, moving story about decades of change in the school system of Shaker Heights, Ohio. To try to achieve better schools, students are bussed, schools are closed, schools are opened, Black students are welcomed into honors classes, honors classes are abolished. But the Shaker community stubbornly, admirably, never gives up."

—**Don Graham, former publisher,** *The Washington Post*

"Journalist Meckler debuts with an in-depth analysis of desegregation efforts in her hometown of Shaker Heights, Ohio. . . . Throughout, Meckler draws on extensive interviews with parents, teachers, community leaders, and students to present the various controversies from multiple perspectives, resulting in a nuanced and impressively detailed study of the barriers to racial equality. Policymakers and social justice activists should take note."

—*Publishers Weekly*

"Meckler is one of the most independent-minded reporters on the education beat."

—*The Grade*

"What if the country had never given up on the goal of integrated schooling? *Dream Town*, a new book by *Washington Post* education reporter Laura Meckler, offers something of an answer, almost an alternate history."

—**Chalkbeat**

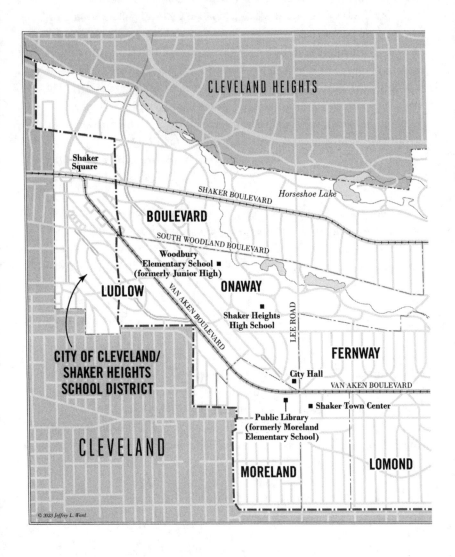

CLEVELAND HEIGHTS

Shaker
Square

SHAKER BOULEVARD   Horseshoe Lake

BOULEVARD

SOUTH WOODLAND BOULEVARD

Woodbury
Elementary School ■
(formerly Junior High)

LUDLOW   ONAWAY

VAN AKEN BOULEVARD

Shaker Heights ■
High School

LEE ROAD

CITY OF CLEVELAND/
SHAKER HEIGHTS
SCHOOL DISTRICT

FERNWAY

City Hall ■   VAN AKEN BOULEVARD

CLEVELAND

■ Shaker Town Center

Public Library
(formerly Moreland
Elementary School)

MORELAND   LOMOND

© 2023 Jeffrey L. Ward

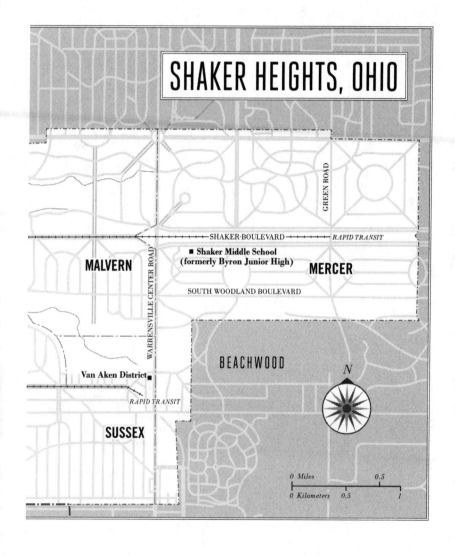

SHAKER HEIGHTS, OHIO

GREEN ROAD

SHAKER·BOULEVARD ———— *RAPID TRANSIT*

■ **Shaker Middle School**
(formerly Byron Junior High)

MALVERN

MERCER

WARRENSVILLE CENTER ROAD

SOUTH WOODLAND BOULEVARD

BEACHWOOD

N

Van Aken District ■

RAPID TRANSIT

SUSSEX

| 0 Miles | | 0.5 |
| 0 Kilometers | 0.5 | 1 |

DREAM TOWN

Shaker Heights and the Quest for Racial Equity

LAURA MECKLER

A Holt Paperback
Henry Holt and Company
New York

Holt Paperbacks
Henry Holt and Company
Publishers since 1866
120 Broadway
New York, New York 10271
www.henryholt.com

The Library of Congress has cataloged the hardcover edition as follows:

Names: Meckler, Laura, author.
Title: Dream town : Shaker Heights and the quest for racial equity /
    Laura Meckler.
Description: First edition. | New York : Henry Holt and Company, 2023. |
    Includes bibliographical references and index.
Identifiers: LCCN 2023017026 (print) | LCCN 2023017027 (ebook) |
    ISBN 9781250834416 (hardcover) | ISBN 9781250834423 (ebook)
Subjects: LCSH: Shaker Heights (Ohio)—Race relations. | Shaker Heights
    (Ohio)—Biography | African Americans—Ohio—Shaker Heights—
    Social conditions. | Educational equalization—Ohio—Shaker Heights. |
    Discrimination in housing—Ohio—Shaker Heights.
Classification: LCC F499.S52 M43 2023 (print) | LCC F499.S52 (ebook) |
    DDC 305.8009771/31
LC record available at https://lccn.loc.gov/2023017026
LC ebook record available at https://lccn.loc.gov/2023017027

ISBN 9781250834409 (trade paperback)

Our books may be purchased in bulk for promotional, educational, or business
use. Please contact your local bookseller or the Macmillan Corporate and
Premium Sales Department at (800) 221-7945, extension 5442, or by e-mail at
MacmillanSpecialMarkets@macmillan.com.

Originally published in hardcover in 2023 by Henry Holt and Company

First Holt Paperbacks Edition 2024

Designed by Gabriel Guma

Map designed by Jeffrey L. Ward

Printed in the United States of America

1 3 5 7 9 10 8 6 4 2

For my parents

TABLE OF CONTENTS

A community is known by the schools it keeps.

—Shaker Heights City Schools slogan

1

DREAM TOWN

The shiny hallways of Shaker Heights High School were silent and the classrooms empty, students and teachers scattered for summer vacation, when Hubert McIntyre walked through the door. He had an urgent question on his mind.

He took the seat at one end of the table and folded his five-foot-eleven-inch frame into the chair. He looked me straight in the eye, the sort of look I imagined he had given many of his students over his thirty-seven years teaching high school here, the look that said, *I'm on your side*, but also, *Don't even think about messing with me*. McIntyre glanced down at the pages printed out in front of him. It was a copy of a newspaper article I had written about Shaker Heights, Ohio, my hometown. I could see he had marked it up with handwritten notes.

He zeroed in on one paragraph—one word, really.

I had been spending this July day inside one of the empty classrooms. Boxes from the school district archives sat on a cart, folders inside waiting to be opened, one by one, in a hunt for details that would shed light on the promise and problems of Shaker Heights, a place that for decades had been on a quest for racial equity. But the boxes could wait.

A few days earlier, I had spent hours with McIntyre, a lanky, soft-spoken Black teacher known by teachers as Mac and students as Mr. Mac. He explained how he had won respect from even the toughest kids, and recounted the pranks he and other Shaker teaching legends had played when they were young and bold. He talked through why Black students too often fail to thrive in this well-resourced, racially integrated community and about how he had helped a group of academically successful young Black men create the Minority Achievement Committee, a national model for positive peer pressure. I heard why he's still hanging out at the school, still nurturing students nearly a decade after his official retirement. He hadn't found all the answers, but he was still looking. "That's a good question," he would say. "I've asked myself that question."

Now Mac was here again, and this time he wanted to ask me a question. My story, published in the *Washington Post*, centered on a controversy involving a young Black woman named Olivia and her Advanced Placement English teacher. It raised all sorts of questions about who was in these advanced classes and who was not, and why.

"Hearing Olivia's story got me thinking about my own," I had written. "I was in AP classes, and sometimes I struggled, too. Kids in my class were crazy smart, and it seemed to come so easy for them. But I never considered that my classmates might think I didn't belong there. It never crossed my mind that I didn't belong."

"It never crossed my mind," Mac read aloud to me, *"that I didn't belong."* Belonging. He turned the word over as he put the question to me: *What has to happen for students to feel like they belong? What does belonging feel like to you?*

Reporting this story for the *Post* had been eye-opening. So much was comfortable, familiar, even three decades after I graduated. The red brick school, constructed in 1931 as wealthy Clevelanders migrated to the growing suburb, sat on its grassy oval, iconic bell tower on top. Outside, the quiet road curved around the campus, a signature of this prototypical garden suburb, and testing ground for generations of student drivers learning to parallel park. Inside, the air still carried that familiar scent of adolescent sweat mixed with a whiff of cafeteria food. The hallways were silent until the clanging of the bell, then filled with shuffling feet, laughter, shouts, and the banging of locker doors. And up and down, the walls were alive with student murals painted through the decades. With each generation, new murals had been added to the tableau, so the faces of Tupac Shakur, Bob Marley, and Ray Charles now presided over a row of lockers, greeting people as they walked through the front door. From an earlier age, Jim Morrison's giant face still stared out, haunting an obscure corner of the second floor. A row of four cartoon Betty Boops, dating to 1985, still kicked their legs high in a chorus line.

The full-fledged planetarium was still tucked into the science wing, showing off the planets to elementary school field-trippers. Behind a wall of windows was the central office, where guidance counselors had for decades steered top-notch students to the Ivy League. And outside the office hung a tall plaque listing members of the school's Hall of Fame: performers, politicians, business executives, judges, writers, and more. Most famous was the actor Paul Newman, and for generations students joked that they had Newman's locker, though in truth nobody had a clue which locker had been his, and once, when he was asked about it, he replied, "I had a locker?"

But while nostalgia often feels good, returning to Shaker was deeply unsettling. Shaker Heights—a suburb of about twenty-nine thousand people, located just east of Cleveland and situated high above the city—had a decades-long, nationally recognized track record of racial integration, but also a persistent achievement gap in education. I had come back to better understand these contradictions. I expected to find some Black students who felt that Shaker was not supporting them academically. I knew there was systemic racism and bias. In America, with its vile racist history, how could there not be? But I did not realize how widespread it was. Even as they appreciated much of what Shaker had to offer, virtually every Black student had a story. So, it seems, did every Black parent.

How did this happen?

Shaker had been founded as a wealthy and white enclave of privilege, an escape route for Clevelanders looking to flee the city. Housing covenants sought to exclude Blacks, Jews, and Catholics, and, until the 1950s, they were particularly effective when it came to Blacks. Then things changed. Black and white families came together to create and maintain integrated neighborhoods. It started in one neighborhood called Ludlow and spread to other parts of town, with people of all races making a conscious effort to get to know one another, fight real estate agents intent on keeping neighborhoods segregated, and resist the forces of racism and white flight. Shaker won a national reputation as an integration pioneer, featured in the pages of *Look* magazine, *Reader's Digest*, and the

New York Times, on the airwaves of ABC News, and in countless academic papers.

The school district began voluntary busing to integrate its elementary schools in 1970, even as communities across the country, including Cleveland, right next door, were resisting doing the same. Later, boundary lines were redrawn to make the schools more integrated, while similar line drawing elsewhere had the opposite intent. Student groups dedicated themselves to Black achievement, race relations, and cross-racial friendship. One, the Student Group on Race Relations, was still leading conversations about race more than three decades after it was created. Hubert McIntyre's Minority Achievement Committee was still crowning high-achieving MAC Scholars after more than twenty years.

It's almost a mantra for Shakerites Black and white: If any place can navigate the complex issues of race in America, it's Shaker Heights.

While many inner-ring suburbs flipped from virtually all white to almost entirely Black over time, the city of Shaker Heights remained majority white, and the schools were about 40 percent white and 45 percent Black decades after the first Black families moved to the city. The community showed that racial integration was possible in housing, and Shaker became a national model for other cities seeking alternatives to white flight. I saw it up close.

Through it all, the schools built and maintained a reputation for excellence, sending large numbers of students to elite colleges and developing robust Advanced Placement and International Baccalaureate programs. The theater and arts programs were top-notch. Students could take classes in French, Spanish, German, Latin, Greek, and Mandarin. It wasn't unusual for the high school to sponsor a half dozen international trips for students. Taxpayers, including some of the wealthiest people in the Cleveland area, approved one tax levy after the next, driven by the slogan "a community is known by the schools it keeps."

It was, in short, an American dream town. That's how *Cosmopolitan* put it in 1963, when the magazine put Shaker Heights on its cover with the headline THE GOOD LIFE IN SHAKER HEIGHTS. The magazine reported: "The wealthiest city in the United States boasts practically no unemployment, no slums. Back-yard swimming pools are commonplace, nearly everyone belongs to a country club and most kids have new cars."

"Here," *Cosmo* announced, "is the inside story of an American dream town come true."

They were talking about the American suburban dream, of opulence and wealth, of excellent schools and fine services, of beautiful architecture and stately trees and picturesque lakes. To be sure, *Cosmo*'s description was an over-the-top exaggeration, but the overall tone rang true.

And yet for decades, Shaker had aspired to be another sort of American dream town as well. It was the dream articulated, a few months after that *Cosmo* cover, by Dr. Martin Luther King Jr., speaking to some two hundred thousand people gathered at the Lincoln Memorial to demand that this country live up to its ideals.

King, with a marble Abraham Lincoln towering behind him, spoke of what might be. "I have a dream," he preached. "I have a dream that my four little children will one day live in a nation where they will not be judged by the color of their skin but by the content of their character . . . one day, right down in Alabama, little Black boys and Black girls will be able to join hands with little white boys and white girls as sisters and brothers."

Shaker Heights was trying to make this dream come true, too.

———

Growing up, I was all in and on message. As a white child in a white family, I felt enormous pride that I was from Shaker Heights, imagining that I held a sort of superiority trump card in the category of race relations.

I grew up in a neighborhood called Sussex that was racially diverse then and remains so today. My first teachers about race lived right next door. Diane and Jim Lardie were white parents with six children—five adopted, four of them biracial or Black. Their daughter Betsy was my first best friend. Betsy laughed loudly and drew people to her with a natural charisma. She seemed scared of nothing, while I was scared of almost everything. I remember as a very young girl asking my father why Betsy was half Black and half white. "Because one of her biological parents was Black and one was white," he told me matter-of-factly.

Years later, I learned how the Lardies landed on Scottsdale Boulevard. Jim and Diane met in fourth grade, growing up on the east side of Cleveland, in a white neighborhood home to many Irish Catholics. One by one, Black families arrived. Jim recalled his grandmother taking him by the hand to greet one of the first, who moved in across the street. She told him they were going to do what they did for every new neighbor—bring Irish soda bread. "I never read in the good book where you love your neighbor unless they're colored," his grandmother told him.

"The faith was real clear, and it was pounded into us," Diane said.

They saw their neighborhood flip from white to Black before their eyes, spurred by real estate agents who scared white homeowners into selling. Diane said her parents were the second-to-last white family on the block.

Jim and Diane married and had a daughter, but Diane was unable to get pregnant again, so they decided to adopt, which is how a white infant named Jimmy arrived. Soon after, the Lardies told the adoption counselor they would like to adopt again and asked if she knew any children who needed homes. "I have some, but they are unadoptable," she told them.

"That changed our lives," Jim told me. The idea that any child was unadoptable was unacceptable to them. Jim ultimately quit his job and became a full-time advocate for children in need. The Lardies eventually adopted four more children—hard-to-place kids. Their multiracial family grew and thrived in their brick colonial on Scottsdale Boulevard.

For me, that's what Shaker always was about. A place that would welcome the Lardies.

My parents, Bill Meckler and Marsha Cousens Meckler, moved to the Sussex neighborhood in 1966 just as it was starting to draw Black families. My dad, who grew up in an adjoining suburb, remembered feeling as though a certain sense of prestige came with moving into Shaker Heights. He also recalled being aware that the neighborhood they chose was integrating, and of that being a plus.

They had already worked and lived with Black people to a degree that was unusual among their white peers. They were both attorneys and met at their first jobs out of law school, at a program representing juvenile defendants. The project's other lawyer, Clarence Rogers, was Black, and the three of them were friends. Rogers remembered my parents as engaged and interested in issues of race. "You could not ignore race as a part of what we dealt with," he said. All three volunteered on the mayoral campaign of Carl Stokes, the first Black person elected to lead a major American city.

My parents, each in their own way, had been prepared to take their place in an integrated community.

My mother grew up in a Jewish family in Detroit. Her father, Leon Cousens, was a labor attorney and a field worker for the Socialist Party. Her mother, Frances Reissman Cousens, was even further to the political left, a communist who joked that she married her husband even though he was a "mere socialist." (Later they settled in as more conventional Democrats.) After her husband died, Fran earned her doctorate and became research director of the Michigan Fair Employment Practices Commission, charged with examining whether employers were discriminating against workers based on race, and, in 1969, she authored a significant study of employment discrimination. She also was an expert witness in a case accusing real estate agents of racial steering and blockbusting in Detroit, and went on to serve for many years as a sociology professor at the University of Michigan–Dearborn.

People of color regularly turned up at my grandmother's home for meetings and dinners, my uncle, Mark Cousens, recalled. "The entire concept of white people interacting with Black people was simply something we took for granted." Race, he said, "was central to our conversations." Mark also remembered his mom receiving harassing calls from real estate agents seeking to scare white people like her into selling by stoking fears of racial change. "Those absolutely infuriated her," he said. My mom and her siblings attended a magnet high school that was integrated well before the courts ordered the Detroit schools to desegregate.

My father was raised in a more conventional family, in a Jewish community in University Heights, just north of Shaker. He remembered being taught that Black people were just as good as white people, and he recalled that his father, who was a dentist, cared for Black patients as well as white ones—something he knew would scandalize his clientele and that he consequently did after hours and under the radar.

Still, race relations were more of a theoretical matter. The only Black student in his high school was the daughter of a janitor. But when he arrived at Ohio State University, he made Black friends, and by the time my parents married in 1966, they were primed for Shaker, and just the sort of people the community was attracting—the type of people who would reinforce the community's emerging values.

It wasn't just racial diversity that made Shaker special. It was excellence. Academically, Shaker schools were the pot of gold at the end of the rainbow, at least for students like me. The education I got there was expansive and rigorous, and I landed at college supremely prepared. College was in some ways easier than high school, and definitely less competitive. At Shaker, everyone in my academic circle knew who got the high score on the math exam, who was a National Merit semifinalist, who had been admitted to an Ivy League school. In a class my senior year, the teacher asked students to talk about how they were feeling about the college admissions process, and one student spoke of his profound fear that he would not be admitted to Princeton. Later, everyone found out that he didn't get in and had to "settle" for the University of Michigan. It's one of the best schools in the nation, but he was embarrassed and disappointed. After his freshman year, he transferred to Harvard.

"I built my identity around academic success and achievement. That's who I was," he told me later. "If I didn't measure up, I was nobody."

Beginning in kindergarten and straight through high school, I was so insecure that I spent hours wondering how others might be judging me, worrying that I wasn't measuring up. Was my haircut okay? Could everyone in AP Calculus see that I was confused? Why wouldn't my mom buy me Izod alligator polo shirts so I could dress preppy like the wealthier, more popular kids all around me?

There was precious little mental space left for me to consider whether I was actually the one with all the advantages. I knew that my AP courses were filled with white people. It was impossible to miss. But why? I remember asking our congressman, Louis Stokes, who was Black, that question when he spoke at the high school, the same school his own children had once attended. I don't remember his answer, but years later, when I met Stokes as a reporter in Washington, I reminded him of the moment. "You were asking hard questions even then," he said. But he still didn't have an answer. Neither did I.

Now, with the benefit of time and distance, I was looking for answers again.

One answer was economic: the economic divides in Shaker are heavily correlated with race. They are deep, and over time they have grown deeper. Thirty years ago, the typical Black household in Shaker earned about 65 percent as much as the typical white household. By 2020, white median income had risen, while Black family income had dropped to

35 percent that of white families. Moreover, the portion of Black Shaker families living in poverty had nearly tripled, to 14.7 percent, while white poverty inched up to 3.8 percent.

In most of America, children from poor and low-income families attend different schools than those who come from wealthy homes. People tend to cluster with others just like them, either by choice or because they have no choice. The result is that schools in wealthy communities enjoy all the advantages of wealth: parents who have the time, money, and education to help their children succeed when they hit academic roadblocks, and who can contribute those resources to the school itself. They are populated with children who don't have to worry about basic necessities and can concentrate on advancement. Meantime, schools in poor communities face the significant challenges of concentrated need: children who may not have enough food to eat or a quiet place to study, whose parents might work odd hours and who can't afford academic camps and tutors. Unlike most of America, Shaker was trying to educate children from both these worlds, side by side.

Most of the country has abandoned the deliberate pursuit of racial integration, yet decades of research have shown that it is one of the few things that works to close racial achievement gaps, largely because segregated schools serving mostly Black students tend to be both underresourced and home to concentrated poverty. Nationally, the gap between reading scores of Black and white students on standardized tests fell by half between the early 1970s, when desegregation began in earnest across America, and 1988, the height of integration. The math gap also closed, though not as dramatically.

Rucker C. Johnson of the University of California, Berkeley, an economist who studies poverty and inequality, tracked the long-term outcomes for thousands of students born between 1945 and 1968. He compared those who were educated in segregated versus desegregated schools—even comparing siblings where the older child graduated before desegregation and the younger experienced it. He found that for Black students, desegregation significantly increased educational and professional achievement and earnings, decreased the likelihood of incarceration, and improved health outcomes. Separately, a 2004 study found the desegregation plans of the 1970s reduced high school dropout rates among Black students by 2 to 3 percentage points. And a 2022 paper found Black children who were young when desegregation orders were implemented in their counties went further in school and did better economically as adults.

The studies found these policies had no negative economic or educational impacts on white students, dispelling any misplaced fears that white students would be hurt.

A 2022 study by Harvard University's Raj Chetty and others found similar results based on an analysis of 72.2 million American Facebook users: low-income children who grew up in economically diverse communities had higher earnings as adults. Simply being exposed to higher-income peers provided opportunities for connections and friendships that boosted them into a higher economic class.

And in a study in Montgomery County, Maryland, researchers at the RAND Corporation compared the impact of two strategies. Some low-income families were assigned to live in public housing scattered across affluent areas, so the children attended schools in those neighborhoods. Separately, the county invested $2,000 more per student in high-poverty schools to, for instance, reduce class sizes and provide teacher training. Despite the additional funding in the high-poverty schools, researchers found that poor students in the wealthier schools did better over time.

So what Shaker Heights has been attempting matters. Integration matters. But has it worked as well as it should in my hometown?

Back in Shaker, I dropped into an eleventh grade English class where the topic was a graphic novel set partly in Iran. In a small group discussion, students were asked to consider taboos in American society, and a Black girl named Ananda Watson turned the discussion to Shaker. Why, she asked, are Black students at Shaker disciplined more often than whites? Why are elite courses predominantly white? "Do we as a minority feel uncomfortable being in a predominantly white class?"

Ananda was one of the sharpest kids in the room. She enthusiastically participated in the discussion, offering one insightful comment after the next. I wasn't surprised when she told me she had started the year in AP English. But she left after one day. "I just felt really uncomfortable being one of three or four minorities. I felt like I'm not supposed to be here," she said. Her counselor could have tried to talk her out of it, pushed her to stay, found support for her, talked to teachers about making sure she had a good experience. But she let Ananda slide down to honors level.

The system had delivered her its message: you don't belong in AP.

I began to think more about Betsy Lardie (whose name is now Mary

Allen), my next-door neighbor and childhood best friend. She had been pulled out of Shaker schools after elementary school and sent to Catholic school. Why?

"At the end of sixth grade, I had three daughters who could not write a simple sentence," her mom told me. "The Shaker schools were wonderful for a motivated kid like you." But she said they were not wonderful for kids who were less academically motivated. I wondered: Even if Betsy wasn't motivated, why couldn't a district like Shaker, with all its resources, help her succeed anyway? Didn't Betsy belong in Shaker?

—————

Many communities were already grappling with questions of racial equity when in May 2020, a Black man named George Floyd was murdered by police in Minneapolis. His death sparked national and global outrage, rallying around the Black Lives Matter banner, and igniting a movement for racial justice that touched virtually all corners of public life. Schools were among them, and many vowed to look deeply at their policies and practices through the lens of racial equity. Districts reconsidered the use of police in their school buildings. They reexamined discipline practices with an eye toward rooting out racial bias. Some worked to diversify their faculties, and some broadened their curriculums to include more experiences and voices of people of color.

Predictably, those efforts led to backlash. Conservatives labeled any effort to address systemic racism, either through policies or in classrooms, as "critical race theory," a once arcane academic construct that holds that racism is systemic and baked into American law. They pushed back through loud protests at school board meetings, and at least eighteen laws were enacted in fourteen states governing how race could be discussed. Details varied, but many reflected the intent and spirit of a 2020 Trump administration rule that outlawed federal employee trainings promoting the idea that "the United States is an inherently racist or evil country or . . . that any race or ethnicity is inherently racist or evil."

The new laws and heightened scrutiny prompted many teachers to self-censor, not knowing where the line was and what might get them into trouble. In New Hampshire, for instance, a new law barred teaching that people of certain races or genders are inherently superior or inferior to people of another. Jen Given, a tenth grade history teacher at Hollis-Brookline High School in Hollis, New Hampshire, found the wording so vague that she wasn't sure what she could or couldn't do. She used to teach students about racial disparities in economics partly by tying the relative lack of Black wealth to Jim Crow laws and discriminatory mortgage policies known as redlining. She stopped. "We started avoiding modern parallels in order to avoid any question coming up that we were, by including this information . . . somehow suggesting one group is better than the other," she said.

Those sorts of debates were never on the table in communities like Shaker Heights, which is overwhelmingly liberal in its politics. But that doesn't mean there weren't debates over how to address difficult questions surrounding race. In the quest for racial justice, for instance, communities including Shaker began unraveling their academic tracking systems—mixing kids of different achievement levels in order to give students of color, who were far less likely to enroll in advanced classes, more access to challenging coursework.

The hope was that by exposing lower achievers to a rigorous curriculum in a classroom that included more advanced students, they would think of themselves as learners who could handle challenging material. "If you are told in sixth grade, 'You're in a lower math track,' that changes your mindset and your belief about yourself," said Jo Boaler, a professor at the Stanford Graduate School of Education and a leading advocate for detracking. "Going forward, they think, 'Math is not in my future.'"

But even in Shaker Heights, there was considerable anxiety and opposition to this change. None of this is or has been easy.

———————

My story about Shaker Heights was published in the *Washington Post* in November 2019, part of a series of stories about schools and racial integration. And while it was a long story, it still left me wanting to know more, to go deeper. The headline was, THIS TRAIL-BLAZING SUBURB HAS TRIED FOR 60 YEARS TO TACKLE RACE. WHAT IF TRYING ISN'T ENOUGH? Here's a little secret. When a newspaper headline asks a question, it's often because the writer doesn't know the answer, or there are conflicting views, or mixed evidence. And the story will lay all that out for readers. But, for me, this was not just any story. This was the story of a place that means something to me, the story of home. And I wanted to answer the question: *Has trying been enough?*

The questions raised by the story of Shaker Heights go right at the fabric of American life: How can and do people of different races live together? And what does it take to make diverse communities succeed? For white families, particularly those of means, it stirs questions of priorities and values. Do they value diversity simply in theory, or enough to live and learn alongside people who are racially, socially, economically, or academically different? What do they owe their own children, and what do they owe all children? The questions lurk whenever a family considers public versus private school, a diverse neighborhood or one where everyone is the same. For families of color, the Shaker story asks whether integration has delivered on its promise. What does it take to feel like they truly belong?

Belonging is a tricky thing. McIntyre, who taught Health Science for years, asked me about the AP Calculus class I had taken as a high school senior. I never really felt smart enough in that room, I told him. I remembered another kid blithely telling me that if he couldn't remember the formula for a particular problem, he would simply derive it. I didn't have a clue how to derive formulas. Yet no one else had to know that I was struggling. I fit in. I fit in, in large part, because I am white.

"No one's going to look at me and say, 'What's she doing here?'" I told him. "You know, I can fake it. Even if I don't necessarily understand calculus, I can fake it 'til I make it."

"I love that phrase: 'Fake it 'til I make it,'" he said. "It gives me time. It also gives me courage, hope, and a belief that I'm going to be able to pull this off." But imagine the person of color in that same class also feeling like she doesn't belong, who has eyes on her, who's fending off microaggressions—little insults and dismissals. McIntyre painted a picture: How might she feel, say, if the teacher asked students to divide into groups and everyone groups up with their friends and no one asks her to join because these are not her friends? How much harder does this make it for her to fake it 'til she makes it?

The conversation with Hubert McIntyre about belonging reminded me of something someone else had said to me. Stacey Hren, a white mom, had been president of the Onaway Elementary School parent-teacher organization. She tried to figure out why it was mostly white parents who came to their events. Events were not just events—they were gateways to networks and knowledge and connections that help navigate the system. Many theories had been posited, but Hren landed on a simple idea: belonging. "My sense is it's the feel of the room," she said. "If you are a mom or dad or a grandma or aunt or uncle of color, why would you walk into that space if it doesn't look like a space for you?"

Shaker long ago declared it was a space for everyone, trumpeted to one another and on the front pages of newspapers. But was this true? And were white people willing to give up any of their privileges to create a more equitable community? Could one place dream both dreams—be the dream town of *Cosmo* and the dream town of Dr. King? I would ultimately conclude that while Shaker Heights is far from perfect, this is a place that has defied the odds, not once or twice, but over and over again. Much of what Shaker tells itself is myth. Much of what has transpired is kept out of the brochures. But it's worth asking: How does one place in a nation full of places transform itself from a racist haven for the elite to a community striving, even if imperfectly, for racial equity? What has worked, and where has the community come up short? And why has the story of Shaker Heights unfolded so differently than the stories in most of America?

I was back home, trying to figure that out.

At the end of the rainbow lies—Shaker Village.

—Van Sweringen Company advertisement for Shaker Heights

2

THE VAN SWERINGEN BROTHERS

The Van Sweringen brothers were as close to each other as two brothers could be.

Oris Paxton, known as O.P., and Mantis James, or M.J., were both shy and reclusive, with big ambitions. They were two years apart, but one writer described them as "twins by choice." They were "almost like two halves of a single personality."

Growing up, they had almost nothing. No family money, that's for sure, and not much education. Their ancestors, who arrived in America in 1656, were of notable Dutch lineage, but their father, James, had been injured fighting for the Union in the Civil War and struggled to provide for his five children.

The family bounced from home to home in Ohio. O.P., the fourth child, was born in 1879, and M.J. arrived in 1881. Just five years later, their mother, Jennie, died of consumption at age forty-one. James moved the family to Cleveland, hoping for more opportunity.

He never really found it. Hamstrung by his war injuries, James worked as a watchman, an engineer, and in advertising, but the jobs didn't last long.

It would be different for his two young sons. As kids growing up near Cedar Avenue and East 105th Street, O.P. and M.J. operated a bicycle repair shop and worked for a butter-and-egg man. They lit gas-fueled street lights. They delivered newspapers, and that's what first took them east into the undeveloped woodlands known as the Heights. They returned to the area for a summer job tending cattle. "We used to sit up there and day dream," O.P. told a writer for the *Cleveland Press*. "It was then only sparsely settled, but its beauty was tremendously impressive."

As teenagers, both boys worked in the office of an agricultural fertilizer firm. In April 1897, just shy of his eighteenth birthday, O.P. seemed to be living the life of a much older man. "I have been quite busy lately and have been working till seven and nine o'clock, standard time, most every evening," he wrote to his father, who was away that spring and summer, "and upon looking at the small clock on my desk, find it is now after seven o'clock and as [sic] have not had any supper yet."

O.P. had determined that by age twenty-one, he would go into real estate, and that's what he did. And once again his younger brother followed. "They were always together," wrote Taylor Hampton, a friend of the brothers and author of an expansive biography of the pair published in the *Cleveland News*. M.J. was the doer, she wrote, and O.P. the dreamer.

They pocketed $100 on their first sale, turning over a house on Carnegie Avenue within twenty-four hours, and repeated the trick on a second house a few weeks later. Their beginner's luck ran out when in 1902 they tried to sell a string of lots on what later became Cook Avenue in Lakewood, a suburb emerging on Cleveland's west side. The properties were foreclosed upon, and for two years, the brothers did business using their sisters' names. Once they finally settled the Lakewood mess, they reconstituted themselves.

Their last name as children was simply Sweringen. The brothers now resurrected the "Van" portion of their family name, which had been dropped years earlier for unknown reasons. It's not clear why they took it back; Taylor Hampton speculated they may have been seeking a dose of prestige, or perhaps putting distance between themselves and their Lakewood failures. Whatever the reason, they would soon be known as "the Vans."

They now looked east to the Heights, where they had once delivered newspapers and tended cattle. They began developing residential property in Cleveland Heights, subdividing the territory into large lots for grand homes on what would become North Park Boulevard.

With success at their backs, they turned to the nearby land once occupied by an obscure religious sect called the Shakers.

The original Shakers were small in numbers but not ambition. They were out to build a utopia.

They envisioned a world of peace and communal living, where men and women were on equal, albeit separate, footing, and where people of all races and classes were welcome. They refused guns and weapons, aimed to be charitable and honest, strove for simplicity and discipline. Dancing was an act of divine worship, and in prayer, they would shake and jerk, sing and whirl, confessing their sins aloud as they shook them away. Sometimes their palms would turn upward, followed by an inward motion, symbolizing the receiving and giving of spiritual gifts. They were an outgrowth of the better-known Quakers, and their demonstrations of religious ecstasy gave rise to the name Shaking Quakers, or, for short, the Shakers.

The group was founded by Ann Lee, who left her homeland of England in 1774 to escape religious intolerance. She and her followers settled in upstate New York and began spreading their philosophy to colonies dotted across the Northeast and, eventually, to the West.

One future site sat in northeast Ohio, on a five-mile-square swath of land called Warrensville Township, which had been surveyed in 1796 by Moses Cleaveland. Early settlers here included Jacob Russell, a veteran of the Revolutionary War from Connecticut. In 1821, one of his sons, Ralph, traveled to a Shaker community in southern Ohio and returned a convert. He formed the North Union Shaker Community in 1822 and called the land "the Valley of God's Pleasure."

Shakers advocated for the abolition of slavery and for the rights of Native Americans, with Native and Black people welcomed into their ranks. They did not vote because doing so would make them part of a discriminatory system, and they chose to expand into Ohio in part because Ohio was a state free from slavery. The North Union colony included at least seven Black members, at least two of whom had escaped enslavement. And in 1856, the colony hosted a visit from Sojourner Truth, the leader for women's rights and abolition who was herself born enslaved.

Shaker communities were organized into larger "families" of as many as a hundred people, with everyone surrendering personal possessions to share with the whole. Their innovations were expansive. Shakers are credited with inventions ranging from the common clothespin and the flat broom to the circular saw and the one-horse wagon. Their herbal medicines were sold far and wide. Handcrafted Shaker-inspired furniture, renowned for its quality and simple designs, is still produced today. The North Union colony erected buildings across what had been wilderness and dammed a stream called Doan Creek, powering a grist-mill and a sawmill and creating two lakes.

Some of their other practices were less practical. During one of her jail stays in England, Mother Ann, as founder Ann Lee was known, had had a vision. Sexual lust, she concluded, was standing in the way of Christ's work. "Sex," she said, "is the root cause of all the ugliness in human life." The Shakers imposed strict rules of celibacy, with men and women sleeping, eating, worshipping, and working apart. Even their graveyards were divided by gender, with men on one side of the cemetery and women on the other.

All this was a tough sell to young people coming of age. It's one thing to commit to communal living and quite another to a life of celibacy. Not producing any children of their own, they depended on orphans and converts to maintain the population. It wasn't enough. "Youth shall ever be our burden," one Shaker wrote in his diary. He reported that fifteen young people had "gone to the world" in less than two weeks.

The North Union colony disbanded in 1889, and the twenty-seven elderly Shakers who remained left to join other colonies, leaving the area to deteriorate into a veritable ghost town. The land was bought by a group of Clevelanders. One evening the group was discussing over dinner what to call the area, according to Henry Avery, one of the people involved. His wife said, "Why don't you call it Shaker Heights, after the Shakers, and because it is high up on the hills." The group agreed, and thus was born the Shaker Heights Land Company, which began to develop roads and worked out an agreement to set aside a swath of land for parks. Before it would go any further, the company sold its 1,400 acres to a land syndicate based in Buffalo, New York, for $316,000 (about $10 million in 2022 dollars).

The Buffalo syndicate laid out lots, built another boulevard, and planned to develop the land. Then the depression of the 1890s hit, and the prospect of quick profits disappeared. They decided to hold off. The land's future would be charted by a pair of brothers who, at this moment, were just little kids in a family barely scraping by forty miles to the south.

By the time the Van Sweringen brothers came along, the neglected territory was in rough shape. The dams, mills, and communal buildings erected by the Shakers had fallen into ruin. Brambles, brush, and weeds covered the ground. The lanes and roads were impassable. But now that the depression of the 1890s was over, Cleveland was on the rise again, and the brothers saw great potential.

The Vans didn't have the kind of cash needed to buy the land outright, but they didn't need it. In late 1905, they met with the land agent for the Buffalo group and reached an agreement: the Vans would find buyers for the land, using the proceeds to pay the syndicate, which would then be obligated to give them twice as much land to sell, and so on. They made sale after sale, acquiring more and more property, all without putting up any money of their own, a pattern they would repeat through their careers as the numbers and stakes grew larger. Eventually, they organized a syndicate of Cleveland investors and bought up the remaining Shaker acreage.

As they sold lots, the Vans also set out to refurbish the territory, clearing the brush and rebuilding the old dams. They preserved two Shaker-made lakes and built two new, smaller lakes. "It was a rugged job, but I loved it. Carving a city out of wilderness is the most satisfying of experiences," William J. Van Aken, who worked closely with the Vans and served as Shaker's mayor from 1916 to 1950, told the *Sun* newspapers.

They meticulously planned a community typical of the garden suburbs of the era, based on the principles developed in Riverside, a suburb of Chicago, by the famed architect Frederick Law Olmsted. Trees lined the streets, and lawns were set in front of homes. Wide thoroughfares moved east-west and north-south, and in between, roads curved, taking advantage of the topography, a hallmark of a planned community. The Shaker map was not a grid, but a series of arcs and ovals, with open space set aside for parks and trees, for schools and churches. The homes were set back from the street, with greenery unfolding in front of each home, creating the sense that one was not just near a park, but living inside one. Business was restricted to a few chosen areas.

The Vans offered incentives to attract the first wealthy buyers— "people of the right sort"—reasoning that early settlers would then draw their friends, who would draw their friends, and so on. Their work began during a heady time for Cleveland, an industrial powerhouse that was home to steel and iron manufacturers and the headquarters of John D.

Rockefeller's Standard Oil Company, among many other thriving concerns. By 1930, the region would rank as the third-largest metro area in the United States, after New York and Chicago.

The initial homes in Shaker were large. Perhaps the grandest of them all was built in 1912 by the brothers for themselves across from Horseshoe Lake, a stone mansion on South Park Boulevard, with a steeply pitched roof, a pair of stone chimneys, a prominent turret, and seven bedrooms, which would grow even grander with a renovation a decade later. Nonetheless, O.P. and M.J. were said to have shared a bedroom, sleeping in twin beds beside each other.

As the Vans marketed their new community, they sold not merely lots but a new suburban dream, a place that made clear not just anyone could belong. Like the Shakers, they imagined they were creating a utopia. But instead of a utopia built on communal values and shared possessions, theirs embodied the capitalist spirit of rewarding the rich with the finest things money could buy.

In the 1920s, the Vans placed weekly advertisements in *Cleveland Topics*, a magazine of culture, society, and politics aimed at the area's elite. One 1923 issue featured five pages of society announcements with news such as "Mr. C. A. Selzer sailed Thursday on the Majestic to spend the summer in Europe," and "Mr. and Mrs. Ralph T. King have opened their country home, The Pinery . . . for the summer season." The advertisements for Shaker Village were surrounded by ads for theater, motor cars, fine tailoring, artistic brass lamps from England, and steamship lines sailing to Europe and the Mediterranean.

The Shaker advertisements painted a picture of a community awaiting those who appreciated refined living and wished to be shielded from the unrefined.

"On every family's horizon is a rainbow," said one advertisement in the 1920s, "and for many the pot of gold at the rainbow's end is Shaker Village. For the pot of gold . . . turned out to be contentment and that is what Shaker Village offers—contentment, forever assured by protective restrictions."

The promotions assured potential buyers that restrictions would ensure the area's exclusivity long into the future and promised an idyllic escape from the dirt and grime of the city.

As early as 1905, the Shaker Heights Improvement Company, the Van Sweringens' firm, promised residents would be safe from "saloons, manufacturing and business establishments, flats, terraces and double houses, unsightly bill boards and everything else inconsistent with the highest ideals of a residential park." An ad in April 1923 denigrated the new arrivals to Cleveland, which it estimated at six thousand to seven thousand per year. "Do you wonder that the fine home districts are being inundated with refugees who are crowded out of industrial districts by this influx?" it read. "Shaker Village has permanent security for those who want homes beyond this tide area." And in 1928, an ad decried the tons of soot dropped into the city each month. "Try to find a speck of it in the Shaker Country Estates!"

The Vans set strict, conservative rules for architecture, and building plans had to be approved by their company to ensure standards were met. The only styles accepted were colonial, English Tudor, and French country. Buyers were required to hire architects whose qualifications, drawings, and knowledge constituted the "highest and best in architecture." Only certain color schemes and material types were allowed, with charts serving up detailed guidance. For English residences, for instance, gray-brown walls were to be married with dark brown trim, shutters, and door. Garages must not look like garages but "have the same design, treatment and quality as the house itself." Bungalows and similarly humble houses were not appropriate for the community that Shaker Heights "is destined to be," so "we have thought it necessary to exclude all buildings of that character from our property." Shingles, slate, and tile were acceptable for a roof, though tile was not appropriate for a colonial house, and of course tar, composition sheet roofing, and asphalt shingles were all banned because they "have neither character nor beauty."

Written permission was needed for open sleeping porches. All houses had to be two full stories in height, and homes were to be set close to the ground, allowing for a sense of "beauty and coziness" not afforded by a flight of steps.

Shaker was to be not just a wealthy enclave, the Vans made clear, but a tasteful one. "Good taste calls for well-designed residences that combine things that make for comfort and convenience with the things that make for beauty," instructs the 1928 edition of "Shaker Village Standards," a booklet given to prospective buyers. "The most pleasing is never conspicuous—never flashy." It seemed no detail was too small for specification. Genuine lead bars, not zinc, for instance, were to be used in glass work. "The effect of zinc is flashy and therefore not in good taste."

The rigid planning drew national attention. In 1936, a piece in *Architectural Forum* called the Vans' planning unprecedented in its scope. "There had been no instance in the history of American real estate development where any man or set of men had set such a definite plan for the development of so large a piece of property along such rigidly controlled lines as the Van Sweringens set for the development of the Shaker farm tract," the magazine declared. Lord Rothermere, an English newspaper tycoon, once visited Shaker Heights and told the Vans, "You have developed the finest residential district in the world."

Soon the Shaker school system became part of the attraction, too. At first, classes were offered inside the real estate office. The Vans also recruited a trio of private schools, and in 1914, they unveiled their first public school building, named Boulevard, with nine others opening over the next seventeen years. (By 1957, there would be nine elementary schools, two junior highs, and a high school.) The system would serve the children of wealthy, educated parents, a recipe for excellence that Shaker achieved and nurtured. One way—maybe the easiest way—to build excellent schools is to start with a population of advantaged families, and that's exactly what Shaker did.

None of this was explicitly about race, yet race hung over the entire enterprise. The unstated rules put new homes off-limits to Blacks, Jews, and Catholics, though exceptions were made—for instance, for wealthy Jews such as Salmon P. Halle, who with his brother owned Cleveland's finest department store and who began construction in 1927 of what would become one of Shaker's most notable mansions. No such exceptions were made for Black buyers, who typically did not have such wealth or connections.

The rapid growth of Shaker Heights in the 1920s unfolded just as the Great Migration was bringing thousands of Black Southerners into Cleveland, a mass population shift that began in World War I and would continue for decades.

Cleveland had been known as a place more progressive on racial issues than many other northern cities. During the years leading up to the Civil War, the city was home to many abolitionists and was an important stop on the Underground Railroad, known to those escaping enslavement by its code name, "Hope." Most schools, restaurants, and public spaces were integrated, and the Black population was dispersed around town.

Attitudes and housing patterns shifted as Black migrants arrived to Cleveland, escaping the punishing violence and racism of Jim Crow. They were initially drawn north during World War I as factories faced a labor shortage and dropped policies barring Black hires. Southern Blacks often came to Cleveland up the rail lines from Georgia and Alabama, looking for factory work, migrating in large numbers in the decade following the war. The Black population in Cleveland rose from about 8,500 in 1910 to nearly 72,000 by 1930, and rather than dispersing, they became concentrated in certain areas. In 1910, no census tract was more than 25 percent Black; ten years later, ten tracts were, with two of them more than half Black. On the flip side, a rising number of neighborhoods had no Black residents at all. Thousands of new arrivals were forced into an increasingly overcrowded Cedar-Central ghetto, which stretched for dozens of blocks east of downtown Cleveland. As Blacks arrived, white immigrants moved out. A few African Americans were able to escape to outer neighborhoods, farther to the east, but in general, racist policies and practices kept the Black community trapped in conditions that grew more dire by the year.

Cleveland Topics warned in a 1925 editorial that the Black population had already grown from 8,500 to 50,000 in ten years. "More are on the way," it said, ominously. It suggested the new arrivals were different and frightening. Cleveland's Black population during the "old, regular, well ordered days," the editorial said, tells us nothing about "this new population or of the problem it presents."

"These southern negroes are not welcome here. Please do not delude yourself, or delude them," the editorial concluded.

Some early suburbs overtly banned Blacks. Shaker never put it in writing, but the Vans kept them out nonetheless, partly because they controlled the real estate and decided who and who not to sell to. In marketing the new community, they played on white fears and prejudices. A January 1924 advertisement for Shaker described East End white Cleveland families as "desperately clinging to homes of former comfort and luxury." The advertisement continued: "Many have read the signs aright and safeguarded the future by resetting their homes in Shaker Village—where such experiences cannot happen—have you? See us today—delay is expensive."

That's not to say Black buyers never got through. Details are sketchy, but in 1924, a prominent Black undertaker named J. W. Wills bought a home in Shaker Heights and was then, according to the NAACP, subjected to a pressure campaign to sell, reported the *Cleveland Gazette*, Cleveland's oldest newspaper serving the Black community. The *Gazette* also suggested Wills might have bought the house hoping to turn a profit by selling to bigoted neighbors who wanted to keep him out.

Soon after the incident, a Black doctor named Edward A. Bailey bought a house in Shaker, and O. P. Van Sweringen saw it as another shakedown attempt. "We've been bled once, and we won't be again," he said. But the Vans had other tools available to drive the doctor away.

From the start, the Vans knew that growth depended on convenient access for commuters to downtown Cleveland. Earlier, in developing a portion of neighboring Cleveland Heights, they had persuaded the Cleveland Railway Company to extend its streetcar line beyond Cedar Hill and out to Fairmount Boulevard, enabling easy commutes into the city. Now the closest stop was two or three miles from the new Shaker homes, and the Vans needed another extension to facilitate mass sale of houses.

The brothers pushed the railway company to extend its line again, but the company's president refused, seeing it as a losing proposition. So the Vans came up with a new plan. They would build their own light rail line covering the six miles between Shaker Heights and downtown Cleveland. Poring over maps, they noticed a thin black line—a natural ravine called the Kingsbury Run—stretching along the perfect corridor. They began to buy up property along the run, including four acres in the heart of Cleveland for a terminal that could service their Shaker transit line and other interurban routes. Construction began.

The final two miles they needed were controlled by another railroad, the Nickel Plate, which was owned by the New York Central Railroad. Luckily for the Vans, the New York Central had its own problem. It was being investigated by the Justice Department because one of its services competed with its Nickel Plate route, a possible antitrust violation. So the company was under pressure to shed the Nickel Plate, and the Vans offered themselves up as buyers.

On its face, it was absurd that suburban land developers would purchase a 539-mile railroad simply to fill a two-mile gap in a modest transit line. And yet that's what happened. Helped along by creative financing, in February 1916 the Vans bought the entire railroad for $8.5 million (roughly $232 million in 2022 dollars), spending just $525,000 from their own bank accounts, with most of the rest promised in notes that would be paid from profits.

"The size of an undertaking never awes these boys," a writer in the *American Magazine* gushed in 1917. "I submit that buying a transcontinental railroad in order to assist in the development of a piece of suburban real estate is a bit out of the ordinary, a trifle beyond the imagination of the average real estate operator. It's typical of the Van Sweringen way of going ahead."

As the brothers' local and national profile rose, they remained introverted and averse to publicity. A newspaper reporter hired to handle their public relations recalled being called into O.P.'s office after about three months in his position.

"You have been working as our public relations man now for three months, and there has not been a single story about us in the newspapers," the boss began.

"Well, sir," the PR man stammered, "you see . . ."

"Splendid work!" O.P. interjected. "Keep it up!"

The brothers belonged to country clubs but rarely appeared there. They didn't drink, rarely if ever took vacations, and never, to anyone's knowledge, became involved in any serious romance. Their homes were huge and well appointed, but they did not entertain. Neither played sports, aside from a fleeting interest by M.J. in horseback riding. A room in their mansion was devoted to Charles Dickens and contained many first or limited editions of his books, but neither brother spent time reading them. The only friends they are known to have had were their business partner Benjamin Jenks and his wife, Louise, and the only real pleasure the Vans appeared to enjoy was time at their Hunting Valley country estate, nicknamed Daisy Hill, on property that neighbored the Jenkses'.

"The Van Sweringen brothers are conveniently regarded by the business world as one man," *Fortune* magazine wrote in 1934. "And with some reason. For no men of their prominence have ever so successfully merged their identities." O.P. was taller, heavier, and was said to love sleep. M.J. was a bit more athletic, but also beset with high blood pressure. But their similaries ran far deeper.

Their minds were fixated on business. Once, the brothers were persuaded to attend an Ohio State University football game in Columbus by Horton Hampton, vice president of the Nickel Plate Railroad. At a key point in the action, O.P. leaned across his brother to ask their host, "Horton, do you have any idea how many cubic yards of concrete were used in this stadium?"

The purchase of the Nickel Plate launched the Van Sweringen brothers into railroads, a venture that eventually included some thirty thousand miles of track. This put the Vans on the national scene in a way a single suburb never could. More importantly for Shaker Heights, they now controlled the full Kingsbury Run and could complete the Shaker transit line. The new light rail would ferry Shakerites downtown in as little as fifteen minutes, and, in a profitable turn, bring domestic workers—maids and gardeners—from the city into Shaker Heights, creating demand for trains in both directions.

Operations began on April 11, 1920, between Public Square in downtown Cleveland and Shaker Heights. Two sets of tracks traveled through Shaker, putting trains within easy reach of the entire suburb.

———

The completion of the rapid transit in 1920 set off a stage of explosive growth for Shaker Heights. Over the next ten years, the community would grow from sixteen hundred residents to nearly eighteen thousand. But as that growth began, and as more lots became available, the Vans became concerned that their elite community might attract the wrong sort of people along with the right sort. They could control whom they sold to, but what if a homeowner later sold to someone beneath their standards? Looking to protect their vision of a selective community, they added a new restriction to property deeds, which became known as Restriction No. 5 and required any future buyers of the house be approved by the Van Sweringen Company. The company deployed scare tactics to pressure—to bully, really—existing homeowners to add this restriction to their deeds.

In the summer of 1925, the company sent three increasingly urgent letters to Helen Luthi, who owned a lot in the Ludlow area of Shaker Heights. The language was no doubt replicated, at least in part, in many similar missives. The first letter, dated June 15, 1925, began with an all-caps opening paragraph, lest the recipient fail to grasp the importance of the matter at hand. "THIS LETTER IS OF VITAL INTEREST TO YOU AS A RESIDENT OF SHAKER HEIGHTS AND MAY BE THE MEANS OF PREVENTING UNDESIR-

ABLES GETTING INTO YOUR NEIGHBORHOOD—DO NOT LAY THIS LETTER ASIDE
UNTIL YOU HAVE READ IT AND ACTED UPON IT."

The second letter was sent two weeks later, complaining that Luthi
had not yet responded to the first plea and that the matter was urgent
enough that it merited another letter. "What would you do if tomorrow
an undesirable bought and occupied the premises next door to you?" the
letter asked. It said the choices would be to buy him out, an expensive proposition, or to live next to someone even though the home "will have lost all
of its charm and pleasure for you." With that, the Vans made plain their
view of living beside a Black or perhaps a Jewish family.

Despite this heavy hand, three more weeks passed, and Helen Luthi
still had not authorized alterations to her deed. Writing to her again, A. L.
Sackett of the Van Sweringen Company addressed qualms about whether
the proposal was in Luthi's best interest. Sackett assured her that a meeting had recently been convened to address this question and that seven
Shaker lawyers approved of the plan.

———

In Shaker, the racial element of the restrictions was implied. In much of
the rest of the country, it was stated outright. The first private racially
restrictive covenants began appearing in exclusive American suburbs in
the 1890s, and the practice picked up steam after the Supreme Court
ruled in 1917 that racial restrictions via city ordinances and zoning rules
were unconstitutional. Around this time, Black migrants began arriving from the South, further prompting real estate developers to insert
racial restrictions into deeds. They often imposed these rules on entire
subdivisions, banning ownership or rental by "any person other than
of the white or Caucasian race" or specifically barring groups including
Negroes, Africans, Chinese, Japanese, Mexicans, Puerto Ricans, American Indians, and Jews (who were referred to as Semites or Hebrews).

In 1926, the Supreme Court affirmed the legality of these covenants.
The next year, the National Association of Real Estate Boards distributed standard language for these restrictions and encouraged local real
estate boards and homeowner associations to adopt them. Many did.
A 1928 study of deeds in 84 suburbs found that 40 of them included
racial restrictions. They were seen as an element of city planning, analyst
Helen C. Monchow wrote. "The device seems to be in rather general use

in the vicinity of the larger eastern and northern cities which have experienced a large influx of colored people in recent years." They were also common on the West Coast, directed against people of Asian descent.

The National Housing Act of 1934 introduced the practice of redlining—the drawing of lines on city maps indicating where banks could safely invest and issue mortgages. Black neighborhoods were outlined in red, leading to a devastating, decades-long disinvestment in these communities and giving developers incentive to restrict occupancy by race. Developers and landowners who wrote racial restrictions into their deeds kept their areas from being redlined. By keeping Black people and other minorities out, they assured investment would continue to flow.

So the out-and-out racism on display in these deeds was not the function of a few bad actors. It wasn't something that caught on in a community or two. It was widespread, pernicious, encouraged, and enforced from the top—and broadly accepted as not just the way things were but how they should be. The result: Black people couldn't get mortgages in their own communities because they were redlined as risky, even hazardous— and they couldn't buy into white areas because deeds barred the sale. The use of covenants persisted even after the Supreme Court, in *Shelley v. Kraemer*, ruled in 1948 that they were unenforceable.

In Shaker Heights, Helen Luthi finally gave in, though it took a while. On May 26, 1926, a new deed including the restrictions was registered at the Cuyahoga County Recorder's Office. By then, Shaker Heights had learned that keeping itself all white was not a given.

———

D r. Edward A. Bailey was a member of the Black elite when he arrived in Cleveland in 1912. He had been born in 1883 in Texas, where, according to the *Cleveland Gazette*, his father was a "large landowner." His medical degree was from the noted Meharry Medical College in Nashville, where he also earned a gold medal for excellence in medical studies. In Nashville, he had met Clara Hodgkins, whose father was an attorney and whose sister was married to the president of Tennessee State College. The couple wed in 1914.

In Cleveland, where Dr. Bailey added a law degree from Cleveland Law School to his medical credentials, he and Clara were mainstays of the society pages of the *Gazette*. In 1923, the couple traveled to California for an American Medical Association meeting, a trip the

Gazette covered in gushing detail, taking a vicarious pride in the Baileys' journey. The Baileys were the only Black members of the traveling party, which made its way through Chicago, Omaha, Denver, Colorado Springs, Salt Lake City, and Los Angeles before arriving in San Francisco. "In each of these places, the large party was housed in the very best hotels, and shown the sights of the cities," the *Gazette* proudly reported. "At Colorado Springs and in San Francisco the entire party was photographed; Dr. and Mrs. Bailey being included of course." The couple then returned to Cleveland via the northern route of Portland and Seattle, through the Canadian Rockies, staying at a hotel that they reported was "nearer a palace."

The trip went off without a hint of racism or discomfort, the *Gazette* reported. It was "a most delightful trip in every respect."

So when the Baileys moved from Cedar Avenue in Cleveland's East End to 2869 Huntington Road in Shaker Heights in 1925, the couple was not trying to flip the house and make a quick profit. They intended to make it their home. A few years earlier, the Baileys had bought a home on East 105th Street, well east of the central Black ghetto, to the delight of the *Gazette*, which called the purchase "more substantial evidence of prosperity." Now they were headed into Shaker, and the Gazette reported the development with palpable enthusiasm.

"Their new home is a beautiful one in exceptionally beautiful surroundings as far as the eye will reach," the paper said. The double garage, it said, will house Dr. Bailey's Dodge coupe and Mrs. Bailey's new Lincoln. Their arrival to Shaker was, to the *Gazette*, a step forward for whites and Blacks alike at a time when Blacks were being terrorized in the South and often subject to racism just as hateful in the North. "When our successful business and professional men and women locate in the better and best residential sections of any city, here in the North at least, they not only help the race's progress but they also furnish the other group a much-needed object lesson, particularly in these days of the K.K.K."

The Baileys' new neighbors in Shaker Heights failed to share the *Gazette*'s enthusiasm. They saw the doctor and his wife not as elite citizens advancing the progress of race relations but as the leading edge of an invasion. Detractors fired shots at their new house. Attempts were made to burn their garage. Stones were hurled at their windows. Their chauffeur tried to protect the house, firing a shot at vandals to scare them away. When the Baileys sought protection from the Shaker Heights authorities, the police stationed a guard at the house who seemed most interested in searching Dr. Bailey, members of his family, and his servants for concealed weapons each time they went in or out of the house. The police claimed the chauffeur's shot justified that approach.

Bailey took the city to court, seeking an injunction to stop the police from harassing the people they were allegedly protecting. Common Pleas judge A. J. Pearson denied the application. He said the Baileys had the right to live where they pleased and were entitled to police protection, but that a damage suit, not an injunction, was the proper course. Bailey informed the *Gazette* that he planned to do just that, and the newspaper cheered him on.

"Good!" the paper wrote. "'Hold the fort,' Doctor! Make them realize fully that Cleveland is not Atlanta, Georgia; Wilmington, N.C., or Houston, Texas. Those persons who are injuring your property and otherwise disturbing your family are a lawless lot of kluxers which the police of Shaker Heights either are unable to cope with or will not handle properly. Therefore, it is up to you to protect your family and your home, your castle, and the law will back you up in whatever you do in order to do so."

The incident coincided with a similar fight in the Wade Park Allotment, on the east side of Cleveland. A Black man, Dr. C. H. Garvin, had bought land and was building a house in another white enclave. Before buying the property, Garvin had bought a lot in Shaker Heights, but sold it—at a price "far in excess of its real value"—after learning he could not get police protection from antagonists. But he made clear that this was not his aim. "I am not trying to 'shake down' anyone," he told the *Gazette*. "I am building a home in which I intend to live." His purchase in the Wade Park Allotment now prompted an uproar, with white neighbors circulating a racist handbill. And after construction was complete, neighbors twice set off dynamite bombs on the property.

Still, racial violence was far less common in Cleveland than in cities such as Chicago and Detroit, according to the historian Todd M. Michney, who studied Black migration out of the Cleveland core, and Garvin and others later reported some degree of friendship and neighborliness once they arrived.

Back in Shaker Heights, citizens were ready to take action, and not the neighborly kind. In September 1925, about four hundred residents met at Shaker Heights High School to protest the presence of a Black family in the community. They formed a "protective association" and a blue ribbon committee to recommend next steps. The association was to collaborate with the Van Sweringen brothers and consider ways to ensure that current property owners would control future property sales. All citizens need to work with the Van Sweringens to impose new restrictions, John L. Cannon told the meeting. Another man made clear that the objections were "not only to Negroes but also to Jews and any other persons not satisfactory to the residents of Shaker Heights."

The *Gazette* had been confident that the Baileys and Dr. Garvin would win their battles to live in white neighborhoods, referencing the 1917 Supreme Court decision in *Buchanan v. Warley*, which unanimously struck down a Louisville ordinance that had prohibited Blacks from living on blocks where a majority of residents were white. It appears that the Baileys stayed for a time, and, intriguingly, the Cleveland *Plain Dealer* listed Mrs. Bailey as a hostess for an upcoming musical performance sponsored by Plymouth Congregational Church, located near their Huntington Road home. The event, in January 1926, was set, of all places, at the Van Sweringen mansion, and hosted by O.P. and M.J.'s sisters, Carrie and Edith. But details of Mrs. Bailey's participation, if she did indeed participate, were unclear.

In any case, the Baileys departed Shaker Heights before long. It's not clear exactly when, but records show that by January 1927, the property was in the hands of another family.

———

The nine-member Committee of the Shaker Heights Protective Association was formed on September 25, 1925, and just three weeks later, it issued its findings.

"The time to protect the property on your street is today—tomorrow may be too late," the report began, placing these words in large print for emphasis. The report raised the scary prospect of property purchased by "an undesirable person" and referenced the recent buyouts of Black would-be buyers. Race was never explicitly mentioned, but there was no doubt whom the Protective Association saw as the undesirables.

The association cast itself as progressive, rejecting harassment and violence. Better to fix things with clear rules. It compared homeowners' interest in choosing their neighbors with the interest private clubs have in choosing members; clubs often required unanimous consent to admit new people. If anything, the report put forth, one cares even more about neighbors than it does about club members. Besides, the report concluded, no one with "sufficient pride" would want to live somewhere "in which he is not desired."

As for solutions, the committee reported that it had rejected some ideas, which it did not detail, as either legally unenforceable or impractical. The answer, it concluded, was already before them: the Van Sweringen restrictions.

The committee made some modifications to what was already known as Restriction No. 5 and recommended that all property owners voluntarily return their deeds to have the new requirement added. Property with the restriction attached could not be sold or occupied without consent of the Van Sweringen Company. If the company refused, the owner could appeal to his immediate neighbors. That included the homes surrounding the lot in question—five on either side, and eleven across the street. Only those with the restriction in their own deeds got a vote.

The report, which apparently was distributed across town, included letters of endorsement from a bank, an insurance company, and two prominent law firms. Committee members signing the report included the pastor of Plymouth Congregational Church, as well as Shaker resident Newton D. Baker, former mayor of Cleveland and secretary of war during World War I. A card was included that homeowners could send back, agreeing to add Restriction No. 5.

By 1927, three-quarters of Shaker property deeds had been revised and returned. Restriction No. 5 was now in force across the suburb.

The Vans, meantime, were busy with yet another ambitious project: building a grand train station in the center of Cleveland to serve several railroads, including their own. Overcoming opposition from a preexisting, competing plan for a lakefront terminal, they set out to construct not just a grand terminal, but also a hotel, a department store, and an office building. The project required the purchase of 17 acres around Public Square and the tearing down of about fifteen hundred buildings. The first stone was laid on March 16, 1927.

The result was the Terminal Tower, the iconic Beaux Arts skyscraper that stretched fifty-two stories into the air, with a wedding cake top. It was, at the time of its completion, the second-tallest building in the world, giving Cleveland the look of a first-class city. Inside, commuters, shoppers, and executives would travel along brass-railed stairways and marble concourses. Outside, the Terminal Tower created a new city center and instantly defined the Cleveland skyline. The first passenger train entered the unfinished station on December 1, 1929, with M. J. Van Sweringen on the platform for the occasion (though he ducked into the tiny yard-master's office as the train rolled in to avoid being photographed, the *Plain Dealer* reported). It was a notable moment, as neither brother was known to attend any event of public interest.

The following June, a who's who crowd of governors, senators, entertainers, and local luminaries assembled for a luncheon in the tower's chandeliered grand concourse, marking the official inauguration of the Terminal Tower. Light beamed out, red lights near the tower's top and bright floodlights all around. Absent from the event: O. P. and M. J. Van Sweringen, who were at their estate, listening in via a special telephone hookup.

Buying the Nickel Plate Railroad set the Vans on a course that would prove historic in the story of American railroads. They soon built a rail empire, acquiring one railroad after the next. By 1929, the Van Sweringen holdings were worth some $3 billion—what would be $52 billion in 2022 dollars. But it was all built on a financially dubious pyramid, a set of interlocking holding companies dependent on a mountain of borrowing. When the stock market crashed in 1929 and the nation fell into a deep economic depression, important local banks failed and their empire came tumbling down. Train travel slowed, and so did income to the Vans, who were unable to meet their payments on the debt that underpinned their holdings, which began to unravel. A congressional committee probed their finances. Separately, in 1934, O.P. was indicted by a Cuyahoga County grand jury for allegedly manipulating bank statements about their holding company's finances.

In August 1935, M.J. entered Lakeside Hospital suffering from high blood pressure. O.P., meantime, was engaged in a fierce battle to save the business after it was put up for auction, and that November he was embroiled in complex bankruptcy proceedings connected to the Missouri Pacific, one of their railroads.

At home, M.J. only grew weaker. He contracted the flu, fell into a coma, and died of heart disease on December 12, 1935. He was fifty-four.

He left everything to his brother: the value of his life insurance policy and $3,087. After soaring to the heights in real estate and railroads, these were his remaining assets upon his death.

At the funeral, O.P. could manage only this: "I've always been able to see a way, but to this there is no answer."

Each morning, the grieving brother went into the office that had belonged to M.J. inside the Terminal Tower and lit his lamp. Each evening, he would return and extinguish it. He insisted M.J.'s office remain as it was. In 1936, the Van Sweringen Company, responsible for developing Shaker Heights, declared bankruptcy, even as O.P. kept trying to rebuild. "The only weapon he had against loneliness was work," wrote friend and journalist Taylor Hampton.

On November 22, 1936, less than a year after M.J.'s passing, O.P. traveled overnight to New York on one of his Nickel Plate trains. A small accident held things up, and around eight o'clock the next morning, O.P. complained that he was tired and retired to his bedroom on the train. When his secretary came to wake him at noon, he found O.P. dead. He was fifty-seven. Cause of death was a heart attack, though some called it a broken heart. After his death, the probate court calculated that he owed debts equal to nearly $81 million. His estate was valued at $534,994.

The Vans died financially broken, but they had set Shaker Heights on its way, and the community continued to thrive as an exclusive, wealthy enclave. In 1955, *Trains* magazine said Shaker "has the reputation of being one of the Midwest's most desirable suburbs." In 1962, the Census Bureau reported Shaker was the wealthiest city in America among places with at least 25,000 residents.

The brothers were buried side by side at Lake View Cemetery in Cleveland beneath a common headstone. VAN SWERINGEN, it read along the top, with each man's name and dates. Below that, simply, BROTHERS.

Before we even moved in, the house next door went up for sale.
—Beverly Mason

3

TED AND BEVERLY MASON

The neighbors were not sure what was happening, but they didn't like it.

It was the spring of 1955, and the sight of Theodore Mason and three other Black men looking around the vacant lot on Ashwood Road, on the edge of Shaker Heights, was enough to cause not one but three families to call the police. Learning the truth about the situation did little to calm jangling nerves. Mason was the new owner of the lot, and he had brought a contractor and a land surveyor with him to lay out plans for construction of his new home.

The neighborhood was called Ludlow. Along the tree-lined, curving streets sat neat, two-story single-family homes, complete with tidy yards, all part of the original Van Sweringen vision for a garden suburb. Like all Shaker neighborhoods, Ludlow was named for the elementary school that sat at its center, geographically and socially. The streets formed concentric ovals around the two-story brick school, built in 1928, which featured the classic neo-Georgian architecture with the traditional Shaker bell tower perched on top.

Just a block away was Van Aken Boulevard, the town's unofficial economic dividing line. On the other side were the lakes left behind by the original Shakers and the mansions erected under the Van Sweringen vision of prosperity. But Ludlow's homes, too, had much to recommend them. They were set within walking distance of the rapid transit and a straight shot downtown, at an affordable price for the professional middle class.

Beginning in significant numbers in the 1940s, Black families had migrated out of the overcrowded Cedar-Central area and into a handful of Cleveland neighborhoods farther east, including Glenville and, on the edge of Shaker Heights, Mount Pleasant. The Black "pioneers," as they were called, were often following the route Jews had taken out of the central ghetto and toward the suburbs. In a chicken-and-egg situation, their arrival was enabled by the white families departing, and also spurred more whites to leave once they arrived. That, in turn, opened up more housing for more Black buyers.

The Ludlow neighborhood was still entirely white in 1955 when the Masons arrived, ready to pioneer a new frontier.

For Ted Mason, the journey to the front lawn of 3166 Ashwood Road had required both determination and subterfuge.

The determination came naturally. Mason, a fourth-generation Ohioan, had grown up in the Appalachian foothills of southeast Ohio, in a little town called Cadiz. The family matriarch (Ted's great-great-grandmother), Susan Bowman Mason Johnson, was a free woman who had married an enslaved man. Her husband was supposed to have been freed upon the death of his enslaver, but the white man died before drawing up the paperwork. Susan's husband was sold and shipped to Louisiana, and Susan and her sister migrated to Ohio.

Ted Mason, born in 1923, was named for one of Susan's sons, a man who died on a Southern battlefield fighting for the Union in the Civil War. A gifted athlete and hometown football hero, Ted won a scholarship to Western Reserve University in Cleveland in 1940. He was first in his family to go to college, and his sights were set on medical school.

In 1942, he left college and signed up to become an aviation cadet in the U.S. Army Air Corps and the next year was sent for flight training at Tuskegee Army Air Field in Alabama, where Black units that executed missions during World War II learned to fly. In 1945, he was assigned to a unit in Fort Knox, Kentucky, and for Mason, it was a time of awakening as he encountered the blatant racism of the Jim Crow South. On base, there were two officers' clubs, one for trainers (all white) and one for trainees (all Black). This ran against official War Department policy, but allowances were made for local laws in the South. Then Mason's unit moved to Freeman Field in Indiana, and the army again established separate, and unequal, clubs—one of many insults and inequities the Black airmen faced.

In April 1945, they decided to act, and sixty-one men from Ted's unit were arrested trying to force their way into the white officers' club. Most of the charges were dropped, on the grounds that the rules had not been clearly communicated. But to make sure there was no misunderstanding going forward, a new segregation regulation was drafted, and the army forced Black officers to sign a statement acknowledging they had read and understood it. Ted Mason refused to sign: Yes, he had read the statement, but no, he did not "understand" it, he later told his son Paul. He was one of 101 men arrested for refusing to sign.

Mason had not been one of the main protesters. He had not tried to enter the white officers' club. "But when the moment came for him to make a choice, it was clear to him that he would stand against the demand to use a segregated facility," Paul Mason said.

After national attention, most of these charges were dropped, and the incident helped lead to the integration of the armed forces. Ted Mason was honorably discharged a month before his release date, in time to return to college.

The entire matter served as a wakeup call for Mason and a turning point. His family had experienced hardship when he was growing up—dinner was sometimes raccoon or groundhog they caught themselves, and he had just one pair of pants, which his mother dyed blue for the winter and bleached khaki in the spring. But this hatred and disrespect was something different. He headed back to Cleveland having seen raw racism up close. He was angry.

"The experience changed him," Paul Mason said.

Ted returned to Western Reserve University and finished his undergraduate degree. The university's medical school would admit only two Black students each year, and both spots were taken, but Mason was admitted to the dental school, and he played on the school's football team. One day he was in the cafeteria, wearing his football letter sweater, when he caught the eye of Beverly Sinkford. "That's who I'm going to marry," Beverly told a friend. After a failed attempt by friends to set up a blind date—he wasn't interested—they met on their own.

Beverly had been raised in prosperity, certainly by the standards of the day for Black families. Her grandfather, George Sinkford, was a light-skinned man, which likely eased his way. He was born in Tazewell, Virginia, but later moved to Bluefield, West Virginia, opening a funeral home in 1911. His son followed him into the family business, and by the time Beverly was born, it was a thriving enterprise, serving Black coal miners and their families, among other Black clientele. The family lived above the business—mortuary on the first floor, living quarters on the second. Bev had close relatives who had attended elite colleges. An aunt went to Juilliard in the 1920s and later was invited by the Black scholar and activist W.E.B. Du Bois to sing in salons attended by artists and writers during the Harlem Renaissance.

Nonetheless, race and racism hung heavy over Beverly's childhood. "I think as a child I was ashamed," she said in an interview for a 1966 documentary. "I had nothing to be proud of, I didn't want to be Negro. I really wanted to be something else. And it wasn't until I was an adult that I worked through these feelings."

There was little doubt that Bev would go on to higher education, as had a brother and all seven of her sisters. She attended Bluefield State, a prominent Black college in West Virginia, and then came to Cleveland to earn her master's degree in social work at Western Reserve.

After grad school, Beverly and Ted married, and they were among the first Black people to move into the Hough neighborhood of Cleveland, which was predominantly white at the time. It was 1949. She worked in a settlement house, and he opened a dental practice on the east side of Cleveland, at 80th Street and Cedar Avenue.

Ted was still a superb athlete and an excellent golfer, with a handicap of one. So he would drive eight miles east, down the boulevards of Shaker Heights with their stately colonials and oversized lawns lining the way, through Shaker and out the other side, to Highland Park Golf Course, the only club in the area that would let Black people play. Sometimes he was stopped by the Shaker Heights police, who asked where he was going and suggested he move on quickly.

His son Paul imagines his father's response to the cops was along the lines of, "I'll fix you." This was a man with a graduate degree, who was building his own life in the professional middle class. He had come from poverty, but he was no longer poor. With an intensity that came through his steely eyes, Ted Mason was a man on his way—on this day, he was on his way to golf, and on all days, he was on his way to prosperity. "Nobody was going to tell my parents where they could and couldn't be," Paul said.

———

By the early 1950s, the Masons had two young sons and a third on the way. *Brown v. Board of Education*, the case that would outlaw the legal system of segregated schools in the South, was making its way to the Supreme Court. (Ted Mason, in fact, sat on a panel discussing the case at a local church in 1953.) In Cleveland, the schools were segregated—a federal court would later find the city intentionally created and maintained a segregated system. But the original *Brown* decision didn't even apply to the North, so accessing better-funded white schools would require different strategies on the part of families of color.

Around this time, there had been at least one or two Black students in the Shaker schools, though details are unclear. The Masons didn't know any of them, but looking at their options in 1955, they wanted the best schools they could find for their kids, and that meant Shaker Heights.

Soon a plan took shape, with the help of a white friend of Ted's named Morrie Friedman, an old teammate from Western Reserve football. The Masons owned two parcels of land at 153rd Street and Harvard Avenue in the city of Cleveland—property they had bought as their family grew. Friedman owned a plot in a residential neighborhood of Cleveland on the edge of Shaker Heights—so close, in fact, that it was part of the Shaker Heights school district. Crucially, the parcel did not carry the deed restrictions that the Van Sweringen Company had worked so hard to persuade owners to adopt.

The two men traded properties, a turning point moment that may explain why Mason kept Friedman's business card in a jewelry box on his bedroom dresser for decades. Of course, the Masons knew this was a dicey proposition, knew how hard it would be to build in an all-white area, knew someone might try and stop them. "We were young," Beverly said. "We decided to try anyway."

The initial transaction flew under the radar of real estate agents and bankers who conspired to keep Black people in Black neighborhoods. The Masons hired a Black architect to design the house, but they knew he could not show his face and expect to get the building permits that were needed. So the architect asked a colleague at a white firm to take the plans to the Shaker Heights Architectural Board of Review for approval. They also needed permission from the City of Cleveland, and Mason asked a friend who served on the City Council to bury the application in a pile of other matters he was asking the building department to approve.

All those tactics worked. Now Mason needed a loan. He made a preliminary inquiry at Central National Bank, where he had an account, and when he explained where the property was, he was told, "You're wasting your time," Ted Mason recounted in a 1962 interview. Later, Mason elaborated in telling the story to his son Paul. He said the banker argued that he was just stating facts: Mason could apply, but getting a loan to build in a white area was not going to fly. "I'm just being truthful with you," he said.

Mason then approached a Black-owned bank, Quincy Savings and Loan. Bought by eleven Black investors in 1952, Quincy quickly saw a steady stream of Black customers who had been rejected by white banks. Within five years, it had made loans on twelve hundred homes, and by 1959 it controlled more than $5 million in assets. "We don't care whether it's an area that has been penetrated or not," said A. B. Heard, a Quincy board member.

The loan was approved, and Mason closed his account at Central National and moved his money to Quincy.

None of this sat well with Shaker Savings & Loan, where the bank president got word that a loan was being issued for a Black family to build in the Shaker school district. It's not clear how he knew; maybe the Central National bankers tipped him off. In any case, the bank president asked the president of Quincy to come in for a meeting.

The Quincy banker arrived with Ted Mason and a minister Ted brought along.

"What are you doing making a loan on Ashwood?" the Shaker banker pointedly asked his Black counterpart. It's a white street, he said.

"I've been there," the Black banker replied. "That asphalt is gray."

Not amused, the banker demanded to know: What is your interest in this lot? "I'm going to provide a home for my family," Ted replied.

Truth be told, Ted later confessed to his son, he thought the sale would be blocked somewhere along the line. These were uncharted waters. But he had it in him to go for it, to push the boundary.

Banks had been blocking sales like this one for decades, part of a suite of discriminatory lending policies driven by racism and the assertion—

advanced by federal agencies, banks, and others—that the presence of Black people would lower property values. This included redlining and other practices used by banks to deny loans and investment. Together they go a long way to explaining why many Black Americans have persistently been unable to build wealth.

But in this case, the Shaker Heights banker had no power to stop the Mason transaction, and it went through. Now it was the spring of 1955, and Mason was eager to get construction underway. He arrived at his new lot, architect in tow, and his neighbors called the cops.

Mason showed them his deed and building permit as upset neighbors watched. The police saw that everything was in order. "Go on home," an officer told the neighbors.

"Before we even moved in, the house next door went up for sale," Beverly Mason told the *Dayton Daily News* in 1968. She was in the hospital at the time, giving birth to her third child, when the man next door announced he was moving, giving the "usual excuse that he was going to Florida," she said. "Of course we knew that he wasn't going." The departing neighbor, as it turns out, sold to another Black family.

The architect, Arthur Saunders, later told Paul Mason that they had been inspired by the Tuskegee experience, the fight for their rights when in the service. "For us, the first step was this house," he said. "We knew this was a revolutionary act."

———

The Masons' neighbors also saw revolution, and they weren't about to allow it to unfold in their neighborhood. In November 1955, a group of several hundred homeowners met at Ludlow Elementary School to discuss the developments. The Mason house was nearing completion, and another home in the neighborhood, for a Black attorney and his wife, was also underway. The meeting's purpose echoed the gathering at the high school thirty years earlier, when Dr. Bailey and his family moved in: to keep "undesirables out of the neighborhood."

The group's leader, Marie J. Chader, lived across the street from the home being built by the lawyer. At the meeting, she proposed forming an association whereby members would agree only to sell their homes to people approved by the association, another version of Restriction No. 5. "This is not a racial matter. At our meeting one or two tried to make it a racial matter," Chader said, according to the *Cleveland Press*. "We want to keep out racketeers and hoodlums." Under her plan, violators would be required to pay a fine to the association. When someone at the meeting noted that one of the Black buyers had already begun construction of a house, a speaker replied, "Well, he hasn't moved in yet."

One resident described the atmosphere as "one of fear, panic, and bitterness." An observer said the meeting's leader had "left no doubts in anyone's mind that she included Negroes among the 'undesirables' she wanted to keep out of the neighborhood."

"The proposal received large support, although several persons objected that it was not American," the *Plain Dealer* reported. "Another meeting is to be held next Thursday to act on it."

Perhaps she didn't like the way this idea looked in print, or maybe she felt her words had been misunderstood, because after the article was published, Mrs. Chader called the newspaper to protest that the goal was to protect building restrictions, not to restrict "undesirables." The Cleveland *Call & Post*, a Black newspaper, wasn't having it. It called the gathering a "Klan-Type" meeting, referring to the participants as race haters plotting "the newest hate movement."

If anyone present remembered what unfolded in 1925, when the Baileys moved onto Huntington, the events unfolding in Ludlow would have felt familiar. And yet there was something different this time. While walking home from the meeting, several residents talked among themselves about what they had just witnessed. Something had to be done, they decided, to counteract the hostility on display. A group of about twenty-eight residents met at the home of Gilbert Seldin, who lived on Becket Road, to plan a new way forward. The group included the executive director of the Cleveland Community Relations Board and the principal of Ludlow Elementary School. Experts told them any agreement to keep out "undesirables" was illegal, and that studies had shown property values did not fall when Negroes moved in unless panic selling followed. Soon after, Seldin reported on their work to the Cleveland Clearinghouse on Civil Liberties, saying media coverage of the school meeting had been helpful in halting the opposition.

The group was cautious, opting against mass meetings or formal organization. "We did not have the right to preach our morals to the neighborhood, nor could we effectively do it," said one person involved, according to an account by Kent and Karen Weeks in an unpublished history of Shaker Heights completed around 1968. The group decided on a low-pressure campaign to urge their neighbors against panic selling. They would keep their ears open for blockbusting, the real estate technique of scaring white people into selling by warning that soon the neighborhood would be all Black. A loose committee of four people was formed to keep an eye out over the neighborhood.

Construction on the Masons' house was completed in September 1955, and the family moved in.

All this angst and anger, and the Masons' house was not even in Shaker Heights proper, but in a slice of Cleveland that was part of the Shaker Heights City School District. But just as bigoted white Shakerites had feared, it would prove the entry point for the first wave of Black families into the Shaker community.

⸻

The school district's odd boundaries dated back to around 1912, soon after Shaker Village was established. Families living in Shaker had wanted their children to attend a newly built nearby school in the city of Cleveland, and the city agreed, according to historian Virginia Dawson, who has studied the development of Shaker Heights. In exchange, Shaker promised to educate children living in a different swath of Cleveland on the Shaker border, mostly farmland at the time, which later included the Shaker Square shopping center.

Boundary lines between school districts are no small matter, especially when it comes to race. There's often debate over where attendance lines are drawn between schools inside any given district. But an even larger factor in explaining segregation are the lines that divide entire school districts from one another. That's obvious every time someone looks up the school district when house hunting. Parents and future parents talk about wanting good schools, and "good schools" usually means schools with lush resources, where poverty is scarce and, not coincidentally, test scores are high. Wealthy people cluster into certain districts, leaving low-income families in others.

School district boundaries make this sorting possible. In 2019, I collaborated with Kate Rabinowitz, a data journalist at the *Washington Post*, to analyze the effect of school district boundaries on racial segregation in the nation's 13,184 traditional public school districts. The analysis found that school segregation was far more pervasive among school districts in a metro area than within them. That means that individual school districts might look integrated, with systems doing a decent job maintaining racial balance in their schools. But when you zoom the camera out and look at children in an entire metro area, segregation is pervasive, because the districts are so different from one another.

Imagine you have one school district that is 90 percent white, and it does a reasonable job sprinkling the 10 percent students of color around its schools. Now, imagine there's a nearby school district that is 90 percent Black, and it does a good job sprinkling its non-Black students around as well. In one sense, each district, viewed on its own, looks integrated because the individual schools reflect the district as a whole. But when you look at this hypothetical metro area as a whole, it's not integrated at all, because one district is overwhelmingly white and another is overwhelmingly Black.

"When you move to an area, you're told by Realtors or by social contacts, 'These are the places to live that have these kind of schools that we think are more like you,'" Erica Frankenberg, who directs the Center for Education and Civil Rights at Pennsylvania State University, told me. "When I came to Penn State, people were like, 'This is the district you should live in.'"

When the deal was struck around 1912 to include the slice of the city of Cleveland in the Shaker Heights school district, nobody was thinking about race or integration. Everyone on both sides of the border was white. But decades later, almost by accident, the district's boundary lines facilitated a diversity not present in most communities, setting up both a challenge and an opportunity.

———

The Cleveland suburbs grew rapidly through the first half of the twentieth century, and by 1960, nearly half of Cuyahoga County's total population lived outside the city of Cleveland. Almost all these suburbanites were white; 98 percent of the county's Black population remained inside Cleveland. And while they once were spread throughout the city, Black residents now were concentrated in certain neighborhoods.

Housing segregation in twentieth-century America was tied directly to federal government policy. The Federal Housing Administration, established in 1934, was created to guarantee mortgages for working- and middle-class Americans, but in effect, only in white neighborhoods for white people. Black people were prohibited from participating by underwriting guidelines; appraisers often were told that projects did not qualify for federal subsidies if they included Black residents and loans were denied for all-white projects if they were too close to Black neighborhoods, under the belief it would "risk infiltration by inharmonious racial groups" and present a financial hazard to the federal insurer.

Public housing also drove segregation. Originally created to ease the housing shortage, the federal government mandated segregated projects, even segregating previously integrated neighborhoods. Real estate agents who belonged to all-white associations were barred by their ethics code from facilitating sales that would lower property values in a neighborhood, which was interpreted to mean they could not sell homes to people of color in white neighborhoods.

If none of that worked to keep an area white, residents had a toolbox of strategies, including violence and intimidation. They'd deny a building permit or, if a Black family managed to move in, send police out to harass the new arrivals on manufactured pretexts. They'd rezone newly purchased lots, or preemptively rezone areas before Black families could buy them. Land once ripe for homes was suddenly available for industry. And many Black families simply could not afford houses in the suburbs.

Shaker Heights was one of the first spots where Black buyers were able to gain a foothold, starting in Ludlow, where the Van Sweringen restrictions failed to do the job intended. While the Supreme Court's 1948 decision outlawing the restrictions did not put an end to their use, it made it harder to insist upon them.

Still, it was not easy for these early families, who were leaving the nurturing and safe spaces of the Black community in search of better services, safer streets, great schools, and the chance to build home equity. "African American pioneers were in a difficult position," said Andrew Wiese, an expert in American urban history at San Diego State University. "They were literally risking their lives to find better places to live."

Yet in some cases, they were moving just a few blocks away. Cleveland's Mount Pleasant, for instance, bordered the Ludlow neighborhood— making a move to Shaker Heights both a natural evolution and also something of a radical act.

As the calendar flipped to 1956, the Masons had moved in, and construction was nearly complete on the other house that Ludlow neighbors had been worked up about the previous fall. The new $40,000 two-story brick house at 13601 Corby Road belonged to John G. and Dorothy Pegg.

John Pegg was one of the most prominent Black attorneys in Cleveland, an active member of the local Republican Party, and a local campaign manager for Republican senator Robert A. Taft. He had graduated from Western Reserve University law school, and in 1944, married Dorothy Singleton, the daughter of a teacher and a physician in Washington, D.C. Dorothy had three degrees of her own, was a correspondent with field directors at the American Red Cross headquarters during World War II, and a teacher in D.C., Baltimore, and then Cleveland. She was also treasurer of the Cleveland League of Women Voters.

The Peggs had spent two or three years looking for a house. In a 1960 interview with a political scientist in Cleveland, John Pegg explained that they wanted a "good neighborhood," adding: "And when we say in a good neighborhood, we don't mean in a good colored neighborhood, but we mean in a good neighborhood." Pegg, who died in 1979, didn't clarify his meaning, but this comment seems to imply that they saw a white neighborhood as an upwardly mobile step, a next-level achievement. They ran into brokers who wouldn't show them homes, or who would cancel appointments after learning they were Black. Once, they saw a listing that interested them in the newspaper and called the agent, who suggested they go see the house. After Dorothy Pegg looked at it, the agent called her back and demanded, "Why didn't you tell me you were colored?" Mrs. Pegg replied that she didn't think it was necessary. "Well," the broker replied, "we can't sell that home to you."

They found the lot on Corby through a tax sale, sending someone who appeared to be white to bid in Dorothy Pegg's name in order to avoid suspicion. It was the only bid, and the property was theirs, but they still faced the Van Sweringen restrictions. John Pegg was convinced that the rules requiring permission would not hold up in court, but he sought permission anyway from the local officials responsible for enforcing the rules, and was denied. Nonetheless, the Peggs moved ahead. While they heard rumblings of pressure to try to block the sale, no one stopped them.

Despite the Peggs' impeccable pedigree, they were turned down for a loan from their own bank, Cleveland Trust Company, who told them they wouldn't make the loan unless the street was already at least 50 percent Black. The Peggs turned then to the Black-owned Dunbar Life Insurance Company. In a repeat of the Masons' experience, an executive with Shaker Savings & Loan called in the Dunbar banker and tried to "beg, persuade, induce, browbeat, threaten" him to cancel the loan. "It ended up with them cussing each other across the table," John Pegg said. Dunbar held firm.

The Peggs set out to build a center-hall colonial. When they put the job out for bid, they got only two proposals from contractors, both well over the price expected. They later learned there was a boycott in place, so Pegg hired an out-of-state contractor. But then no one would sell him lumber, forcing him to buy it in Akron, forty miles south of Cleveland.

"They were determined that no colored family should move this close to Shaker Square or Shaker Heights," John Pegg said, referring to the Cleveland lumber companies in particular but in fact describing the entire enterprise. "They seemed fearful that it would destroy property values and that, well, it just wasn't to be. They seemed to pull out all the stops to prevent it."

Things did not improve once construction began. Vandals broke windows. A woman phoned the Peggs and said she hoped there wouldn't be "any bombings" in the neighborhood. A second caller objected to the size of the windows in the home under construction and to the garage entrance facing the street. (The Peggs maintained that they had carefully studied the Van Sweringen deed restrictions and zoning rules and that they were in compliance.)

Then, at about a quarter past seven on the evening of January 3, 1956, neighbors heard an explosion. A black powder "super bomb" had been planted in the Peggs' garage, still under construction. Its detonation destroyed the garage, ripped open the west wall of the home, and shattered windows on two sides. The force was equal to ten sticks of dynamite, police later said, inflicting $2,000 in damage (or about $22,000 in 2022 dollars). The house next door was also damaged, with basement and second-floor bedroom walls cracked by the force of the explosion.

John Pegg immediately blamed the incident on what newspapers dubbed "racial feeling." The police weren't sure, and they considered the possibility that the bomb was planted in retaliation for the Peggs' use of nonunion labor. Sheet metal workers the Peggs had hired, for example, were nonunion, though the contractor later explained why: the sheet metal union barred Negro membership.

Cleveland mayor Anthony J. Celebrezze ordered police to use "every resource" to solve the crime, but they never cracked the case.

Some made the connection between the neighbors who had tried to stop the Peggs from building the house in the first place and the bomber at large who tried to stop them near the end. "The morons who do bombings get tacit encouragement from people high in society," said Cleveland councilman Charles V. Carr, a leader in the Black community who would ultimately serve on the council for thirty years.

"If this is meant to intimidate us, it is a sad failure," John Pegg told the *Call & Post*.

But he was also encouraged by an unexpected response from his future neighbors.

Immediately after the explosion, the group of residents who had been upset by the meeting at the school gathered again at the home of Gilbert Seldin on Becket Road. "We are alarmed and indignant over the bombing and will take whatever steps are necessary to combat hoodlumism and promote respect for law and individual rights," Seldin told the newspaper.

That Saturday morning, the weather was bitterly cold, with snow flurries and temperatures topping out at the freezing mark. But just before ten o'clock, about thirty people from the neighborhood joined a dozen Cleveland clergy, including several leading ministers, in clearing the debris from the explosion. Some women served coffee; others passed around cakes and cookies. The *Call & Post* called the event "one of the most significant exemplifications of interracial unity and goodwill seen in this area for many years." John Pegg said he and his wife were "deeply impressed."

A few days after the cleanup, Seldin's wife received a telephone call. The caller hurled obscenities and threatened to bomb their home "even worse than Pegg." Three letters containing obscenities and threats arrived. Police ordered special protection.

Police also provided the Peggs with protection for the first two or three weeks after they moved in, but it proved unnecessary. They received hundreds of letters and phone calls, mostly welcoming. "Yes we were afraid during those early weeks, but we were determined to do it," Pegg later said, though he added: "We might not have risked all of this if we had had children."

At the time of the bombing, about seven other houses for Black families were under construction. Soon after, many more homes went onto the market and, driven by pent-up demand by middle-class Black families, many flipped from white to Black. This got the attention of some in Shaker Heights who talked about buying up property to forestall the movement or implementing a quota system, neither of which came to pass.

By year's end, Marie Chader, who had riled up the neighborhood upon first sight of Black arrivals, had moved away. In the Ludlow neighborhood she and her husband left behind, the work of Gilbert Seldin's small group was just getting started.

4

IRV AND EMILIE BARNETT

It was 1956, and Irv and Emilie Barnett were a young white couple, living in a $65-per-month one-room basement apartment near Shaker Square, one of the nation's first shopping centers, on the border between Cleveland and Shaker Heights. They had one son, and when Emilie became pregnant with a second, they decided it was time to buy.

Irv had grown up in a working-class, largely Jewish section of Shaker Heights and wanted to move back to Shaker, though most of the homes in the community were well beyond their means. He was earning just $100 per week in his struggling law practice, and the couple had no savings to speak of. But they managed to find a house they could afford, with help from their parents for the down payment. It cost $17,500 and was set on Becket Road, in the Ludlow neighborhood of Shaker Heights.

In September 1956, they moved in, and in November, their son Bill was born. Between the cold winter weather and caring for a newborn, the Barnetts spent most of that winter inside. When spring arrived, Emilie, twenty-three years old, bundled her young sons into a buggy and set out for a walk.

She was shaken by what she saw. There were For Sale signs all up and down her block. Emilie wondered: Had the neighbors found out she and Irv were Jewish? She knew Shaker Heights was overwhelmingly Christian. Soon she learned the truth. Word was out that a newly built house on their street would be occupied by a Black family, and white flight was underway.

The calls from real estate agents started coming. "I hear you want to sell," they'd say. "You know your neighbor has his house with me. You better sell now while the prices are ripe. If you wait you'll lose your shirt." In 1956, For Sale signs were posted in front of about 25 percent of Ludlow homes, according to historical notes documenting neighborhood history. Within six months, half the houses on their block had changed hands, white to Black.

Irv considered himself an open-minded liberal. He had known Black people before—family maids growing up, and some of his clients. He didn't have anything against them, he thought. But did he want Black children in his neighborhood, playing with his kids? He didn't know. He found himself in utter panic, unable to sleep at night, deeply rooted prejudices spiraling through his mind in the silent house. He was terrified property values would fall, crime would arrive, that the school quality would plummet. "Will we be the only white family left?" he wondered.

There may also have been pressure from his parents, immigrants who had little experience with or understanding of other races. The Barnetts' daughter, Laura Barnett Webb, remembered her grandmother liberally used the word "shvartze," an offensive Yiddish word for a Black person, and making derogatory remarks about "the Blacks."

At a meeting of an investment club Irv was part of, a man who sold carpet relayed that he had just carpeted the home of a Negro couple on Becket Road. The husband was okay, he said, but he disparagingly dismissed the wife as a cleaning lady sort of person. "Boy, I wouldn't want to live there," he said. Irv kept quiet, too embarrassed to disclose this was his street.

Yet as Irv walked to the rapid transit he couldn't help but be impressed. An old house across the street that had been bought by a Black family had been transformed before his eyes—new lawn, new garage, new paint.

In any case, the Barnetts felt they had little choice but to stay. They couldn't afford to move. So Emilie, who had never before spoken with a Black person, screwed up her courage and crossed the street to introduce herself to one of her new Black neighbors. Mr. Price, a postman, was out mowing his lawn. She learned that he, too, was dismayed by the For Sale signs, lamenting that his soon-to-be-former neighbors had not gotten to know him before deciding to leave. He invited her in to meet his wife, but Emilie declined. "I said thank you, no, and I'm embarrassed by the fact," she said years later.

He told her a few neighbors were meeting to talk about how to stem the white flight underway. Emilie wasn't sure what to say, but she promised to talk it over with her husband.

Soon after, Irv and Emilie were at home one evening when the doorbell rang. A tall Black man named Drue King Jr., a Harvard-educated doctor, was at the door, dressed in gray flannel slacks and an oxford shirt. He said he had heard from Mr. Price that they were interested in stabilizing the neighborhood and invited them to attend a meeting of neighbors. Emilie was struck by Dr. King, who was far better educated than she was and, particularly on this evening, far better dressed as well.

For years later, Emilie would tell this story with a humbling spirit— remarking upon how associating with Dr. King made her feel like she was moving up in the world. That attitude turned centuries of American racism on its head—a white woman seeing a Black man not just as an equal but as someone soaring far above. But it's worth noting, not for the last time, just how accomplished a Black man had to be to win over even an open-minded white couple. Mr. Price, the postman, laid the groundwork. A Harvard-educated doctor sealed the deal.

Not everyone was as taken with Dr. King, who had moved to Becket Road in 1957 with his wife, Frances. A few months after arriving, a white boy who had been playing with their daughter approached Mrs. King, distressed. "We're moving away," the boy told her. "But Carol and I are such good friends—can't she move with us?" Mrs. King later said, "How could I tell him that his parents were moving because of us?"

Emilie attended the meeting that King invited her to, which included community relations professionals to help guide the discussion. It seemed the conversation was going in circles, so she offered a simple idea: maybe people needed to simply meet one another. It was summer, so she proposed a barbecue, which the Kings hosted in their backyard.

Soon the group was gathering for coffee klatches and other meet-and-greet events. The neighbors, Black and white, were beginning to get to know one another, house by house, block by block. Individual block associations formed to keep the mingling going.

While the first Black families faced enormous hurdles to buy into Ludlow, now that the neighborhood had a substantial Black population, the white families faced the same barriers, from real estate agents and also from banks.

A white couple named Joanne and Joseph E. Finley heard about Ludlow around 1959 and were drawn to the idea of living in an integrated community, but they were pushed away by one broker after the next. "You don't want to live there," the agents would tell Joanne when she phoned about Ludlow, she later recalled. "You don't want to live anywhere near Shaker Square. Within five years, it will be all Negro." She said that after a while she would call real estate agents "for sport" and when they warned her away from Ludlow, Finley would "bawl them out" and say "I wouldn't think of using you" and then hang up. It was "a little educational procedure of my own," she said.

They found their house by driving the streets of Ludlow and seeing a For Sale sign. Then came financing: they were turned down by three banks before getting a loan with Ohio Savings, she said. Just as banks worked to block Black people out of a white neighborhood, now that the area was integrated, banks worked to keep white people out. Joanne remembered one banker who stood up and walked to the window, put his hands behind his back, and said, "Isn't this terrible that in this day and age I have to say this." Then he rejected them. "They just simply considered it foolish, a poor risk, all the mess about property values [falling] and they could not invest their money through us in this community," Finley said.

Lewis and Elinor Polster, another white couple, also had trouble getting financing. They had moved to the neighborhood in 1953 and were renting on Keswick Road when they observed the arrival of the first Black families. Their family was growing, and they wanted to buy. They loved the neighborhood and the Shaker schools, particularly Ludlow's well-regarded principal, Marjorie Foss. A house across the street was for sale, and they put in an offer. They were well aware that integration was underway and didn't care, Elinor Polster said.

"It was fine with us because we wanted our children to be exposed to different people," she said in an interview. It was also a practical decision: "We looked in other parts of Shaker and either the houses were too expensive for what we could pay or they weren't what we wanted." The house they bought had been on the market for two years and seemed undervalued at $36,000, but the Polsters believed that values would stabilize because the Black families moving in were "professional people who could take the responsibility of owning their homes."

"You had to be an optimistic person to do what they did," their son Dan said later. "They thought it would work. They believed in themselves and others."

They were denied a loan by their own bank, prompting them to pull their money out, Elinor Polster said. She said they also faced blowback from their parents, who were "shocked and upset."

"We weren't asking them 'should we do this?' We did it. They were upset with our associating with Black people," she said.

Polster said her father's views shifted after he picked up his grandson from a Little League game one day and saw that the coach was Black. He was impressed that the coach required him to identify himself before allowing the boy to leave with him in an era where such checks were far from routine. "Our parents gradually came around," she said.

Their friends also thought they were crazy. One told her, "I wouldn't live where you live." She mentioned Elinor's young son. "Aren't you afraid Dan will marry a Black girl?" Polster recalled her asking. "She probably didn't use the word 'Black.'" In a recent conversation that included her son, Polster made clear she was not afraid. "Afraid? Of course not! You were six years old!"

After moving into their new home, the Polsters, like the Barnetts, joined with their neighbors, Black and white, first on their block and then with the larger community, seeking to test the proposition that Ludlow's fate could be different from that of neighborhoods everywhere else.

The neighborhood meetings began on streets that were already integrated and moved into the portion of the neighborhood that was in the city of Shaker Heights, across what some saw as an invisible line that would not be breached by Black buyers. Early meetings were frank discussions about integration—its possibilities and challenges. In the fall of 1957, they formed the Ludlow Community Association, officially incorporating the next year. While Emilie was in the kitchen making coffee, her husband, Irv, was elected its first president.

The association began as a federation of block clubs, explicitly open to all races and religions, with the goal of maintaining standards and stability of the community. Committees were formed to deal with traffic, empty lots, membership, hospitality, sanitation, building code enforcement, zoning, schools, and recreation.

As the neighbors organized themselves, white flight continued, as exemplified by the group's treasurer, who sold his house and moved away without even telling the other board members. Integration proponents preferred to tell the story of a white family who fled to another suburb only to find that a Black family had moved in next door.

The problem was not just retention of existing families. Potential white buyers faced the same barriers that the Polsters had encountered, financial and social. Aggressive real estate agents would approach white residents by phone and letter, encouraging them to sell. By late 1959, white agents had abandoned Ludlow altogether, and not a single white family moved in for the next eighteen months. The portion of Black residents in the neighborhood was rising each year. A community research project found the white percentage in the neighborhood had marched steadily downward, from 75 percent in 1958 to just under 50 percent five years later.

This was a classic pattern, one that had already played out in communities across America and in certain Cleveland neighborhoods. Black families arrived, and white families departed. The white flight was sometimes slow and sometimes fast, but the whites almost always departed, a process known as resegregation. Almost nobody else was trying to do what Ludlow was trying to do. At one point around 1958, the association invited a sociologist to help plot their course. The sociologist told the group that any community with at least 40 percent Black residents was at a tipping point that would turn the neighborhood into "a ghetto." "I'm sorry to report that your chances of success are slim. You are doing all that you can but it won't change history," he told them. As he left, he dropped an envelope on the table. Irv Barnett opened it and read it to the group: "Services rendered—$25.00."

"We went into hock to learn that we are failures," he recalled.

They also battled developers and city officials who were working to rezone land to allow apartments and commercial activity where the Van Sweringens had intended single-family housing. Those deed restrictions were still in force, at least on paper. Yet the foundation responsible for enforcing the rules, created after the Van Sweringen Company went out of business, was waiving them. So in a bit of irony, the Ludlow association brought lawsuits to enforce the provisions and challenged development before city zoning boards. The association's goals were not that different from the original Van Sweringen goals—essentially, to maintain certain economic standards and keep out those not up to them. The difference was that the Vans were creating and preserving an all-white

Shaker Heights, while Ludlow was working to create and preserve a racially diverse community.

The group's central focus was housing, working to resist the pressures of the real estate industry and the banks and to recruit white buyers. The forces were arrayed against them. "There are still many homes for sale in our area," an association summary of the state of affairs in 1959 read. "If these homes are not sold to white families it will be impossible to maintain this as an integrated neighborhood. We must, therefore, reach out beyond our borders to the community at large and attract many more white buyers."

To be clear, it's not that white people living in Ludlow decided one day that it would be great to live in an integrated neighborhood. They didn't invite Black families in, or particularly encourage them. Their work toward integration was meant to prevent a full neighborhood flip from white to Black. Integration was happening whether they liked it or not. Their aim was to control it, to slow it, to preserve an integrated neighborhood in the face of social forces that usually led to resegregation and that were pushing Ludlow in that direction. What was different in Ludlow, though, was the white people there decided that rather than abandon their homes and their neighborhood and move elsewhere, hoping to find an all-white neighborhood that would stay that way, they would embrace the idea of living with people different from themselves—they valued it, appreciated it, and grew to love it. And with those convictions in hand, they sought to test the conventional wisdom that white flight was inevitable.

Ludlow was beginning its work toward integration just as the question of race was rising to the national stage. In the late 1950s, the civil rights movement accelerated the drive to dismantle Jim Crow segregation and deliver equal rights under the law to Black Americans, with violent responses from the powers that yearned to keep the racist order in place.

In August 1955, just before the Masons moved into their new home, Emmett Till, a Black fourteen-year-old from Chicago, was brutally beaten and murdered while visiting family in Money, Mississippi, for allegedly flirting with a white woman. His corpse was disfigured, but his mother insisted on an open casket so the world could see what had been done to her son. In December 1955, just before the Peggs' garage was bombed, Rosa Parks refused to give up her seat to a white man on a Montgomery, Alabama, bus, sparking a yearlong bus boycott. And in 1957, just as the Ludlow Community Association was forming, enormous attention was focused on Little Rock, Arkansas, where federal troops were needed to escort nine Black students into Central High School over the protests of a screaming mob.

Even outside the South, most white Americans were resistant to racial integration, certainly in housing. In September 1958, a Gallup poll found that half of white respondents said they would definitely move "if colored people came to live in great numbers in your neighborhood" and another 30 percent said they might. Forty-four percent of white people said they might or would definitely move if "colored people came to live next door."

There were of course pockets of support. Many of the movement's white allies were Jewish, and it's not surprising that in Shaker Heights, many of the early integration supporters—people like the Barnetts and the Polsters—were Jewish, too.

Nationally, other white ethnic groups also faced discrimination but responded by insisting they should be considered "white" at a time when they were not always seen that way, according to Cheryl Lynn Greenberg, a historian at Trinity College in Connecticut who is an expert on Black-Jewish relations. Jews, by contrast, were more likely to see themselves in common cause with Black Americans, seeing both a moral imperative and a self-interest in eradicating discriminatory laws, both before and even more so after six million European Jews were exterminated in the Holocaust. Jews were reeling in the wake of World War II, and vowing that such a horror should never happen again.

"They did have this direct understanding of what could happen with racism. The end of racism is gas ovens," said Greenberg. Supporting civil rights was seen as a Jewish obligation. "It wasn't just common cause. It was, 'We know what this is like. Your cause is our cause. We're in this together.'"

In 1964, two young Jewish men working to register voters in Mississippi, Michael Schwerner and Andrew Goodman, were murdered along with their fellow activist James Chaney, who was Black. In 1965, Rabbi Abraham Joshua Heschel, a leading Jewish theologian, marched side by side with Dr. King from Selma to Birmingham, Alabama. Jews were among the founders and earliest supporters of civil rights groups, including the NAACP, and Jewish groups filed amicus briefs in civil rights cases.

In Shaker Heights, both Blacks and Jews were initially kept out by design. Now, as the 1960s dawned, hundreds of miles away from the epicenter of the battle for civil rights, the first stirrings of a Black-Jewish alliance were appearing in Ludlow.

⸻

Early on, members of the Ludlow Community Association understood they were selling an idea as much as a house, and worked to market the area as "socially desirable" to the "prestige conscious" middle-class members of the greater Cleveland community. The key, they felt, was to somehow persuade white agents to bring their clients to the neighborhood, though how to make that happen was not at all clear.

Irv Barnett met with the executive secretary of the Cleveland Real Estate Board, told him of the program in Ludlow, and sought backing for their work. The man sat back in his chair, lit a cigarette, and said, "Irv, your association work is wonderful but futile. Never in history has there been an example where white families move into a community where there is a substantial Negro population." He noted that Ludlow was adjacent to a lower-class Black Cleveland neighborhood. "There is nothing I can do to induce whites to move there."

Another official with the real estate board was even less charitable about the work in Ludlow. In a candid interview around this time, he asserted that white people in Ludlow were there only because they couldn't afford to move or because they planned to move soon. "There are a very small percentage of homeowners living in the Ludlow area who are white and who are staying there by choice," he asserted.

To fund a promotional campaign, the Ludlow association won $7,500 from the Cleveland Foundation, the first of many critical contributions by Cleveland's private foundations toward the work of integration in Shaker. The announcement of the grant served as a coming-out for Ludlow to the greater Cleveland area. In July 1959, the *Cleveland Press* reported that the funding would help the group "preserve their neighborhood as one where Negro and white families live next door to each other."

Funding in hand, the association approached the top advertising firm in Cleveland to create a promotional brochure, and it agreed, with one proviso, Irv said. "We just don't want you telling anyone that we did it. You understand, don't you?"

"We understood," Irv said later.

The brochure was called "Ludlow, a Community Report," and while it did not mention integration explicitly, it included photos of Black and white children and adults playing and talking together. The association unveiled the publication in December 1960 over champagne and steaks at a dinner for city leaders at Stouffer's Shaker Square Restaurant.

At the dinner, the association laid out the challenge explicitly: banks would not provide financing for white families seeking to buy in an area "in transition," and white brokers wouldn't take listings. Association members urged the businessmen present not to abandon the community and said Black residents as well as white wanted to prevent a wholesale racial flip of the neighborhood.

"We do not want to see the area become a Negro ghetto," John Pegg said at the dinner. "Negroes have no dreams or anticipation of taking over Shaker Square. They want you to keep it and maintain the same standards it has always had."

William Burton, vice president of the Shaker Heights school board, who was white and had been working behind the scenes to support Ludlow's work, delivered the main address at the dinner. He offered a warning. "Just remember," he said, "if nothing is done the result is clear, even guaranteed. If the objects of the Ludlow Community Association can be achieved and the neighborhood kept integrated quietly, peaceably, the results can be magnificent."

The pitch was successful, to a point. Churches, universities, and brokers asked for copies of the brochure, and people in Ludlow felt as if they were beginning to change attitudes. Yet the neighborhood continued to draw new Black—but few white—home seekers. By 1963, 72 percent of the students at Ludlow Elementary were Black.

———

Not everyone in Shaker Heights was as enthusiastic about integration as those in Ludlow. The mayor, Wilson G. Stapleton, would not even attend Ludlow block parties as a show of support. "To say that he was cool to the idea was putting it mildly," Irv Barnett recalled.

Stapleton, an attorney and dean of the Cleveland Marshall Law School, had been mayor of Shaker Heights since 1956 and enjoyed touting the city's features: top-notch schools, excellent planning, rapid transit straight to downtown Cleveland. He also liked to mention a low tax rate made possible by the inheritance tax, which at the time sent considerable dollars to the city. In 1961, he bragged to the *Plain Dealer* that the death of one man, a newspaper publisher who owned two large construction firms, brought $750,000 to the city. That paid almost the entire cost of a new $900,000 police station.

He also worked to distance the community from neighboring Cleveland. Around 1959, there was a spate of crimes in the Cleveland section of Kinsman Road, one of the major east-west roads that also ran through Shaker Heights. In response, the city renamed the Shaker section of the road Chagrin Boulevard, after the bucolic suburb of Chagrin Falls even farther east of Cleveland. Stapleton also spoke out in favor of a plan to barricade two side streets, cutting off access from Cleveland into Shaker, though that proposal was defeated.

"As mayor of this community, I certainly am not going to go out and promote integration in the face of our citizens who would not favor it. I am not a crusader," he said, according to an account in the *Call & Post*.

At one point, Stapleton suggested countering a controversial proposal to drive a freeway through the Shaker lakes and parks by moving the route to Scottsdale Boulevard, the southern border of Shaker, according to Albert M. Pennybacker Jr., who was pastor of a local church at the time. "I'm sure that this is conceived then as a racial barrier. And they're kidding themselves," he said in a 1964 interview. (In the end, after a vigorous opposition campaign, no freeways were built in Shaker.)

Stapleton and members of Shaker's City Council also suggested that the school board cede to Cleveland schools the portion of the Shaker Heights school district that was in the city of Cleveland, in an attempt to remove from the Shaker schools the Black children who had moved into the district, according to an account from Burton, a school board member at the time. In 1964, Burton said the school board had little interest in this plan and replied by pointing out that ceding this territory would mean losing property tax revenue from Shaker Square, a thriving shopping area, that supported the schools and would lead to a tax increase for Shaker residents to make up the difference. A similar account was given in a separate interview by Alan Geismer, another school board member at the time. Burton recalled telling city officials that integration in Ludlow was going well, adding, "There is no such thing as a Chinese wall."

The so-called Chinese wall would have kept white people in Shaker Heights divided from Black people in Cleveland and was indicative of how racism manifested itself in the North. While the elites of Shaker

Heights were not preventing Black people from voting or mandating separate water fountains or lunch counters, many whites wanted racial segregation that kept Black people away from white spaces, schools, and neighborhoods.

Mayor Stapleton soon learned that racial diversity in Shaker Heights could not be contained to Ludlow. In the fall of 1960, James Robinson, a dentist, and his wife, Lelabelle Freeman Robinson, a pediatrician, attempted to buy a two-story red brick home at 16306 Aldersyde Road, just a block from Shaker Heights High School and more than a mile from the Ludlow neighborhood. The builder refused to sell to the Robinsons, so a white couple bought the house and, three days later, transferred the deed to the Robinsons. They were believed to be the first Black couple to buy a house outside Ludlow, and the so-called straw purchase prompted a lawsuit by the builder alleging fraud and conspiracy.

At first, Stapleton actually seemed open to the sale. The day the lawsuit was filed, the mayor spoke to the Greater Cleveland Ministerial Association, telling 130 assembled pastors that they must assist in bringing about integrated housing throughout the Cleveland area.

"There are too many people in your churches who pray there on Sunday and prey on their neighbors the rest of the week," he said. He added that the "letter of the law" already provided equal housing rights but the "spirit" of the law had yet to be realized, and he suggested that it would help a great deal if ministers would exhort the biblical principle "I am my brother's keeper."

"We live in a changing world, and we have changing neighborhoods," he said.

His comments were printed in the *Plain Dealer* the next day, and perhaps they didn't go over well, because that evening he reached out to the newspaper to "clarify" his comments to the pastors. In fact, he now said, Shaker residents had "social rights" that he would defend against "infiltration."

"No matter what the right of the individuals may be legally," Stapleton said in a statement to the newspaper, "he is still obligated to respect the social customs. And as the mayor of this community, representing the majority of the people who look to me, I shall respect not only their legal rights but the social right which they hold dear. Hence, not only shall I vigorously oppose a frontal attack on any neighborhood in my community which does not desire infiltration, but I shall use every persuasive force I have to suggest to those who choose so to infiltrate that they should proceed very cautiously in the light of the wishes of their would-be neighbors."

A few days later, he spoke to the Cleveland Real Estate Board and reported that he had received a great number of telephone calls and letters supporting his position. "If you neglect the outer perimeter, you will have to defend the inner perimeter later on," he told them. He said he opposed the NAACP's tactics, which he described as "unless you sell to me I'll hit you with a bat." But he also urged the brokers to resist panic selling and white flight.

"Gentlemen," he told them, "where there are changing neighborhoods it is your obligation to stabilize these neighborhoods and not let them panic."

If Stapleton thought he was taking a nuanced stand, it did not go over that way in the Black community. Addressing a rally at Euclid Avenue Baptist Church that month, the Reverend Ralph D. Abernathy of Montgomery, Alabama, compared Stapleton to racists in the South. "The mayor of Shaker Heights is no different from a senator from Mississippi," he said. "In many ways, he is worse, being the dean of a law school and going the opposite way of the law."

And in a letter to the editor of the *Plain Dealer*, Joe Finley, Joanne's husband and a white leader of the Ludlow Community Association, expressed his deep dismay. "He ought to remember that blind defenders of the status quo are the buffoons of history. His stand is nothing more than a brand of silk-stocking bigotry," he wrote. "Those who think they can solve problems of human and social relations by burying their heads in the sand like Mayor Stapleton, or moving farther and farther away, will one day discover they have no place to hide."

In Ludlow, Joe and Joanne Finley, the Barnetts, the Masons, and many others were still working to make those words a reality.

The Ludlow Community Association's membership was growing, panic selling had died down, and the association finally had some money for publicity. But the brochure had failed to draw white buyers to the neighborhood. So they adopted something of a radical solution. They would create their own housing program. If white agents wouldn't bring clients to see houses for sale in Ludlow, Ludlow would do it for them.

The association gathered lists of houses for sale and went looking for buyers. They began by collecting prospects' names from residents and soon reached out more broadly. They distributed the brochures to universities, hospitals, and businesses in Cleveland, asking that they pass them along to new recruits moving to town. They hunted through newspapers for job announcements, looking for leads on new hires. They advertised in the program of the Cleveland Orchestra, in newspapers, and on an FM radio station that played classical music. They talked up the neighborhood's advantages—good schools, fine homes, public transportation— but also a social mission that might appeal to some at a time when the civil rights movement was accelerating. "THERE IS PRESTIGE TODAY IN BEING AMONG THE THOUGHTFUL," one advertisement read. "COME AND LIVE WITH US IN LUDLOW, CLEVELAND'S MODEL INTEGRATED COMMUNITY."

In the spring of 1961, six white couples—potential buyers—were invited to a house-hunting party. They began with a social hour in a Ludlow home, and then each couple was accompanied by a neighborhood resident to see homes for sale that met their criteria. Afterward, they reconvened at another home for a lasagna dinner, where leaders of the association answered questions and the principal touted the school. The result, the association newsletter trumpeted, was a sale on Becket to a young professor at Case, a rental for a minister, "lively interest" from a University Hospital doctor, and a request for details from a pair of musicians who played for the Cleveland Orchestra—all of them white. The Ludlow association newsletter celebrated the results in rhyme:

Let's see
That score
Equals four
There's more . . .

A fifth couple was coming back to see a house again that they liked. And there was already enough interest to host a second house-hunting party two weeks after the first, at which a psychiatrist, a personnel director for a small business, and another minister were all expected. "And we haven't even mailed out invitations yet." Many more house-hunting parties would follow.

That's how Alan Gressel and his family landed in Ludlow. "I met these wonderful people, both white and Black, who were going to show me around and give me a potluck supper afterward," he said in a 2004 interview with ABC News. Gressel, who had never lived in a racially diverse area before, said he wasn't particularly seeking integration. But he reasoned it was coming to almost every neighborhood, and if the arrival of Black families was going to lower property values, it made more sense to buy in an area where that had already occurred.

No white families had bought into Ludlow since the summer of 1959. Now, between May and December 1961, nine white families purchased homes there. There were still far more Black buyers, but the association seized on positive news and highlighted successes even when they weren't entirely sure success was at hand.

In the summer of 1961, the association won a second grant—another $5,000 from the Cleveland Foundation. It used the occasion to announce that in the previous two months, seven white families had moved in. The *Courier*, a Black newspaper, declared Ludlow was "fast becoming the model community for racially integrated living in the country." The suburban *Sun Press* published a "Ludlow Progress Report," in which it declared, at the top of the front page: INTEGRATION WORKS, WHITE FAMILIES MOVING IN, complete with short profiles of several couples.

Still, white families would have trouble buying if they couldn't borrow the needed funds. That led to another innovation, and a controversial one. In February 1961, the association's executive committee discussed the idea of creating a financing arm to help fill the gap left by banks that would not write mortgages in the neighborhood. The idea, debated at community meetings that spring, was difficult for some to swallow: they would be subsidizing white but not Black buyers. Some found the notion morally offensive, saying the association should be helping those who face far more discrimination—namely Black buyers—before aiding whites. Backers argued there was no other way to bring white families in, which was needed to maintain integration.

On a vote of 52–6, the association agreed to form the Ludlow Company, a for-profit entity that sold stock and used the proceeds to make secondary loans of up to $5,000—a mini–mortgage company. The project was championed by Shaker Square business executives, who had a vested interest in Ludlow's future and feared they would suffer financially if the community became all Black.

The association then hired a full-time housing coordinator to keep track of homes that were for sale and to show them to prospective buyers. Joanne Finley, who had battled to find a real estate agent who would show her a house in Ludlow, took the job in November 1961 and became a driving force in the nascent program, which showed homes to white house hunters without commission or fees. Remarkably, neighborhood organizers, on their own, had recreated much of the real estate infrastructure to replace the professionals who had abandoned them.

In 1962, Finley got a call from Lavona and Bush Olmsted, a white couple with four children and a fifth on the way. They told her they were interested in a house on Keswick Road that bordered Ludlow Elementary School but felt the yard was too small for the swing set or sandbox they hoped to set up. Soon, Mr. Olmsted received a call at work from the president of the school board. "You need some property for a sandbox?" he asked. As a result of the conversation, the school board agreed to move the school fence over to enlarge the yard so the Olmsteds would buy, which they did.

This work also had a deeply unsettling side. Ludlow was discouraging—sometimes out loud, sometimes in quiet conversations— Black house hunters, a painful situation for many of the Black leaders of the association. Blacks who sought information were directed to the Metropolitan Cleveland Committee for Democracy in Housing, which was working to facilitate Black buying in other predominantly white suburban areas. Black callers were told about the community's desire for racial balance and asked to house-hunt elsewhere.

"It was far from easy to tell a fellow Negro who inquired about a house, 'Don't buy here. Help us win. Maybe we can help you find a house in another neighborhood,'" Black Ludlow leader Joseph Battle, a real estate agent and open housing advocate, told *Reader's Digest* in 1968. "But Ludlow had to remain integrated if we were going to retain its advantages and character."

One Black buyer, William L. Percy, was so angry about the response he received upon inquiring about Ludlow that he considered filing a discrimination suit against the association. He succeeded in buying a house in Ludlow, and then changed his view, eventually becoming president of the Ludlow Community Association. In a letter to the community in October 1964, he mentioned his concerns but concluded: "The fact remains that, were it not for the [housing] Program, the exodus of white families from Ludlow would probably be complete by now."

The larger Black community was also not enamored with Ludlow's approach. By February 1962, the *Courier* was no longer holding up

Ludlow as a model community. It gave voice to critics with a headline that read, NEGRO STATUS SEEKERS GUILTY OF SEGREGATION. "Critics charge, among other things, that the integrated community is itself guilty of rank discrimination against Negroes; that a quota system is in effect," the *Courier* reported. "That Ludlow is, at best, a noble experiment, where liberal whites believe they are making the supreme sacrifice while living among 'you people;' where status seeking Negroes delude themselves by hiding behind a high garden wall of their own prejudices."

To address the critics and perhaps their own guilt, in 1964 some Ludlow activists helped to create a licensed real estate firm called Fair Housing Inc. The primary goal was to help Black families buy into all-white areas, and to give them somewhere to turn other than Ludlow. The new firm sold some houses, though the numbers were smaller.

Ludlow, meantime, was making steady progress toward its goal. In February 1962, two hundred people showed up to an open house meant to showcase a model racially integrated community, with fourteen homes open to visitors. Beverly Mason now chaired the Ludlow association's Housing Committee. In the group's November 1962 newsletter, she reported that over the previous year and a half, twenty-five white families had bought homes, "disproving the theory that white families will not move into an 'area in transition.'"

"We have all had our lives enriched by the experience we have shared," she wrote.

But while Beverly was proud of her work with the association, she was keenly aware of the trade-offs. "If you're honest, you know that this too is discriminatory," she said in a 1966 interview. "But on the other hand, those of us who believe in it have sort of salved our guilt feelings by saying that the end does justify the means because if we don't do this then we can see that in a few years this might become a totally Negro community . . . I feel like if Ludlow goes down the drain, then any other community who's trying this will feel that if we haven't been successful, then neither can they."

Discrimination was not the only thing that created challenges for people like Mason. White residents embraced a color-blind philosophy that felt progressive to them at the time, but could leave some Black people feeling unseen. "I always felt that the white people in Ludlow did not want to acknowledge that we were black," Beverly Mason said in an interview for a book commemorating the seventy-fifth anniversary of

Shaker Heights. "I never felt they were unkind. In fact, they were quite the opposite. But I always felt like I wasn't there. They accepted me as another person, but never looked at me as black."

———————

Ervin and Thomasine Mason had watched his brother and sister-in-law, Ted and Beverly, successfully integrate the Ludlow neighborhood. Now it was 1962, and Erv and Thomasine were ready to make their own move to the suburbs.

Erv and Ted were exceptionally close. Erv had followed his big brother from Cadiz, Ohio, to Western Reserve, to the football squad, and to dental school. In the summers, they played golf two or three times a week. Were Ludlow not actively trying to recruit white buyers, and were Ted and Beverly Mason not leaders in the association, his brother might have bought nearby. Instead, he looked a little farther north.

"We didn't want to just keep flooding into an area that was already well populated" with Black families, Thomasine, known by her nickname Tommie, said in a 2021 interview. So, like Ted and Beverly before them, they would move into a predominantly white neighborhood where they might not be welcomed. Tommie later said she and her husband accepted this reality. "Black people weren't wanted in most areas."

Around this time, Bernard and Barbara Grenell, a white couple, were preparing to move from their home on Aberdeen Road in Shaker Heights to Beverly Hills, California, where he was setting up a new sportswear company. The couple's Tudor-style brick house, with a curved turret on the corner, had been designed by George Howard Burrows, an influential local architect responsible for nearly a thousand homes over four and a half decades. It was just a few blocks from the Aldersyde home that a Black couple had bought with some subterfuge two years earlier. Like Aldersyde, Aberdeen was on the north side of Van Aken Boulevard in the Onaway district, an area that was virtually all white.

The Grenells believed in integration and saw race relations through the lens of justice. The Urban League's Cleveland affiliate had a new program matching financially qualified Black home seekers with homeowners in white neighborhoods on the east side of Cleveland. In the summer of 1962, Barbara Grenell called the Urban League and said she was looking for Black couples who might be interested in buying her home at 3320 Aberdeen Road. The program connected her with the Masons.

The Masons saw the house and liked it. Barbara Grenell thought they would fit well into the neighborhood and chose them over two other potential Black buyers. They signed a sales agreement on July 20, 1962, for $29,250. Grenell warned Tommie that the purchase might not be easy and said if there was trouble with the neighbors, it would probably come from Charles R. Bechtel, who lived across the street. He, Grenell said, was "the bigot."

Around this time, word was getting out to the neighbors on Aberdeen that the Grenell house had been sold to a Black family. Bechtel got a call from a neighbor with the rumor. "Don't go into a panic until we find out the facts," he replied. A meeting was planned for a few evenings later. Alexander Mintz, a banker with Shaker Savings & Loan, told the group a contract had been signed with the Masons but argued it was not valid because only Barbara Grenell had signed; her husband was already in California. The banker warned the group that their property values would fall if the sale went through.

So the neighbors agreed they would put their money together to buy the house themselves and then sell it to someone more suitable. They quickly raised $8,500 for a down payment, and Mintz offered a $21,000 mortgage.

It was one of many times that Mintz would use the power of his bank to try to prevent Black people from buying in Shaker Heights, according to numerous people who knew and worked with him. "He feels that this is really too bad that the Negroes have begun to move into this community, that it should be fought . . . that this holds nothing but misfortune for this community," said one. It was an ironic turn; Mintz was Jewish, and he had helped open Shaker Heights up to Jewish buyers. But he was evidently unable to sympathize with Black people, who also were facing discrimination.

Alarmed by this turn of events, Bernard Grenell flew back from the West Coast and met with his former neighbors, who pressured him to cancel the sale. Grenell, in turn, pressured the Masons to cancel the contract. Grenell visited Erv Mason at his brother's home. He told him about the neighborhood opposition. Then he called Mason, twice, pleading with him to reconsider. "I told him I expected the commitment to hold," Erv Mason later said.

On August 27, 1962, the Masons received a letter from Grenell indicating he was canceling the purchase and returning the $100 check given to his wife as a deposit of sorts, referred to as earnest money.

The Masons were not having it. Two days later, they filed suit against the Grenells and twenty-four neighbors for housing discrimination and conspiracy. Their lawyers included Joe Finley from Ludlow and attorneys from the NAACP, who saw the case as a key test of open housing. The case was assigned to Common Pleas judge Joseph H. Silbert, who offered an initial ruling favorable to the Masons. He enjoined any further efforts to sell or occupy the home and delivered a lecture on race to the courtroom. "I am satisfied that if the plaintiff was not a Negro, this whole thing would not have come about," he said.

But the court case dragged on. Erv Mason, just thirty-two years old, seemed more sad than angry over his would-be neighbors. He told the *Cleveland Press* that he suspected many of them regretted their resistance. "Many people, in their desire to conform, will climb aboard a wagon without really thinking things out. To a degree, I think that is what happened here." He said he had no malice and that the objective of his suit was simply to win "the home of our choice in the neighborhood of our choice."

"That is our privilege—our right—and I intend to see that we get it," he said. That was probably about as angry as a Black man could get in public, regardless of the provocation, without hurting his own cause.

The Masons remained resolute. Tommie had grown up in a mostly white town in Illinois, with just ten Black children in her school, so the idea of being a minority didn't faze her. No matter where they moved, she reasoned, they would run into racism and pressure. "We made up our minds and we decided: this was the house we wanted," she said.

As the case made its way through the courts, Bechtel moved out of Shaker, to a suburb farther east, even as he continued to defend his position. "I am not bigoted. I have many Negro friends. All I have been trying to do is protect property values," he told reporters covering the trial. He said in an interview that neighbors had offered to help the Masons move elsewhere, but they objected to "being just another Negro moving into an already integrated neighborhood." He charged that Mason had "admitted he had only looked for a home in all-white neighborhoods." He also disclosed that he had offered to let the sale go through if the Masons promised to cover any losses if home values fell. "Our worry is primarily

economic, but the impact on the Shaker schools could be another problem," he said. "No integrated neighborhood has ever worked." He noted
that Ludlow school had become largely Black. "We all agree the Negro
must have better housing. But is this the way? Must we suffer heavy
financial losses to do it?"

In April 1964, twenty months after signing a contract to buy the house,
the Masons won their suit, and soon after, they moved onto Aberdeen.

Once they arrived, the opposition seemed to disappear. Tommie
Mason found next-door neighbors on one side of their new house friendly
and welcoming. On the other side, she said, the neighbors took some
time to come around, with the husband deciding that their arrival was a
good time to plant bushes along the property line between them. "That
soon simmered down," she said. "He liked my husband and they became
friends."

Their two little girls, and later a son, grew up not knowing most of
the story and feeling at home on their street, which remained mostly
white for many years. Hilary Carrington Mason King remembered
roller skating in backyards and swimming in a neighbor's pool. She said
one white mom made a point to introduce her daughter, who was the
same age. The two became close friends, and their moms would often
meet for coffee. "I had no sense of really the hostility there had been,"
she said. "Once they met our family as people instead of this caricature
of a family, that made all the difference." Her brother, Ervin Proctor
Mason Jr., said he rarely heard his parents speak of the court battle.
"My impression was always like they didn't want that event to taint our
relationships going forward."

But throughout the trial, Tommie Mason kept a collection of newspaper clippings and letters sent from friends and strangers alike about the
controversy. Decades later, after their father had died and as their mother
was preparing to move out of the house, the kids found the pile, hidden
in the back of a living room cabinet. Some of the letters were openly
hostile. "You certainly have a lot of nerve trying to force yourself in
where you are not wanted," read one anonymously sent letter in October
1962. "If you negros [sic] weren't so agressive [sic] you would obtain
greater respect, but as it is you are only getting the whites to dis-like
your race more and more." But there were also offers from strangers to
sell their homes to the Masons, and a copy of a letter to Alexander Mintz
of Shaker Savings & Loan, telling him that his behavior in the Mason

case had prompted the writer to close his accounts. Another note urged the Masons to keep up the good fight: "Your courage and conviction in expressing through action stands as an example to all decent citizens of our community."

In the middle of the stack was a newspaper clipping from July 21, 1962, just weeks before the lawsuit would be filed, from the *Plain Dealer*. At the top of the front page was a photo of Erv's sister-in-law, Bev Mason, along with her three-year-old daughter, Elisabeth, talking with a group of junior high school students about life in an integrated neighborhood.

"Mrs. Mason," the newspaper reported, "told her visitors that neighbors had been cordial and that her children had had no trouble making friends."

By 1962, at last, white families were routinely buying homes in Ludlow. A newspaper headline in February 1962 carried the association's message to greater Cleveland: 24 WHITE FAMILIES MOVE INTO LUDLOW IN 10 MONTHS. Real estate agents started to realize they were losing business to the association, which was essentially selling homes without charging a commission, and began to bring white families to the area. Some Black families moved out and sold to whites. And Mintz, the Savings and Loan banker, was persuaded to issue mortgages to white families buying in Ludlow, likely concluding that a mixed neighborhood in his territory was better than an all-Black one.

Economic similarities helped to smooth the way. While many Black people living in the central city were struggling to get by, these Black suburban pioneers were accomplished professionals.

Throughout the 1960s, the Ludlow leaders courted local and national journalists, whose desire for an unexpected story combined perhaps with their interest in racial justice to deliver overwhelmingly positive coverage. Lengthy stories appeared in the *Wall Street Journal* and *National Review*, with some notes of skepticism but mostly marvel at what was unfolding.

Look magazine devoted eight pages to Ludlow in 1964, with large photos showing Black and white adults and children playing and living together, emphasizing the economic similarities between Black and white residents. It featured Ted and Beverly Mason and their four children. The article patronizingly described them as "a family of educated, working, money-saving Negroes" who were "moving into the normal American world, just as though they were white." The writer, Julius Horwitz, a native of Cleveland, alternated between admiring the integration he observed and expressing doubt that it would work. "The white folks and the colored folks of Ludlow and neighboring Shaker Heights live in harmony, work together for the common good, visit each other's houses, share meals, watch their children play together, take them to school in car pools and behave as though everybody is a human being," he wrote. "But ask *some* people, as people do ask: 'Would you like your daughter to . . . ?' And the answer is evasive: 'Time will tell . . .' or 'We haven't got that far yet . . .' or 'Mmm—well-ll.'"

The association's reputation began to spread as national and even international figures started to identify and lift up Ludlow as a shining example of what might be. In June 1964, Hawaii governor John A. Burns spoke to four hundred people in Ludlow, praising the work underway, and pointing to the rich diversity of his own state. "We rob ourselves when we identify only with people of our own kind," he said.

In late 1962 or early 1963, Emilie Barnett read an article about diplomats from African countries who had been denied service at restaurants en route from New York to Washington, D.C. Upset by the message her country was sending, Emilie managed to connect with someone at the State Department, who arranged to send invitations to several African ambassadors to visit Ludlow, where a dinner was held for them in February 1963.

That laid the groundwork for something even bigger. In June 1965, Ludlow hosted ambassadors from five African countries, Jamaica, and the Netherlands for a weekend of events—a monumental undertaking by a neighborhood association pulled off with the help of some two hundred volunteers. The weekend included dinners, city tours, a theater trip, brunches, and a visit to a NASA facility in Cleveland. Ludlow families housed the ambassadors for the weekend and hosted a succession of parties at which the guests ate potluck casseroles, and a Nigerian movie played in a backyard. On Sunday evening, Ambassador Franklin Williams, the U.S. representative to the United Nations, capped the weekend with an address at the high school. He praised the work of the Ludlow volunteers but warned that the Ludlows of the nation were "doomed to die" unless governments stepped up action toward fair housing legislation. His comments were met with a standing ovation.

In November 1965, Ludlow scored yet another big name, hosting the entertainer Lena Horne, a civil rights activist who was among the Black performers most popular with white audiences, at a reception at Stouffer's Shaker Square restaurant. Horne, in Cleveland to promote her memoir, had dinner with a small group from Ludlow and then mingled with more than four hundred others during a reception. Members of the community told her the Ludlow story, and, according to the Ludlow association newsletter, Horne saw connections to the larger civil rights movement. She spoke of Ludlow during a radio interview soon after.

All this—the governor, the ambassadors, Lena Horne—was prologue for the following spring, when the association hosted the legendary jazz singer Ella Fitzgerald for a fundraising concert. The $20 tickets sold out in five days and drew an integrated crowd to the first jazz concert ever held at Cleveland's storied Severance Hall, home of the Cleveland Orchestra. "The patrons were standing in the aisles and they would have been hanging from the rafters like bats had there been any rafters to hang from," reported the *Cleveland Press*. Fitzgerald sang the blues—her own version of "The Saint Louis Blues"—plus "Hello, Dolly!" and "The Shadow of Your Smile" and after two hours she joked to the crowd that she was running out of songs to sing. The crowd leaped to its feet as the concert came to a close, and the reviews of the evening were glowing. "To say that they loved her would be in the nature of a gross understatement," wrote the *Cleveland Press*. "It was something closer to worship."

The concert program touted the Ludlow integration story, concluding: "After ten years, Ludlow can be termed an unqualified success." An advertisement for Ludlow in the program read: "a nice place to visit, but I'd rather live there. Integration works."

After the concert, some five hundred top ticket holders partied into the early morning hours at a champagne supper, drinking French bubbly and snacking on ham, turkey, fried chicken, salads, relishes, and sweets. At eleven thirty, Fitzgerald herself appeared in a black cocktail dress to mingle, sign autographs, and make conversation. The event raised $10,000 for the Ludlow Community Association.

And crucially, the numbers at last started to move, backing up the association's swagger. The Ludlow Community Association had done what the sociologist said was impossible: they had attracted white families with children to the neighborhood. By November 1963, the percentage of white students at Ludlow Elementary School had fallen to 27.6 percent; by 1966, it had climbed to 36 percent.

They had fought back not just against individual racism but against the system itself—against federal law, which mandated segregated housing; against banks, Realtors, and restrictive covenants, which enforced segregation; and against a political and economic system that expected, reinforced, and insisted upon separation of the races.

The Fitzgerald concert was followed in 1968 with another fundraising performance, this time by Nancy Wilson and the Fifth Dimension, which raised another $15,000. "The Ludlow mystique, which cannot be captured in fact, but which is everywhere in the success of Ludlow, flowed freely on June 21, 1968, filling Music Hall with the exuberance and grandness that is Ludlow," the Ludlow association newsletter reported. "The buzz and excitement of the crowd was proof that Ludlow had done it again."

———

The biggest legacy of these years, though, may be the experiences of the children who grew up in a special place at a moment when racial tensions were ripping the country into pieces.

"We played together. We had sleepovers at each other's homes. We sometimes had lunch at each other's homes and it didn't matter who it was," said Lynne Adrine, who is Black and was just five years old when her brother, sister, and parents moved to Ludlow. "We just hung out together."

Her sister, Leslie Adrine Goggins, described an integration magic dust that so many Ludlow kids, Black and white, from that era felt. Their family's old neighborhood in Cleveland had no white people. Now, in Ludlow, their next-door neighbor, Jimmy, wasn't just white but also Jewish. Leslie learned about the Jewish holiday of Hanukkah and how Jewish kids receive gifts for eight straight nights. "I went to his house a few times for dinner, which was a completely different experience for me," she said. When she came home, her mom would quiz her about the foods and whether she ate the gefilte fish served to her.

"I think it was probably the best experience I had in my entire life," said Diane Krejsa, a white woman who grew up across the street from the Adrines. "We went to each other's birthday parties, we played together without noticing right away that there were any distinctions."

She credited the Ludlow experience with all sorts of perspectives later in life: support for civil rights, openness to people of different cultures and sexual orientations. "A lot of things I'm comfortable with now that I might not have been without those experiences, without Ludlow."

Eventually, some of the leaders of the Ludlow association began to depart. In the mid-1960s, the Finleys moved to a bigger house elsewhere in Shaker. The Barnetts also wanted a bigger house, and in 1968, they found one inside Ludlow. But the sellers backed out at the last minute, and they wound up across Van Aken Boulevard on Chadbourne Road. "We ended up moving just a few blocks away," their son, Bill Barnett, said years later. "It was actually a world away."

They left feeling good about the work they had done in Ludlow, confident it would persist. "I have seen that the patterns of history can be changed, because I have been involved in a project that did it," Irv Barnett wrote in his memoir around the time of their move. He said that friends who lived elsewhere in the area were now experiencing the same shock and fear he and Emilie did upon the arrival of Black neighbors. "They call regularly for help, advice, and counseling."

"But I know that they too will survive," he concluded, "and think in the end there will be good housing for all everywhere."

It was a happy note to end on, but a little pat. Victory may have been at hand in Ludlow, but maintaining it would not be easy, and no one was sure how the rest of Shaker Heights would react when integration moved beyond the borders of one small neighborhood.

Now, where do we go from here?
—The Reverend Albert M. Pennybacker Jr.

5

THE REVEREND ALBERT M. PENNYBACKER JR.

Every one of the 445 seats in the auditorium at Woodbury Junior High School was occupied, and organizers had to set up chairs in the aisles. Still more people stood in the back. It was September 17, 1963, and the evening's topic was "The Negro in Shaker Heights."

While the Ludlow neighborhood had been grappling with integration for eight years, the rest of virtually all-white Shaker Heights was only starting to realize that race might be their concern, too. The idea for the discussion had come from the Shaker Democratic Club, which never guessed so many would turn out. The room was full in part because local real estate firms had required agents to attend. Open housing legislation that would bar racial discrimination in rentals and sales was on the table in Columbus. Redlining and blockbusting were coming under increasing scrutiny. There was good reason to worry that their business model was at risk.

The panel featured Joe Finley, the Ludlow leader who advocated for open housing, and former Shaker mayor Wilson Stapleton, who argued you can't "legislate human behavior." But the most profound speech delivered that evening came from someone new to Shaker Heights.

The Reverend Albert M. Pennybacker Jr., thirty-two years old and white, had moved to town that spring as the pastor for Heights Christian Church. His new church was set in the Lomond neighborhood, a middle-class part of Shaker Heights originally marketed as perfect for young couples who could buy a starter home and then move up to larger Shaker houses as their finances improved. At this point, a handful of Black families had moved to Lomond, and white residents of the neighborhood were starting to organize a group modeled after Ludlow's work. Appearing on the stage, Pennybacker was stunned by the turnout. He hadn't even realized there were racial tensions in Shaker Heights until about two weeks before he came to town, when he caught wind of the hoopla around Erv and Tommie Mason's purchase in the Onaway neighborhood.

At Woodbury, Pennybacker began by reviewing some basic facts: nearby areas such as Harvard-Lee and East Cleveland that had been recently all white were now home to many Black residents. The number of Black high school and college graduates had doubled, and there was pent-up demand for better housing. Already, some Black families were living in Shaker, and not just in the Ludlow neighborhood.

In spite of all that, he said, some people seemed to think staying all white was an option for Shaker Heights. It wasn't, he said. Can't be done. The real options were two: allow Shaker to become entirely Black, or work for a balanced, integrated community. "This, it seems to me, is the only real option," he said. "I am convinced that this kind of balanced community can be realized."

After laying out the logic of the situation, he turned to the area where he could claim more expertise: morality. This, he said, is a moral issue, and a simple one at that: "Is a man a man, without regard to the color of his skin?"

Pennybacker—known as Penny to his friends—had been thinking about race his entire life. Raised in Chattanooga, Tennessee, in the heart of Jim Crow, he went to schools that were segregated by law. Once he attended a concert at a progressive church in town where a renowned Black singer performed. "After the concert," he recalled decades later, his Southern accent still discernible, "one of the elderly ladies said to her, 'All the music is wonderful. I loved to hear you sing. I closed my eyes and thought your soul was just as white as mine.'"

His father, Albert M. Pennybacker Sr., was the general secretary of the local YMCA, and used his position to advocate for the Black community. He would meet with Black pastors for strategy sessions in their homes and was a founding member of the Interracial Committee of Chattanooga, which his son described as "not the most popular thing" in the white community in 1927. As part of a statewide YMCA project, his father supervised Myles Horton, who would create the storied Highlander Folk School, a training camp for labor organizers and, later, the civil rights movement. Pennybacker Sr. would let Horton, who was white, use the YMCA to raise money for Highlander, a decision that at one point put his job in jeopardy.

"Myles was highly controversial in the white community and to some extent in the whole community," the younger Pennybacker recalled. "He would come to our home for dinner and Mother would pull the shades down because they were afraid of drive-by shootings. When the shades went down, I knew Myles was coming for dinner."

Pennybacker Jr., born in 1931, was active in the youth movement of his church, where racial issues were front and center. He recalled traveling with an interracial group to Indianapolis, where the Black people in the group were told they could not eat at the restaurant the group had chosen. "They said the whites could stay," Pennybacker said. "We all, of course, walked out." He attended a segregated Vanderbilt University, where he drew attention to racism as editor of the school newspaper, then headed to Yale Divinity School, where he learned alongside white and some Black students. His first postgraduate posting with the Christian Church (Disciples of Christ) was in Youngstown, where he took up the cause of a Chinese family who were barred from burying a friend in the church cemetery because the cemetery's charter allowed only whites to be buried there. Shocked and appalled, Pennybacker engineered a swift change in the rules. In 1963, he was invited to pastor Heights Christian Church in Shaker Heights, replacing a minister who had died in a car crash the previous year.

He had been there for only a few months when he was asked to speak on the panel at Woodbury Junior High. "I thought it was an opportunity to speak about the future of the community," he recalled. "And I thought that was church business."

After laying out his case, he proposed a new city-sanctioned citizens commission to look at the issues facing Shaker Heights, including questions related to banking and real estate.

Pennybacker concluded by asking listeners to consider the passage in *Peter Pan* in which Peter tells the Lost Boys what to do if they encounter wolves in the woods: bend over double, put their head between their legs, and run backward, in hopes of scaring the wolves away. Now Shaker had a choice, he said: "Shall we face the future with our heads between our legs running backwards, hoping that our wolfish fears will run away? Or shall we assemble our resources in an intelligent, responsible, morally sound manner and together walk erect into our community's future?"

The speech made waves and was covered by the local press. Soon after, the mayor of Shaker Heights and a member of his congregation, Paul Jones, came to ask the pastor what he had said and why he had said it. Pennybacker assumed Jones had been sent by others to "keep his preacher in line." Jones reminded him that he was new to the community and suggested that he didn't really understand how decisions were made. The mayor acknowledged that yes, race relations were an issue, but said it really wasn't the pastor's business. "It was that kind of talk," Pennybacker said years later. "We left with some differences still on the table."

Others responded in writing. Critical notes included one postcard signed simply "a member," presumably of his church, who demanded: "Why not be a preacher & stop playing community politics. Don't you have enough to do?" He also received notes praising his comments, including letters from a leading local rabbi, a *Plain Dealer* columnist, and an official with the League of Women Voters. Joanne Finley, who headed Ludlow's housing effort, wrote with a list of suggested names for his commission, and with a thank-you, calling Pennybacker "a good new wind blowing in our community." She concluded: "We have worked terribly hard, but now we are not alone."

Pennybacker didn't wait for official blessing to begin implementing his vision. Three days after his speech at Woodbury, he solicited names for a citizens commission, and two weeks later, forty-eight people met for two hours on a Monday evening at Heights Christian Church to organize themselves. The group set out an expansive agenda, including looking at Black housing demand, lending policies of area banks, real estate agencies and their practices, the impact of change on the school system, and impact of integration on property values. City officials were still trying to figure out what to do about their changing community. This group of private citizens was pushing ahead.

―――――――

While Rev. Pennybacker put forth the moral argument, others were operating from a position of fear.

As superintendent of schools in the early 1960s, Donald G. Emery was wrestling with the realities of integration. He held what was at the time something of a mixed view: he thought exposing children of different races was positive and dismissed a parent who complained because his child had a Black teacher. But he saw a dilemma in whether the schools should allow Black and white children to dance together socially.

In November 1963, after hearing Pennybacker's speech, Emery wrote a memo to the school board about integration and marked it confidential. He said that until a few months earlier, his view had been that the schools should simply educate children who are legal residents of the district. Now, he said, his point of view had changed.

He detailed eight risks the district faced if and when more Black students enrolled, each based on negative stereotypes of Black families. Among them: It may be harder to recruit and keep experienced teachers. Schools could be less attractive to young families, and market value of homes will drop. Black parents may fail to understand the important work of reinforcing lessons at home.

He concluded that integration was inevitable but didn't need to be negative if it could proceed "under some type of planned approach." Black families don't want the community to change wholesale, either, he wrote. They "prefer a genuine integration and the benefits of the community as it is when they first arrive—not as it may become."

He proposed that a group of "carefully selected representatives from the city government, the Board of Elections, the religious community and the community at large" be formed. This group, he said, "could cause a planned integration to proceed without panic and without erosion of property values and without the downgrading of our school system."

His reasoning was less noble, but like Pennybacker, Emery was pushing for a city commission to manage the integration underway. He wanted it to be "planned," another way of saying slowed, or controlled. If Black families moved in too quickly, white residents would flee. It was, in reality, the same approach Ludlow was taking. Ludlow residents talked about the value of living together, while Emery talked about the risks that Black arrivals posed. But they were all talking about moving slowly down the integration road.

———

This wider conversation was unfolding as Black families began to move into Shaker neighborhoods beyond Ludlow and, in particular, into Moreland—a neighborhood that, like Ludlow, bordered the city of Cleveland, but was just a bit farther east.

Unlike the rest of Shaker Heights, the houses in Moreland were not developed under the Van Sweringen rules. The neighborhood, like others on the south side of Shaker, was originally part of East View Village, which was annexed to Shaker in 1920. Buyers working for the Vans had snapped up property in other neighborhoods, but the Moreland area was developed by others, featuring the types of houses typically found in Cleveland and often not up to the same quality standards that the Van Sweringen Company required of new construction. The Moreland houses typically featured front porches, and they included bungalows and "Cleveland Doubles," which were two-family houses with top and bottom porches. They were set close together, with smaller yards.

In the 1940s and '50s, Moreland was a working-class, largely Jewish neighborhood, home to institutions including the Orthodox Kinsman Jewish Center, the Jewish secular Workmen's Circle, the Hebrew Shelter Home, Temple Beth-El, and a drama center run by the Jewish Community Center. A 1958 study estimated that Moreland school was 70 percent Jewish. Many of these families had fled east from Cleveland neighborhoods such as Mount Pleasant and Glenville, both making space for Black families and fleeing as they arrived.

Now the pattern was set to repeat. In the early 1960s, Black families began crossing the border from neighboring Cleveland into Moreland—people such as Earline and Lorenzo Hooper, a Black couple with two young children who had been living in the Rosedale neighborhood of Cleveland.

One day in 1963, the Hoopers visited their son Sam's second grade classroom. The principal didn't want to let them into the class, but Lorenzo insisted, and the Hoopers were unimpressed by what they saw. The room felt uninviting, and the academics seemed weak. They had friends from church who had moved to Shaker Heights, and that evening the Hoopers started talking more seriously about doing the same.

Earline Jenkins had been born in Birmingham, Alabama, brought north to Cleveland in 1946, when she was fifteen, by her grandfather, who had migrated there first and bought a home for the family. "He wanted us to improve our education," she said. "He said, there's a better life for you in Cleveland." Earline graduated from Cleveland's Glenville High School and then from Ohio State University, where she estimated she was one of maybe fifteen Black women. She had met her husband before college and, after graduation, they married. He worked for the U.S. Postal Service, and she became a teacher. They bought a two-story house on Pennington Road in Moreland, with a front porch and a small lawn. Many white families lived on the street when they arrived. Slowly they disappeared.

Paula Hooper, Earline's middle child, was two years old when the family moved to Moreland and remembered living next door to a white Italian family and down the street from a Jewish woman. "We used to go to her house and she'd give us little treats and things," Paula said. The Italian neighbor would offer special Italian cookies. She recalled a group of girls, including one or two white girls, running together through the sprinkler in bathing suits, then lying in the sun. "I went home to my mom and said, 'I need a towel so I can lay out in the sun and get a tan.'" Her mom replied, "Honey, you don't need a tan. God already gave you one."

Soon the Jewish lady down the street was gone. So were the Italian neighbors next door.

"There were [real estate] agents out on the street knocking on doors of what they perceived as being the white families, saying, 'Maybe you want to move. Maybe it's time for you to get out. I can get you a good price,'" Steven Minter told an interviewer in 2017. He was Black and his wife, Dolly, was white. One day she was home alone when the doorbell rang and a white real estate agent began to give his pitch, she recounted in a 1992 commencement address. "Negroes were moving in. Our neighborhood would be undesirable," he told her. "You better sell now." He said he would help. She politely replied that she wasn't interested, but later wished she had called out his racism. A few days later, when a plumber warned her to be careful since this was a "changing neighborhood," she made clear that her neighbors, Black and white, were fine people.

Jerry Greenberg, who is white and grew up in Moreland around this time, recalled the reaction when one Black family moved in across the street in the early 1960s. "All the white people put their houses up for sale within a year," he said. He would overhear the conversations: "'So and so is moving . . .' As a kid, I didn't understand what was going on."

His own family could not afford to move, he said, and stayed until his parents divorced in 1968. At that point, they sold the house to a Black family.

———

In April 1964, the Pennybacker commission, now called the Shaker Heights Citizens Study Group on Racial Change, reported results from a comprehensive study of property values in Shaker Heights. The group had examined 4,350 homes to find 417 that had been sold at least twice between January 1955 and November 1963. The study meticulously documented gains and losses for every sale, organized by neighborhood, and concluded that the arrival of Black families had not depressed prices. In fact, in Ludlow, property values had risen on average by 5.9 percent, second in gains to the Mercer area, one of the most expensive parts of the city. In Ludlow, 83 percent of twice-sold homes showed a price gain, the group found, higher than all other eight Shaker neighborhoods.

"There has been no panic selling in any Shaker Heights school district as a result of Negro occupancy," Pennybacker told a crowd at Fairmont Temple on April 22, 1964, where he presented the results.

The study had its flaws, which critics were quick to point out. It was a small sample because not many homes changed hands twice, and it omitted sales in the Cleveland portion of Ludlow. It was possible that the prices had already dropped before the first sale. "Those who wanted to believe in the results did, and those who had felt that the presence of Negroes in a neighborhood had a depressing effect on property values were skeptical of the report's findings," Kent and Karen Weeks wrote of this period in their unpublished manuscript.

———

Driving east from Ludlow, the next neighborhood is Moreland, followed by Lomond, and this is the path that integration in Shaker took. Both Moreland and Lomond sought to emulate Ludlow's approach to integration and formed community associations modeled on Ludlow's. Moreland began its work in 1962, with some four hundred people showing up for an organizing meeting, and Lomond followed in 1963, even before Black residents arrived.

Both neighborhoods were ripe for integration, the stage set by Black families who arrived in the early 1960s to the adjacent Lee-Harvard neighborhood in Cleveland. Black brokers were eager to open the area up to Black home buyers, as illustrated by what happened on a Sunday in August 1961 along Scottsdale Boulevard, which marked Shaker's southern border with Cleveland in the Lomond area. A parade of fifteen cars drove slowly down the street, stopping periodically to let Black people out to look at the houses. Kenneth Jay Suid, who later wrote about this incident in his thesis at Princeton University, took down license plates and contacted the drivers. Nine of the fifteen told him they had been asked by real estate brokers to participate in the event so they could see the homes that might soon be available. "Evidently, the agents figured that the time was propitious for precipitating panic on Scottsdale Boulevard, even though no Negro had purchased a house on the street," Suid wrote.

It took two years before the first Black families would purchase homes in Lomond, with five sold on Scottsdale in summer 1963. Soon white real estate brokers abandoned Scottsdale, and For Sale signs began to pop up everywhere. The March 1964 *Lomond Newsletter* conveyed the ongoing concern about blockbusting agents and warned residents that they might receive "telephone solicitations by certain unethical brokers." If so, the newsletter urged them to report the calls to the city's law director.

Similarly, in Moreland, many white brokers stopped bringing white clients to see houses, and brokers of both races were pressuring white residents to sell. One resident told the Weekses that her family had been solicited fifty times in the summer of 1963: "There were deliberate attempts to frighten people. If you hadn't even thought about selling, you certainly would, with brokers ringing your doorbell beginning about nine o'clock on Sunday morning."

Trying to stem panic, the Lomond Association lobbied sellers and brokers to take down the For Sale signs and then lobbied the city to pass an ordinance banning them altogether, which Shaker did in April 1964. Both neighborhoods also established housing programs aimed at attracting white buyers, again modeled on Ludlow's work.

The Lomond Association's message to the neighborhood was that integration was an asset, not a burden, encouraging newcomers while working to persuade existing residents that they should stay put. The March 1964 newsletter projected this attitude ahead of the spring selling season, the first following the arrival of Black homeowners: "Spring is fast approaching and with it the usual flurry of buying and selling houses. We think it is a time for reseeding of lawns and philosophies. The arrival of the first Negro families in Lomond has been greeted by the overwhelming majority of our residents in a mature, calm, intelligent, and considerate fashion. Most of the people we have had a chance to talk to in our discussion groups and over the back fence have recognized the inevitability and the *moral* right of Negroes to move to areas where they can obtain better housing and schools. They have long since learned the importance of judging people as individuals rather than prejudging them in groups."

All this unfolded at a time of open warfare in the South over civil rights. In January 1963, Alabama governor George Wallace declared, in a fiery speech vowing to resist federal desegregation of schools, "Segregation now, segregation tomorrow, segregation forever," a new rallying cry for racist forces fighting civil rights. In June 1963, NAACP state field director Medgar Evers was murdered in his Mississippi driveway. In August, Dr. Martin Luther King Jr. delivered his "I Have a Dream" speech from the steps of the Lincoln Memorial. In September, a bomb planted in the 16th Street Baptist Church in Birmingham exploded, killing four girls. Throughout American history, there have been moments where the issue of race has taken center stage in the national debate— and with the civil rights movement reaching its apex, this was one of them.

The April 1965 *Lomond Newsletter* addressed the point directly: "We do not feel that criticizing Selma, Alabama relieves us of our responsibilities for Shaker Heights, Ohio. Negroes need decent housing." Nonetheless, by the summer of 1965, the Weekses reported, more Black residents had arrived, and there had been no white buyers. Both Lomond and Moreland associations won foundation funding for their housing programs and kept battling.

As the neighborhoods of Shaker were grappling with integration, the City of Shaker Heights itself moved more slowly. It did take some steps toward curtailing white flight, though city leaders appeared motivated mostly by a desire to control the arrival of Black residents. In 1961, the City Council passed an antiblockbusting ordinance, which made it a misdemeanor for any person to use the threat of racial change in a neighborhood to induce homeowners to list their houses for sale. Fines ranged from $50 for the first offense to $500 for subsequent violations. Officials bragged it was the first law of its kind in the nation, though it's not clear whether anyone was actually fined, and blockbusting continued to be a problem.

In April 1964, five days after Pennybacker presented the results of his group's property study, the council voted 5–0 to approve the ban on For Sale and Sold signs. Real estate agents and their attorneys questioned the constitutionality of the ban, calling it an infringement on free speech. Black brokers (known then as Realtists) were also opposed; they had been denied access to the listings service, and the signs let them know what was for sale. But city officials defended the policy as economically sound, and other communities soon followed suit. The ban would remain in place for more than three decades, until these ordinances were ruled unconstitutional.

In 1964, the city gave in to pressure and appointed a five-member Citizens Advisory Commission, charged with making integration an "orderly and constructive process for the entire city," recalled Bernard Isaacs, a Ludlow activist who served on the panel. Members toured the integrated parts of Shaker and encouraged city officials and residents to accept integration as a fact of life. The school system had already been dealing with integration for several years, but the mayor and the City Council needed a shove, one commissioner told Kent and Karen Weeks. "We tell the mayor and the council, 'This is your chance to be remembered for doing something significant, not sitting on your hands.'" Attitudes of the commissioners also shifted. "I've come a long way," one member said. "I see integration as a practical economic fact of life. I see it with less emotion than several years ago."

In the fall of 1965, the commission recommended that Shaker create a central office to support the three neighborhood associations, and the following summer, it suggested the city take over the entire enterprise. The question was put to the associations. Ludlow was divided, recalled white Ludlow resident Carolyn Milter, who voted no. She feared the city would never tend to and care for the program the way the people living in Ludlow did. "I thought the government was only interested in trying to keep Ludlow from going all Black," she said. Alan Gressel, who had run Ludlow's housing program, made the case for the centralized office, arguing that Shaker's money combined with Ludlow's talent would create an effective program.

The vote in Ludlow—as in other neighborhoods—was yes, and later that year, the Shaker Communities office was created, with housing coordinators reporting to a director employed by the city. Ultimately, it would employ fourteen part-time staffers, with a $100,000 budget funded by the city and, in what may have been a first, the schools. In 1968, it was renamed the Shaker Heights Housing Office.

The office focused on drawing white buyers to Ludlow, Moreland, and Lomond. It placed advertisements in elite national publications such as the *Saturday Review*, the *New Republic*, and the *Village Voice*. It hosted a dinner for some thirty business executives at Shaker Country Club. It approached area universities and companies, looking for leads on new recruits moving into the city.

It was a bold program that would win Shaker an enormous amount of national publicity over many years. In 1973, *Money* magazine cited Shaker in a piece about property values and integration: "Anyone seeking horror stories to support the view that a declining neighborhood is the price of integration must look somewhere other than Shaker Heights." In 1977, officials from Southfield, Michigan, visited to study Shaker's housing program in hopes of replicating it. Other communities that came calling for advice included Dayton, Ohio; Oak Park, Illinois; Teaneck, New Jersey; Silver Spring, Maryland; and Fort Wayne, Indiana.

In 1979, *U.S. News & World Report* wrote about Shaker under the headline WE FEEL GOOD ABOUT OURSELVES. The story showed how Shaker had successfully turned what was for many the frightening prospect of Black migration into a positive new self-identity. Integration wasn't a challenge; it was a selling point. "We've taken this potentially explosive problem, turned it around and now we advertise it. We say our diversity pays dividends," Joe Szwaja, director of community relations for the school system, told *U.S. News*.

But the housing office was not promoting integration for the sake of integration. It was promoting integration in areas where Black families had already moved, as a way of preventing resegregation. The housing office did not serve Black buyers or encourage integration in the mostly or all-white Shaker neighborhoods. In May 1969, a *Plain Dealer* reporter wrote that he had accompanied a Black man to the housing office. The man asked for a place to rent in Shaker Heights for about $180 per month ($1,460 in 2022 dollars) and was given a list of rental units outside Shaker.

Workers were careful about how they spoke about race, said

Isabel Ann Lewis, a white mother of four who had moved to the Lomond neighborhood with the help of the housing program and then worked for the office for two decades. "I would just say 'diverse areas,'" she recalled. "I wouldn't say 'integrated'—it had a bad connotation."

Another Shaker Heights Housing Office employee, Renée Schecter, explained how she would only show apartments to prospective white renters between 10 a.m. and 3 p.m. because after 3 p.m., children were out of school.

"There would be an awful lot of Black children in the street," she said. "And Black families who came into the area always have two or more children. So at that time every Black face was more visible than it is today, you know." She added: "To someone coming in who'd never seen Black people living, they've only seen Black domestics, and in some cases never seen a Black person at all, seeing three or four Black children playing in the street, my God, that was like, oh, scary, especially if they were teenagers, you know."

When the three community associations asked the commission and the mayor to endorse the idea of open occupancy, declaring that Shaker Heights welcomes all residents, the commission declined. A commissioner told the Weekses that the city had to respond to conservatives living in Shaker Heights. "If we attempted to facilitate the movement of Negroes into other parts of Shaker Heights, we'd lose the confidence of much of the people and we'd lose our effectiveness." Another commissioner told them: "People already ask us, 'Are you guys quietly bringing in Negroes?'"

So while the housing office was Shaker's innovative answer to integration, it did not exactly operate from a position of racial justice. It was selling Shaker and the benefits of diversity in general, and integration in areas where it was already underway, while downplaying the actual presence of Black people.

In July 1965, Rev. Pennybacker was on vacation visiting the Carlsbad Caverns in New Mexico with his wife, their three children, and her parents when he received an urgent phone message at the hotel from two of his parishioners, Joan and Paul Campbell.

"Guess what?" they began. "We're going to have a Nobel Prize winner speak in our church."

"Oh, who might that be?" Penny replied, knowing full well who they meant.

The Campbells, as well as Rev. Pennybacker, had been involved in the mayoral campaign of Carl Stokes in Cleveland, and Stokes's supporters included the Reverend Dr. Martin Luther King Jr., who periodically came to town to boost his campaign. That summer, campaign officials were discussing the idea of King visiting a white suburban church and Joan spoke up to suggest hers—Heights Christian in Shaker Heights. "We'd be happy to have him!" she said.

On the phone from New Mexico, Pennybacker told the Campbells he was all for it and suggested they call the chairman of the church board.

The board chairman was less enthused. The church was composed of upper-income establishment types, not all of whom were ready to embrace King, who was labeled a communist in some circles and whose reputation was far more controversial than one might remember given how he would come to be venerated after he was assassinated. The chairman informed the Campbells that, wouldn't you know, urgent redecorations needed to be done right away and the sanctuary would not be available on the day King planned to visit. They agreed on an alternate plan: King would speak from the back porch of the church, and the crowd could gather on the lawn outside.

Pennybacker got another call, this time from a lawyer representing a leading member of his church, a railroad executive, who said if King spoke, this man would leave Heights Christian and take a third of the congregation with him. Pennybacker kept his resolve.

On the morning of July 28, 1965, Joan Campbell accompanied Dr. King to the church. Before his speech, King asked to see the sanctuary. Campbell was horrified by what he would see—the sanctuary in a state of disrepair due to the "urgent" redecorations that were now underway. She figured he would see that this mess could have been avoided if the church had wanted to avoid it. "Well, well, well," King told her, "I must be a very popular man that they can take the whole church apart for me." Campbell remembered him adding, "I know what a risk this is. I want you to understand that I know my presence will not make your life easier, but I also think it will give you a life of things that matter." That moment, she said, changed her life.

Police estimated the racially diverse crowd at three thousand, Pennybacker recalled. There were some protesters, carrying picket signs as they paced the perimeter, but the vast majority listened with rapt attention. "I still have faith in the future, and I believe we're going to solve this problem in America," King preached. "I submit to you that if the inexpressible cruelties of slavery couldn't stop us, the opposition that we now face will surely fail."

After the event, Pennybacker had to deal with the blowback within his congregation. A group of angry church elders called him to a meeting at which they leveled a long list of charges against him related to the King visit. He recalled replying something to the effect of, "Every one of you knows that the future of this congregation does not lie with bigotry and hatred and racism, and when I'm out of town I have every right to expect you to do what is best for this congregation, and there was an absence of your leadership in this instance." After that, he said, the railroad executive who had threatened to leave sheepishly retreated, saying he found Pennybacker to be "an honorable man."

Pennybacker capped the evening by telling the group he expected to see each of them in church every week for the next three months, saying that their presence should quash the circulating rumors that they were trying to oust him. Half joking, Pennybacker added, "When anybody asks you about this rumor of wanting to get rid of me, you tell them we've got the greatest pastor in the country."

The debate inside the church led to a grappling with race that had never happened before, Pennybacker said, and to efforts at becoming more racially inclusive. An interracial couple, he said, was welcomed into the church. And a church member who was a senior vice president for Republic Steel, a big Cleveland company, started questioning why his company had an all-white executive team when it was boasting of inclusivity.

"It was time to confront an issue we should have been confronting for years," Pennybacker said.

In the end, just six families left the church in protest.

———

Keeping white residents in the Moreland neighborhood had proved especially challenging for Shaker Heights. It sat on the edge of an urban corridor, with car dealerships erecting bigger and brighter signs just around the corner from people's homes, and its housing stock was less appealing compared with the rest of Shaker. "Unfortunately, these homes are not attractive to families with adequate assets and thus are being purchased by families of marginal means," Alan Gressel, president of the Ludlow Community Association, said in a 1965 letter to the mayor.

In 1966, the city hatched an urban renewal plan aimed at increasing property values, decreasing what was seen as blight in Moreland and bringing that neighborhood into closer aesthetic alignment with the rest of Shaker. The master plan's new civic center for cultural organizations would require tearing down seventy-five Moreland homes in the middle of the neighborhood, and a new city service center to process Shaker's garbage would require demolishing fifty-four homes. Planners also recommended a luxury high-rise apartment building and a town house development meant to attract white residents.

Urban renewal projects like this, many of them much larger and in bigger cities, were meant to revitalize neighborhoods, demolish slums, and eliminate substandard housing. The federal government spent $13 billion on these programs between 1949 and 1973, displacing some two million residents and often destroying the social and economic fabric of neighborhoods, sometimes plowing a highway right through a community. Often these were Black neighborhoods.

In Shaker Heights, the architects warned that without their urban renewal plan, Moreland could become a "ghetto" inside Shaker. But Moreland residents questioned how much they would be paid for their homes and whether they'd be able to afford something else in Shaker Heights. They charged that the real goal was to reduce Moreland's population and eliminate affordable housing. At a meeting to discuss the proposal, the *Sun Press* reported that "several residents attacked the civic center proposal as a thinly disguised containment program for Moreland's Negro population."

"Where can we go for open housing in Shaker? You are moving the Negroes out of Shaker," a woman identified as Mrs. Johnnie Mae Reeves said at a contentious meeting of the City Council that drew a record three hundred people.

In response to these critics, the plans for the civic center and the high-rise apartments were dropped, but a citywide vote to fund the town houses and the service center moved ahead.

A group led by two Ludlow Community Association leaders formed to oppose the bond issue that was to pay for the project. Alan Gressel called the proposal one of "Negro removal" that undermined the work of integration in Moreland. But the bond measure passed, and the projects were built. The city retaliated by firing two Ludlow veterans from the housing office—Alan Gressel, as well as Sue Spetrino, whose husband, Ron, was another vocal opponent of the bond issue. It was particularly galling to many that Sue Spetrino was fired because of the actions of her husband.

The Ludlow association protested the firings to no effect. In one sense, the community had scored a victory: the program was scaled back in response to critics. On the other hand, it was the civic center that was eliminated and the service center that remained. As of 2023, Shaker's garbage was still being collected and processed in Moreland.

———

As the 1960s gave way to the '70s, there were signs the Ludlow Community Association was beginning to fray.

The association lacked the volunteer power to produce an annual report in 1969, and seven committee chairmanships were vacant. After growing year after year, membership in the association peaked in 1970 at 610 families and then began to decline.

In 1970, the association was bitterly divided—not over race, but economics. At issue was a proposal by the City of Cleveland to put fourteen public housing units into the neighborhood—ten town houses and two two-family homes. Carolyn Milter recalled that many white people in Ludlow felt it was their neighborhood's responsibility to be part of the solution at a time when demand for low-income housing far outstripped supply. She remembered the proposal as modest and was among those who endorsed it. "We had to do our part," she said.

But many Black Ludlow residents were "extremely angry" at the prospect, she said. Many of them had grown up in the city of Cleveland and moved to Shaker for the suburban dream, not to live alongside those in poverty.

After negotiations with the developer and the public housing agency, the association endorsed the plan. The *Plain Dealer* said it was the first time an outlying area in the region had supported public housing in its own backyard. Opponents were so angry that they briefly broke away from the Ludlow Community Association. They argued that the proposal would devalue the neighborhood and that the proposed units were overly dense.

After one emotional meeting, a Black woman made clear to a white friend and neighbor that their situations were not the same. "You can move to Lyman Circle now, but I can't," she said, referring to a white part of Shaker.

In the end, the units went up.

"There were people who carried feelings afterward for a long while," Milter said. She said neighbors suddenly realized they were coming from very different life experiences. "It affected people's feelings about each other."

In the 1971 annual report, the president of the North Ashwood block club reviewed the controversy and concluded: "If someone from outside the Ludlow Community was making an effort to disrupt or destroy our community, he or they were doing one helluva job; for what was once a very unique street club was now vastly deteriorating."

In an address delivered in January 1971, Ludlow Community Association president Jerry Berner began, "My chief goal will be to try to redevelop a sense of community in Ludlow." In the annual report written at year's end, Berner suggested not much progress had been made. "People do not seem to be as actively interested in the housing activities of LCA as in the past, when the need to maintain a stable integrated community was more unique and seemed to be more pressing," he wrote. Hospitality chairman Peggy Fuller reported that the first chair resigned midyear and that one of the parties that year "met with disaster as only five couples attended."

At the same time, more people began questioning the underlying philosophy of the housing program. The association had always defended the uncomfortable practice of steering Black buyers elsewhere in order to maintain integration. In the 1972 annual report, the president said that was changing. "In the housing program, we began to rethink Ludlow's role in the Shaker Communities' program. The question of steering—by us, the Shaker housing office, and by the Realtors—has come under scrutiny." The next year, the association officially repudiated its own unwritten policy of steering.

Hard work toward racial balance had moved the percentage of Black students at Ludlow Elementary School from 72 percent in 1963 to 54 percent in 1970. But that half-white/half-Black balance didn't last. In the fall of 1971, the share of Black students rose to about 57 percent; a year later, 69 percent. In the fall of 1974, Black students again made up 72 percent of Ludlow students.

That year, the association's coffers were low, according to the annual report, but there was little enthusiasm for a major concert or event. The main issues dealt with that year involved safety and security, and plans were underway for crime prevention.

The Ludlow Community Association had reached heights that Irv and Emilie Barnett, that Ted and Beverly Mason could never have conceived of in the earliest days. They had defied the sociologist's discouraging predictions and made water run uphill, at least for a while. They had recruited white people into a neighborhood where Black people already lived. They even had Ella Fitzgerald raising money for the cause at Severance Hall. But economic divides proved tricky, and this was just the beginning of Shaker's work to reconcile divisions of class as well as race. Now the association morphed into something closer to a normal neighborhood group, with the mantle of integration in the hands of the City of Shaker Heights.

Negro children suffer serious harm when their education
takes place in public schools which are racially segregated.
—United States Commission on Civil Rights, 1967

6

JACK LAWSON

John H. Lawson was getting ready to leave his house in Shaker Heights when the front doorbell rang. It was February 24, 1970, and Lawson, the superintendent of schools, was heading to a school board meeting where he would present his recommendation for a busing program aimed at desegregating the district's nine elementary schools, in particular Moreland, which was overwhelmingly Black.

He had been quietly selling his proposal to the school board for months, and a couple of weeks earlier, its outline had been released publicly. Now he was ready to talk directly to the community about his plan to bus Black students from Moreland to the predominantly white schools elsewhere in Shaker. Before leaving his office that afternoon, he had received a frightening phone call from a Shaker Heights resident who delivered a warning: "If you recommend the integration of the Shaker Heights elementary schools, you won't leave alive. I have a gun, and I will bring it with me to the meeting to kill you." The man then hung up. Lawson figured it was a crank call, but a colleague recognized the guy and insisted Lawson tell the police. The police assured him they would be out in force at the high school that night.

Now Lawson was home, getting ready to leave again for the school board meeting that evening. He answered the doorbell, and this time, he was greeted by a pair of friendly faces, two Black women who worked for the school district. One was Beverly Mason, whose purchase of a lot

in Ludlow back in 1955 had started the Shaker schools down the road
to integration. Mason was now a social worker for the schools, and, with
a colleague, she presented the superintendent with a petition they had
circulated supporting the plan, signed by a majority of teachers from
each of Shaker's nine elementary schools. The pair also handed Lawson
a bottle of expensive whiskey and suggested he would need it after the
meeting.

———

John Lawson, known universally as Jack, hadn't been focused on issues
of race when he took over as superintendent in 1965. Tall, lanky, and
silver-haired, he was rarely seen without a suit, tie, and reading glasses at
the ready. Maybe it was his Boston accent or perhaps the nickname Jack,
but to some, he came across as Shaker's version of John F. Kennedy. In
fact his roots were far more modest. Lawson had grown up in Gloucester,
Massachusetts, in poverty, the son of an alcoholic father who died young.

He came to Ohio from nearly all-white school districts in Massachusetts, where race relations rarely came up. His son John didn't recall
much conversation about race at home, and remembered having exactly
one Black classmate in his classes before arriving at Shaker in the eleventh grade. "Just one kid, and he disappeared halfway through the year,"
he said. "I don't think my father had a lot of actual experience with the
racial issue." But he said his father sent him to a basketball camp run by
Bill Russell, a Black superstar for the Boston Celtics and a civil rights
activist, and voted for Edward Brooke, a Black man who ran for various Massachusetts offices and eventually became the first Black person
elected to the Senate by popular vote. And when his dad saw a Black
lawn jockey on the lawn of his father-in-law's house, Jack "called him a
racist, and they had a fight all afternoon," his son remembered.

Lawson had been drawn to Shaker by the beauty of the community
and its reputation for educational excellence. Students were at the top
of virtually every measure of academic achievement, and the faculty
was exceptionally well qualified, with many teachers holding advanced
degrees. The curriculum was rich, with extras such as foreign language
classes in elementary school. Citizens regularly voted for tax increases
to pay for it.

Lawson arrived as the number of Black students was rising each year.
In 1965, his first year, Black students made up 14.5 percent of the dis-

trict, up from 10.5 percent a year earlier. The school board considered his positive attitude toward integration one of the chief criteria in hiring him. Time and again, residents told him, in a mantra that would be repeated over and over through the years, "If integration could not succeed in Shaker Heights, it could not anywhere." His predecessor, Donald Emery, had left Shaker for Scarsdale, New York, a virtually all-white community. Now a new leader had arrived with an opportunity to examine the situation with fresh eyes.

It didn't take long for Lawson to see the complex racial dynamics at work in Shaker Heights. When he and his wife, Helen, were house-hunting, real estate brokers steered them away from certain neighborhoods, saying places like Moreland and Ludlow were too Black, and areas like Mercer were too Jewish.

Once he took office, Lawson noticed that the mostly white schools had been constructed more recently and had better facilities. One of his first acts was to recommend a bond issue to pay for libraries and improved facilities in older buildings. He pushed his leadership team to hire more Black teachers after seeing the faculty was virtually all white, and by 1970, a Lawson aide reported that the number of Black teachers on the five-hundred-member faculty had risen from two to thirty-five. And he redrew boundary lines to racially balance the two junior high schools: Woodbury was 35 percent Black; Byron had almost no Black students. Complaints came from parents and real estate agents, but the school board unanimously endorsed the change.

Now Lawson had his eye on a more profound challenge: the elementary schools, where there were sharp racial imbalances.

———

In 1967, Jack Lawson had been superintendent for two years when he addressed the district's teachers on the topic of integration. It had been thirteen years since the Supreme Court ruled, in *Brown v. Board of Education*, that schools segregated by race were inherently unequal and a violation of the equal protection clause of the Fourteenth Amendment of the Constitution. Still, most school districts had yet to comply, and segregation was widely seen as a problem of the South, where schools were segregated by law.

Lawson spoke at length, emphasizing that neither educational quality nor property values had fallen as the district added more Black students.

Then he dropped something of a bombshell. He said the shift in student assignments for the junior high schools had gone well and that now the administration was studying elementary school "patterns and alternatives . . . in order to provide every boy and girl with integrated education at the elementary level." Shaker neighborhoods were defined by their elementary schools, and changing school assignment in the primary years was sure to be far more controversial.

The nine elementary schools were situated differently when it came to integration. In those north of Van Aken Boulevard, there were almost no Black students on October 1, 1967, when a census of students was recorded. Boulevard Elementary, the first Shaker school, constructed in 1914, enrolled 6 Black students out of 352 in the school. At Onaway, the neighborhood where Lawson lived and where Ervin and Thomasine Mason had fought to buy a house, there were 14 out of 365. Mercer, a heavily Jewish area built in 1952 to serve the newest homes in Shaker, had 4 Black students out of a school population of 656. And Malvern, deep in the wealthiest section of old Shaker where the largest, grandest homes sat, had exactly 0 Black students.

A very different story was unfolding south of Van Aken. At Sussex School, in the southeast corner, integration was just beginning, with twenty-six Black students, or 6.7 percent of the total. At Lomond, the next neighborhood over, nearly one in four children was Black. At this point, Ludlow Elementary was 59.5 percent Black.

And then there was Moreland, the onetime working-class Jewish neighborhood. In November 1963, the school had been 29.7 percent Black; by October 1967, it was 89.5 percent Black, a classic example of resegregation driven by white flight.

The virtually all-white schools were just as segregated as Moreland was, but from the start, Moreland was the focus of the district's attention. Lawson and his staff consulted with teachers, principals, administrators, and staff, working to keep the work under the radar so as to avoid rumors that might mobilize opponents. Lawson considered closing Moreland altogether but quietly settled on an alternate but still dramatic proposal to bus fourth, fifth, and sixth graders out and create what he would call a "special services school" at Moreland. Elementary school students from across the district would rotate into Moreland for six weeks of special enrichment activities each year with experts on hand in math, reading, science, and French (the foreign language of choice). Another idea was using Moreland to co-locate special service providers including speech therapists, guidance counselors, psychologists, social workers, dental hygienists, and optometrists.

This idea was considered provocative because it involved busing white children "into what is now seen as a Negro school," wrote a young Lawson aide named Gardner P. Dunnan, who was charged with developing the plan and documented the process for his Harvard University thesis. But Dunnan and Lawson saw it as an opportunity to not just address racial imbalance but to fill a wide range of unmet needs.

In a memo outlining the plan, Dunnan offered a robust argument for integrating Shaker's schools, saying racial isolation was harmful to both Black and white children and that Black children who attend integrated schools have higher self-esteem, test scores, and success later in life. He ticked through a list of alternate approaches and explained why each would be difficult to implement in Shaker. For instance, instituting "racial quotas" for each school would solve the segregation problem but would have to be sold to the community on the basis of integration alone and would disrupt all nine elementary schools. The memo also raised the prospect of a possible civil rights lawsuit challenging school segregation if the district did nothing; it's not clear how serious or specific that threat was.

The school board discussed the proposal at a May 1968 work session that Lawson deliberately scheduled immediately after a school bond issue was handily approved by voters. Lawson had been confident it would pass and he was right. That, plus a couple of other unrelated developments, put the school board in "an extremely positive state of mind," Dunnan wrote in his thesis. In addition, he wrote, a consultant had made some proposals regarding school integration as part of the discussion of the city's master plan, which put some pressure on the school board to devise its own solution. The school board gave Lawson the go-ahead.

In February 1969, Lawson applied to the Ford Foundation for funding for the special services school, and the foundation responded with a $165,547 grant. That fall, he returned with a developed plan and presented it to the school board in a private executive session. It's unclear how much, if at all, he consulted with the Moreland community itself about the details or even the general concept. A meeting in November 1969 suggests any attempt to win buy-in was minimal.

On November 20, four months after winning the grant and three months before he would unveil his integration proposal publicly, Lawson met with eight Moreland leaders who were part of a group called Concerned Citizens for an Integrated Moreland School. They presented him with a proposal for two-way busing, backed by a petition signed by six hundred people from the neighborhood.

The Moreland group's seven-page proposal made many of the same points Lawson and his staff had about the need for integration, but it asked for "voluntary cross-enrollment," with white students bused to Moreland as well as Moreland students bused out. Bringing more white children to Moreland School would make the neighborhood more attractive to white home seekers, they said, so it was important that the board make an "exhaustive" effort to find white parents willing to participate.

"We believe it is essential that plans be worked out with the active participation of Moreland parents," they wrote. "We do not wish to be confronted with a plan at the last minute and be placed in the position of defensively reacting to it."

Lawson was vague about where he was in the planning process. He told them he had been working on "various integration plans" for the past two years and expected to finish work within the next few weeks. In fact, on the day of the meeting, the plan for a special services school was fully developed and funded with the Ford Foundation grant.

There are other indications that the Black community was not feeling heard at this moment. A few days before Lawson would announce his proposal, Shaker's PTA Council drew an overflow crowd of seven hundred people to a community conversation titled "How the Blacks Have Changed Our Schools." Some objected to the panel's title, saying it was racist on its face. Jack Robinson, a high school senior and leader of Students for Black Identity, spoke from the audience to say, "Black students may go to the school but they do not feel it is their school. They feel they can excel as a Black student but they don't feel welcome." A student at Byron Junior High School asked, her voice quavering, "How are you dealing with the racism of teachers at Byron?" Lawson, who was moderating the panel, responded with surprise and said he doubted such an attitude was widespread. He invited the girl to speak with him after the meeting, but it's unclear what, if anything, he did to address her concerns—or to ascertain whether such attitudes were in fact widespread.

Resistance was also coming from the opposite direction. Before an official announcement, Lawson and school board president Robert

Rawson explained the plan to Shaker's mayor, Paul Jones, who a few years earlier had admonished Rev. Pennybacker for his comments about embracing integration in Shaker. It didn't go well. Jones "was very negative and hostile and told me that I was destroying Shaker Heights by desegregating the schools," Lawson wrote in an unpublished memoir. "Bob and I knew that Paul was not especially fond of the racial changes that were happening in the city so we were not surprised by his reaction."

In February 1970, another group, this one called the Moreland Parents Committee, wrote to the school board and made clear, again, that any plan to turn all or part of Moreland into a special services school was unacceptable to them. They suggested that white parents would accept two-way busing if the district would explain why it would do no harm. They made clear: "WE WILL NOT ACCEPT A PROGRAM OF ONE-WAY BUSSING."

A two-way busing plan asking or requiring white parents to send their children to a mostly Black school would be far more controversial for people with the power in town than the plan Lawson had in mind. And documents show that he was also committed and excited by the idea of the special program at Moreland, regardless of whether people in Moreland wanted such a program. That program would not be possible with a two-way busing program.

Two days later, on February 10, Lawson announced his plan. It had not changed much in the two years since Dunnan had written his proposal: Moreland students up to grade three would continue at Moreland, but those in grades four, five, and six would be bused to the six predominantly white elementary schools. (Two elementary schools, Lomond and Ludlow, would not receive Moreland students because they already had substantial Black populations of their own.)

The space freed up at Moreland would be used for what was now described as an Enrichment School, which would offer opportunities such as homemaking, industrial arts, music, social studies, theater, math labs, science, foreign language classes, and programs for students with learning disabilities. Students in upper elementary grades would spend five weeks each year at the center, meaning students would be bused to Moreland for these weeks. However, no student who lived outside the neighborhood would be assigned to attend Moreland as their primary school.

Lawson launched the plan and was ready to fight for it. Integration, he said, was needed to improve learning—and to prepare all children for life in a multiracial world. He cast the imperative in moral terms, saying the "very survival" of the community depended on understanding that the issue was not whether to desegregate Moreland, but how.

Interest in Lawson's plan was intense. More than fifteen hundred people turned out for the first meeting at the high school, and a subsequent session brought out nearly fourteen hundred. Meetings were added to the schedule, both big, open sessions in schools and smaller gatherings in homes, arranged by the PTA Council, the League of Women Voters, the Dads' Club, and the teachers union. News coverage was robust, with the *Sun Press* running its own unscientific reader survey on the proposal (showing 71 percent opposed). Shaker used the *School Review*, a newsletter for parents, to explain the plan and answer common questions about it.

Nervousness was evident in a March message from the principal of Sussex Elementary School, which in attempting to help calm parents also reinforced prejudice and stereotypes. He assured them that each class at Sussex, which had a small Black student population, would see only a few new students, "therefore, no major change will be observable." He also set up expectations that the Black students would be trailing academically. He said "it is probably true" that more of the new students were in "the lower range" but said parents should "remember that there will be only four or five in the class." He added: "I believe that many benefits will accrue if we are finally fortunate enough to be part of it."

Straight-up opposition to the plan came from Black parents in Moreland, who opposed the unequal burden of busing put on their children, and from white conservatives elsewhere in Shaker, who opposed integration at all. On February 24, the day of the first public meeting on the plan, the Moreland Community Association formally came out against it. "Any meaningful solution must involve a coming together of the entire city in a spirit of equality," the association's president wrote to Lawson. Again, the community made clear: "We will not accept a program of one-way busing."

The *Plain Dealer* reported that in addition to concerns about fairness, Moreland residents worried about the loss of their neighborhood school. Some were afraid white kids would not accept the Black transfers. Others wondered where Moreland children would eat lunch, given that all students walked home for lunch. "The white kids aren't going to invite these kids home," said Gessie G. Clark, president of the association. "We don't want the children to grow up feeling that they're any different. All we want them to do is get the same treatment as anyone else."

Tensions persisted through the spring, including a prickly back-and-forth over whether Lawson would appear at a Moreland forum on the plan. (He didn't, ostensibly objecting to the format, though the ongoing tensions likely were at work.)

In his memoir, completed in 2000, Lawson emphasized Black support for his plan, but most of it appeared to come from Ludlow, a higher-income area that was home to the Black doctors, dentists, and lawyers who first desegregated Shaker Heights—people like Drue King Jr., who was now serving as the first Black member of the school board. King's support for the plan, Lawson said, helped bring along the rest of the school board. Still, those from Ludlow were unaffected by it personally.

Lawson faced organized opposition from some white Shakerites, too. He recalled being booed for fifteen minutes at the start of one public meeting. "I remember saying thank you over and over," he wrote. He said he would receive telephone calls in the early morning hours—between midnight and 3 or 4 a.m. Callers would make vile and racist comments such as "nigger lover," he wrote. "I would listen and hang up."

The Western Reserve Women's Republican Club of Shaker Heights organized a campaign against the plan, urging its members to attend the public meetings and to call or write the school district. And a newly formed Shaker Taxpayers Association circulated a petition demanding that the plan be put to a public vote, filing 3,634 signatures with the district. The group's stated objection was to its cost (though the foundation grant covered much of the expense). "Taxpayers have a right to know what is planned and how much of a tax burden he is forced to carry," said the group's chairman, Larry Selhorst.

Lawson and the school board had no interest in putting their plan up for a vote. At one of the public meetings, Rawson, the school board president, dismissed the idea. "It would be a good way for the board to escape its responsibility, but we are elected by the people," he said. He was interrupted by applause—a sign that, as is often the case, the loudest voices do not necessarily represent the majority.

Hundreds of calls and letters poured into the district's administrative offices, roughly divided between supporters and opponents.

Among white people in town, some of the opposition centered on the value of neighborhood schools. Housing in Shaker—and across the country—has long been segregated, a situation created in part by government, banking, and real estate policies. As a result, most neighborhood schools have been inherently segregated, too. Some opponents in Shaker said the real answer was to integrate housing in Moreland, something that the city was working on but finding easier said than done. And while there are very real advantages to neighborhood schools, support for them is also an argument that would be deployed across the country for decades to come by those who opposed desegregation plans. And it must be said, in this case, no one was taking away the right of anyone to attend a neighborhood school—except for students living in Moreland.

Some opponents cast their views as sticking up for Black students, expressing concern, for instance, that they would be unable to go home for lunch.

But others were blatantly hostile and overtly racist. One caller, Howard Bacon, phoned the district offices and charged, "All liberals are liars." He said if the district tried to bus his children he would "resist with whatever force is necessary from words to bullets," according to notes taken on the call. The summary continued: "He restated the 'bullets' . . . He said the Board asked for citizen reaction and THIS IS HIS!"

A postcard to the district asked simply, "When does your course on interracial marriage begin?"—no matter that the children involved were all under the age of thirteen.

Jack Weingold, a father from the Mercer area, wrote that he had always supported tax increases for the schools, but if the busing plan was approved he would never vote for another. "Why should someone who pays 30% of the taxes I pay be given the same privileges? Is this a communistic community?"

James M. Wilsman, who lived near Fernway School, was among those who said he would not have bought a house in Shaker Heights if he hadn't supported integration. But he also bluntly asserted that he expected his children to be with families like his own. "I purchased my home because it was in a neighborhood that had families of the same general background and professional attainment as my own," he wrote. "I cannot believe that the parents in the Moreland School District want their children to be bussed to another district, isolated, unable to go home for lunch, and be generally 'set apart' from the other children in the school to which they are bussed."

To be clear, the opponents of this plan were not being required or even asked to change the schools their own children attended. They were simply being asked to accept a handful of Black students bused into their schools, and for their own children to travel with their classes to Moreland for a five-week rotation once a year for enrichment services.

While the opposition was intense, supporters were enthusiastic. They argued that desegregation was the right thing to do, and agreed with Superintendent Lawson that it would help prepare their own children for life in a multiracial world while helping those at Moreland.

The plan won support from a large number of Shaker organizations including the teachers union, PTAs, and churches, as well as individual community members. Mr. and Mrs. Michael Wipper, who lived in the wealthy Malvern neighborhood, wrote Lawson to say they assumed many of their neighbors had moved to Malvern because it stood as "the last 'enclave' of exclusiveness" for elementary school. "We have never felt that way. We are ready to welcome the Moreland children when they arrive."

"Hopefully, one day our children will look back and wonder what the furor was all about," wrote Glenn and Ruth Frye. Mrs. John Piepgras wrote, "I cannot see where busing the Moreland students will hurt my child."

Stephen Alfred, a future mayor, wrote to say that the Shaker Heights Democratic Club was unanimously in favor of the plan but was not taking a public position for fear it would "only encourage other organizations to take the opposite stands in public."

Others, though, said the vocal opposition had prompted them to speak up. "It is time for those of us who agree with your Moreland School Policy Decision to stand up and be heard," wrote Katherine McWilliams, a white Shaker mom and future school board member. "My hearty congratulations for your forward thinking! Don't back down!"

Soon after the plan was made public, Dottie Curtiss, a past president of the local League of Women Voters, sent a friendly postcard to Jean Gaede, a member of the school board. Curtiss reassured Gaede that the plan was going over well with the public, notably because it was so modest. Her note made clear that many in Shaker had been anticipating something more sweeping—perhaps the two-way busing plan that Moreland parents had demanded.

"Your phone ear must be so flattened I haven't the heart to call," she wrote. "But 'early reports' are beautiful! . . . The plan is so much milder than people expected that they're saying they'd love to have black kids in their Malvern classes, etc! It's the fear of the bussing into Moreland that was the worst!"

Parent Aaron Salzman complimented Lawson on judging the climate of the community "to within 1/10 of 1 degree." He supported bringing Black children into his neighborhood elementary school, called Fernway, but said he would not approve of busing his daughter to another school. "I do not feel it would improve her education opportunities, formal or informal."

Nonetheless, something unexpected was percolating among other white people living in Shaker. They began to recommend the same thing that Moreland parents had been demanding for months: run the buses two ways—into as well as out of Moreland.

In March, a newly formed citizens' group, the Committee for Voluntary Cross-Enrollment, sent Lawson a detailed proposal for a two-way busing plan open to all students in grades one through six.

Individual white parents also wrote to say they supported a two-way program, and several volunteered their own children to be part of it. Marge Townsend wrote in March to say her only regret was that the Lawson plan "calls for shoving black people around . . . Isn't it time we white people shouldered some of the inconvenience?"

Her husband, Norman W. Townsend Jr., made it clear their backing was not just theoretical: "To indicate my support for the concept of cross-busing, I volunteer to have any of my children to be part of a cross-busing experiment."

———

In the ten years following the Supreme Court's *Brown v. Board of Education* decision, schools in the South did almost nothing to implement it, thanks in part to the court's oxymoronic directive that desegregation proceed "with all deliberate speed." They preferred the deliberation over the speed. Despite a few high-profile desegregation attempts—like the arrival of six-year-old Ruby Bridges at a New Orleans elementary school in 1960, accompanied by four federal marshals—most systems avoided desegregation with mass resistance, total disregard, or school choice programs that deliberately kept whites and Blacks apart. That state of affairs started to change with the passage in 1964 of a civil rights law that cut federal funding to any district that segregated students by race, giving federal officials a baton to wield in forcing compliance. In 1969, the Supreme Court, having lost patience, ruled that desegregation needed to begin immediately, and in 1971, the court blessed mandatory busing as a legitimate tool for unraveling school segregation.

The *Brown* decision covered only the seventeen Southern and border states that explicitly segregated children, but civil rights activists made the case that the segregation in place in the North and the West—what was called de facto segregation—often had been created through deliberate choices and also was unconstitutional. In 1973, the Supreme Court agreed, ordering Denver schools to desegregate and launching a string of court battles where plaintiffs sought to prove that school systems had deliberately divided children by race. Through the 1970s, those battles raged, including in Cleveland.

Debating its desegregation plan in the winter of 1970, Shaker Heights was far ahead of the curve. Still, a district like Shaker clearly would have seen the legal challenge that was coming, as early as the mid-1960s. "It was very much in the air," said Matthew F. Delmont, a history professor at Dartmouth College who has studied the history of busing. "This is something that was clearly going to be on your doorstep sooner or later."

━━━━━━

Lawson was not convinced by the suggestion that the schools bus students both in and out of Moreland. He took the three-page proposal from a group of white parents and, in the margins, scrawled a series of questions and criticisms, the work of someone looking for reasons to say no. For instance, where the proposal concluded that two-way busing "significantly improves racial imbalance," Lawson wrote, "? How (?)" Where the proposal says that it will retain "Moreland's neighborhood identity," Lawson wrote, "for whom?" (Seems obvious—for the people living in Moreland.) In a list of seven objections handwritten at the bottom of the third page, Lawson penned a criticism more likely to have been leveled by opponents of school desegregation in general: "destroys neighborhood concept thruout district."

Lawson was not alone in his preferences. When forced to desegregate, many communities closed the predominantly Black schools and bused their students to schools perceived as better. Thousands of Black teachers and administrators lost their jobs, and Black students lost their role models, a debt American education is still paying. The burden of desegregation fell harder on the shoulders of Black students, even though the white schools were just as segregated.

Lawson asked three top aides to analyze the proposal for voluntary cross-enrollment. Their memos to him listed some concerns, including the challenge of recruiting enough white volunteers, but they all mentioned upsides, too, with two of the three seeing real potential in two-way busing. These memos also hinted at the fact that Lawson was committed to the special services school, and looking back now it seems possible his investment in the idea played an outsize role in his opposition to two-way busing.

Lawson summarized the staff's view in a two-page memo to the school board that nitpicked at the details of the voluntary cross-enrollment program and concluded it would not work, in part because the number of volunteers was unpredictable. It also called the impact on neighborhood schools a "radical departure" from the original plan. And he said the change could slow down the entire program. Then, in what appears to be a disingenuous summary of his aides' input, he concluded, "The staff feels that this proposal does not have much opportunity for success."

Yet Lawson came around. Advocates presented a list of names of white parents who said they were willing to send their children to Moreland. It's unclear whether the school board pressured Lawson to change his recommendation, or proponents simply wore him down, or if seeing the list of volunteers was enough to overcome his reluctance. In his memoir and in an article he wrote about the integration process, Lawson made no mention of the pressure he was under to shift course or the Moreland community's insistence on two-way busing.

On May 5, 1970, the Shaker Heights school board unanimously approved what would become known as the Shaker Schools Plan. It called for Moreland students in grades four through six to be bused to other schools, though parents could opt out. White students elsewhere in grades one through six could request transfer into Moreland. The enrichment services that Lawson envisioned for the special services school would be offered elsewhere, where possible. (It's not clear whether or how those services were offered.)

"In short, we believe the proposed program is a practical, sensible, conservative and straight-forward course of action, supported by persua-sive education experience and research," the board said. In an apparent effort to reassure opponents, the statement added: "This program is not intended to be an interim step to something else."

It was a landmark moment. Only a handful of school districts had done what Shaker did—voluntarily desegregate their schools, absent a court order. Elsewhere, resistance and sometimes violence met manda-tory busing plans. In Shaker, the district acted voluntarily, as did the families who would participate.

A year after the plan began, Dorothy M. Uhlig, a researcher at the Harvard Graduate School of Education, contacted Lawson's office. She had heard the story of how Shaker had put in place a voluntary deseg-regation plan and was interested in learning more, including about the Black community's original objections and how the program evolved into a two-way busing system. "If it is even half true, it is a rather special case and really worth looking into," she wrote.

Rather than being flattered by the attention from Harvard, a Lawson aide replied on his behalf defensively. He objected to characterizing the Black community as opposed to the original plan and said the final plan was "initiated by the superintendent and the school board," even though the record shows it was pushed by the community and the district went along.

Lawson was the man who led Shaker to this moment, and he deserves enormous credit. But either the opposition from Moreland to his original vision was irrelevant to his decision to change course, which would be stunning, or he was ungracious in acknowledging the role Black parents played, both in his memoir and in his response to the Harvard professor. Perhaps he was embarrassed by those details. Or perhaps he was dis-playing the sort of paternalistic, anti-Black attitude that was ingrained into many white Americans, even many who were not overtly racist. Or maybe there's another explanation that is lost to history.

———

By June 1970, the debate was over, and the district began to sell the plan to Shaker parents before it would take effect that fall. In the June 1970 *School Review*, the district appealed to the community to help Shaker "stand as an example to our nation, which everywhere faces the challenges and opportunities of integration."

Lawson and his aides had been doubtful that enough people would volunteer if busing were optional. Now it was time to find out.

Earline and Lorenzo Hooper were among the Black parents from Moreland concerned about the original one-way busing plan. Now they had gotten what they had asked for—a voluntary two-way plan—and the neighborhood was buzzing with conversation about whether to participate. The Hoopers attended every meeting about the matter. They had moved to Shaker for better schools. Now they were being told that integrated schools would serve their children better.

"There was a lot of research showing that separation was not equal education and that if you put the races together, the study showed that you would get better education," Earline said years later. Their oldest, Sam, was already in junior high, and their youngest, Emily, was not yet in elementary school. But their daughter Paula would be assigned to Malvern Elementary School, twenty minutes away, unless the Hoopers requested she stay at Moreland.

Lorenzo Hooper loved to drive, and he would take his children on drives around Shaker just for fun, ferrying the family in his light brown Ford LTD station wagon with wood paneling. One afternoon, he asked Paula if she wanted to go see Malvern, and the LTD made its way to the far wealthier north side of Shaker.

The back row of the station wagon was flattened down, and Paula lay on her back in the rear, looking up. The first thing she noticed was how quiet it was. She turned her head and out the window she saw trees, beautiful trees. "They were so green," she said. "Big trees, tall and lush." Then she sat up and saw the houses. They were gorgeous—classic Shaker colonials and English Tudors, enormous homes with as many as eight bedrooms inside, lush gardens, and expansive lawns. Paula's mouth fell open. Then they rounded the corner, and there was Malvern Elementary School, tucked into a quiet corner of the leafy neighborhood. Her home school, Moreland Elementary, was a similar kind of building, but set at the intersection of two main streets, the rapid transit running across the street from the school's front door.

"We came to this school that looked like a castle on a hill. That was Malvern," she recalled. Next to the building was a huge playground. Paula thought, *Wow, I get to go to school here? Amazing.*

"Do you want to go to school there next year?" her dad asked.

"Of course, it's beautiful," she replied, and she lay back in the station wagon again and looked up at the trees some more. Paula would attend Malvern that fall.

By the time the Shaker Schools Plan took effect, Irv and Emilie Barnett were living in the Onaway school district, having left Ludlow, where they had helped create the community association, for a bigger house. When the chance came to advance Shaker's next integration effort, they signed up again.

Their daughter, Laura, went to Moreland for fifth and sixth grades. It was notable for her, partly because it was so ordinary.

"I don't remember it being particularly special or different, honestly," she said. "Sometimes you feel divisions when whites and Blacks hang out together. I didn't have any memories of that. It was just one of those things that I did."

Participating in the plan was an easy decision for Katherine McWilliams. She had long worked with the Black community through her church and had spoken up in favor of the district's desegregation efforts, so when the district went looking for volunteers to go to Moreland, she signed up her fourth grade son, Doug. She instilled in him the idea that what he was doing was important, that he was part of something bigger. It wasn't always easy, and Doug remembered sometimes getting picked on during recess. But the experience was transformative.

"As a white male going through life, it's pretty easy to always take the perspective of the privilege the majority provides or offers. That was a circumstance where I was not the majority, I was not the dominant culture. I had to figure out my way," he said.

In September 1970, the school year began with 146 children bused from Moreland to other schools, and 66 children bused into Moreland. That transformed Moreland from 88 percent to 50 percent black and marginally increased the Black percentage at six other schools, a triumphant accomplishment of integration that the community began to embrace as a core part of its identity. On the first day of school, Moreland students were greeted with signs reading, WELCOME and FRIENDSHIP, and Principal Lesora Greene, the first Black principal in the district, escorted them into school.

The district vigorously studied the plan's implementation and reported its findings in February 1972. A sociogram—a student survey that helped map social networks—showed most children developing cross-racial friendships. Academic achievement tests showed students at the receiving schools did not lose ground and those who were bused performed as expected, or, in the case of fourth and sixth graders bused into Moreland, significantly better.

Questionnaires sent to parents of participating students across the district found strong support for the plan: 87 percent said their children benefited academically and 96 percent said they formed new friendships. There was less support among parents of other children, with 42 percent calling the plan "desirable," 22 percent saying it was "undesirable," and 22 percent saying it made little difference. About seven in ten teachers in grades four through six said they did not adjust academic expectations and goals, though 18 percent said they did. Just over half said they did not adjust their teaching techniques; a third said they did.

The report also considered a wide range of concerns raised by parents and tried to address them. Some were logistical—when the buses ran and how long students had for lunch, which bused kids now ate at school. But some pointed to problems that Shaker—and schools across the country— would have to contend with for years. One person worried about isolation of Black children and said there should be at least two Black children in each class. The district replied that it was trying. Another parent advised: "Eliminate the double standards of discipline for students." The district denied this was a problem.

And another raised a point that would course through debates in Shaker for years to come, saying there should be an effort to "match the scholastic achievement of the assigned pupils with the receiving class." The district said all classes have diversity but "grouping within classes helps the teacher adjust lessons to levels appropriate for a particular student."

In the aftermath of the decision to adopt the busing program, some bad feelings lingered.

In May 1970, after the decision had been made, a twenty-five-year-old Lomond mom who signed her name Mrs. George Griffiths wrote Lawson a long letter bristling with fury and tinged with sarcasm. Her letter no doubt represented a lot of rage that went unspoken at the time and put down a marker for how significantly Shaker's identity and the views of people living there would change.

"If the Negroes in Moreland don't like an 88% black school . . . fine . . . let them move!! After all they are the ones that moved in there to make it 88% black and I can't recall anyone complaining about moving into there!!" she wrote. "It's just another instance of a small group of people making waves and then getting their way. Perhaps all the Jews, Italians and Germans start demanding that they attend schools in proportionate numbers. It sounds ridiculous, but then that's no more ridiculous than your plan to bus children.

"I am sick to my stomach of hearing about integration, and now to have this busing thrust upon us, is just too much!! Yes, maybe I am a bigot, but I too have racial pride, although no one seems to pay too much attention to people with white racial pride. After all, our illustrious community of Shaker boasts of many intellectuals who think it beneath them to have any bigotry at all. Please spare me from all these people!!"

Late into the fall of 1970, as the busing program got underway, Lawson recalled taking his regular seat at a Cleveland Browns football game, behind five men who would typically drink their way through the event. On this day, with the weather particularly frigid and the wind whipping off Lake Erie into Municipal Stadium, the group grew drunker than usual. One asked Lawson to write down the score of the game at the end so they could tell their wives, since it was clear they probably wouldn't remember. Lawson said sure.

Then, without warning, one of them turned to Lawson and started shouting, "Now I know [who] you are. You are that bastard superintendent of schools who integrated the schools in Shaker Heights." The man then used a vile racial slur. Lawson, in his memoir, recalled not reacting and the men leaving him alone. At the end of the game, he handed them a note with the score. Cleveland had won.

As the district prepared to go to the voters for a tax increase in the spring of 1971, Lawson and his aides were nervous. An organized group campaigned against the tax levy, and Lawson recalled spending fifty-nine of sixty consecutive evenings speaking to voters to promote it. It passed with 58.5 percent approval—a solid majority but a lower margin than was typical. Since 1933, the schools had gone to the voters for additional taxes twenty-three times. All but one levy had been approved, and eighteen of the twenty-three had passed with at least 60 percent of the vote.

The plan was an important milestone in the community's emerging sense of itself as a racially progressive place and as a national model for voluntary integration, a reputation that had begun with the housing program. But it continued Shaker down a road that not everyone cared to travel, and some who were opposed moved while others who might have chosen Shaker bought elsewhere instead. Larry Selhorst, for instance, who had led the opposition to the busing plan, moved farther east to Moreland Hills soon after the plan was approved. In an interview decades later, Selhorst, at age eighty-eight, said that his family wanted a larger house and a better school system for his children, but that the changing community was also a factor. "We felt defeated and we felt that the whole community had moved to the left," he said.

Until this time, integration had been a reality only in parts of Shaker Heights. As an article in the *Plain Dealer* put it in 1970, on the north side of Shaker, "integration is more of a cocktail party discussion topic than a fact of life." Now Shaker was taking a step that would affect many more families.

"I attended the School Board Meeting last Tuesday evening," began a letter that May to Lawson, signed by Mrs. Robert Rich, "and I must express to both you and our Board the pride I feel living in a community that has had the foresight and courage to make the decision that was made concerning education in our schools."

"These types of voluntary programs were incredibly rare," said Richard Kahlenberg, an expert on school integration. The approach was both forward-looking and unusual, he said, in that it recognized the benefits of integration for all children, and that the burden of moving to another school did not rest solely with Black students. Elsewhere at this time, he said, some Black students attended predominantly white schools. "There was almost never a comparable program in which white parents sent their children to Black schools."

In 1975, the *New York Times* wrote about the integration plan with the front page headline AN INTEGRATED SUBURB THRIVES IN OHIO. After describing Black and white students living in Shaker, the newspaper declared: "They are among the first generation of black and white children to grow up side by side, from toddler to teenagers, acquiring friends of both races, in one of the country's most dramatically successful, long-term ventures in racially integrated housing in the suburbs."

<hr>

Lawson remained in Shaker until 1976, when he left to become superintendent in Lexington, Massachusetts, his home state—partly because his wife had been diagnosed with breast cancer and they believed medical treatment would be better there. In 1981, he became education commissioner for the state, where he played a central role overseeing the contentious court-ordered busing program to desegregate Boston's schools.

There is little question that Lawson's leadership was critical to improving the racial balance in the Shaker schools—first the junior highs, and then the elementaries. That's not to say he didn't have blind spots, notably his apparent lack of concern as to what the Black parents in Moreland wanted for their children.

Even so, his reputation for integrity became the stuff of legend.

In one notable example, Lawson noticed that all the head custodians working for the district were white while the assistants were Black and he asked why. He found out that many of the Black custodians could not read and thus could not pass the test needed to advance. Lawson set up a reading program for them.

He also applied this sense of fairness to his personal life. When his son, John Lawson, was a senior in high school in 1967, he applied for admission to Harvard University. An admissions officer told the superintendent that Harvard had decided to accept five students from Shaker that year, and four of the spots had been filled. The final spot, Lawson was told, was set to go to a young man who would become the first Black student from Shaker admitted to Harvard. However, the admissions officer told Lawson, it was possible to give that spot to his son instead. The officer then asked Lawson which of the two he would like them to admit.

"His statement placed me in a difficult position," Lawson later wrote. (And, it should be said, it was outrageous of Harvard to put him in that position.) He told them it wasn't up to him to decide who should be accepted and Harvard should decide on its own. His son was rejected and wound up at Middlebury College. Decades later, John would tell this story about his father with pride.

In his memoir, Lawson identified numerous racial injustices he encountered during his tenure and explained steps he took to solve or at least mitigate them. Early on, before the busing plan, he heard from a group of Black Moreland parents who complained that a kindergarten teacher was biased against their children. He talked to the teacher and asked to sit in on her class. He noticed that when talking with white students, "she would place one of her hands on the back of their heads and tell them they were doing good work." Yet when she checked the work of Black students, "she told them they were doing fine without placing a hand on their heads."

He shared this observation with the teacher, who quickly acknowledged it and said she had not realized she was doing this. "Within days, the black parents told me that their children had changed their feelings towards their teacher," he wrote. It's a story that is in some sense reassuring—it was the late 1960s, and he was taking allegations of implicit bias seriously. And yet it seems doubtful—if not downright delusional—to believe that this teacher's implicit bias disappeared with one simple conversation, or, for that matter, that similar problems didn't exist in other classrooms.

Similarly, he told the story of attending the honors assembly at Byron Junior High School, where about 15 percent of the ninth graders honored were Black. During a reception, he talked with Black students and parents and learned that none of the awardees planned to take advanced level courses at the high school. They all reported that their guidance counselor had discouraged it, saying those classes "are very difficult and you might not do well." He urged these students to reconsider and later met with the principal and the counselors, who were defensive. "The next year, I noted that most of the black honor students were enrolled for high school A.P. and high level courses in the major subjects," he wrote.

It sounds like a happy ending to that particular problem. In fact, the problem of Black students sorely underrepresented in advanced courses was only just beginning.

7

HERLINDA BRADLEY

Like so many Black couples before them, Jean and Henry Bradley moved to Shaker Heights for better housing and excellent schools. A year after they moved into their new house on Scottsdale Boulevard, their daughter, Herlinda, was born.

Herlinda began elementary school in 1978 at the school down the block, Sussex, where thanks to the Shaker Schools Plan, the racial balance almost perfectly reflected the district as a whole. Without busing, 23 percent of Sussex students would have been Black; with it, the Black student percentage was 37 percent.

Herlinda loved the school, and remembered one teacher in particular, Mildred Talbot. Her mother requested that Herlinda be placed in Mrs. Talbot's second grade since she hadn't yet had a Black teacher. It was a transformative experience.

"She looked like the people that I knew—my mom, my grandmother, my aunts, my mother's friends," Herlinda said. "It was something about having a Black lady being your teacher that felt good. I just remember adoring her."

Sussex was a positive experience, too, for how it exposed Herlinda to differences. She fondly recalled a Jewish teacher who took her and a few other kids to Sands Delicatessen at the nearby Van Aken Shopping Center for lox and bagels. It was the first time she had tried lox, and quite liked it. Her immediate neighbors were Black, but she played with a lot of white kids. "We were all friends," she said, rattling off the names of a half dozen white friends she played with. "It was almost as if race didn't matter back then. We were all just in school together."

———

As Shaker schools grew more diverse, the district developed and expanded its system of sorting children into academic buckets called levels. With each step toward integration came more and more leveling, with white students moving into top classes at higher rates than Black students from the start.

Initially, advanced classes were only for a handful of the top students. Shaker schools first offered Advanced Placement classes in the mid-1950s, as the AP program was introduced to U.S. high schools, but most students remained in regular classes. In 1955, the district bragged that gifted classes were not generally needed because, much like in fictional Lake Wobegon, all the children were above average. "In a sense, our whole school system is organized for the very capable child because our average I.Q. is 117," Superintendent William Slade wrote in the *School Review* in December 1955.

Tracking saw its first big expansion in 1964, when the district adopted a new and sweeping Levels of Instruction system, with courses classified as levels 1 (the lowest) through 5 (the highest). The high school was now about 7 percent Black, and while the district did not publicly tie the change to the changing demographics, it also was no longer bragging that all Shaker students were gifted.

"Experience has forcefully demonstrated that an individual student often has varying aptitudes in various subjects in the curriculum," the *School Review* explained in November 1964. The new system, the article said, would challenge highest achieving students, while for "less able students," would offer "a class nearer his ability [where] he can be more successful in a realistically planned course."

Under the new system, most students were expected to be in level 3. Those needing extra help were in levels 1 and 2, and level 4 was honors. Level 5 was Advanced Placement, for which students were chosen by staff for enrollment. Officials decided to offer an incentive, or a reward, to students taking harder classes, so higher-level courses received higher point values in determining grade point average and class rank.

Two years later, the leveling system was expanded again after the district redrew the boundary lines to better racially balance the two junior high schools. Again, the district's communications suggested this was a way of reassuring parents who might oppose the new boundary lines by promising that their children could segregate in high-level classes. Byron created three levels for English and a similar "individualized approach" for science. Woodbury's new system considered test scores, teacher recommendations, and parent conferences to individually sort students into multiple courses. The district explicitly tied this change to growing diversity.

"Woodbury, as the community knows, has participated in a dominant change of current history: the opening of educational gates to Negroes," the district said in the newsletter article in which it announced and explained the new levels system. "Woodbury has quietly achieved a racially-integrated school population. Has this change affected educational standards at Woodbury? The answer of evidence is a clear no."

Then, in 1970, as the district moved to desegregate the elementary schools, officials again reassured parents that the levels system was there to stay at the older grades, reflecting general nervousness in the community. In the October 1970 issue of the *School Review*, Superintendent Lawson wrote, "Grouping of students by ability has long been a typical practice in American secondary education and we expect it to continue." The high school, in fact, was adding more level 4 and 5 courses, partially made possible with the addition of a new science wing. "In short, we anticipate an expansion of the level system at the upper levels."

As leveling expanded, Shaker increasingly became two school systems within one. Both academically and socially, Black and white students were together—and also apart. They were arriving at the same high school, but the south-side entrance was colloquially dubbed the "Black door," and one on the north called the "white door." (Since Black students were concentrated on the south side of Shaker, many arrived at that door.) Students ate lunch in the same cafeteria, but one side was mostly Black students and the other mostly white. And, perhaps most important, as time went on, the upper-level courses were filled with white faces, while the lower-level classes became dominated by Black ones.

Herlinda Bradley never knew a world that was not racially integrated. Not so for her parents.

Henry and Jean Bradley had been living in Cleveland when they decided it was time for a move. He was a teacher in the Cleveland schools. She worked for the welfare department downtown.

It was the mid-1960s, and like other Black families before them, they were hearing good things about Shaker Heights.

"Everybody knew about Shaker Heights," Jean recalled. "I knew Shaker had a wonderful reputation. They had lovely homes. The community was nice. No crime. And it was just, just a good place to live and start a family."

Before moving to the Sussex area, they rented a small apartment in the Ludlow community, among the most affordable areas in town. A couple of years later, the Bradleys went looking for a larger apartment in the area and were shocked by the result. They were turned away from the apartment they wanted because they were Black.

The man in charge of the rental explained why: the community was trying to maintain racial balance and needed to reserve that apartment for white renters. In fact, most of the apartments in the Ludlow area had traditionally been populated by white renters, one factor that kept Ludlow's overall population in racial balance. Jean was furious, fuming. She understood their reasoning but didn't care. She wanted that apartment.

It all felt ironic given where she'd come from. She was born in Winston-Salem, North Carolina, in 1934, when Jim Crow laws were in full effect. Though her parents owned their own home and had good, steady jobs that sent her to college, segregation surrounded her.

Her fondest wish as a child had been to sip iced tea in the restaurant of the Robert E. Lee hotel. As she would get off the bus in the steaming summer heat and walk to the movie theater, she'd walk past the large picture windows of the hotel named for the Confederate general and see white people inside enjoying their iced tea. When she reached the theater, Jean would climb the stairs to the balcony, the only place Black people were allowed to sit.

Now she was living in that rare suburb where Black families were actually welcome—except when they weren't. She complained up the chain about the apartment, reasoning that she was there first.

"Then someone tries to explain that it's for the best of the neighborhood, yada, yada, yada, yada," she said. "And I'm still saying, 'But

I still want that apartment. It's available.' And they're saying, 'Sorry, but you can't have it.' You know, I thought it was terrible. But that was their policy."

The Fair Housing Act, signed in 1968, had yet to become law. That would attempt to put an end to this sort of overt discrimination, whether motivated by good or ill, though Shaker Heights would continue to steer Black buyers away from already integrated neighborhoods for years to come.

For now, the Bradleys settled for another apartment in the same area. A few years later, in 1971, they were ready to buy a house, and found their three-bedroom, three-story brick home for $35,000 in the Sussex neighborhood. It was a neighborhood of midsized houses where Black families were arriving but was still overwhelmingly white.

In October 1972, Jean gave birth to Herlinda.

———

Over the years, administrators in Shaker cast the levels system as an educational victory for everyone involved. Upper-level students would be challenged; struggling students would get focused help. Those assertions were questioned very early on, in 1969, when the system was still quite new.

Alan Geismer Jr., who graduated from Shaker Heights High School in 1966, was part of a family that went back to early days in Shaker Heights. His grandparents moved there in 1928, and though they were Jewish, their ownership of the Stearn Company, a high-end furniture retailer, and their prominence in the Cleveland community may help explain why the Van Sweringen brothers let them in. When Alan was in high school, his father, Alan Geismer, served on the Shaker school board.

The younger Alan recalled his father, a lawyer, as not being particularly interested in civil rights. "He sort of believed in it but didn't fight for it," he said. "They probably would have gone nuts if I had come home with a Black girlfriend." But his aunt and uncle lived in Ludlow, and Alan was more tuned into issues of race than his parents were. As a high school student at Shaker in the mid-1960s, Geismer noticed his upper-level classes were entirely white, while the lowest-level classes at Shaker were dominated by Black students.

Geismer went on to Harvard for college and, as a junior, took a sociology class for which he wrote a paper about his hometown school district, helped by access to administrators by virtue of his father's position on the school board. More than a half century later, he didn't remember writing it, but his paper, "Counseling Services, the Level System and Racial Polarity," must have been given to someone who worked for the school district, because it was tucked into the back of a box of documents on a high shelf at the end of a winding passage crowded with files in a storage room in the basement of Shaker Heights High School.

The paper presented a reality starkly different from the one that Shaker was showing the world, a reality that would, in the coming years, become plain to many in the community. It was an image that cut directly against the story of Shaker as the poster child for peaceful integration. Without change, he wrote, Shaker may be guilty of "practicing discriminatory education behind the facade of a desegregated structure."

The paper laid out the situation: the cafeteria was segregated by race; the school social room was used almost entirely by Black students, while school dances were mostly white. Academically, he wrote, the levels system worked well for students of all races who came up through Shaker schools. But Black students transferring in from Cleveland were pushed into lower-level courses—not because of lower aptitude but because of lack of preparation. Once a student was placed in a given level, he wrote, it was "almost impossible" to move up.

At that time, he wrote, 16 percent of the high school was Black. The upper two levels were "almost totally white," level 3 had about 20 percent Black students, and levels 2 and 1 were, respectively, 75 and 90 percent Black.

Geismer quoted the assistant principal for guidance, Albert Senft, who called the levels system "our biggest problem." It had expanded too fast, was misunderstood by parents and students, and had led to segregation. "The policy is not designed to be racist, yet it has evolved to that point," Geismer concluded. Students had a fair bit of say about what classes they took. But if Black students wound up in lower-level classes, either because counselors recommended them or because that's where their friends were, that could drive white students into higher-level courses "simply to avoid being in an all-Negro class," even if that was not the right academic choice for them.

Student assignments were driven by guidance counselors, he wrote, and counselors were too busy to help students who needed it most, too quick to shunt new students into lower levels without considering their potential to do well in more challenging classes. Black parents, he wrote, "because they are often so awed with the school," didn't think to question the counselor's recommendation. "When the school has PTA programs to explain things like the level system, it seems that only the parents who already understand it come."

He also noted that weekly student meetings with counselors, called "group conference," where subjects such as careers, tests, and applications were discussed, became unnecessarily segregated based on the schedule. Groupings for these conferences were based on gym classes, and gym classes were based on results of swim tests, and Black students were far less likely to know how to swim.

The paper ended on a hopeful note, reporting that administrators were working to fix some of these problems, though Geismer argued the district should go further and also hire a Black counselor. With the right effort, he wrote, "Shaker can once again begin to move along the line from desegregation toward truly integrated education."

This forgotten, unpublished paper marks the first known critique, certainly on paper, of the levels system. And while Geismer voiced optimism, the problems he identified so presciently would vex the Shaker school system for decades to come.

———

Throughout these years, Shaker continued to build a national reputation for proactive racial integration. Students ran into racism but didn't always talk about it.

Dan Polster had grown up white in Ludlow during the heyday of the Ludlow Community Association's triumphs, arriving with his family, at age two, in 1953. When he got to high school, there was a moment when his up-close education about race faced a serious test.

All students were evaluated in swimming, and those who failed were required to take swim class in school. Polster knew how to swim well, but he repeatedly came up a second short in the time required to complete two laps, so he was required to take swim class. He remembered being the only white boy there.

The fact that many Black students failed the swim test was hardly surprising given the historic lack of access to swimming pools. Municipal pools weren't often built in Black neighborhoods. Black people were frequently kept from using segregated facilities in white areas and were sometimes chased away by violence if they tried. The debate would come to Shaker, too, in the 1960s, when the city built a municipal pool and barred use by Shaker school families who lived in the Cleveland section of the school district, a decision the Ludlow Community Association battled for years before the city finally gave in.

On the first day of swim class for Dan Polster, the swim team coach walked into the pool area, looked over the group, and declared that he would not be teaching them anything. "He said, 'Blacks can't swim, so I'm not going to teach you how to swim,'" Polster remembered. The coach walked out and the guys spent the next six weeks playing football in the pool during what was supposed to be swim class. And the Black kids in that class were not taught to swim.

Polster, who went on to serve as a federal district court judge, was then sports editor of the *Shakerite*, the high school newspaper. He could have exposed it. "If I had just put that in my article, he would have been fired. And I didn't do it." He doesn't know why. He never talked about it. And he regrets it. "There was racism then."

Ron Adrine's family had moved to Ludlow when he was in junior high school, too late for the sort of idyllic childhood that his sisters and many other Black and white Ludlowites experienced. He had a good experience in Shaker, but also encountered racism.

When he got to high school, in 1962, Black students were a distinct minority—there were maybe seventy-five at the time, out of some two thousand students. During his sophomore year, he became friends with a popular white girl, a cheerleader, and during their junior year, he found their friendship tested.

The cheerleaders were staging an auction to raise money for the prom, offering themselves at auction as dates. The "prizes" lined up on a platform in the girls' gym, the audience seated on the wooden floor before them. Ron and his friends decided to pool their money and bid on a date with Ron's white friend. "They thought it would be funny," he remembered. It worked. They won her for Ron.

Then it got awkward. The girl thought to herself: *What have I gotten myself into? How am I going to navigate this?* Her parents, who lived in Lomond, an area Black families were beginning to move into, supported integration. They were happy to live in an integrated community. Her rabbi, Arthur J. Lelyveld, was an outspoken supporter of the civil rights movement who had traveled to Mississippi in 1964 to register Black voters and been beaten by a pair of white segregationists wielding tire irons. But in a 2021 interview she said she wasn't sure if she had talked to her parents or anyone else about the date situation at the time.

She approached Ron, distressed. She just couldn't do it, she told him. She offered to refund his friends' money.

"What do you mean?" Ron replied, and he was peeved. "I paid for the privilege. So I think you are going to have to do that."

Ron recalled her responding that, given his race, her parents wouldn't understand. And he replied that she should have thought about that before signing up to be auctioned off.

Ultimately, they agreed that the "date" would take place in the cafeteria at school and that she would reimburse him for the auction bid. They ate lunch together and that was the end of it.

"I was a little hurt," he said many years later. "But I wasn't mad at her. I recognized she could have a problem with her parents. It's not like we were completely impervious to the world we lived in."

"It was a hard situation because I was fond of Ron," she said in an interview. "I felt trapped and couldn't figure any other way. You live in the times you live in, so that was part of the reality at that time . . . I didn't have the guts to or the courage to make a different choice."

The woman spoke on condition that she not be identified. She feared, nearly sixty years later, that she would be judged poorly for her actions as a teenager. "At [age] seventy-four, I don't want that to be my legacy." She regretted her actions from that day forth. One year, on Yom Kippur, the Jewish day of atonement, she wrote Ron a letter of apology. But Ron, who had become a lawyer and served for thirty-six years as a judge on the Cleveland Municipal Court, didn't feel he was owed an apology, exactly. "I recognized that I lived in 1964 America. And things were what they were. She was actually more acute in assessing what the likely dangers might be than I was."

A year before Herlinda Bradley started kindergarten, informal concerns about the scant Black participation in upper-level courses grew formal. A new group of Black parents called Concerned Parents formed in 1977, worried their children were not represented in upper-level courses at the high school or in the junior high courses that served as prerequisites for advanced work in high school. The group pinned the problems on systemic racism, sought professional development for teachers district-wide, and encouraged Black parents to confront teachers when they saw disrespectful or exclusionary attitudes and actions.

Around the same time, the district was notified of an investigation by the U.S. Department of Health, Education, and Welfare's Office for Civil Rights. The agency was shifting its focus away from desegregation, reflecting both President Nixon's opposition to busing and growing discomfort on the part of Northern members of Congress since the Supreme Court ruled that school segregation in the North was also unconstitutional. Instead, the federal government began focusing on discrimination, disparate discipline based on race, and course assignment.

In the 1976–77 school year, the agency requested data on Shaker's levels system, including enrollment data by race. The district reported that of 802 students in honors, Advanced Placement, and enrichment programs, 734 were white—91 percent. Of the 245 students suspended or expelled in the previous year, 74 percent were Black.

"These statistics are very difficult to rationalize when one keeps in mind that the district is composed of 35% minority youngsters," Mark Freeman, who managed federal grants and relations for the district, said in a message to colleagues in February 1977. "Perhaps we need to work at plans to recruit minority children into honors and special programs, or we need to examine the criteria or current recruitment process."

The district added programs to try to address the gaps. In 1979, a high school tutoring center was established (and one for elementary schools in 1980). That year, the high school also established an academic conferencing and monitoring program for underachieving students in grades nine and ten, with regular conferences and communication with parents.

Shaker also saw the chance to address these problems through participation in a program called PUSH Excel (short for PUSH for Excellence). In 1975, the Reverend Jesse Jackson, then a young civil rights leader, had launched a movement aimed at prodding Black youth to improve their lives and futures. Jackson told audiences, "If my mind can conceive it and my heart can believe it, I can achieve it!" and bellowed out his signature call and response: "I Am—Somebody!" His program focused on values like discipline and hard work, high achievement, and self-help.

In 1978, PUSH Excel established an office at Shaker Heights High School, and one of its first acts was to gather data on achievement, with results broken down by race. The data was presented to administrators, teachers, a community advisory committee, the Concerned Parents group, and others, and it revealed sharp gaps: more than 60 percent of Black males had grade point averages below 2.0, and half took at least one of the lowest-level classes.

"What I was seeing was a lot of underachieving African American males," said Mary Lynne McGovern, who had bused her son to Moreland as part of the desegregation program and now worked with PUSH Excel. Helping Black young men change that dynamic would become her life's work.

———

As is the case with many preteens, social interactions changed profoundly for Herlinda when she got to middle school. Suddenly race mattered, with the cafeteria divided between Black tables and white tables. Friends were divided, too. It used to be no big deal for Herlinda to belong to a Pixie and then Brownie troop with Black and white girls. Now cross-racial friendships were the exceptions. "I just remember all of a sudden my friend group became all Black, and my interests became all Black." That meant rapping and beat-boxing, hip-hop, and Run-DMC.

"I didn't mind it at all," she said. "It was comfortable in a different way. I remember being perfectly happy."

The self-segregation that starts to unfold in middle school stems from the development of personal identity—and specifically racial identity—that begins in earnest in adolescence, according to Beverly Daniel Tatum's book *Why Are All the Black Kids Sitting Together in the Cafeteria?* Black students start to realize that the world sees them as Black—sometimes through positive experiences and exposures but often through experiences and observations of racism.

It may be that Black students see advanced level classes are filled with white faces. Sometimes it's the accumulation of microaggressions—small offensive comments by teachers or others that telegraph to Black students that the world sees them as, first and foremost, Black. If a student hears a racially offensive comment from a teacher, she is more likely to get support and understanding from a Black friend than from a white friend, so that's who she sits down with at lunch.

"Not only are Black adolescents encountering racism and reflecting on their identity, but their White peers, even when they are not the perpetrators (and sometimes they are), are unprepared to respond in supportive ways," wrote Tatum, president emerita of Spelman College. "Joining with one's peers for support in the face of stress is a positive coping strategy."

In 1980, the Urban League of Cleveland began an investigation that put Shaker schools on the defensive like never before, challenging the district's image and public insistence that it was a model of excellence for all students. The Urban League was a storied civil rights group with a big megaphone, and it planned a deep investigation into the levels system.

In February 1980, Mark Freeman, on behalf of the district, met with the Urban League's education director to discuss the group's study. In a follow-up letter, his irritation with the matter seemed clear. He wrote that the district already knew the problems and didn't need a study to say so. "I hope I made it clear that identification of this problem will not be a revelation to the school district. We are aware of this disproportionate representation of minority children in these classes," he wrote. He said he hoped the Urban League would make some suggestions for fixing the problem and not just dwell on the problem.

The Urban League issued its report in summer 1980. It covered both Shaker Heights High School and the neighboring Heights High School, serving Cleveland Heights and University Heights, two integrated school districts where classrooms were racially segregated through leveling.

"Are blacks gaining an equal education in Shaker Heights and Cleveland Heights? The answer is 'no,'" the report said.

The numbers were damning but also familiar. At Shaker Heights High School, 611 Black students made up 39 percent of the enrollment.

Of them, more than 75 percent were in the lowest level in social studies, more than 70 percent were in the lowest level for English, and more than 60 percent were in the lowest level for math. Less than 3 percent of Black student enrollment were in the top two levels.

In the lowest levels, the report described a self-fulfilling prophecy. "Already perceived by tests and/or recommendations as lacking intellectual ability, students in the lowest level begin to perform according to expectation. Teachers no longer teach; students no longer learn."

It acknowledged students were free to choose their own courses, but said racism was a driving force in those choices. It got less attention, but the report also put significant responsibility on Black parents. It said they had failed to engage in community life, partly for economic reasons (parents had to work hard to afford those suburban homes) and partly because they didn't feel part of the community. Their sense of isolation led to . . . more isolation. Parents didn't play an active role in the schools, where decisions about class placement were discussed and managed, because they did not truly feel a sense of belonging.

This problem didn't exist in the same way for the first Black families to arrive, the report argued. Those families emphasized the importance of education and the need to strive and participate in the life of the community. Not so with newer arrivals. "Having made it to the suburbs, black parents too often expect the public school system automatically to work for their child without their involvement," the report said. "Black parents expect superior education. What they fail to realize is that superior performance in the classroom and on standardized tests requires a family life committed to achievement and academic excellence."

Finally, for Black students, the report suggested many experienced confusion over what path to take and scorn from Black peers if they competed with white students.

Its chief recommendation was that all courses include a mix of ability levels—an end to the leveling system, with training for teachers to work in heterogeneous classes. But Shaker had no interest in dismantling its levels system.

Ahead of the report's release, the district defended the levels system as the best way to address the fact that "ability to learn is not uniformly apportioned among human beings." Writing in the May 1980 *School Review*, Superintendent Jack Taylor cited a range of efforts underway to boost achievement, including a tutoring center; training to help teachers treat all students equally, particularly regarding expectations; and work to involve more parents at the elementary level.

The Urban League report was publicly released in August, and it was front page news in the *Plain Dealer* and the suburban *Sun Press*. The district responded by pointing to its policy of open enrollment. The levels can't be racist, it said, because students choose their own classes—a view that downplayed the significant role teachers and counselors play in guiding these choices. In a position paper, the district struck a confident tone: "Overall, we are certain that no other school district in the nation is addressing this concern in as comprehensive a fashion."

On September 16, 1980, the school board voted unanimously to continue the levels system. The district resolved to do a better job of explaining the options to parents and students and began a study with Western Michigan University to examine how the levels system might be improved. That study engaged many community members and, a few months later, made a range of recommendations. But it reaffirmed the basic approach of ability-group leveling.

═══

When Herlinda Bradley got to high school, she enrolled in a mix of classes, and remembered few Black students in the upper-level courses she took. Her grades were never very good and her counselor was always pushing her to try harder.

"She was like, 'Herlinda, clearly you're a smart kid. Why are you getting Cs?' I did just enough to be on the pom-pom squad," she said. Strong ACT scores got her admitted to Ohio University in spite of her grades, she said. Her friends didn't pressure her to ignore her academics, but they didn't pressure her to improve them either.

Her mother remembered Herlinda coming home every day complaining about one particular teacher who appeared to be treating white and Black students differently. "The same answer was wrong for (Black students) but right for white students," Jean Bradley said. She wasn't going to have it. She scheduled an appointment with the teacher and confronted her with the disparity. "I suggested to her she needs to stop that behavior and if she didn't, the next time I would contact the Board of Education." Herlinda was thrilled by her mom's intervention. She hated that teacher and said it's possible she was moved to another class.

Growing up, one of Herlinda's close friends was Wendy Newberry, who lived next door. The pair made their way together from Sussex Elementary all the way through high school. Wendy and her brothers represented a split-screen version of life for Black students in Shaker.

Her brothers, twins who graduated in 1982, were pushed toward a remedial program housed in the high school basement. Their parents were skeptical. Her dad was a high school teacher who had earned his doctorate and then taught at a community college, and her mom, a social worker, had her master's degree. Education was so important in their family; even an ancestor who had been enslaved, the story went, had found a way to get an education and was nicknamed "professor."

So when the recommendation came for the twins to join the remedial program, their father had questions. "My dad was like, 'Who is in those classes?' And all the names were Black student names," Wendy recalled. "My dad was like, 'absolutely not.'" Instead, the twins were put into regular classes. One did fine academically, she said; the other struggled after hooking up with the wrong crowd. But both successfully graduated.

Wendy, by contrast, was always in advanced courses, and she suspected she had it easier because she was a Black girl rather than a Black boy. "The Black males for some reason were just cast aside. There were very few Black males in those Advanced Placement classes that I can remember, if any. Maybe one or two."

In seventh grade, Wendy was in advanced math (and English) and realized that the cool kids, the ones she wanted to hang out with, were elsewhere. She decided to stop doing her math work in a poorly planned scheme to get bounced down to regular math. The result was that her teacher warned her that she might fail—a prospect that terrified Wendy and got her back on track in short order. "That was just not an option for me to fail." Years later, she remained thankful to this teacher. She realized she'd have to figure out another way to get a social life.

As for Herlinda, she graduated from Shaker schools in 1991 unconvinced that they were quite as wonderful as advertised. And yet, in spite of any concerns, she knew she had received an excellent education and made lifelong friends. For the senior prom, she remembered the white students wanting a band and the Black students a disc jockey. At the after-prom party, they had both—a band at one end of the hall, a DJ at the other, and casino games in the middle where the groups mingled. She had nurtured her Black identity and also been part of a diverse school system.

After high school, Herlinda earned a social work degree from Ohio University and then a master's degree in public administration from the University of Akron. She reconnected with a high school friend and they began dating. She became pregnant, and in September 2001, she married her boyfriend, though she said she knew it wouldn't last. In February 2002, she gave birth to a baby girl, Olivia, and, as she'd predicted, five months after that, the marriage fell apart.

Herlinda worked for the City of Cleveland, which required employees to live within the city limits, and Olivia attended a Catholic school for kindergarten and first grade. Then the city lifted its residency rule, and Herlinda and Olivia moved into her childhood home on Scottsdale Boulevard with Herlinda's mom, who had been alone since her husband died a few years earlier. Herlinda wanted her daughter to attend Shaker schools.

Things work out best for those who make the best
of the way things work out.
—Winston Richie's family mantra

8

WINSTON RICHIE

Winston Richie was back in the Shaker Heights City Council chamber where he had spent twelve years as a councilman. It was 1987, and he was here to discuss his current mission, one quite unexpected for a Shaker enthusiast like Richie. He sought to talk people out of moving to Shaker.

Specifically, his job was to talk Black people into moving somewhere else. By the early 1980s, Shaker Heights had realized that if Black home seekers did not have other options, they would continue to flock to Shaker in large numbers, making it all but impossible to maintain integrated neighborhoods. The city hatched an effort to open up other suburbs, and Richie was its leader.

This was not exactly the work he had trained for. In fact, he had been a dentist for thirty-three years. But when Shaker launched the suburban housing initiative, Richie saw the chance for a midcareer shift to something he believed in, and took charge of the program.

Richie, who was Black, had practiced what he preached, repeatedly blazing a trail into white spaces. He grew up in a predominantly white neighborhood in Cleveland. Richie and his wife, Beatrice, were among the first wave of Black pioneers into Ludlow. And then they pioneered again, moving to the wealthier neighborhood of Mercer at a time when there were few, if any, Black families there.

So Richie wasn't asking Black house hunters to do anything he hadn't done himself. That didn't make it easy, though.

Speaking at the public meeting in 1987, he commanded the room with a calm and clear voice, using humor to cut the tension of what was by any measure a controversial if innovative program.

"I find myself trying to tell people what's better about Mayfield (Heights) than Shaker," he said, but said he was reluctant to disclose what those advantages were. With the hint of a smile, he added, "I don't want to start an exodus." He then mentioned lower taxes, prompting knowing laughs.

He explained how his group does its work and mentioned public service ads running on television, albeit in the middle of the night. "We like to think that maybe insomniacs buy houses too."

It was a classic Winston Richie performance. Funny, committed, engaging, and passionate, deploying a natural optimism about the future, and the gift of language to defuse and delight.

And at six foot two and well over two hundred pounds, he did not go unnoticed. Richie's booming, sonorous voice and gregarious nature would announce his presence, and he moved easily in spaces where Black men before him would have been reluctant to set foot—in business, in housing, in church. "Win could always say something that would lessen the tension and bring people together," said Patricia Mearns, who later served as mayor of Shaker Heights. His daughter Laurel said his superpowers were "charisma and passion." There was something, she recalled, about the way he walked into a room.

"He was able to show up in places that lots of other Black people at that point in time didn't show up because he was approachable and easy to be around," Laurel said. "He had an uncanny ability to infiltrate power structures."

He had succeeded in business, running a successful dental practice, first in Cleveland and then in Shaker. He had succeeded in politics, elected and reelected to City Council. And he had succeeded in life, with a joyful marriage and four children poised to follow in his footsteps.

He would need all those skills, and more, for the next challenge before him.

———

Born in 1925 in New Jersey, Winston Richie grew up among the professional class of Black families in the mostly white Mount Pleasant and Glenville neighborhoods of Cleveland. His father was a pharmacist and a dentist, and his mother an active volunteer in her church and with civic organizations including the National Urban League and NAACP.

Growing up, of course, Richie encountered racism. As a kid, he rode his bicycle through the Italian neighborhood of Murray Hill, chased by white boys riding after him. In college, as the only Black player on the Western Reserve University basketball team, special housing arrangements were necessary when the team traveled, as he was not allowed to stay in the same lodgings. Once, Richie was asked to stay home when the team traveled to play in Louisville, Kentucky. "I accepted it," he said later.

He followed his father into dentistry, earning bachelor's and dental degrees at Western Reserve, determined to take advantage of the opportunities life presented. He had a hard time understanding when others didn't do the same. He told the story of another Black man in his class in dental school who never showed up for class. Day after day, this man's name was called during roll, and finally they gave his spot away. Richie later saw the man, who was working as a mailman, he told Cynthia Richter, who wrote her PhD dissertation about Shaker Heights.

Richie told him, "You know, they called your name," and asked him why he left the program. "He said, 'I didn't think I could make it.' And I thought to myself, what a waste." To him, it was almost unfathomable to be given an opportunity like this and let it slip away.

When he married Beatrice Jourdain in 1953, the pair were already prominent enough to merit a lengthy story in the *Call & Post*, which captured details down to the white orchid design on the bridal fan that Bea carried. But this could not protect them from the America of the 1950s. On the night after their wedding, the hotel in New Hampshire where he had made reservations turned the Richies away.

Richie thought it would be safe—the hotel had advertised in *Ebony* magazine, for God's sake. But when they arrived, everyone sitting on the porch was white. Some started to harass the newlyweds, and the hotel offered him his $5 room deposit back. "I was happy just taking the five dollars and getting the heck out of there because I wasn't up for getting tires slashed or any harassment," Richie said later. "We had a lot of traveling to do."

When he returned to the car and explained the situation to his new wife, she wanted to push back, wanted to fight for their rights. But he wanted to leave, and they left. His work to enter and win acceptance—to win respect—in the world of white America would come later.

Soon after they married, the Richies were living in the Cleveland neighborhood of Glenville when they decided to join their friends, Ted and Beverly Mason, in the Ludlow neighborhood of Shaker Heights.

Their new house on Livingston was back-to-back with the Masons, a shared swing set in the space between them, the children hopping back and forth over a low fence dividing the backyards. Bev, who worked for Shaker schools, and Bea, who had a master's degree in library science, became best friends, and when the phone rang first thing in the morning, it was Bev calling Bea to catch up, or the other way around, a daily ritual for many years.

Each family had two parents and four children, and they were quickly outgrowing their houses. The Masons moved first, building a bigger house on Onaway Road, still in the Ludlow neighborhood. The Richies decided it was time to pioneer somewhere new.

Their choice was unexpected. They found a lot in the Mercer neighborhood, on the very eastern edge of Shaker Heights, the street farthest from the city of Cleveland and among the wealthiest and whitest in Shaker. Winston Richie felt strongly that if Black families continued to concentrate themselves in Ludlow, Ludlow would never be able to maintain a racial balance. New neighborhoods needed to open, and he set out to open this one himself.

Their resolve was inspired or at least reinforced by the March on Washington in 1963, where Dr. Martin Luther King Jr. delivered his "I Have a Dream" speech. Winston and Bea Richie had traveled to D.C. with a busload of Clevelanders for the speech, leaving their children with his parents, a rarity that happened only because this was such an important opportunity. They heard King's vision for a nation where children would be judged not by the color of their skin but by the content of their character. They felt the winds of change blowing in America, and they tried to answer the call they heard at the Lincoln Memorial that day.

"I strongly believed in an integrated experience for my children," Winston Richie later said. "I wanted them to be able to compete in the world, to become part of the mainstream, and when they grew up, to have self-confidence and pride in their ability to make it as blacks. I wanted them to know that there are some good whites and some bad ones, just as there are good and bad blacks."

His four children, a boy and three girls, were in training—in training for life in a white-dominated world—and Richie was determined to set them up for success. As he trailblazed, his tools of choice were humor and language. With a turn of phrase or playful pun, he would disarm tension and cut through the noise to identify a core bit of truth.

"I think Blacks don't do justice to their kids if they confine them to Black neighborhoods," he told Richter in 1995. "I facetiously say sometimes that I wanted my kids to know some dumb white kids, that there are some dumb white kids in this world. I wanted them to go to school with whites so that they could compete at college, in the corporate level, or wherever else they wanted to go."

So Richie was thinking ahead when he looked to buy the lot at 2741 Green Road. But acquiring it would require the same savvy and determination deployed by the first Black families into Ludlow and across Shaker. As with other pioneers, the sale was made possible with a straw purchase: A white couple who lived in Akron, James and Eileen Dougherty, bought the land in June 1963 with the intention of transferring it to the Richies, according to children of both couples who recalled their parents telling them the story. Records show the deed was transferred in December 1963 to the Richies from the Doughertys.

"He was a man of his convictions," Eileen Dougherty Knittel said of her father, who was a labor union activist. She was fourteen at the time and remembered him talking about the sale over dinner. "I was of that age and really proud of him. And still am."

Even that wasn't enough. Buyers were still required to submit applications to the Van Sweringen Company, and in June 1964, the company would not approve the sale. A letter to Dougherty cited the deed restrictions and required Richie win consent of his neighbors, saying this would be in the "best interests" of all. "It is very necessary that they have a chance to meet each other and become acquainted before The Van Sweringen Company considers the transfer," the company president wrote. Richie would need a majority approval from five owners on either side of the lot and the eleven owners across the street, the scheme devised back in 1925 and spread in the wake of Dr. and Mrs. Bailey's arrival to Shaker Heights. Richie set out with pen in hand.

One of the first neighbors he approached was a banker who said he needed to think about it. A Jewish woman across the street said no. "Her attitude was that if the Jews let the blacks in, then the Jews would not be admitted to the next neighborhood to which they might want to move," Richie later said. He had better luck when he approached

Thomas Boardman, editor of the *Cleveland Press*, who didn't just sign but insisted on helping Richie collect additional signatures among his neighbors, according to historian Virginia Dawson.

He got the needed signatures and, at last, the Richies were able to build and, trepidatiously, move into their new home.

Two years after the Van Sweringen Company forced the Richies to jump through its racist hoops, Richie gently poked the company's president with a brief but pointed letter. As a young newlywed, he didn't want to risk a tire slashing in rural New Hampshire, but now he seemed to relish calling out the racism of the company in his own way.

His letter noted that two homes had recently changed hands within five houses of his and yet he had not had the "chance to meet my prospective neighbors" first, echoing the language of the directive requiring him to go door to door. "I do hope the Van Sweringen Company will apply the same screening methods to all who approach them for consent," he wrote, knowing full well it would not.

Richie hoped his own experience of moving to an all-white neighborhood would motivate other Black families to do the same. In May 1967, he published an article in the Ludlow newsletter arguing that it was important for other families to follow his lead. "The consensus of those most active in the field of integrated housing," he wrote, "is that significant progress has been made in overcoming all obstacles except one—FINDING NEGRO BUYERS." Not every Black family who wants to move to the suburbs can fit into Ludlow. "THE WAY TO ACHIEVE INTEGRATION IS TO INTEGRATE."

———

The move to Mercer made a dramatic impact on the Richie children, in different ways given their six-year age span and the rapidly changing racial environment. Winston Jr., the oldest, was in fifth grade when he entered Mercer Elementary School for the first time in 1965. Records for the previous school year indicated there were two Black students, but he and his sister Beth recall being the first and only.

"You knew everybody was staring at you," he said. "It was all the things. Touching your hair, touching your skin because they had never seen a Black person. Sometimes I would say yes, sometimes I would say no. The thing I remember is they wanted to touch."

To prepare for the move, Winston's fourth grade teacher at Ludlow gave him extra help in math, to be sure he didn't show up behind the other students. "By the time I got to Mercer," he recalled, "I was ahead of them."

His new classmates were not hostile. In fact, Winston was elected class secretary just a month or two after he arrived, winning with a campaign slogan modeled (somewhat awkwardly) after a cigarette ad at the time: "Winston is good as a secretary should."

Beth Richie, the second eldest, recalled an odd and uncomfortable sort of welcoming. One June day in 1967, her fifth grade teacher excitedly asked her to stand up before the class. "Beth, stand up. This is a really important day," the teacher instructed. Thurgood Marshall had been nominated the nation's first Black Supreme Court justice. The teacher said: "Beth, tell us about Thurgood Marshall." Beth had barely heard of Thurgood Marshall and felt called out, even as she knew her teacher meant no harm. Her brother's election as secretary and the excitement around Marshall felt, to Beth, almost too much—"a certain kind of exceptionalism."

For Laurel Richie, the third child, the move to Green Road was less complicated and more thrilling. She and her siblings got to put their footprints into the concrete poured for their new patio. Her mom let her pick out special pajamas for the first night in the new house. Her teachers were invited home with her for lunch every year. "My mother did lots of things like this, and made growing up exciting and joyful," she said.

Anne Richie, the fourth child, started kindergarten at Mercer in 1966, the year after the move, the only Richie child who never attended Ludlow Elementary. She recalled being completely comfortable with white people. In fact, one day she visited Ludlow with a friend and recalled being uncomfortable there.

At Mercer, she remembered walking to school with a friend, who observed the housekeepers walking from the rapid transit to the homes where they worked. "Here comes the maid brigade," her friend said. At her friends' homes, she found it awkward being around the Black women cleaning the house, not because they would be working hard as she and her friends played but because her mother insisted she call the housekeepers by their last names, including the appropriate Miss or Mrs., and Anne didn't know any of their last names. Her friends all called them by their first names. "I knew my mom felt a certain way about showing respect, but I couldn't really do that."

Then, when Anne was in fourth grade, the Shaker Schools busing plan began, and it was a culture shock. "I was happy. Life is good. I'm invited to all the birthday parties. All of a sudden there was this bus of Black children coming to the school, and I felt like I was being discovered."

The new Black students were complete strangers to her, but her mother wanted to be welcoming, and insisted that Anne invite her new classmates over. "Every week I had to invite a different Black student home for lunch. It was, 'Who are these people?' They were like Martians to me." Years later, she recognized a "colorism" at work—the Black children she had been around until then had a much lighter complexion than many of the children from Moreland.

As the Richie children moved into junior high and then high school, they responded differently to the multiracial environment before them. Both Beth and Laurel had Black and white friends, but Anne felt she had to prioritize Black friendships. Her elementary school friends were all white, and other Black kids taunted her, referring to her family as "Oreos"—Black on the outside, white on the inside. Anne already felt accepted by her white friends, and longed to be accepted among Black kids, too, so she sought out Black friendships.

"For me, it was a choice. I chose to try to round myself out in that way," she said. "Part of it was because of the pressure of getting called 'Oreo.' That didn't feel good. It was probably also wanting to make sure I was comfortable with my own. Subconsciously, maybe I was tired of being the only one."

———

Shaker Heights continued its work promoting housing integration and faced a central challenge: demand for suburban housing among Black families was spiking, but the racist practices of the real estate industry and others meant just a few neighborhoods were open to them.

In 1971, St. Ann's Church in Cleveland Heights documented what Shaker and Cleveland Heights were facing. They sent out seventeen Black and white volunteers to look for houses, with Black and white participants matched into pairs, similar in age, family size, and income, to test whether they would be treated similarly—or not. They all asked to see homes in eastern suburbs other than Shaker and Cleveland Heights. The study found Black volunteers were steered to these two suburbs, and in general received far less service from the agents.

Black volunteers had to make 88 percent more phone calls to secure a first appointment. Real estate agents volunteered to show whites but not Blacks additional homes for sale and were more likely to make follow-up calls to white seekers. One Black volunteer was told the owner was not available to show a house at 7:30 p.m. on a particular day, while a white volunteer had no trouble making the same appointment.

All this despite the 1968 Fair Housing Act, which barred discrimination on the basis of race and other factors when renting or buying a home, obtaining a mortgage, or engaging in other housing-related activities. The law enabled private lawsuits that alleged discrimination but had little enforcement power beyond that, which limited its reach. And communities and owners seeking to keep people of color out still had their suite of tools: threats and attacks directed at those who integrated new areas, discrimination by banks in mortgage lending, discriminatory zoning to keep out smaller homes and multifamily dwellings.

"The federal law may have stopped open, blatant discrimination, but it hasn't ended the subtle kind," Suzanne Nigro, chair of the church's housing committee, told the *Sun Press*. The study was circulated widely, she later reported, making it to Ohio governor John Gilligan and shared with regional offices of the U.S. Department of Housing and Urban Development.

There had been early efforts to address the problem. There was Fair Housing Inc., the real estate agency formed in 1962 by activists in Ludlow. It offered financial assistance and advice finding homes for Black buyers in all-white neighborhoods—to help more people do what Winston and Bea Richie had done on their own. It also aided white people buying in integrated areas.

"We've got to urge Negroes not to live in clusters," Stuart E. Wallace, the real estate broker who ran the company, told *Newsweek* magazine in 1966. By the time Fair Housing Inc. closed in 1971, the firm had sold 350 homes, including 199 to Black buyers.

The other strategy was litigation to deter discrimination in housing. That was the approach of Operation Equality, a project of the Urban League led by Joseph Battle, the Black real estate broker who lived in Ludlow. But without more options for Black homeseekers, neighborhoods like Ludlow and Lomond would always be battling to remain integrated.

Winston Richie wanted to run for the Shaker Heights school board, and would have been the first Black member, but he didn't get very far. In 1970, he sought endorsement from the Shaker Heights Citizens Committee, a group that interviewed candidates, made endorsements, and funded campaigns, holding unusual sway over who was elected to public office in Shaker Heights.

One influential member saw Richie as "too militant," Richie later recalled, without elaboration. Carolyn Milter, his friend and former Ludlow neighbor, guessed his move to all-white Mercer explained why he was seen that way, though she considered the idea ridiculous. "There were a bunch of us who were a lot more militant than Winston," she said. "Winston had such a wonderful personality and he had this ability to relate to whoever he was with. He was never going to be a hater. He was always gracious, always wanted to get along with people." Nonetheless, the Citizens Committee made sure Richie wouldn't run for school board by putting him on the nominating committee.

Ultimately, another Black man from Ludlow, Drue King Jr., was endorsed and elected, just in time for the school board to consider its pathbreaking busing plan.

The next year, Richie ran for Shaker Heights City Council in a city-wide election, and this time he was victorious. "I think by that time people were of the mindset that there ought to be some black representation on Council," he said in an interview published in 1987. He embraced, or maybe created, the nickname Win during his campaign, manifesting success for himself.

While victory would break another racial barrier, he hardly positioned himself as a revolutionary. He told the *Call & Post* that his experience made him "keenly aware of how little we know about each other and how much more we ought to listen to each other."

Of course racial tensions were all around, but Richie would often disarm those feelings. On a camping trip with other Ludlow families, he and a white dad were partners in a canoe race, calling their team "Black Power and the Great White Whale." As he campaigned for City Council on a slate with two white candidates, he'd close out remarks saying that all three were good choices "but perhaps Win Richie is a shade better."

He was elected in 1971, then reelected in 1975 and again in 1979.

Richie's drive to belong and excel in predominantly white spaces extended to religion, traditionally one of the most segregated aspects of

American life. On Sundays, the Richies would drive into Cleveland to their Black church, driving right past a white church, Fairmont Presbyterian, on the edge of Shaker. Eventually he asked himself: Why? In conversations with friends, Black and white, the couple talked about their aspirations and vision for their lives and community. A white friend who attended Fairmont offered a provocative thought: "If you really believe this [integration], you should come join our church," Richie recounted. The Richies visited the next Sunday, were welcomed by the pastor, and joined, prompting a few white families to leave in response. They joined the church, Richie said later, because that's how he thought things ought to be in this country.

To be sure, Richie was involved in many civil rights and Black organizations, including the NAACP, the Council on Human Relations, and Fair Housing Inc. But as with church, he embraced a growing list of memberships and hobbies in areas where Black Americans were underrepresented. He served on Shaker organizations, including the Thornton Park Committee, the Shaker Recreation Board, the Chamber of Commerce, and the Shaker Lakes Regional Nature Center. He was a Boy Scout leader, a master bridge player, and a regular on the tennis courts. He moved his dental practice to Shaker and was proud that his roster included white as well as Black patients.

He understood that all these things, these little things and big things, were adding up to something meaningful, creating a different sort of world for his children.

Carolyn Milter recalled Election Night 1967, when Carl Stokes was elected Cleveland's mayor, the first Black mayor of any major American city. Carolyn had volunteered for the Stokes campaign, and as the returns came in, she and her husband, Burt, headed to the Rockefeller Building in downtown Cleveland to celebrate. She recalled spotting Winston with his son, who was called Roddy then. "Winston, what are you doing with Roddy up this late?" she asked, knowing full well what the answer would be.

Richie turned to Milter, serious. Looking at his young son, he said, "I know he won't remember this," she recalled. "He's falling asleep in my arms. I just wanted him to be here."

———

The Shaker housing office continued to draw national praise for its embrace of integration, and also barbs.

Real estate brokers objected to its very existence, arguing the enterprise was selling real estate without a license, and without commissions, providing unfair competition. In 1974, the Cleveland Area Board of Realtors asked the state to investigate the housing office, and in 1977, it filed a lawsuit, though the challenge was ultimately unsuccessful.

Other criticism came from those who saw the work as inherently discriminatory because the office was helping white house hunters and not Black ones.

An early flare went up in 1972 when Operation Equality accused the housing office of "passively accepting continued discrimination directed at blacks." A position paper charged: "No efforts are being made to support open housing in unintegrated areas of the city."

Then controversy exploded in April 1979 when six housing office employees resigned to protest what they described as a racial double standard. They asked whether the office's goal was containment of the Black population or integration of the city. They interpreted the city's response as containment.

The event that set them off was when Renée Schecter, a worker in the office, showed a white family a house in the mostly white Fernway neighborhood without discussing it with a colleague who was responsible for finding homes for Black families in this area. The housing office was allegedly committed to moving Black buyers into white areas, and now this.

At the center of the controversy was Lucille Anderson, who directed the office. In the early 1960s, she had seen racial change coming to her Lomond neighborhood and got involved recruiting white families. She was committed to recruiting white buyers, serving as a counterweight to a racist realty industry that worked against integration. "She did an extraordinarily good job," Stephen Alfred, a city leader during this period, said in a 2023 interview.

But over time, Anderson came under scrutiny because the housing office did not see the same need to serve Black buyers.

Decades later, Ann Lewis put it bluntly: Anderson, she said, "didn't want to show Blacks homes in white Shaker." Milter saw the same: "Her goal was to keep Blacks out of Shaker, quite frankly. She would have seen it as success if we could limit the number of Blacks in Shaker."

There was some irony in the leader of an integration effort being accused of racism, and to Anderson, this might have felt like goalpost moving. She had been hired to keep neighborhoods integrated, which meant drawing whites, and that is what she was trying to do. The criticism surely stung given her dedication to this cause. Charles Bromley, a fair housing activist who knew Anderson, said Anderson's view was "limited by her time." But he said charges leveled against her seem unfair. "A racist would have packed up everything and gone to Highland Heights," he said.

In April 1979, after the resignations, the housing office drafted a new policy stating it would assist Black buyers who wanted to move into white areas but made clear it would continue to focus on white home seekers moving to integrated areas. A few months later, the controversy was evidently still simmering as Stephen Alfred, then a member of City Council, wrote a letter to the *Sun Press* defending the city and arguing that it was not possible to maintain integration and treat the races equally. "Promoting integration of necessity results in unequal treatment," he wrote.

Pressure continued to mount. In June 1980, a Black Shaker resident named Mary Blair telephoned the housing office and was connected with Anderson. She gave Anderson a fake name and told her she was interested in buying a four-bedroom home in either the Sussex or Fernway neighborhoods, both mostly white areas, indicating her price was up to $85,000, according to an account Blair shared with a raft of Shaker officials. Blair already knew there was a house for sale in the Fernway area with an asking price of $79,900.

According to Blair, Anderson asked her race and when Blair said she was Black, Anderson suggested she might be interested in the Moreland area. "I stated that I was not interested in Moreland, but wished an area such as Fernway," Blair wrote. "At this point Mrs. Anderson said the purpose of the housing program was to assist whites in moving into integrated areas of Shaker. She suggested I contact a broker."

If true, this story indicates that not only was Anderson unwilling to help a Black woman buy into a white part of Shaker, but she was steering her to the most heavily Black neighborhood, undercutting the housing office's stated mission. Anderson died in 2010, and it's not clear how she responded to these allegations. Tom Webb, a city councilman, at one point defended her, saying her version of events differed.

That month, the Ludlow Community Association board invited city officials overseeing the housing office to a meeting at the home of the Milters. Board members were fuming. The city housing office had grown out of their cherished Ludlow housing program, and now it was being run by a woman they saw as untrustworthy. (Milter couldn't help but recall the close vote by which Ludlow turned its housing program over to the city. "I've said many times—I want it on my tombstone when I die that I voted against the housing office.")

Among those in the room was Winston Richie, now on City Council and a member of the housing office's governing board. Richie said he knew they wanted Anderson fired but that it wasn't likely, given her strong support on the governing committee and "throughout Shaker Heights."

But the Ludlow contingent pressed their case, according to notes of the meeting written by one of the Ludlow residents who was there and confirmed by Milter. The housing office would lack credibility in Ludlow as long as Anderson was in charge, they said. Joe Battle, the fair housing activist from Ludlow, said he could document cases of discrimination. One woman told the story of a caller to the housing office who was asked "if she would mind having a black landlord!" The group admitted that the Ludlow Community Association, too, had not served Black house hunters, but they argued that was different. Back then, it was a demonstration project meant to test whether a viable integrated neighborhood could even exist. They set up programs like Fair Housing Inc. to help Black buyers find options elsewhere. And perhaps most important, all this took place before the Fair Housing Act had made discrimination in housing illegal.

———

The housing office's mission was not the only policy Shaker supported that was seen by others as racist.

In 1972, a group of moms of young children living in the Lomond neighborhood grew concerned about traffic. Cars were speeding down Avalon Road from the city of Cleveland, past their houses to a nearby commercial area. They complained about whiskey and beer bottles tossed from cars, noise, and hazards to children. In response, two barricades were set up at the border between Cleveland and Shaker Heights along Scottsdale Boulevard to control traffic, first as a test. Then, in 1978, they were made permanent.

Furious, the City of Cleveland retaliated with barriers of its own and a boycott of Shaker businesses. A Cleveland city councilman erected a sign across Lee Road, on the Cleveland-Shaker border, reading, ENTERING APARTHEID SHAKER: HOME OF BARRICADES. In 1987, another Cleveland councilman told the *New York Times* that the barriers had become "a symbol of racism." The City of Cleveland filed suit challenging the barriers (winning in lower courts but ultimately losing at the Ohio Supreme Court).

Shaker officials strongly denied racial motivation. The neighborhood involved, Lomond, had a substantial Black population. Were critics arguing that Black people were racist against other Black people? Local officials argued that the barriers were needed to maintain Lomond as an integrated neighborhood.

"The more traffic on a street, the less safe it is, the less attractive it is to live on, the lower the housing values, and the worse the chances to maintain integration," Webb, the councilman from Lomond, said. In other words, if traffic ruins the neighborhood, white people will be more likely to leave.

While the racism charge was questionable, there were clear questions of economics and class at work. People of all races in Shaker were wealthier than those living in Cleveland, and they sought to keep it that way. "It's more of a class struggle than it is a racial struggle," James L. Hardiman, president of the Cleveland chapter of the NAACP, told the *Times*. "Shaker Heights doesn't want the riff-raff of Cleveland contaminating their city."

Shaker weathered the storm, and the barricades remained. It wasn't the last time tensions between race and class would play out in Shaker. Black pioneers such as Winston Richie understood that common ground in Shaker had been forged through shared class status, with similar levels of professional and academic achievement bringing people together. Economic integration would be harder.

"I think that if we could solve the race problems in Shaker, we will have done a whole heck of a lot," he told Cynthia Richter. "I feel strongly that people ought to be economically integrated also, but I think if you bring that into this mix, then you're going to hurt this mix. I mean, you know, somebody needs to do it, and I support it. But I think the more you water down what we're trying to do, the more difficult it'll be."

Ted Mason, his close friend, expressed a similar sentiment. He said the shared professional experiences of Black and white neighbors made people in Ludlow of both races comfortable living together. "If I live next door to a person who has similar experiences as I have, then I'm more comfortable feeling that he will seek the same for his children that

I will seek for mine," he told Richter. "If I live next door to a high school dropout, his experiences after dropping out are *far* different than mine, and can I have great hope that his aspirations for his children are the same as mine? No, I can't have any great hope."

The economic differences were rarely spelled out so bluntly, but many of the Black families arriving in the 1970s and beyond were less wealthy than the first wave in the late 1950s and '60s. Shaker would have to confront not just racial divides, but economic ones, too.

―――――――

By early 1982, opposition had grown to Lucille Anderson's leadership at the housing office, and a palpable anxiety was spreading in parts of Shaker Heights about the city's ability to maintain integrated neighborhoods. In March, the City Council, the school board, the mayor, and the schools superintendent met on a Saturday for what members considered one of the most important meetings in many years, a daylong session meant to chart a new course for the city's housing program.

The Housing Office Governing Board, chaired by Winston Richie, convened the session and saw the situation as dire and urgent. Problems included "total lack of support" in the Black community for the office, weakening of community associations, low visibility of the program, Anderson's leadership of the program and resistance to change, and the fact that white buyers and renters had become "harder and harder" to find.

Members left the session convinced new leadership and a new approach were needed, and soon after, Anderson was forced to resign. Interviewed thirteen years later, Anderson seemed somewhat bitter about her experience.

"From the housing office perspective, you could never do it right," she told Richter. "The blacks would be angry because you wouldn't help them. The liberal whites, the real liberal whites would be angry because you were discriminating against blacks. The conservative, reactionary whites would be angry at you because you encouraged black people to move on their street, or ten streets away. You name it, it didn't matter who, you were always wrong, and it was always on me."

With Anderson out, the city planned a new housing program that would expand financial incentives, and they plotted a new campaign to sell the program inside and outside Shaker. The housing office "will serve all areas of the City and serve people of all races and religions," said an April 1982 memo by Mark Freeman, the school district official who had managed federal grants. The fact that a school official was put in charge of such a sensitive and important transition in city housing policy underscored just how closely the issues of housing and schools were tied together, and how important the school district saw housing to its own interests.

Meantime, the city had its sights set on bolder ideas to keep Shaker racially balanced: "We must go outside Shaker in pushing integration," Tom Webb, the city councilman, wrote in a March 30 memo. "Look at all the eastern suburbs."

It wasn't clear at the time, but Winston Richie would become, more than anyone else, the person to see this vision through.

Throughout this period, as Shaker officials were trying to figure out how to adapt their integration program for a new era, the politics were changing. Republican Ronald Reagan was now president, and rather than encouraging integration, his administration was boosting a colorblind vision that undercut their work.

In May 1983, the Justice Department opened a new initiative under the Fair Housing Act to go after entities that sought to limit Black residents in order to maintain integration. The department began by charging a California housing developer and manager with employing a racial quota system to limit the number of nonwhite tenants.

"This practice, euphemistically labeled 'integration maintenance,' is designed to put a lid or cap on the number of minorities allowed to move into a housing complex or neighborhood," William Bradford Reynolds, assistant attorney general for civil rights, said in a 1983 speech to the National Bar Association, an association of Black attorneys. He also called out "subtle forms of racial steering, race-conscious solicitation practices, preferred tenant lists" as examples of prohibited activities. "Exclusionary housing practices based on race find no haven in the law, whether they be for purposes of 'integration maintenance' or for any other purpose." He said the Justice Department planned a "major enforcement effort" under the Fair Housing Act targeting these programs.

Shaker viewed this development as a significant threat to its goals. "Mr. Reynolds' approach must be stopped," a city official wrote in letters to Representative Louis Stokes and Senators John Glenn and Howard Metzenbaum, Democrats representing Ohio. "He must not be allowed to prevail in this attack on the interests of Shaker Heights and the other but all-too-few integrated communities."

———————

In the fall of 1982, Shaker hired Don DeMarco to replace Anderson, and he was far more comfortable talking about race. A white man married to a Black woman, with four children, DeMarco had been doing similar work in the Chicago suburb of Park Forest. "I am dedicated to integration in both my personal and professional life," DeMarco told the *Sun Press*.

Many years later, DeMarco recalled being driven on a tour of Shaker by a housing office employee when he was in town to interview for the job. "We were driving around and we get to Moreland and my escort tells me, 'This is the most heavily integrated area.' And of course it's the most segregated area and not integrated at all," he said. She was using "integrated" as a euphemism for "occupied by Black people." In general, the staff avoided discussing race, and when they did, it was to note the area's embrace of integration.

Anderson had not been interested in being part of the larger fair housing movement in the area, DeMarco said. "She had kind of this 'I don't see race' attitude, and of course, if race matters, and it has to matter if you're going to be doing work to engineer integration, you have to be able to talk about these things and justify them."

DeMarco saw his work as connected with the larger regional fair housing movement. In an interview with the *Sun Press* for a story announcing his hiring, DeMarco said he would take a regional approach to integration, saying Shaker cannot maintain racial balance unless other communities become available to Black residents. "What happens outside of Shaker will have an impact on Shaker," he said. A few months later, he told the *Sun Press* that Black buyers who approach the Shaker Heights Housing Office would be directed to virtually all-white suburbs such as Lyndhurst and Solon. "The communities which are virtually all white are happy with it [segregation]. But that does not make it okay."

In July 1983, Shaker Heights, Cleveland Heights, and University Heights, together with their school boards, formed a new organization to formally steer Black house hunters to the Hillcrest suburbs farther east:

Lyndhurst, Mayfield Heights, South Euclid, Mayfield Village, Highland Heights, and Richmond Heights. They called it the East Suburban Council for Open Communities, or ESCOC. According to Gary Orfield, a leading academic studying and promoting desegregation, it was the first of its kind in the nation. He said the cooperation between cities and school boards had been almost unheard of before this.

I n 1983, Richie decided to run for mayor instead of seeking reelection to City Council. Ahead of the race, Carolyn Milter recalled six or eight of his Ludlow friends, mostly Black, meeting in hopes of talking him out of it. "They were worried he wouldn't win," she said. Beverly Mason, she said, was among those concerned he wasn't willing to do what he needed to do to win—namely do all he could to turn out the Black vote in Shaker.

Nonetheless, he decided to run, and Milter was "nominally his campaign manager," she said. "He was his own campaign manager and that was the problem."

"Winston always had this glass is half full thing," she said. He thought he could win with support from white Shaker voters "instead of working on building support in Moreland and Lomond and Ludlow, where for sure they would vote for him."

"I have support in all of the city's neighborhoods," he told the *Call & Post*.

The newspaper wrote glowingly of the path Richie had forged: there were now Black people working across city government, Dr. Martin Luther King Jr.'s birthday had been designated a city holiday, police officers had been suspended and punished in response to derogatory racial remarks. Nonetheless, the *Call & Post* endorsed Stephen Alfred, a white candidate, for mayor, suggesting he would be better able to handle an ongoing dispute with neighboring Cleveland over the traffic barricades. The endorsement took Richie to task for having entered the race belatedly.

"He who hesitates is lost," the paper said. "Decisiveness, commitment and a hard nose instinct separated the good guys, from the good guys who win."

Richie's children said their father's heart didn't seem to be in the race. He was interested in public service, not in political strategy, and he thought that his accomplishments and willingness to serve should speak for themselves. Beth recalled going to the polls with him on Election Day and he barely wanted to hand out materials. "People have made up their minds," he told her.

Alfred won. Richie came in third (though he won in a few precincts in majority Black areas). His wife was "so heartbroken," their daughter Laurel said, hurt by the people who didn't support him. She recalled her dad as more accepting. "He was like, 'I ran and I didn't cater to anyone. People will make up their minds. It's fine.'"

Bromley, who befriended Richie through housing work, recalled him as more unsettled than that. He remembered Richie blaming the Black community for not turning out. Richie, he said, was under the impression that Black voters believed he would not be effective in the job because of racism he would face.

Just as Richie lost his race, the city was looking for someone to lead the new housing office, ESCOC. Richie had been closely involved in the creation of the program, and now he was available to run it. He retired from his dental practice and devoted himself full-time to integration—a bold new regional approach to fair housing that went beyond calling out individual acts of discrimination and tried to diversify entire communities.

Richie threw himself into this new line of work—trying to persuade people to move to a place they had no particular desire to go and that had no particular interest in receiving them. He starred in television advertisements promoting the Hillcrest area to Black Clevelanders. ESCOC printed a twelve-page color brochure promoting the other suburban options, with information about the schools, services, and housing available in each. It was titled "You're Welcome." It also offered $3,000 grants to Black families to move into all-white areas.

ESCOC opened an office in its target area. The team reached out to Black brokers to bring clients to the area, and to white agents to work with them, sometimes inviting them to the same luncheons and making introductions. Marilyn Brown, a white woman from the area, was hired to work with local leaders and neighbors, while Richie focused on publicizing their work locally and nationally as well as working with Black families who were considering the move.

Working with Black agents was more challenging than expected, Richie said, because they were unfamiliar with the territory and found it more convenient to sell Shaker and Cleveland Heights. "It's much easier for them," he told a group in Shaker in 1987. Black agents also had their own listings in familiar areas, he added, meaning they didn't have to divide the commission with another agent, as was the case in the Hillcrest suburbs.

Richie had a way of putting people at ease, Brown recalled. Once when a family was visiting with two excited children, he came out of his office, stooped his large frame down to their level, and asked what they wanted in a new house. All they wanted was a yard and a safe place, neither of which they had in their Cleveland home.

When families came in, Brown said, she would try to reassure them about the communities they were considering, while Richie talked about being a pioneer.

"Often they would have questions about how it would feel to be one of very few or the only Black family in a community—those were questions that he could answer and nobody else could answer," she said. "He said it could be tough, but you're tougher and it will pass and more Black families will move in and we will help you."

Local officials were not particularly excited about the help. But ESCOC looked for creative ways around that, DeMarco said. It might give somebody in an all-white suburb an award for equal opportunity and present it with some fanfare, and encourage the Black press to cover the event in hopes of changing the way Black residents in the wider area viewed that community.

"It was in our interest for them to have a better reputation so people of color would feel, 'Maybe I should look at options there,'" he said. "Rather than badmouthing the communities who were seeking to deflect Black housing traffic and schools traffic, the response was to good-mouth them, even if they didn't want it."

ESCOC itself got death threats—nooses sent through the mail and other harassment, Brown said. It also suffered a major embarrassment when it was learned that an interracial couple ESCOC had helped was hosting swinger parties, where couples swapped sexual partners. Brown recalled this as an all-out crisis, made worse when Phil Donahue featured the tale on his popular TV talk show. But Richie handled it perfectly, she said.

"Winston was so calm," she said. She remembered a large meeting with angry neighbors gathered. "He told them we don't vet their sex lives. Would they want somebody to vet their sex lives?"

In 1985, the City of Shaker Heights added a fresh strategy to its integration toolkit. With funding from local foundations and donors, the Fund for the Future of Shaker Heights began offering mortgage assistance to families—white and Black—who bought homes in areas where their race was underrepresented. The fund provided financing at below-market interest rates to help provide down payments or otherwise supplement mortgages, in amounts ranging from $3,000 to $6,000. It was an echo of the financial incentives policy pioneered by the Ludlow Company more than twenty years earlier.

Shaker had a particular interest in stabilizing the Lomond area, where sales to whites had fallen from 81 percent in 1981 to 47 percent in 1985. The new loans were available to people of all races, but in the first five years of the program, 71 of its 75 loans went to white buyers, almost all of them buying in Lomond. It had an impact, with annual percentage of sales to whites in Lomond rising as high as 70 percent and consistently representing a majority. A 1990 study by a Federal Reserve Bank economist found that the probability of a white person buying in an integrated area rose by 20 percent and that housing prices rose by 5.8 percent annually. (The Fund for the Future continued until 2012, when its leaders said demand for the loans had faded.)

This program helped Shaker win fresh national attention for its housing work. In 1988, ESCOC and the cities of Shaker and Cleveland Heights were recognized with a $100,000 prize for racial integration incentives by Harvard University's John F. Kennedy School of Government. In a video promoting the award, Mayor Alfred said they were working to create a "third America," where Black and white people live together.

"Cleveland's just like every other major city. It's segregated," Richie said in a video produced in conjunction with the award. "And this condition will not correct itself." He added: "We have shown where people want to live in a diverse community, it works."

By 1990, ESCOC had helped about four hundred Black families move to mostly white suburbs. Richmond Heights schools, for instance, had almost no Black students in 1980; by 1987, Black students represented 9.6 percent of the district. But just a few years later, ESCOC fell apart. Richie resigned, and while his letter of resignation did not specify what the disagreement was, he was clearly angry and frustrated. He wrote that "proposed new directions" approved by the board would be "detrimental to improved race relations" in the Hillcrest communities. He declined to tell a reporter what the proposed new directions were but said he was tired of "feeling like I'm beating my head into a brick wall." He also said that he wanted ESCOC to expand its scope to a larger territory.

In a 2021 interview, DeMarco gave another version of the story. He said the controversy was over whether ESCOC should serve Black renters, or only Black buyers. DeMarco said Richie wanted ESCOC to concentrate solely on Black buyers because they were better representatives of the Black community than renters were. That approach wasn't okay for Shaker and Cleveland Heights, which funded ESCOC and were looking to divert Black renters as well as buyers, he said.

Marilyn Brown was gone by then, but DeMarco's explanation rang true to her.

Richie "believed home buying was the way to have Black families earn equity and have a stake in the community and renters didn't do that," Brown said. "And he felt that if more Black renters entered any community in new numbers that it would be a negative on what we were trying to achieve." His primary goal was not to relieve pressure off Shaker and Cleveland Heights, she said; his goal was a measured and stable integration of the Hillcrest suburbs.

In 1991, the program was dissolved, and the city contracted with other organizations that it hoped would do similar work, including one run briefly by Richie.

That November, Richie ran again for City Council and was elected once again. DeMarco concluded his days in Shaker were numbered, found another position in Philadelphia, and departed. Richie remained on City Council until 1995. He also realized he liked selling houses and earned his real estate license. In 1997, he sold more than $3 million worth of property.

When asked, Richie said his legacy would be his children, and by that measure it is an impressive one. Winston Jr. worked as an insurance executive and volunteered in politics. Beth went into academia and became a pioneer in activism and scholarship on gender-based violence. Anne founded a debt fund for businesses owned by women and people of color. And Laurel became the first Black person to head a major U.S. sports league, the WNBA.

Laurel also served as president of the Board of Trustees of Dartmouth College, her alma mater. She spent her college years not far from the hotel that had turned her parents away on their honeymoon.

> To believe in places is to know hope and to know
> the emotion of hope is to know beauty.
> —Adrienne Kennedy, *Funnyhouse of a Negro*

9

EMILY HOOPER

John Gray didn't mind offending people. In fact, he bizarrely appeared to revel in it. One morning in 1983, he took the stage at Shaker Heights High School and began ranting. His performance was always the same. He'd talk about attending a Ku Klux Klan rally, and assert that Black people get what they want by violence. He would refuse to take a question from someone because she appeared to be Jewish. If someone asked a question with a foreign accent, he would snap that he should "speak like Americans."

The audience was horrified and incredulous as students broke into small groups to discuss what just happened. They were supposed to consider how stereotypes block communication, how attitudes affect behaviors, and how to develop the skills to cope with bigotry. Then they gathered again in the auditorium.

John Gray took the stage once more to a chorus of boos. He then flashed a slide of himself with his Black family: "I'd like you to meet my brothers and sisters and mom and dad."

"You could hear a pin drop," said history teacher Terry Pollack, who helped plan the event. Gray was a stage name. He was actually a light-skinned Black man named Ted Paynther, a professor at Kent State University, with an act aimed at challenging students' assumptions. "It was really quite an assembly," Pollack said later. "It was really quite powerful."

Emily Hooper and her friends were not impressed. In fact, they were pissed off.

"It's not okay to play people like that," said Emily, a junior at the time. "I was angry at the school for having used that as a ploy to address issues that I felt were important and should have been addressed. It felt like, you can't do this kind of thing as a onetime thing. It has to be a discussion that continues."

She was part of a tight, racially diverse group of friends who had been having intense conversations about race and life since junior high school. That day, the group decided that complaining wasn't enough. They wanted to do something.

———

Earline and Lorenzo Hooper's daughter Paula had ridden on the first buses that carried Black students out of Moreland, across Van Aken Boulevard and into the mostly white elementary schools. Now it was the spring of 1975, and their younger daughter, Emily, was in third grade and would be eligible for the busing program the following year. The Hoopers weren't sure it was a good idea. Emily was a little more sensitive than Paula, Earline recalled, a little more concerned with what the other kids might think of her. She was a little too focused on trying to "satisfy everybody, which is impossible." Maybe, her parents thought, it would be better for Emily to stay at Moreland.

It was a few years into the voluntary busing plan, and interest was beginning to wane. In the first year of the program, 250 students participated, but by 1974, that number had fallen to 108. As the novelty wore off, the appeal of neighborhood schools tugged families to stay at their home schools.

Emily was insistent. For her, it was simple. Her sister got to ride the bus, so she wanted to ride the bus. It's not that she wanted out of Moreland. At her neighborhood school, she felt a real sense of community, and, thanks to the busing program, had both Black and white friends. "I was happy at Moreland, but I wanted to get on the bus because she [Paula] was riding the bus. It seemed like a cool thing to do." Her parents relented. So in 1975, Emily, like her sister, began fourth grade at Malvern Elementary School, in the oldest, wealthiest, most opulent section of Shaker Heights.

The Hoopers had moved to Shaker Heights for the schools and were laser-focused on delivering the best education possible to their three children. Earline was a teacher, and Lorenzo believed deeply in the power of education. "It was just central for us," Emily said. "Our father always tried to help us believe we could be anything." The word "can't" was akin to a profanity, something never to be uttered around him. "He would look at you like you sweared when you said 'can't.'"

Their house was typical of the Moreland development. It was small—and by Malvern standards, tiny. Downstairs consisted of a compact living room, a small kitchen and dining room, plus a small bedroom where her grandmother would stay. Upstairs, there were three bedrooms for five people. Emily remembered early in her first year at Malvern being invited to a sleepover party in "this huge, huge Shaker mansion." She came home and told her dad about it.

"I want to live in a big house like that," she told him.

"No you don't," he replied. "Those houses are haunted."

Emily thought to herself, "*Really*?" But she believed him. "I never wanted to live in a big house again. It was his way of making me feel like whatever we had was enough, as it should be."

The Black students from Moreland were divided among six elementary schools, and at Malvern, Emily was one of just a handful in her grade. Before the busing plan began, Malvern had no Black students. It was not always easy. "When I was in fourth grade, I was called the n-word on the playground," she remembered. "I never told my parents." She did tell a teacher, and the boy was reprimanded and forced to apologize.

"I just didn't want to tell my parents," she said. "I felt angry, and I was not sure how to respond."

Fifth grade, though, was magical. Emily described it as a "transformative year," all because of her teacher—Mary Krogness. "She was just one of those once-in-a-lifetime teachers."

On April Fools' Day, Emily and some friends decided they'd play a trick on their teacher. They made arrangements to come to school early and turned the entire classroom into a spider web, with dark thread close to the floor—hard to see—and yarn up high. "If you started walking you wouldn't see the thread on the floor," Emily remembered. "We thought she would get caught in the web."

They were a little scared they'd get in trouble. In fact, Mrs. Krogness was so delighted that she called the local newspaper to come take photos.

"There was just a way that she had to encourage us to think differently, really supporting our creativity."

Junior high school brought new challenges. Moreland, her neighborhood school, and Malvern, her elementary school, both fed into Byron Junior High. Emily was still riding the bus across town, this time with all the Moreland kids. She also had her overwhelmingly white elementary school friends from Malvern. She had a foot in both worlds, with friends both Black and white, but the racial dynamics were complicated and at times hard. One of the Black kids teased her, called her an Oreo. That was confusing to Emily, who had always felt a deep connection to the Black community—from her church, from her early years at Moreland, from her neighborhood, from her family. Some of her close friends were Black kids from her early days at Moreland. Still, one Black friend told her that they could talk on the phone at night, "but I'm going to keep my distance from you at school, because you have a different set of friends than I do."

Earline remembered her daughter struggled to maintain both Black and white friendships. Some Black students would accuse her of rejecting them. "It hurt her an awful lot," Earline recalled. Emily didn't get invited to some of the Black parties. Sometimes her mom had to pick her up from school so she wouldn't have to take the bus home with other students from her neighborhood.

Classes presented another challenge for Emily. She was in advanced classes, and their makeup was mostly white. She missed being with a diverse group of kids—culturally and academically. She also felt a new pressure to always have the right answer, because if she was in this class, obviously she was supposed to fit some sort of academic ideal. "There were times when you didn't feel comfortable asking a question because then it seems like you don't know something you're supposed to know." Emily had to figure out who she was in this new space. "I felt like I had more than one identity."

Her answer would come through theater, which connected Emily to a new set of friends. The theater adviser was a Black teacher named Zachary Green, who was also pursuing a graduate degree in counseling. He wanted to share some of what he was learning about psychology and personal development with some of his students, so he formed a peer counseling group, a mixed-race collection of students. They met in his classroom after school on Fridays, and sometimes dropped in at lunch, when his classroom was open to students.

At the time, they were just a group of kids, looking for friendship, exchanging ideas. They had no idea what this peer counseling group would lead to.

———————

When Terry Pollack arrived as a new teacher at Shaker Heights High School in 1964, he encountered what he now calls "old Shaker." The man who hired him said, off the cuff, "You're only the second one of your kind that I've ever hired." Pollack knew that he meant he was only the second Jew, but he replied, "You mean I'm only the second male?"

Pollack stood out as something of a raging liberal, both politically and culturally, on a conservative faculty in a preppy town. He and a handful of other young teachers were questioning the United States' involvement in Korea and in Vietnam; a year earlier, two teachers had been fired for teaching controversial topics and openly opposing the Vietnam War. One day Pollack went to check his mailbox in the school office and found someone had slipped the anticommunist book *None Dare Call It Treason* into the slot.

A "significant number" of teachers at the high school were overtly racist, he said, referring to Black students using vulgar racial epithets. The dean of girls would walk the hallways with a carpet square in hand and instruct girls to kneel on the square to be sure their skirts touched the floor. He also faced an unspoken dress code. "Students and teachers won't respect you if you don't wear a tie," an assistant principal warned him. Pollack said he replied, "It isn't wearing a tie that earns respect. It's what you do and who you are that earns respect."

Pollack said he could weather the barbs in part because he had the support of the principal and of Jack Lawson, the superintendent, though Lawson wasn't always happy with him either. Pollack's wife, Maxine, was a leader among the moms at Mercer Elementary School insisting that all children be allowed to stay at school for lunch, which would free mothers up during the day. "My wife was a real gung-ho women's libber. She was a stay-at-home mom but didn't want to be," Pollack said. Lawson was irritated. (In his own memoir, he derided these women, claiming they wanted to "play tennis, golf and shop" and saying he was amused when he was named runner-up for the Male Chauvinist Pig of the Year award by the Cleveland chapter of the National Organization for Women.) Pollack said Lawson would purposely irritate his wife by calling her "Mrs. Terry Pollack," and he once sent Terry a note asking, "Can't you control your wife?" Pollack said he replied by noting that he was acquainted with Lawson's wife. "Come on, there's no such thing as a man controlling your wife anymore."

Pollack saw the district integrate before his eyes. In 1964, when he arrived, there were 131 Black students at the high school—6.8 percent of the student population. That figure steadily increased over the years. He found the Shaker community remarkably progressive on race and decades later, still marveled at the parents who voluntarily bused their children away from their neighborhood elementary school to promote integration. But he also saw the limits of those progressive values.

Once, he said, he was invited by the principal of Mercer Elementary School, set in a mostly white part of Shaker, to speak to the PTA. He asked parents to write questions on cards anonymously. One questioner said her child was white and had no Black friends. "How do I help my child to develop more Black friendships?" Pollack said he responded with a challenge: "How many of you have Black friends or have invited Black residents who live near you to come to your house?" Not one hand went up. "Here's the answer to the question: The kids often role model what their parents do in life."

Meantime, at the high school, Pollack was developing a reputation as an outstanding teacher and starting to think more deeply about how he could promote achievement for all students. He hated the idea of certain teachers teaching only AP courses, which he saw some do. He said teaching AP classes isn't hard. "You teach AP and you sneeze and they're going to write down 'God bless you' in their notes." So in addition to AP U.S. History, Pollack taught regular-level classes, including U.S. History, Economics, and Human Relations. Some teachers complained that lower-level classes were out of control, with students not paying attention or working hard. Pollack found that wasn't necessarily so.

"The way to get rid of poor discipline in the room is to be demanding as a teacher so kids see you are working your rear end off as a teacher, and kids know they have to rise to the occasion and not stay in lower-level thinking," he said. "Teaching is an art where you have to help kids unwind the rust that's in their brain and discover a way to learn."

He recalled one day at the opening of a class he taught called Oppression, a regular-level course that studied how humans could surrender their values to allow evils such as slavery and the Holocaust. It was the first day of class, and a Black male student arrived, stood at the doorway, and observed, "There are a lot of white people in this class and my teacher's a fag." Pollack was wearing a pink shirt that day. He said he replied, "This is a perfect class for you because we deal with prejudice and stereotypes."

Other teachers, he thought, would have gotten angry and maybe tossed the kid out of class. He said he viewed it as him seeking attention, "so let's give him another type" of attention. "You use that as a teaching moment, not as a disciplinary moment. Too many kids are used to being disciplined."

On another day of the Oppression class in 1997 or 1998, captured on film for the movie *Shaker Heights: Struggle for Integration*, Pollack showed photos of three different women to the class, one at a time, and asked what assumptions came to mind. The first was of a white woman with neatly parted hair. Then came a Black woman with a tall Afro. Finally a young woman with a typically Jewish name.

After some discussion, he asked the students, "How many of you have ever . . . been prejudged by your name or your looks?" He turned to one student in particular and asked, "Are you ever prejudged as a Black male?" And the student told the class about how he and his friends were followed in stores. "It might happen to others, too, but I just notice it happens to me a lot," the student said.

In just a few minutes, Pollack had moved a room of students from considering prejudice in the abstract to seeing it right up close, in the form of a classmate living it each time he walked into a store.

Pollack was chair of the Social Studies Department for some fifteen years and would observe other teachers on a regular basis. He knew enough to see that sometimes teachers were the problem. "I saw subtleties of how they called on white students versus how they called on Black students, and kids are sharp enough to pick up on the subtleties." Subtleties, he said, like tone of voice, irritability, sarcasm.

But he also held parents responsible. "You go to the open house and you [would] think Shaker is a 90 percent white school," he said, referring to the school's back-to-school night. "A significantly large number of

Black parents don't go to the open house." Ditto for parent-teacher conferences. But he understood why this was. Many parents were juggling
child care and work and competing priorities. Some felt uncomfortable
at the school. Some of his colleagues would conclude that these parents
didn't care. But Pollack pointed to a deeper question, one of belonging:
"How do you create a hospitable environment where the message is 'We
want you there'?"

A s Emily Hooper arrived at Shaker Heights High School, her father
remained intensely focused on her academics. He warned her that
if she didn't keep up her grades, she could not participate in theater,
which she loved. On one tenth-grade report card, she got a B in French,
despite having won a national French contest in elementary school, and
a C in math. Her dad was upset, but not by the C. He sat Emily down at
home and said, "I will take the C in math because math has always been
difficult for you. I believe you could be doing your best. I will not accept
this B in French. I know you can do better."

At the start of Emily's sophomore year, she was assigned to regular-
level U.S. History. On the first day of class, the teacher said, "This is our
history book and I want you to open up and see this is the table of contents." Emily replied, "If we've made it this far and we don't know what a
table of contents is, we're in trouble." She was sent to the office and when
she got there, declared she wasn't going back to that class. She was told
the only other option was Advanced Placement U.S. History. Her parents
hadn't even known AP History was an option. Emily said, "Okay, I'll take
that," and she landed in Terry Pollack's classroom.

It was, for Emily as for so many others, a phenomenal class with an outstanding teacher. She remembered Pollack leading a conversation about
the levels system at Shaker. "He really pushed the class to talk about how
we felt about it, and I was adamantly against it." She talked about
how it felt to be racially segregated and how they were losing the chance to
learn together with other students. She recalled that one of her classmates
responded, "I could not be in classes with those kind of people."

Emily was shocked—even frightened—that someone would say that.
"There were a lot of us who pushed back against that," she said, and Pollack was among them. "It was not like the class supported her, but she

felt comfortable and confident about saying that . . . I never forgot that she said that out loud."

Her close-knit group of friends from junior high were still meeting, and they would talk through tough issues of race with Zachary Green, their friend and teacher, who had moved to the high school at the same time.

Green had grown up in Shaker Heights and experienced the racial opportunities, and divides, personally. At Lomond Elementary School, in fifth grade, he was asked to be campaign manager for a student running for Student Council president. The idea was that Zachary was a bookworm, and he'd dress in green with some sort of worm costume on his head. A teacher said no, that this was akin to a "minstrel show." She said, "He needs to wear a suit and tie just like every other campaign manager," Green recalled. "That teacher was aware."

In junior high school, he had been recruited into advanced classes because, he said, there were no other Black kids there. He resisted, worried about being the only Black student and also that he wouldn't do well, which would bring down his grade point average.

Zachary's father, Ernie Green, had been a star running back for the Cleveland Browns. He had grown up in the segregated South, and a community like Shaker represented a significant culture shock. It took time for him to learn the ins and outs of the system, but almost immediately, his fame gave Zachary an extra level of privilege, a singling out that other Black kids did not enjoy, both socially and academically. Administrators watched out for him and his brothers, Zachary said. If something was amiss, maybe his mom got an extra phone call. "My [Black] friends didn't get a second phone call, didn't get an extra opportunity."

He remembered a test on *Moby-Dick* in the eighth grade. Someone behind him asked to borrow a pencil, and after removing one from the briefcase he always carried, Zachary left the briefcase open. His notes were inside, and the teacher accused him of cheating, ripping his test in two on the spot. Later, she returned the exam with half credit. Zachary concluded that she must have spoken with another teacher who told her, "That kid's a good one." He suspected a different Black kid would not have gotten the benefit of the doubt.

Now, as a teacher at Shaker high school, Zachary Green saw things from the other side. He worked with a lot of Black students, many of them behind academically. He tried hard, and saw many other teachers trying hard, to help Black kids achieve. They sometimes had to fight teens' attitudes, with social identity trumping academic achievement. Students, in turn, were victims of bias baked into the system. "Teachers didn't think you could do it, and friends reinforced it. So you believed it."

He also saw how Black kids watched as wealthy white students came back from winter break with a mid-January tan, a telltale sign of a tropical vacation, or heard about tennis camp as classes began again in the fall. "That all was part of growing up in Shaker," he said. "That issue, the conflation of the social class issues with race, is a part of the story that doesn't get told."

Green saw that younger teachers at Shaker were trying, even as some older teachers were in mourning for the "pristine" Shaker of old. What was missing, Green thought, was kids talking to each other about all these difficult things.

As a teacher at Byron Junior High, he had begun opening his room during lunch for a small group of students who were interested in learning peer counseling skills from him. It was a rare interracial group, and the students found themselves discussing tough subjects like divorce and health and family but also the challenge of growing up in a community with so much racial, religious, and economic diversity. "Zack was cool and it was fun," remembered Ken Danford, who is white and was one of about ten kids in the collection of students who called themselves Group. Around the same time the students moved up to the high school, so did Zachary Green. Group stayed together. "By the eleventh grade," Danford said, "we were tight."

After the John Gray assembly, where the fake bigot turned out to be Black, Group came together to talk it through with Green.

Decades later, Terry Pollack remained enormously proud of the John Gray event. He had been the one to introduce him, and the pair fake-parried onstage. In an essay for *Shaker Life* magazine celebrating the school district's centennial, Pollack, who had by then been a teacher in Shaker for forty-eight years, singled out this event as a highlight of his tenure.

But in Zachary Green's classroom later that day, the entire Group was livid about the stunt. "We were like, that was some bullshit," Danford said. Allegedly, the discussion was supposed to continue in homerooms. "In my homeroom, we didn't talk about it at all," he said. "It wasn't funny. It didn't prove anything."

Group gathered a day or so later for their peer counseling meeting with Green and resolved: we should do something. Green replied, "What should we do?"

———————

On the high school faculty around this time there was rising concern about the gaps in achievement between Black and white students.

Government teacher Jerry Graham sounded an alarm in a letter to Superintendent Peter Horoschak. "A number of faculty members at the Senior High continue to be quite concerned about the disproportionately large number of our black students who are doing poorly academically," he wrote. Graham wanted to know: How did the district plan to address this? Another memo around this time, from English teacher Bill Newby, said the issue of minority achievement was "a source of chronic frustration" at the high school.

The bleak numbers pushed the district to look for new ideas and fresh strategies to close the gaps. One proposal, for instance, recommended academic interventions at the earliest possible primary grade, compulsory for those who qualified.

"These students begin their school experience getting the message, 'you cannot perform as well academically as others.' This message gets reinforced each year throughout the next 12 years," the proposal concluded. "Such a situation needs to be changed."

———————

In the aftermath of the John Gray hoax assembly, Zachary Green's peer counseling group—Emily Hooper, Ken Danford, and the rest of Group—started talking about where things started to go wrong in Shaker.

They agreed that high school was too late for even a well-done event about racial attitudes. Racial attitudes form much earlier. It's really junior high, they realized, when racial stratification begins. Cross-racial friendships are normal and expected in Shaker elementary schools, but they seemed to fall apart in junior high, as social and academic pressures amp up. By the time high school arrives, Danford said, "Boom, everyone is separated."

"So we said, there needs to be a program where we go talk to elementary school kids and tell them to be aware, be conscious, look around in sixth grade, think about who you want to be friends with," he said. "Zack was like, 'All right, sounds good, let's do it.'"

And they did.

That spring, Green met with the superintendent, and the students met with all nine elementary school principals. They floated the idea of a three-day program for students in sixth grade, the last year of elementary school—one day in the fall, one in the winter, one in the spring. They would talk about trust, race, peer counseling skills—all the things these students had been working through for years in Group.

In June, eight of the students visited seventh grade classrooms to talk with younger students and see if their own perceptions rang true. They did. Visiting junior high again, it seemed the major racial split happens in seventh grade. As a result, students who wanted to maintain cross-racial friendships were alienated from friends of their own race. "The two races tend to fear each other," the students wrote in a summary of their findings. "We found white students who actually expressed physical fear of black students. Conversely, we found black students who fear intellectual inferiority. It was not rare for black students to actually say that they are stupid and less intelligent than their white peers."

That summer of 1983 they submitted a formal proposal for what they would call the Student Group on Race Relations, or SGORR. In a memo to the superintendent and other senior officials dated July 14, 1983, they wrote:

"As a racially and sexually balanced group of juniors and seniors at SHHS we witness daily the problems which exist in the area of racism and segregation in our schools. The situation concerns us greatly; we see tension, termination of friendship, and general distrust as a result of it. We think we all agree that a problem does exist and that we understand the forms in which it manifests itself." They wrote about junior high as the key dividing point. "We have lost friends, experienced alienation, and seen two separate worlds develop. During our years in elementary school, there was no split; a feeling of unity pervaded. Upon arrival at Byron, we encountered our first instances of (voluntary?) segregation."

In just a couple of months, the group developed a remarkably detailed plan for the program, with high school students who were part of SGORR spending three afternoons with sixth graders over the course of their last year of elementary school. In October, they would teach vocabulary words dealing with race, like "discrimination," and watch and discuss a Bill Cosby film on prejudice. In February, students would discuss feelings and preconceptions about junior high school. And in May, they would role-play racially divisive situations with the goal of finding alternatives to polarization.

Green, who was now twenty-seven, was leaving the district after that summer to continue his graduate work. He called Marcia Jaffe, a sixth grade teacher at Mercer Elementary School with whom he had talked frequently about education. He asked her to take on this project. "You're the only person I would trust to nurture this," he told her. She agreed.

They were both impressed with the students' motivation and work on the program. Neither one thought it would last long, but in fact, Jaffe would help nurture and grow SGORR for decades to come. When she died in 2020, Green and more than 20 SGORR members would travel to Baltimore for her memorial service.

———

Like many in Group, Emily Hooper was on the Shaker speech and debate team, at that time a powerhouse in the state of Ohio. One weekend in March during her sophomore year, she traveled with the team to Cincinnati for the state finals tournament, where she competed in the oratorical interpretation event. Her piece was intense and heavy with racial themes, an excerpt from the play *Funnyhouse of a Negro*, by Adrienne Kennedy, which chronicled the final hours and inner life of a biracial woman struggling with race and identity.

Emily had hesitated to go because her father, then sixty-one, had gone into the hospital just before. But he was in and out of the hospital a lot with breathing troubles. "The doctor said go and win it for your dad," she recalled.

Emily performed her piece and received perfect scores from two of the three judges but a low mark from the third, which took her out of competition and which she suspected related to the racial nature of her topic, presented in a conservative part of the state. Emily was furious. She also was frustrated. She couldn't reach her father. No one was answering the home phone.

She came home Saturday night with the team and saw her dad for the last time Sunday morning. He died that evening of emphysema, the day before Emily's sixteenth birthday. On Monday night, Emily's friends from Group, Black and white, crowded into the compact living room of her family's Moreland home, huddled around the coffee table for cake, to comfort their friend, to mark her birthday.

When it was time to apply for college, Emily kept thinking about something her father had told her. He always said, "My baby girl's going to grow up and go to Yale." Emily never knew why he was focused on Yale. Yale wasn't on her radar in particular. She wanted to study acting. But her father meant everything to her, so she went to see her counselor and told her she'd like to apply to Yale.

The counselor looked at her and condescendingly said, "Oh dear, that's going to be a far reach for you," Emily recalled. "People are going to see this C in math. This isn't going to happen for you, sweetie." And Emily replied, "Well, I want to do it anyway."

Emily was admitted—to Yale, as well as New York University, Boston University, Carnegie Mellon University, and others. She visited New Haven and, to her surprise, it felt like somewhere she could learn and grow. With the help of a generous scholarship, she enrolled. Four years later, Emily graduated with honors.

When you don't want to face a hot issue, appoint a committee.
—Carolyn Milter

10

CAROLYN MILTER

In June 1983, something unusual happened. At least it was unusual for Shaker Heights. Voters rejected a proposed tax increase to support the schools.

The schools were facing a huge budget shortfall, but some Shaker residents had lost patience with the repeated tax increases. This request was the third in three years, and a group called Halt Automatic Local Taxes campaigned against the levy, arguing the district should save money by closing schools. Enrollment had fallen from more than 8,000 students at the height of the Baby Boom in 1966 to about 5,300, yet Shaker still had nine elementary schools and two junior highs, in addition to one citywide high school.

School officials were stunned by the loss, and while they made plans to try again that August (and won on the second try), they also took the critics' arguments to heart. Within weeks of the levy's defeat, a high-powered, forty-three-member citizens' committee was formed to study utilization of school facilities.

Among the appointees was Carolyn Milter, a white woman who was raising her daughters in Ludlow and had been active in the Ludlow Community Association, serving as a housing activist, an adviser to Winston Richie, and a vocal advocate for racial integration.

When she walked into the Shaker schools administration building for the first meeting of the School Facilities Utilization Study Committee, she was stunned to see a room full of men. Normally it was the moms who volunteered for school-related activities. But this committee was composed of thirty-five men and thirteen women.

"I don't know how this is going to go," Milter thought to herself. It was moms, she knew, who understood the nuances of school. They understood the ramifications when a school had only one fourth grade class and a parent didn't like the fourth grade teacher.

The committee was carefully assembled to include people from every neighborhood, and to Milter, they each might as well have been wearing a T-shirt emblazoned with their turf. She wondered how they might ever come to agreement.

The panel was led by a heavy hitter—Frederick Snowden, a senior executive at Republic Steel Corporation—and packed with the type of people whose recommendations were likely to carry weight: attorneys, professors, a management consultant, a pediatrician, business executives, city planners, a banker, and a real estate agent, as well as teachers, school officials, and parents, both Black and white, but mostly white. That part didn't bother Milter. "I understood that it was the white people who had the power and if this committee was going to do something and be accepted, it had to be done by white people," Milter said. "Back then everybody understood who is going to be making the decisions: the white people."

Milter, who was tall and slim and wore her brown hair short, had by now been around politics for decades. She started her career as a reporter for the *Cleveland Press* and then worked for open housing, including for the Urban League's Operation Equality program. She served as a press secretary for Democratic campaigns in Ohio for governor and Congress, and in Representative Dennis Eckart's district office. Later, she would work communications for the Cuyahoga County commissioners.

Milter had had her share of run-ins with the city. She blamed Shaker for destroying the housing program begun in Ludlow and thought the city's housing director was an outright racist. She thought the decision to locate the garbage facility in Moreland—and then punish those who opposed it—was shameful. So as work began on this new schools committee, she assumed this was not an assembly that would be overly concerned about racial justice, though the group's mandate did include promoting integration.

And as a Ludlow resident, she feared others might want to close her school. "Because I was from Ludlow, I felt like we were kind of outliers in the overall Shaker power thing, and whatever was going to happen was going to happen to us rather than by us."

———————

Carolyn and Burt Milter had not started out in Shaker Heights. First they tried the nearby suburb of East Cleveland, but it didn't take long before they realized it was not going to be the place of racially integrated living they had anticipated.

It was the early 1960s, and Black families had just started moving into East Cleveland, once one of the region's most prestigious communities. The Milters wanted to live in a racially diverse area, but their white neighbors were worked up, and flyers advertising a community meeting at the local junior high school were everywhere. They decided to attend and were stunned by what they heard. "It was clear the white people were going to try to keep the Blacks out and, if that didn't work, they were going to leave," Carolyn recalled. (In fact, whites would rapidly depart the suburb, as the Black population jumped from 2 percent in 1960 to 67 percent in 1970.)

Around the time of that meeting, someone passed Carolyn a newsletter from the Ludlow Community Association in Shaker Heights. She and Burt were excited to find a neighborhood that was intentionally working toward racial integration, and they contacted a real estate agent, who was Black; white agents had abandoned the area. When the agent didn't have any houses to show, the couple approached the Ludlow housing program. "They really didn't have to sell me on it," she said. "When I arrived on the doorstep of the program, we already knew that I wanted to move there." In 1964, they bought a house on Keswick Road from a Black couple.

Their new next-door neighbor was William Percy, who had once threatened to sue the Ludlow association over its discriminatory tactics. He came over to welcome the Milters and also to offer a small warning. His wife, Percy said, was nervous about a white family moving in next door. She'd always lived around Black people, he explained, and didn't know what to expect. Carolyn was amazed, and a bit delighted. Wasn't it the white people who were usually anxious about living near Black families? "Here is a woman who is nervous about me moving in instead of the reverse."

———————

The Shaker Schools Plan had successfully launched in 1970, with 250 students volunteering to be bused out of or into Moreland Elementary School. Participation fell after that, but the program had become part of the fabric of the district. Shaker won a $135,000 federal grant, so there was now an office dedicated to running and promoting the plan—directed by Beverly Mason, whose family had personally integrated Ludlow in 1955.

The plan was a success, but a limited one, given that this was a district with thousands of students and nine elementary schools. Shaker officials worried their stab at integration might not be enough. In 1976, fewer than two hundred students were participating, and outside pressure was building on the district to take bolder action.

School officials were particularly concerned with events next door in Cleveland, where a school desegregation case, *Reed v. Rhodes*, was making its way through the federal courts. It had been filed by the NAACP in 1973 after the city spent years resisting desegregation through policies such as one allowing white parents to transfer if they didn't want their children to attend a majority Black school. Black students had been crammed into Black schools, while white schools enjoyed extra space. Teachers were assigned to buildings based on their race.

"This school system is a classic case of duality; it's as segregated as any that would have been found in the South and is more segregated than most major school districts in the South today," Nathaniel R. Jones, general counsel of the NAACP, said in 1973. In August 1976, federal district Judge Frank Battisti, who was overseeing the Cleveland case, found the Cleveland schools in violation of the Constitution, but he did not immediately order a remedy, leading to anxiety in Shaker and elsewhere about how broad his order might be.

The question was whether Battisti, or perhaps the state of Ohio, might bring students from adjacent suburbs into the same system as students in Cleveland, with Shaker students bused to Cleveland and vice versa. In 1974, the Supreme Court had set a high bar for including suburbs in desegregation plans of central cities, but the NAACP asked the court to order a metropolitan school plan in the case, and some thought Battisti might go along, especially given the challenge of integrating Black students on Cleveland's east side with white students on the west side.

In Shaker, Superintendent Jack Taylor, who had replaced Jack

Lawson, was repeatedly asked what impact the Battisti decision would have on Shaker. In a September 1976 memo to the staff, Taylor explained the district could face pressure from both the federal courts and the federal education department. "If we are to avoid being included eventually in any plan mandated by the Battisti Decision, we must show that we are in total compliance," Taylor wrote.

Later that month, Taylor spoke to some 350 people at a PTA Council meeting, where an audience member suggested the Battisti decision could destroy neighborhood schools. Devotion to neighborhood schools has long been both a fiercely held value and a common excuse for opposition to integration. Taylor replied that countywide busing was not likely, though not impossible.

In June 1977, Mark Freeman, the director of federal-state relations for Shaker schools, appeared before a congressional committee in Washington and was pressed as to whether Shaker had considered cross-busing with the City of Cleveland.

Also around this time, the Ohio State Board of Education was considering how to force school districts to racially balance their schools. In June 1978, the board would direct the state education department to survey every Ohio school building to determine which had racial makeups that "substantially" varied from their districts as a whole. (That was defined as having a minority student population that was 15 or more percentage points lower or higher than the overall district. Districts out of compliance were to take action to desegregate their schools.)

With these pressures bearing down, in the fall of 1977 Shaker expanded its voluntary busing plan to every school. Now any student could attend any elementary school and either junior high, as long as the transfer would improve the racial balance at the new school. And the district created magnet programs, such as one at Ludlow called Special Projects, which drew students from across the district to a gifted and talented program for students who showed particular creativity. (This program was popular with parents, though it created its own integration challenge: the Special Projects classrooms were mostly white, while those with neighborhood kids remained mostly Black.)

Battisti ultimately ordered busing to remedy segregation in Cleveland schools, and the program began in 1979. The court did not include the suburbs, and the state school board never ordered inter-district integration, either. But the pressure from the case, and from the state, spurred

Shaker to expand its integration efforts at a time when the Black population in the schools continued to climb, rising to 37 percent in 1979–80.

The voluntary busing and magnet programs succeeded in reducing racial imbalance across the district. At Moreland Elementary School, for instance, Black students would have made up 96 percent of students in 1980 if all students attended their neighborhood schools; with the busing plan, Moreland was 72 percent Black. On the other side of town, Malvern Elementary School's Black student population climbed from 5 to 20 percent. Despite these successes, five of the nine elementary schools were out of compliance with the state's 15 percent metric. Moreland and Ludlow had too many Black students, and Malvern, Mercer, and Fernway had too few.

District officials continued to look for new ideas. In 1981, they expanded the magnet program, putting a French program at Lomond and a math and computer program at Moreland, trying to draw more volunteers. It was a common strategy across the country to encourage integration and generally popular because no one was being required to participate. It was all carrots.

Nonetheless, concerns were voiced by some white parents in Shaker, who argued it wasn't fair that these special programs were only available at certain schools. One parent from Malvern, the wealthiest neighborhood in Shaker, said the magnet program had created "curriculum inequity." Of course, the whole idea was to create incentives for families to choose other schools; if these programs existed everywhere, there would be no incentive.

Still, the overall feeling in Shaker Heights was pride in what was being accomplished.

"Virtually no other district has been able to accomplish so much in the same time period *with or without* a *court order*," Arthur W. Steller, assistant superintendent for elementary education, wrote in a June 1982 memo to the school board. "Shaker Heights has once again demonstrated the kind of educational leadership to which every other school district in this country looks to as a model."

━━━━━━

Integration was making a real difference in the lives of at least some of the children growing up in Shaker. This was driven home for Carolyn Milter one evening at dinner with her two daughters, who attended

Ludlow Elementary School. Nancy, then a second grader, announced to the table: "A long time ago, some of us were slaves in America."

Her sister, Joanna, a fourth grader, replied, "Dummy, we weren't slaves ever, but our ancestors were."

Milter found her mouth agape. She had grown up in the 1940s and '50s in the West Virginia town of Ravenswood, along the Ohio River, where virtually everyone was white. In Ravenswood, it's fair to say, white people did not think of themselves—or their ancestors—as being among those who were enslaved.

Carolyn hadn't known any Black people herself, but she grew up hearing stories about her grandfather and great-grandfather, both doctors, who, the story went, had treated a couple of Black families who lived in the county at the time. The first time she met a Black person was at a Methodist church conference. She and a Black student had both been nominated for offices and had to wait in the hallway during the balloting. They introduced themselves and stood in the hallway, talking. That was it.

In high school, Carolyn grew fascinated by the history of slavery. Once, a kid in her class called out something about Blacks not accomplishing much. She shot back, "Have you ever heard of Ralph Bunche?"—a Black American diplomat who was awarded the Nobel Peace Prize for his work in the Middle East. After that, the most popular boy in her class, the star football player, teased Carolyn, giving her the nickname Chocolate Drop. It didn't bother her.

Now her children were students at Ludlow Elementary School, a majority Black school where they were learning through a new lens.

"Weren't we slaves once, Mommy?" Nancy pressed.

Her mom finally replied, "Yes, it's true some of us were slaves once."

─────

As the work of the School Facilities Utilization Study Committee got underway, all of Milter's reservations melted away. Yes, it was being run by a business executive and was full of others cut from a similar cloth, but she came to appreciate what they brought to the table. Snowden, the chair, was "wonderful," she realized. "He absolutely ran this sort of large unwieldy committee in a fair, intelligent way."

Slowly, committee members began to trust one another, Milter said, and grew comfortable enough to talk about the implications of closing school buildings, and about race. Members looked at data, including complex analyses produced by members whose businesses had access to sophisticated programming. These calculations made the urgency of closing schools clear. Malvern, for instance, had a fifth grade class with just twelve students. At Sussex, one fourth grade class had fourteen students and another sixteen. Those small class sizes came with huge costs.

But closing schools, especially elementary schools, was among the most controversial things a district could do. Shaker neighborhoods were built around their elementary schools, most of them set on ovals with parks and playgrounds and parent associations. That's how the Van Sweringens had designed the community in the first place—each neighborhood with its own little village center. Neighborhood identities were tied directly to the elementary schools, with people saying they lived in Sussex or in Mercer or Malvern, and everyone knowing what that meant.

At a community meeting about the committee's work led by Snowden, a succession of parents and homeowners stood to voice opposition to closing schools, with some speaking negatively about integration as well. One man said families already were putting their children into private schools or choosing not to move into Malvern, where he lived, and said closing schools would exacerbate the problem. He appeared to be referring to the voluntary busing plan already in place, which he told the leaders was a product of "well-meaning people such as yourselves" who had made "some major errors."

"I would submit that if schools are closed, you will multiply a problem which already exists, that you will drive additional people out of the district, and that you will ultimately do serious if not fatal damage to this community," he said.

The committee recommended a bold plan that would save $1.7 million per year, about 6.5 percent of the district's 1983 operating costs. Two of the nine elementary schools would close: Moreland, with the highest concentration of Black students, and Malvern, with the highest concentration of white students. The committee noted that the schools were set in different parts of town without stating what was obvious to anyone in Shaker: one was set among the city's wealthiest students and the other its poorest. In addition, the Shaker Heights library wanted to expand and had its eye on Moreland school, Milter recalled. The committee reasoned that Malvern Elementary could be perfect for high-end condominiums, whose sale could raise money for the district.

The committee recommended a "cluster system": Four elementary schools would serve kindergarten through third grade, and three would serve grades four, five, and six. That would allow the district to create a near perfect racial balance in each school, as well as the greatest cost savings because class sizes could be optimized.

In addition, the committee recommended closing Byron Junior High School and consolidating grades seven and eight at a new middle school at Woodbury Junior High School. This would save money but also promote integration, as all students would be at the same school starting in seventh grade. Ninth grade would move to the high school.

When they were done, Snowden celebrated the committee's work by giving each member of the group a faux Monopoly game board filled with Shaker references and in-jokes. The properties were clustered in neighborhoods, with Moreland and Ludlow the cheapest and Mercer in the Boardwalk slot. One square was a property tax: "Pay 10% or move to Chagrin Falls," a tony hamlet to the east. And the word "Monopoly" was rendered as an acronym for Move Other Neighborhoods Only. Protect Our Little Youngsters. Years later, Milter found her copy and was touched all over by the gesture. "It's like when the skiers get bouquets at the Olympics. These Monopoly things were our bouquets."

Opposition quickly emerged, concentrated in the two neighborhoods that were losing their schools. "Malvern was furious," Milter said. She recalled one school board member who lived in Malvern and said he would never vote to close the school. Malvern residents had no interest in turning their school into condos, high end or not.

Katherine McWilliams, who had sent her son Doug to Moreland during the early days of the Shaker Schools Plan, was now on the school board and supported the school closure plan. She saw it as the best way to achieve integration, and recalled traveling to homes around the community, talking with people about the subject. "Everybody wanted to keep their neighborhood school," she said in an interview. Doug remembered his mom coming home late many evenings after these sessions, "frustrated, rarely exhilarated."

Earl Leiken, who was elected to the school board in 1983, also recalled frustration with Shaker's inability to rally around any plan. "They were all receptive to integration, but they weren't receptive to having their little kids bused around," Leiken said. "We were looking for consensus and we didn't get it. We got division."

Peter Horoschak was superintendent now, and he put forward his own twist on the plan, with different schools closing and new protests from those areas. That, too, was unpopular.

The school board mostly punted. In September 1984, it voted to move the ninth grade to the high school, the one idea everyone seemed to agree on, and close Woodbury Junior High, consolidating the seventh and eighth grades into a middle school at Byron. It left elementary schools alone.

McWilliams was irritated. She voted for the modified plan, but drew sustained applause when she said the board should have followed the citizens committee's recommendation for clustering primary schools. "The issue of any elementary school closings in Shaker Heights has simply proven to be stressful, divisive, and highly controversial," Leiken said that night.

———

With all these views swirling, the school board election of 1985 was shaping up to be a referendum on the school reorganization plan. Milter remembered attending a community meeting that spring or summer. It was a nice evening, so she walked there. On the way out, Steven Minter asked if he could drive her home.

Minter, who was Black, was a major player in Shaker. President of the Cleveland Foundation, an important local philanthropy that had repeatedly supported Shaker's integration work, he had also been a political appointee in the Carter administration, helping to create the new Department of Education. And he was a leader of the Shaker Heights Citizens Committee, which endorsed and helped elect local candidates.

"We have to do something," he told Milter as he drove her home. The school board's moves were not good enough, he said, and she agreed. He urged her to run for the five-member school board to push for a bold and fair plan. His encouragement alone was enough to persuade Milter to run. "He was such an important person and I had so much respect for him." She also knew the decisions ahead were critical and saw herself as being in position to look out for Ludlow's interests. One of her children teased her, "Mom, the only reason you're willing to go on the school board is you know there's a big fight about closing the schools." And Milter knew that was true. "I had never in my life walked around saying to myself, 'Someday I want to be on the school board.'"

She ran on a slate with two others, all three endorsed by the Citizens

Committee. She said their campaign platform was obvious. "We didn't say, 'We're going to go in and close a bunch of schools,'" she said. "It was clear what we were sent there to do."

They won and took office in 1986, joining Earl Leiken, who was eager to try again. Leiken, who was vice president of the board and then, in 1987, president, had had some time to think about what had happened and how to avoid a repeat. He now realized community consensus wasn't possible. The board was going to need to develop a plan on its own, get feedback, and then have the courage to make a decision.

─────────

The community remained on edge as the question lurked. Paula Hooper, the daughter of Earline and Lorenzo Hooper who had been bused from Moreland during the first year of the Shaker Schools Plan, was now a second grade teacher at Fernway Elementary School, a mostly white neighborhood with lovely homes, though not mansions, filled with professionals who had long held sway in Shaker politics.

Hooper was working late one night and could hear screaming from a community meeting in the school gym pouring into the hallway. Parents were angrily refusing to send their kids to nearby Moreland school, which some evidently feared might be the plan. "We're not sending our kids across Lee Road!" she remembered one person exclaiming. "We don't want them going toward that area." Some said the value of their homes would drop if students from the neighborhood were assigned to a school in a Black area.

To Hooper, the voices were so racist and so upsetting that she dared not enter the room. Moreland was where she grew up, where her mother still lived. And she truly loved her Fernway students and liked their parents. She didn't want to know who was saying these things.

This time around, instead of going smaller, the school board decided to go bigger. The previous board had been unable to close two elementary schools. In January 1987, the new board announced that four schools would close, but didn't say which ones. Leiken and other board members said the plan was needed because of dwindling enrollment, to save money, and to revitalize an inadequate integration program.

The next month, the board told four hundred people packed into the Shaker Heights High School auditorium that their plan was to close Moreland and Ludlow, two majority Black schools, and Malvern and

Sussex, two majority white schools. The decision was cast as racially balanced. Of 960 elementary school students to be bused the next year, 54 percent were Black. Still, three of the four targeted schools were on the less-affluent south side of Van Aken Boulevard. And of the city's three majority Black schools, two would be closing.

The Moreland community was furious, with some picketing the high school during the meeting. Kathryn Sears, a white parent whose first grader attended Moreland, complained to the *Plain Dealer* that Moreland was being closed so Black students could be "distributed" to other schools, and so Shaker could meet its integration goals. The community found itself not far from where it had started sixteen years earlier: "It's unfair to put the busing burden on one community," she said. Sears also wrote a letter to the editor, where she was harsher.

"It would appear that the white parents are afraid of allowing their children to be bused into a predominantly black neighborhood," she wrote. "Our community needs its own elementary school and it is clear to me that if Moreland closes, it is just one more example of racial prejudice against the people I have come to love and greatly respect."

The Fernway Community Association was also opposed. Even though Fernway had kept its school, the boundaries were being redrawn and some residents would be zoned for other schools.

As it became clear that Ludlow was on the chopping block, Milter met with the Ludlow Community Association. She tried to help her neighbors understand. Ludlow's population was falling faster than most other schools. The school was no longer racially balanced. The board had to find savings. But opposition ran deep.

"If we had known they were going to close the school, we never would have bought the house," said Lorenzo Marsh, who had chosen his home so his children would be a block from the school.

Levin G. Armwood, a Ludlow graduate who had lived in the neighborhood for thirty years, told the *Plain Dealer* that the plan seemed even-handed but still felt wrong. "You just feel that if you're black, no matter what you do, you end up on the short end of the stick," he said.

One of Milter's closest friends let her know how upset she was. She made one request: "Well, we need to keep that playground. That playground is so important." The friend could see kids playing there from her kitchen window, could see how important it was as a gathering place for the neighborhood. The final plan kept all the playgrounds, with money budgeted to maintain them.

In the end, the Ludlow Community Association voted to support the plan. "I was eternally grateful," Milter said. "It just showed how wonderful Ludlow was."

The Sussex community also accepted that their school was closing and quickly began thinking about what other services could land there. (Ultimately, the school became home to several preschool programs.) "Overall, we're more concerned about the city of Shaker Heights rather than our neighborhood," said Jay M. Schonfeld, president of the Sussex association, showing a remarkable amount of perspective. "If it means quality education, we're willing to have our school closed."

Under the plan, the five remaining elementary schools would educate grades kindergarten through four, with boundary lines redrawn to racially balance each school. After that, all the district's students would attend the same school: Woodbury would be reopened as an upper elementary school for fifth and sixth grades; the old Byron Junior High, now called Shaker Middle School, would serve seventh and eighth; all students would attend the high school for grades nine through twelve. The result was that all schools would be integrated, with perfect racial balance starting in fifth grade.

Busing was offered for all students who had to cross a major roadway to get to their new school. Most bused children were assigned to schools relatively close to their homes—except for Moreland kids. They would face a thirty-one-minute bus ride across town to Mercer Elementary School, in an overwhelmingly white neighborhood on the eastern edge of the city. Some Moreland parents referred to it as an "airlift."

Leiken received about thirty phone calls and seventy letters, he told the *Plain Dealer*. Still, he told the paper that the atmosphere was "substantially calmer" than it had been in 1984. Years later, he did not recall any discussion of the transportation impact on Moreland students. "Whether some kids got bused a little farther than other kids—I'm sure we didn't discuss that," he said. Milter also didn't recall that being an issue. "Every once in a while people would toss out a piece of information about how quickly you can get to anywhere in Shaker Heights," she said. "It didn't get to my doorstep that we had to worry about kids being bused too far."

The night of the vote in March 1987, Leiken was exhilarated. After

At the turn of the century, brothers O. P. and M. J. Van Sweringen transformed Shaker Heights from an abandoned swath of land into an elite suburban refuge with exacting architectural standards for wealthy white Clevelanders.

In the process of developing light rail from Shaker Heights into Cleveland, the Van Sweringen brothers wound up buying railroad and developing a grand train depot on Public Square in the center of downtown. Their Terminal Tower became the iconic landmark for the city of Cleveland.

From the start, Shaker Heights was marked by its natural beauty, including Horseshoe Lake, which was created by the original Shaker colony.

Many of the early Shaker homes were large, none more so than the Van Sweringen mansion on South Park Boulevard.

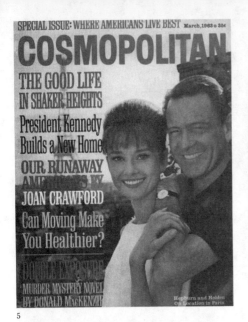

5

6

The Vans set strict, conservative rules for architecture, with only colonial, English Tudor, and country French acceptable.

In March 1963, *Cosmopolitan* magazine put Shaker Heights on its cover with a gushing story about opulence and privilege: "Here is the inside story of an American dream town come true."

7

John and Dorothy Pegg were building a home in the Ludlow neighborhood when, in January 1956, the garage was firebombed. They were among the first Black families to move into the neighborhood, and racial motives were suspected. About thirty people from the neighborhood gathered to help clean up the debris and serve coffee to the workers. The incident set off a drive among Black and white families to build and maintain an integrated neighborhood.

8

The Ludlow Community Association marketed the neighborhood as a rare example of
successful, integrated living. This 1967 promotional brochure contrasted "fury and violence" elsewhere in the country with Ludlow,
where the community "is handling this vast
social change in a far different way." In the
center of the photo, pointing to a map of the
neighborhood, is Beverly Mason. She and her
husband were the first Black buyers in Ludlow.
Later, Mason would run the Shaker schools' integration plan.

9

10

The Van Sweringen brothers developed Shaker Square, on the
edge of Shaker Heights, in the 1920s as one of the country's first
shopping centers, with architectural style and standards consistent with their suburban planning.

11

Students at Ludlow Elementary School, including
Winston Richie Jr., age six (next to the teacher),
participate in a program on patriotism in 1962.
Ludlow was the first Shaker Heights elementary
school to serve a racially diverse student body.

12

Shaker schools superintendent John H. Lawson,
known as Jack, led the district to adopt a voluntary
school desegregation plan in 1970.

Earline Hooper was among the parents—Black and white—who in 1970 voluntarily put their children on buses to desegregate the Shaker elementary schools. "There was a lot of research showing that separation was not equal education," she said.

13

Winston Richie and his family helped integrate two neighborhoods in Shaker Heights—first Ludlow, then Mercer. He served three terms on City Council before leading an effort to integrate other Cleveland suburbs.

14

A Cleveland city councilman erected a sign over Lee Road, at the border of Shaker Heights and Cleveland, accusing Shaker Heights of apartheid. The action came after Shaker erected traffic barriers on side streets that had connected the two cities. A battle over the barricades, which extended for years through the courts, was as much about class as it was about race.

16

15

Carolyn Milter, an activist with the Ludlow Community Association, later was elected to the school board as the district considered a plan to close elementary schools. In this 1978 photo she was working as press secretary for the Dick Celeste gubernatorial campaign.

Reuben Harris Jr. got involved as a volunteer with the Shaker schools after he noticed teachers treating Black and white children differently. He led an organization devoted to helping Black parents navigate the school system and later served on the school board.

17

In 1987, the high school newspaper the *Shakerite* published an article about the racial achievement gap that angered many members of the Black community and spurred a renewed effort to address the problem.

VOLUME 67 • ISSUE 5   FEBRUARY 28, 1997

SHAKERITE

SHAKER HEIGHTS HIGH SCHOOL • 15911 ALDERSYDE DRIVE • SHAKER HEIGHTS, OHIO 44120

Black & White
or shades of gray?

The Problem
Shaker Heights High School statistics

→ 82% of students who failed 1 or more of the Ohio State Ninth Grade Proficiency Exam subtests were black
→ 84% of students who earned an end-of-semester grade of a D or F in one or more academic classes were black
→ In academic years '89-'90 through '93-'94, of all semester grades earned by black students in the English, math, science, and social studies departments, 40% were either D or F.
→ 80% of black students either failed a proficiency subtest or received an academic grade of D or F in at least 1 class, or both.
→ In graduating classes between '92 and '95, the average SAT score of black students was 905 points less than that of white students
—facts compiled from Project Achieve report

The Solutions
to be implemented for the '97-'98 school year as proposed by Project Achieve

→ Early Childhood Intervention Program
  One early childhood specialist for every 2 kindergarten classes to help students who are performing below their peers and the addition of psychologists and learning disability service positions
→ School/community Outreach Program
  Principal George Cannon and Parent liaison Gail Rose are working on ways to increase parental involvement in education, such as evening sessions
→ Professional Development Program
  Workshops to facilitate communication between staff members about achievement
→ Modernization of Technology
  Wiring school classrooms and libraries for computers

Study in achievement between the races
reveals disparity, prompts frustration & solutions

BY NAWAL ATWAN
Co-News Editor

18

Greg Hutchings, shown here at Woodbury Elementary School, began a five-year tenure as superintendent in 2013, promising to address questions of racial equity head-on—thrilling some and alienating others. "In Shaker, we've been talking about diversity, we've been talking about equity for a very long time," he said soon after arrival. "It's time to take action."

19

20a

20b

An uncomfortable conversation between Olivia McDowell, then a high school junior, and her Advanced Placement English teacher, Jody Podl, in 2018 set off a contentious community debate.

21

Olivia McDowell jumped to the stage during a loud and raucous community meeting in November 2018, outing herself as the student who had been admonished in class by her teacher for not having her assignment done. Administrators David Glasner (center) and Stephen Wilkins listened but had little to say.

22

Teachers were among those who showed up in force for the November 2018 community meeting.

David Glasner, who was named superintendent in 2019, initially intended to address questions around academic tracking incrementally but wound up changing the system dramatically in one fell swoop. "If we wait 'til everybody's ready, we'll never be ready," he said.

23

Eric Juli, principal of Shaker Heights High School, questioned whether core values around academic rigor held by many people in Shaker make sense anymore. Each morning, he delivered the morning announcements, always ending by telling students, "Make it a great day, or not. The choice is yours."

24

25

Kim Harris was a young single mom, struggling to make it, when she first moved to Shaker. "I was so out of the loop, I didn't even know I was out of the loop," she said. Later she tried to help other struggling moms and also tangled with school administrators over their priorities.

27

26

The author as a child, in her driveway in the Sussex neighborhood of Shaker Heights, and with her next-door neighbors. In the pool are (left to right) the author's childhood best friend, Betsy, who now goes by Mary Allen; Missy (Lardie) Maroun and Maria (Lardie) Hewitt, who are twins; and the author.

Jim and Diane Lardie, the author's childhood next-door neighbors, adopted five of their six children and devoted their lives to helping children across the state of Ohio. Their multiracial family was the embodiment of Shaker Heights values.

28

three years of debate, the board was acting. Some 250 people crowded into the high school auditorium, and the board heard public comments from about fifteen residents, mostly opposed to their plan.

The vote was called, and the plan was approved 5–0. Then the board went into executive session to consider some mundane matters.

"What are we doing here?" Leiken thought to himself. "I feel like going out and celebrating!"

Milter was proud of the decision too, but in the end she didn't feel like celebrating. She had just voted to close Ludlow, the school that had educated her three children, the literal and figurative center of a community she fell for after reading a newsletter touting integration. Ludlow Elementary was the heartbeat of a neighborhood that had once upon a time defied the sociologists and made water run uphill.

She left the meeting and got into her car. As she drove home to Ludlow, she began to cry.

———

Ultimately, the neighborhoods accepted their fates, and Shaker began to feel good about itself again. Leiken was easily reelected to the school board, though a write-in candidate who opposed school closures received more than a thousand votes. The community's support for integration—beginning with the Ludlow Community Association, and fostered by the city's housing program and the Shaker Schools Plan— had been affirmed again.

Shaker's citywide integration plan took effect, as it turned out, just a year before school integration peaked in America. After that, courts began releasing districts from their mandatory desegregation plans, and progress made in response to *Brown v. Board of Education* began to unravel. In the years that followed, Black and Latino students became more likely to attend schools with students of their own race. In 1968, 64 percent of Black students attended schools that were intensely segregated, meaning 90 to 100 percent nonwhite; by 1988 that had fallen to 32 percent, before rising again to 40 percent in 2018.

Shaker's commitment remained. It had done precisely what integration activists urge communities to do, even today: draw boundary lines so that each school is racially, and economically, diverse. Often, districts have done the opposite, drawing lines to keep wealthy white people in certain schools and poor people of color in others.

In Shaker, children of different backgrounds, races, religions, and family income levels were learning together every day. Wealthy parents and those in poverty shared the same PTAs. And unlike the original Shaker Schools Plan, none of it rested on volunteers. The boundaries were drawn, and if you wanted to attend Shaker schools, you were going to attend an integrated campus.

What few people talked about at the time was what happens when some kids have a neighborhood school and others attend a school in someone else's neighborhood? What happens when some kids can stay after school and play on the playground, fostering friendships while their parents trade gossip and news about the school—and others can't? And was it enough for integration plans to mix students together in the building, while the levels system continued segregation by classroom?

———————

Carolyn Milter served one term on the school board. Later, she would serve on a city task force. She helped plan a fiftieth anniversary celebration for the Ludlow Community Association. And her volunteer work at University Hospitals won her a major award, something she knew her mother, who had been a nurse back in West Virginia, would have relished.

She and her husband remained in Ludlow for thirty years before moving less than a mile away to the stately Moreland Courts condominium building just off Shaker Square, completed in the late 1920s by the Van Sweringen brothers, where some of the Vans' furniture remained on display in the grand mirrored hallways.

The Milters' next-door neighbors in Ludlow, the Percys, became close friends—so close that when Bill died suddenly, his wife, Cleota, called Carolyn for help writing his obituary for the newspaper.

When the phone rang, the Milters were packing to leave for a spring break trip to Florida the next morning. They dropped everything and sped to the Percy home. There they sat with the family, the only white people in the room, and helped Cleota put pen to paper, summarizing her husband's life. And Carolyn thought back to how Cleota wasn't even sure she had wanted a white neighbor, and now here they were.

In 2006, as Carolyn Milter approached her seventieth birthday, she found herself thinking about something that had happened soon after she and Burt moved to Ludlow.

In 1967, Ernie and Jackie Tinsley, a Black couple, were living in the Cleveland portion of Ludlow and wanted to buy a home in the Sussex area, which was mostly white at the time. He was an accountant for the IRS; she was a second grade teacher in the Shaker schools. When they met the real estate agent at the house on Townley Road, the agent suddenly realized he didn't have the key and couldn't show it. Another agent, upon meeting the Tinsleys, said lo and behold, the house had sold the day before. It hadn't.

Jackie Tinsley was furious and took her frustrations out on a pair of socks that she rubbed so vigorously on a washboard that she washed a hole through them. She talked to her minister, who advised her to let it go. "She would not let it go," said her daughter, Debi Tinsley. Her mother thought, "I've done everything I'm supposed to do. I got an education. I'm a teacher. I teach in the damn system! And you're going to deny me a home?"

The Milters heard about the case through their involvement in the Ludlow Community Association and offered to step in to facilitate a straw purchase. They would buy the house, then immediately sell it to the Tinsleys.

Carolyn posed as a potential buyer and took Jackie with her to visit the house. At one point, the real estate agent, confused by Jackie's light skin, asked Carolyn if Jackie was a Negro. No, Carolyn lied.

After that, Carolyn and Burt went back, asked questions on the Tinsleys' behalf, and offered the asking price. The two couples met at the Milters' house with a pro bono attorney to go over details of the transaction. Carolyn arrived to the meeting feeling good about the work she was doing, the fight for justice she was engaged in. At that meeting, though, she was flooded with sadness as she looked at Ernest Tinsley, a decent, hardworking man who was agreeing to buy a house he could not even set foot into first.

Nearly forty years later, Carolyn found herself replaying these events. On her seventieth birthday, in 2006, she nervously drove by the house on Townley Road for the first time since the straw purchase. She wondered what she would say if she saw Jackie. She was too nervous to phone her, though she fantasized about meeting for lunch, or maybe just coffee. As she drove by the house, a landscaper rolled a leaf blower off a truck down the block. It was simply another Monday morning, quiet and peaceful.

A year and a half later, she finally phoned Jackie and the two women met for lunch. Jackie still lived in the house, still loved it. Carolyn had been worried Ernie might have been disappointed, but it turned out he loved it, too.

> Imagine trying to build a sandcastle right next to the ocean. The
> waves keep coming and washing it away. But as long as you have people
> committed to build a sandcastle, most of the time you will
> almost have a sandcastle.
> —Ronald Ferguson

11

REUBEN HARRIS JR.

Aida Harris, a Black girl in an advanced middle school science class, was struggling. One Friday she was instructed to report to a lower-level section. She told her father, Reuben Harris Jr., who wasn't having it. That Monday he went to see the teacher, who sent him to the principal. Harris promised the principal his daughter would succeed, said he'd make sure of it. The principal said it was all right with him for her to stay in the class if it was all right with the teacher, and the teacher said all right.

It was the mid-1990s. Harris ran his own insurance agency, giving him a flexible work schedule. He used that flexibility to do something remarkable—he sat in the front row of his daughter's science classroom, in the corner by the door, every day for six weeks so he could better help her. He started to notice that the teacher, a white man, would joke around with many of the white boys before and after class, often about sports but segueing into college and their futures and the way ahead. He once overheard one kid bragging that he would attend Princeton, even without top grades, because of his dad's connections. During class, these were the kids the teacher typically called on. One day Harris pointed this out to the teacher, who was sure it wasn't true. Just think about it, Harris implored him. A couple of weeks later, Harris said, the teacher told him he realized that Harris was right and vowed to change.

Aida's grade climbed from C − to B+, but it was all embarrassing and awkward for her, having her dad sitting in the front row. It also was liberating. Kids are always blaming their teachers for this and that, she recalled. Her dad knew it was true.

Years later, as an adult, Aida would tell her friends the story of how her dad sat in on her middle school science class to help her bring up her grade. "This is the best example I can give new people who meet me as to what my dad is like."

———

R euben Harris Jr.'s paternal grandfather, Johnson Harris, had arrived in Cleveland in the early 1920s, part of the Great Migration from South to North that accelerated after World War I and continued for decades. He had been living outside Macon, Georgia, working as a share-cropper. After he confronted his boss for refusing to pay him money owed, he was sentenced to thirty days on a chain gang. "Boy, when you get out," his boss told him, "we're going to make you a little taller." Ter-rified he'd be lynched, he headed north as soon as he was released.

In Cleveland, Johnson Harris landed work in a steel mill as a laborer, the worst, nastiest job available and one reserved for Black workers. His son Reuben labored as a truck driver, working his way up from pov-erty into the working class, hauling bricks and building materials for construction. Reuben and his wife, Marie, had four children, including Reuben Jr., their eldest.

In 1962, the Harris family moved to a middle-class neighborhood on the edge of Cleveland called Lee-Harvard, just south of Shaker Heights. When they arrived at their three-bedroom, compact 1940s-era colonial house on Eldamere Avenue, the neighborhood was mostly white. It rap-idly flipped, spurred by Black and white real estate agents alike, who worked together to create panic and fear among white owners and oppor-tunity for Black buyers. The white agents would scare the white owners into selling, and the Black agents would produce the buyers. By 1970, the neighborhood had resegregated and was almost entirely Black.

Reuben Jr. remembered his childhood as having *Leave It to Beaver* wholesomeness. He knew everyone up and down the block. Families kept their yards and homes tidy. His parents hoped young Reuben would go to college one day, but "it was more of a hope than a plan," he said. He was propelled by teachers who saw something in him, did well in school, graduated from Cleveland State University, and began work as an accountant.

By 1982, he and his wife were preparing to adopt a baby girl. They bought a home not far from where Reuben grew up, still in Cleveland, but in the Shaker Heights school district. Aida was born in December 1982. With one look into her dark, deep-set almond eyes, it was love at first sight for Dad.

By the time Aida was ready for school, Shaker had reorganized itself, closing four elementary schools and racially balancing the rest of the buildings. But while this plan was a shining example of desegregation, Harris came to believe that implicit bias coursed through the system. Harris spent time in Aida's classes and saw it with his own eyes. And, in her own way, so did his daughter. In first grade, Aida asked her father, "Why are the Black boys always in time-out?" As she moved into upper elementary school grades, top students would be pulled out for "enrichment," and Aida was one the few Black children in that group. She found herself harassed by her Black classmates. "Why do you think you're better?" they wanted to know.

At the high school, English teacher Carole Kovach, who is white, saw it, too. She joined the faculty in 1993 and noticed that by the late '90s, white students with a range of abilities were moving into honors classes, while Black students with a range of abilities stayed in regular sections. Every year, she said, she would notice five to ten Black students who should have been in higher-level classes. "Certain counselors just wouldn't push it and it was really frustrating," she said.

———

After overseeing the contentious school consolidation process, in 1988 superintendent Peter Horoschak announced he was leaving the district. The school board settled on his replacement without a search: Mark Freeman, who had been with Shaker schools for more than two decades, working his way up from junior high shop teacher to assistant superintendent and now, superintendent of schools.

Over the years, Freeman navigated sticky issues with confidence and aplomb, attending to parent complaints and celebrating student successes. He made news defending the *Shakerite*'s right to publish advertisements from supporters and opponents of abortion rights. He helped calm the community when a Shaker teacher contracted AIDS during the early days of the epidemic. Behind the scenes, he arranged for flowers to be sent on behalf of the school board when a teacher or prominent community member was sick or suffered a loss.

His determination to keep parents happy was legendary, and sometimes controversial, like when he overruled high school staff to let two girls participate in a special end-of-the-year project for seniors even though they had been caught streaking naked across the high school lawn.

Freeman was well aware of Shaker's racial achievement gap. In April 1988, two months before he was named to the top job, the *Shakerite*, the high school newspaper, reported familiar statistics—Black students made up 86.4 percent of students in level 2—the lowest—and 16.8 percent of those in level 5—the highest.

But Freeman tended to emphasize the positive, certainly for public consumption. A flyer published in 1994 or 1995 asked, "How Good Are the Shaker Schools?" It answered the question by highlighting the SAT scores of Shaker students compared with national averages, the number of winners in the National Merit and National Achievement competitions, high enrollment in Advanced Placement courses, impressive college admission rates, and the fact that virtually everyone passed the state's proficiency tests in time to graduate. None of these numbers was disaggregated, or broken down, by race.

The district had a raft of initiatives aimed at building up Black achievement. A tutoring center, established in 1979, offered students free help almost every day after school. In 1985, an intervention was developed for first graders who were not yet reading. In 1986, a special humanities program was added for high school students with low test scores. By 1988, the Student Group on Race Relations had grown to 180 students and was conducting programs for middle as well as elementary students. In 1992, free all-day kindergarten was expanded to all elementary schools.

And the question of how to raise Black academic success was front and center for a faculty committee focused on achievement. The group was chaired by Mary Lynne McGovern, a white woman who had sent her own son to Moreland School as part of the Shaker busing plan and who had been on the front edge of racial achievement issues as leader of the high school's PUSH Excel program. She looked around and realized every teacher in the room knew of high-achieving Black students. Why not ask these students for their opinion on how to reach their peers?

With Black male scores particularly dismal, McGovern invited eight young Black men to a meeting and handed them a printout showing student achievement data broken out by race. "We thought, they're sixteen, you know, they're going to look at us and say, 'Well, what do you want us to do about it?'" she recalled years later. But no. The young men pushed the desks into a circle and together began talking: *Can you believe this? . . . I knew so-and-so's brother was not doing well, but I didn't know things were that bad . . .* The teachers just listened as they talked it through among themselves.

"They were stunned," McGovern remembered. "That's the only word I can think of." The students asked if they could come back the following week, and at the next committee meeting, they explained their thinking. Struggling students were sick of being admonished by parents and teachers about their grades. *Might there be another way?* It was a transformational moment, said Hubert McIntyre, the Black health teacher who also served on the achievement committee. "One of them said, 'Why don't you let us talk to them?'"

The next fall, the students, advised by McGovern and McIntyre, created the Minority Achievement Committee and began crowning MAC Scholars—Black male students with top grades. (MAC Sister Scholars, a companion group, would be created seven years later.) The students from that initial meeting, plus a couple of additions, came up with the idea, the format, and the rules. They held meetings for ninth graders, calling them "potential scholars." Meetings were conducted by the scholars and focused on strategies for success. Scholars and potential scholars wore shirts and ties on meeting days, another student idea. They looked each other in the eye at every meeting as they practiced a firm handshake.

McGovern recruited the potential scholars from the incoming ninth grade classes. She also called the home of every student who was failing or struggling. She asked parents what was in the child's bedroom, and if the answer was electronics, "I ask them to please remove those." She advised them to have their child do homework at a table where parents could see them, with the TV off. "Parents appreciate the calls," she said shortly before retiring in 2017. "I've never had anybody make me feel like it's not my business. They want tools. They want ways to help their kids. They all want their children to succeed."

While MAC Scholars and the other initiatives certainly were helping individual students, none of it was making much of a dent in the statistics writ large. In January 1996, the school board decided to take a big swing at the problem and voted to create Project Achieve, a committee of some 150 teachers, administrators, parents, and community members.

Nancy Moore, who was on the school board at the time, remembered that Freeman, the superintendent, was pushed to take on the issue. "My recollection is this wasn't welcomed," she said. "Anything at that time that pointed to disparity in achievement, or anything less than the way we touted our schools as being the beacon of very high achieving students, anything that pointed to less than that was not welcome. It was like hanging out our dirty laundry." She said the philosophy at the time was that Shaker offered all students enormous opportunities. If some did not take advantage of them, that was due to outside factors. "He believed the causes of the achievement gap were societal and not any failing of the system that caused it."

Freeman said, years later, that he was constantly looking for ways to address the achievement gap. And Jim Paces, who was executive director of curriculum at the time, recalled Freeman championing the work. "Mark wanted people to embrace the effort and not fear it," he said.

Freeman told the committee at the outset that the achievement gaps were well documented and he did not want to waste time or resources to "rediscover the problem." He asked for doable projects and new initiatives that were affordable, manageable, and realistic.

Committee members came up with pages of new ideas: New services and smaller classes for the youngest students. Extending the school day. Professional diversity training. Maybe school uniforms. Classrooms wired for computers. A whole set of recommendations focused on increasing parental involvement in schools such as "You Are Here" maps to help parents find their way around school buildings, holding some parent-teacher conferences in the evening to accommodate more parents, a homework hotline for questions, and parent support groups. In January 1997, Freeman wrote the committee with his thanks, and endorsed almost every suggestion made.

One of the dozens of community members on the committee was Reuben Harris Jr., who had gotten involved with the schools as a parent volunteer. His daughter was doing well, but he was frustrated that so many other Black students were not, and he asked for a meeting with the superintendent. "What can we do to get better outcomes for other students who look like her?" he asked Freeman.

Freeman replied that the district had just formed Project Achieve and asked whether Harris would be interested in participating.

"I felt I had to," Harris said.

He joined a subcommittee that set out to document racial achievement gaps, along with suggesting contributing factors and possible solutions. Harris had assumed there would be racial disparities. He was right.

A memo to Freeman from the subcommittee unsparingly laid out the numbers. From 1992 to 1996, about half of Shaker students were white and about half Black. Yet Black students made up 7 percent of the top 20 percent of the class, and 90 percent of the bottom 20 percent. Similar disparities existed on the state proficiency exam and high school grades.

Black students were doing worse even though they were taking easier classes. The higher the level, the whiter the class. Ninety-five percent of students in the lowest level were Black, and in Advanced Placement, the top level, just 12 percent of students were. Only about half of all Black students took the SAT college entrance exam, and their average math plus verbal score was 813 out of a possible 1600. About 90 percent of white students took the SAT, and their average was 1118.

"We realized we had two schools even though it was one building," Harris said.

The subcommittee had done exactly what Freeman did not want: It had "rediscovered the problem." Its report put hard, cold numbers to the general perception of gaps.

The subcommittee came up with a robust list of possible causes for underachievement, spreading responsibility across all involved. The community as a whole was undervaluing the education of Black children and enrolling too few Black kids in preschool. Parents were unable or unwilling to interact with schools, set low expectations for their kids, and accepted underachievement. Schools and teachers set low expectations for academics and behavior, provided too little attention and counseling, tracked students by ability, and lacked proper communication with parents. Students undervalued education and succumbed to negative peer pressure.

Harris knew the report was a ticking time bomb. Shaker was portraying itself as high-achieving—and that was true, for some. He wondered what to do with the numbers showing it wasn't true for all. If they hid the data, things might never improve. If they publicized them, the community might go nuts.

The decision was made for them. The information was presented at what was assumed to be a routine, but public, school board meeting, and that's where the *Shakerite* first saw the numbers. The reporter, junior Nawal Atwan, who is white and of Middle Eastern descent, wasn't shocked. She was in all AP classes, and they were almost completely white. But she knew this was news—front page news—and the high school paper reported it there for all to see. Still, she didn't think much about what the reaction might be.

"I wrote articles all the time," she said. "I just thought it was going to be another article."

The two-tier headline stripped across the front page read, BLACK & WHITE . . . OR SHADES OF GRAY? The article had very little nuance and not many voices, but it laid out the data accurately, along with some potential solutions.

The response was explosive. Many Black students and their parents were furious. They directed their anger not at the underlying disparities, but at the student newspaper. The story was published on a Thursday, and that afternoon, a small group of Black students staged a walkout, drawing local TV news coverage. About thirty students angrily pressed their case to the newspaper's editors in a face-to-face meeting that afternoon. Atwan was pulled out in the middle of a class and escorted to her car by police, who followed her home to make sure she arrived safely.

Many in Shaker's Black community thought the story made it look as if all Black students were academic losers, that the paper set out to make Black students look bad. The story's headline began BLACK & WHITE, but only Black students were discussed. A fact box at the top of the page, labeled THE PROBLEM, detailed all the academic shortcomings of Black students. No word about their successes. The fact that it was published during Black History Month made it that much worse, they said, particularly because the paper had failed to cover a "Black History Makers of Tomorrow" contest in which four of the twenty-five finalists came from Shaker, with one placing second.

The next day, Principal Jack Rumbaugh sent a letter explaining what happened to high school parents, saying no offense was meant by the article, even as much offense was taken. Over morning announcements at school, he chastised the *Shakerite* for publishing the data.

Student editors also addressed the school over the PA system. Atwan apologized, saying the article "was not intended to be racially biased or incriminating toward Black students." She added that it was wrong to report problems without also reporting achievements. *Shakerite* co-editor Scott Fuller told the school that front page treatment was justi-fied but apologized for failing to mention anything about Black History Month celebrations. "For this, the *Shakerite* sends its deepest apology, for we have acted wrongly."

It seems, certainly in retrospect, an outsized helping of self-flagellation, and a classic case of blaming the messenger. To be sure, the article itself could have been better. It should have included more voices, more per-spectives, more sensitivity, more balance, and more analysis. But the core of the reporting was accurate.

The anger continued to surge toward the student journalists, and it was certainly much simpler to identify errors made by a few students publishing an imperfect article than it was to identify deep and disturb-ing forces that created the disparities in the first place. Threats were leveled against Atwan, the writer, and for a time her parents considered moving her out of the district. Few Black students knew her, she said, except for those in choir, her only racially diverse class. "They called me and said, 'You should come to school. We have your back.'"

The morning after the story was published, a group of Black parents rallied in front of the high school, drawing local news attention. After school, a large group of students, parents, and teachers gathered in the high school auditorium for a conversation that stretched two and a half hours. Students passed a microphone around, steam building.

One Black girl, on her feet and at the top of her voice, railed against a statistic showing low passage rates among Black students on a math proficiency test. "Can you please tell me why they expect us to pass the geometry portion of the test when most of the ninth graders that get here their freshman year take Algebra 1?!" she cried, her voice heavy with emotion and rising in volume. She held the *Shakerite* in her hand until her gesticulation became so intense she had to drop it. "I'm just now in Geometry! I keep failing, keep failing. And I'm thinking like, 'Am I stupid?' I sit home, cry, looking at myself . . . 'You'll never graduate.'"

She addressed other Black students directly: "They talking about all of us. Just 'cause you passed on the first try, don't mean they ain't talking about you." She demanded that the school teach them geometry in the eighth grade so they can pass the test. "We can do it! We can do it!" And as she finished speaking, she walked away from the microphone and students stood and cheered.

Another speaker demanded that the *Shakerite* adviser resign immediately. More cheers. One girl said she and everyone else was trying to work hard. "When you say things like this and you take them and make them one-sided," she said, "you make it look like I did all this work for nothing."

Standing on the edge of the auditorium was Reuben Harris Jr., watching and growing more upset with each speaker. Finally, he took the microphone himself.

"I was one of those people who put those statistics together," he began, left hand in his tan suit pocket, right hand clutching the microphone, his six-foot-four-inch frame pitched forward slightly. "We spent about a year and a half looking at data, statistics." He said he didn't intend for the data to come out how it did, but that part didn't matter. "What really matters is what are we going to do based upon the information. Unfortunately, those statistics are valid and are accurate. But that's really of little importance. What are you going to do to change those? What are your teachers going to do to change those? What are your parents going to do and what are we in the general community going to do to help you to change those things?" Looking toward a previous speaker, he said, "I empathize and I hurt with the young lady because I literally did not sleep for forty-eight hours after I first saw the statistics. I tried"—and at that moment, his voice caught. He looked to the floor, tried to pull himself together. "Take your time," a voice from the crowd called. "I'll speak in a minute," Harris said, and he relinquished the microphone and moved again to the side of the room.

Pressure on Shaker schools was not coming only from inside the district. A few months earlier, the federal Department of Education's Office for Civil Rights had opened a review of racial disparities in enrollment in advanced classes in Shaker schools. In December 1996, federal officials met with Freeman and requested a wide range of data and policies around the question of class leveling, sometimes called tracking.

The investigation was not prompted by a complaint; Shaker was chosen at random by the agency for the review, a spokesman for the federal office said at the time. In a meeting with investigators, Freeman acknowledged there were racially disproportionate course placements but noted that enrollment in classes was voluntary. In a follow-up letter, the district's attorney showed little patience with the entire endeavor. "As you were advised," wrote attorney David Millstone, from the firm of Squire, Sanders & Dempsey, the district saw a request for district data as "time consuming and expensive." He wrote that Shaker was less interested in being investigated and more interested in recommendations for improving the situation. He asked for sources that might fund these initiatives and details about how similar districts had solved the problem. And in a line that reflected a remarkable cockiness, given that Shaker was at the time under investigation for violating federal civil rights law, Millstone added, "We understand why OCR would like to partner with Shaker as it has been recognized nationally as a model for schools seeking to maximize the educational attainment of African-American students."

News of the investigation became public right around the time of the *Shakerite* publication. At the time, nearly a thousand white students were enrolled in at least one Advanced Placement class, the district said, compared to about a hundred Black students.

In March 1997, Freeman addressed the *Shakerite* article and the federal civil rights probe in an open letter to the community and at a meeting with the high school faculty that felt to some there like a damage control session.

Using an overhead projector, Freeman displayed data demonstrating that Black students in Shaker were doing better than Black students elsewhere. The achievement gap, he suggested, was largely driven by uber achievement on the part of Shaker's white students, whose parents were wealthy and highly educated. As long as Shaker was home to some of the smartest, highest-achieving white kids around, closing the achievement gap would be all but impossible.

Teachers jammed into the smaller of two high school auditoriums were told, and many believed, that this had little to do with how they were teaching or whether the district was offering equal opportunities. "It was the fact that these are impoverished students," said John Morris, a white man who had recently started work at Shaker as a student teacher and was in the room. The gaps were also attributed to the fact that Black students were less likely to have begun in kindergarten at Shaker, so they were behind from the start.

The goal was to calm the waters, to reassure everyone that the Shaker ideals of academic excellence and racial progress were alive and well.

"You had that psychological safeguard. We're doing so much better than other districts," Morris said. "I just remember this palpable sense of urgency for us, the district, to address the reasons for this gap. And to rationalize it."

There was truth to Freeman's arguments. Black Shaker students did perform better on standardized tests than Black students elsewhere. But was that the bar the community wanted to set? Was outscoring high-poverty communities like Cleveland really success for a well-funded, prestigious district like Shaker Heights?

Others delivered a similar reassuring message. The Reverend Marvin McMickle, president of the school board and former Cleveland NAACP president, told the *Plain Dealer* that the district fared well compared with others and expressed optimism for the road ahead. And he offered up what was already a mantra in Shaker Heights, a sentiment repeated so often it might as well be affixed to plaques on the school walls: "If it can't be solved in Shaker, I don't think it can be resolved."

Anyone listening to Freeman's explanations, or hearing the school board president's commentary, was bound to feel better about the situation. The message was simple: Yes, there's a problem, but it's been exaggerated by the media and we're on top of it and there's really nothing to worry about.

———

The problems did not begin at the high school. At Mercer Elementary School, white but not Black students were routinely pulled out for special enrichment sessions, said Lisa Hardiman, who began teaching at Mercer in 1995. She was stunned the first time she witnessed the call for students to leave her class for enrichment.

"Every white kid in my class gets up and hits the door," said Hardiman, who is Black. "I'm twenty-five years old. I'm like, you mean to tell me none of my Black kids qualified for this at all?" Their participation wasn't based on test scores or assessments of achievement in class. It was based almost exclusively on parental requests, and Black parents didn't know to make the request.

Mercer's population included students from the neighborhood, one of Shaker's whitest and wealthiest, and also students from the mostly Black, lower-income Moreland area, who were bused about four miles as part of the district's success in integrating its schools. The two groups began on unequal terrain in so many ways. The Moreland kids typically had fewer educational experiences at home as young children, and their parents generally had less education and were less comfortable dealing with the school. It was also not nearly as convenient for them, since the school was across town.

But Hardiman said Mercer exacerbated those gaps. She said the enrichment pullouts were curtailed for a while, following complaints about the racial gaps in the district, and then resumed amid parent demands. Again, she said, the placements were not equitable. The longtime principal was focused on keeping white families at the school happy, meeting their needs, giving them what they wanted. "He let white families in (to enrichment) all the time, based on nothing," Hardiman said. (The former principal declined comment, a district spokesman said.)

And, on the other end of the spectrum, the principal applied a similar double standard for the intervention groups meant for kids who needed extra help, said Derek White, another longtime Mercer teacher. "He didn't want any white kids in there," he said. Hardiman remembered one white boy in particular needed extra help, and the principal argued that no, he didn't. Instead, she said, the principal would ask teachers to tutor white kids before school.

In the aftermath of the *Shakerite* article, Reuben Harris Jr. and other Black parents saw an opportunity for action and demanded it. Project Achieve had put forward a list of ideas for boosting Black achievement, and the district had a long list of plans for closing the gaps. But Harris believed Shaker needed a thorough look from an outsider who might be able to see what 150 people from the community could not.

Harris and other Black parents he was working with came to Freeman with a request. "They said, 'How about you bring in an expert,' and I think to their amazement I said sure," Freeman recalled. "They were suspicious of me."

Harris suggested John Ogbu, a soft-spoken Nigerian-born anthropologist from the University of California, Berkeley, who had gained prominence with research in the mid-1980s positing that Black students saw academic achievement as "acting white." He theorized, controversially, that Black students exhibited what he called "oppositional peer culture"—resisting the proposition that academic achievement was worth striving for and that education and good grades would lead to well-paying jobs later on.

Freeman recalled warning the parents group that Ogbu was an anthropologist, not an educator. But that's who the parents group wanted, and he went along. The district would spend $14,000 plus another $1,783 in expenses to bring Ogbu and a research assistant to study the Shaker schools.

Ogbu was excited about the opportunity, the chance to test the question he'd studied in urban areas in an affluent, academically successful suburb. Over eight months, Ogbu came in and out of the district, while his research assistant moved to the community. They held long meetings with groups of teachers, counselors, parents, and students and observed 110 classes. By design, he focused on the attitudes and behaviors of the students rather than systemic issues.

In a meeting with counselors and others at the middle school, Ogbu heard something that resonated with his own sense of the problem. The principal spoke up to discuss a fourteen-year-old boy he had observed in a class. He knew this boy was smart but noticed he never raised his hand. The principal asked him to come to his office. He wanted to know why he wasn't showing the class how much he knew.

"He said, 'You don't have to ride home on the bus like I do,'" the principal recounted for Ogbu, according to a transcript of the session. "I said, 'You're right. I don't.' 'You don't have to play in the neighborhood with all the other kids.' I said, 'You're right. I don't understand.' He said, 'I don't want 'em to know I'm smart. They'll make fun of me. I won't have any friends.' I said, 'So you'd rather sit there and pretend that you don't know than face kids who might say you're smart.' And he even said, 'Worse than smart.' I said, 'Well, what's worse than that in your world?' He said, 'Where I live, they're gonna say I'm White.' I said, 'Oh.' I said, 'Now I, I think I understand.'"

He also heard complaints about the school system itself. In one discussion with students, for instance, a Black girl said that her mom had to talk to the administration about putting her into an advanced class in middle school. She said her test scores were high enough to qualify and she was doing well in school. "But for whatever reason, they didn't want to put me in those classes," she said.

Ogbu published his findings a few years later, in 2002, in a book titled *Black American Students in an Affluent Suburb: A Study of Academic Disengagement*. Ogbu's provocative and uncomfortable central conclusion put the responsibility squarely on Black students themselves: They were not trying hard enough, not putting forth the same effort as white students. He said he purposely chose not to focus on the system itself because those issues had been examined before, whereas the issues inside the Black community had not.

"We can confidently say that Black students in Shaker Heights from elementary school through high school did not work as hard as they should and could to make better grades than their records show," he wrote.

He said middle school students described their own effort as "just enough to get by." There was a "norm of minimum effort," he wrote, especially among Black males. Students in lower-level classes didn't complete homework, so teachers stopped assigning it.

One Black female told Ogbu that Black students were slacking because they felt inferior. "Once we feel inferior inside, okay, forget it: 'I'm not even going to try.' Once we have that inferior feeling, it's like something turns us off. We're just turned [off] and stop trying." Those feelings of self-doubt, he said, explain why some students avoided honors and Advanced Placement courses. "Doing well in these classes required a lot of effort," he wrote, "and some students doubted their ability to make those efforts." But he said that the disparate class assignment was also partly because Black parents did not understand the leveling system and perhaps did not encourage their children to take the more challenging courses. Pathways were set early; whether a student enrolled in advanced courses in high school depended on whether they were in advanced courses in middle school, which depended on whether they were in enriched groupings at the upper elementary school.

Ogbu dismissed many of the conventional explanations for the racial achievement gap. He said that socioeconomic factors did not explain it because Black academic performance falls below white performance even within economic classes. Racial segregation could not explain the gaps in Shaker because all the schools had been racially balanced since 1987. Low teacher expectations played a role, he allowed, but said that students themselves influence what teachers expect from them.

His 289 pages of text included just 17 pages of recommendations. A few were directed at the school system. He suggested the district expand the MAC Scholars program and work with teachers to raise expectations. He recommended the schools offer programs to educate Black parents about how the leveling system worked and about how to monitor their children's academic standing.

He was more interested in what the Black community could do. He recommended that the community itself offer supplementary educational programs for students. They should lift up academically successful Black professionals so role models would expand beyond sports and entertainment. He urged Black parents to engage in their children's education, and said new programs should teach Black students to work harder and motivate themselves.

"The Black community and Black families," he wrote, "must assume a proactive role to increase the academic orientation, effort, and performance of their children."

Ogbu's book drew national attention upon publication, with coverage by the *New York Times*, *Washington Post* columnist William Raspberry, and *The O'Reilly Factor* on Fox News Channel. It also drew criticism. The Urban League issued a statement accusing Ogbu of blaming the victim. Ohio state senator C. J. Prentiss said he missed the real problem, which she said was lack of school funding. A Black parent from Shaker called him an "academic Clarence Thomas." Other academics criticized his methods as subjective and said he minimized the systemic issues at work.

Emanuella Groves, a Black Shaker mom, had worked with Harris to bring Ogbu to Shaker, and couldn't believe what he had produced. "I felt betrayed because we brought him in to look at [the problems] and give us support we needed to say there needed to be institutional changes. And he kind of flipped the script and blamed the parents. We felt horrible," she said. "It put a cloud on all the work we were doing."

While Obgu was preparing his findings, Harris introduced another expert to Freeman. Ronald Ferguson was Harris's best friend back to middle school and Aida's godfather. Harris, in turn, was godfather to Ferguson's two sons. Ferguson, who was Black, was also an MIT-trained economist now at the Kennedy School of Government at Harvard University. Over the years, they had discussed Harris's concerns about Aida's education in Shaker and Ferguson's burgeoning interest in the field. From the start, Harris thought he could help Shaker.

Ferguson soon launched a large study of forty thousand middle and high school students from fifteen districts around the country who were in the Minority Student Achievement Network, a group founded by racially diverse school districts including Shaker, which were all struggling with the same questions of race and achievement. That was followed by intense study of and consulting with the Shaker schools.

Ferguson's findings stood in contrast to Ogbu's. He found that at least half the gap, and as much as two-thirds, could be attributed to differences in family income and resources. Other factors included the academic orientation of parents, such as how many books are in the house or how often children are read to. But he also found Black and Latino students worked just as hard and cared just as much about school as white and Asian students do. He concluded that the differences in grades between Black and white students weren't about an "oppositional culture," or disinterest in education. It wasn't that Blacks weren't trying hard enough or that they weren't interested in school. It was a lack of skills. The remedy, he said, was more instruction, starting in homes and classrooms in elementary school and sustained as students grew older.

His research found that Black students spend just as much, or more, time on homework compared with white students in the same course levels, but were less likely to complete their assignments. Overall, without accounting for course levels, they reported just twenty fewer minutes each night on homework. That was partly because they didn't have friends to study with, Ferguson said.

"We flipped for teachers their assumptions about why [students] weren't getting their homework done," he said in an interview. "Initially the assumption was they weren't working as hard. The data don't support that."

Parental education made a difference, he found, and in this sense his conclusions echoed some of what Ogbu had reported. Children whose parents had only high school degrees reported that they paid less attention in class, participated less, and saw their studies as less interesting. They watched more television and had lower college aspirations.

In publishing his findings in academic journals later, Ferguson presented the analogy of a race where members of a Black tribe and a white tribe were all competing individually, with each step representing the acquisition of knowledge. It's not that the white runners try harder or run faster. They start ahead, they get extra coaching, and they are channeled more information about strategy. For Black runners, "the only way to catch up is to run faster . . . But is this possible? Simply exerting greater effort while using old techniques and strategies might do little to close the gap."

He added that high-achieving Black kids don't get accused of "acting white" because they get good grades, but because they are seen as acting superior.

"It's things like talking too properly when you're in informal social settings," Ferguson told the *New York Times* in an article about Ogbu's book. "It's hanging around white friends and acting like you don't want to be with your black friends. It's really about behavior patterns and not achievement."

The study launched Ferguson on what would be more than a decade of study of Shaker schools and intense work with the faculty to raise Black achievement. Working in Shaker, he developed a program called the Tripod Project, which focused on three keys to student success: content, pedagogy, and relationships. Teachers need knowledge of their subjects, skills for presenting the information, and the ability to connect with students.

Ferguson led school-wide professional development sessions throughout the year to help teachers apply these ideas, always including students to share their perspectives. One meeting early in the school year, for instance, was about managing student behavior. Students will challenge teachers, Ferguson said. Some will misbehave and see how the teacher responds. Other kids will test the teacher by asking hard questions and see if the teacher has a good answer.

The goal for all students, he said, was to encourage a growth mindset, the idea that they can push themselves to learn. So if a student acts out, the teacher should respond empathetically and try to figure out what the student is actually trying to communicate. The message should be: just because you don't understand this now, doesn't mean you can't. Teachers, he said, should "create a climate where it's safe to seek help."

Shaker now had two theories of the case before it from two very different academics. Ogbu said the problem was unmotivated Black students. Ferguson said it was a system that failed to connect and properly equip these same students. The two were pitted against each other in the media, but inside Shaker, there was little question who held sway. The district spent many years working with Ferguson and trying to implement his ideas. Ogbu died in 2003, and his analysis of Shaker students became a footnote in the district's history.

⸻

But while the district was not acting on Ogbu's results, Reuben Harris Jr. was giving them some deep thought. He believed there was truth in both Ogbu's and Ferguson's findings. After meetings of the Project Achieve subcommittee, Harris would find himself standing in the parking lot talking with Emanuella Groves. She lived just down the street from him, but the two had not met before they served together on the panel, and now they found they had a lot in common. Emanuella and her husband, Greg Groves, both attorneys, shared Harris's anxiety about how their own Black children would fare in the Shaker schools, and about how all Black children were faring.

Together with a handful of others, they formed a new Black parent group: Caring Communities Organized for Education. More than any other group before or since, Caring Communities would focus not just on pushing the school district but on trying to help parents solve the problems themselves.

"We were on a mission," said Emanuella Groves. They knew education was key to upward mobility. "We saw the disparity, the potential that level of achievement would be lost in the next generation." They feared that "the Black middle class would not be sustained."

The group produced a middle school planning guide to help parents understand that there were honors as well as regular courses to choose among. It invited parents into the schools as volunteers in classrooms and hallways. When the district declined to offer summer classes, Caring Communities created its own Summer Enrichment Program for grades kindergarten through eighth, with classes including science, algebra, English, creative writing, African American history, TV production, personal development, and study skills. The district wouldn't fund the program, but it did let Caring Communities use school buildings for free.

A Caring Communities flyer offered tips for study skills, with ideas like flash cards, study guides, and summaries. It asked students to consider whether they worked better in groups or on their own. In 2001, it hosted a parent conference featuring a keynote address by Ron Ferguson and sessions on homework, using the library, and why study groups are effective. In 2003, a parent forum focused on how to get the most from the high school academic experience.

The group also looked for ways to celebrate Blackness and Black identity. It sponsored an essay contest during Black History Month and a Kwanzaa ceremony each December. It helped create a celebration to kick off Black History Month called Sankofa, an African symbol of a bird looking backward, as a way to emphasize the value of understanding the past in order to chart the future. The event always included "Lift Every Voice and Sing," the Black national anthem. Earlier, in February 1998, Caring Communities co-sponsored an Afrocentric and multicultural book fair at the high school. The group also experimented with a Juneteenth event and a pancake breakfast.

In a speech at a local church in 1999, Harris issued a call to action: "We must ask for more from teachers, students, and ourselves as parents. No, we must demand and expect more! Our opportunities must not be squandered! We cannot allow our dreams for our children to be denied or deferred, only to dry up and shrivel like a 'Raisin in the Sun.'

"For too long we have tolerated, ignored and all too often denied the existence and magnitude of this situation, which is somewhat akin to a person denying the existence of high blood pressure. For the short run, denial definitely works, but in the long run, systemic failure may result. Several of you have mentioned your concern regarding this issue. Some have expressed a desire to assist in solution building. Today, I extend an invitation to you to move beyond the rhetoric, beyond the 'excusism,' beyond the racism, beyond the sexism and the other 'isms!' . . . We have a window of opportunity, a chance to make a difference."

Caring Communities offered its summer program for ten years. The program ended only after the district finally offered a summer school program of its own. "We thought they'd put us out of business after a couple years, but it took ten," Harris said.

But even as they turned their living room into headquarters for a Shaker summer school, the Groveses wound up pulling both of their children out of the district.

For their son, Gregory, the problem came in fourth grade, when he was put into a middle-level reading group. His confidence was crushed. He desperately wanted to read a series of books called "The Littles" that

his older sister had read, but the middle group didn't read "The Littles." At age ten, he already was being tagged as slower than others. "If
you're telling me he's not reading fast enough to be in this high group
and therefore you're not going to give him the better part of your educational experience, something is wrong with that approach," his father
said. The Groveses saw the statistics showing scant success among Black
males and were terrified this was their son's future. They moved him to a
private Montessori school, where he thrived, and then to an elite private
high school.

Their daughter, Angela, always did very well academically in Shaker,
but in ninth grade, the Groveses got upset with the girls' basketball
coach. Emanuella inquired with Hathaway Brown, a private girls' school
in Shaker Heights, and was initially told there was no space. However,
after seeing her daughter's grades, the school called and said, "There's
always room for a student like Angela."

It was just two kids, but their experience highlighted a real challenge
for Shaker: If Black children from high-achieving homes like the Groveses'
were not finding success in the district, if they were moving away or choosing private school, the achievement gap would grow larger, because the
remaining Black children would come from families with fewer resources
and more stresses. Over time, the Black population in Shaker did in fact
become less wealthy, driven in part by choices like the Groveses'.

As for the Groveses' children, they both went on to attend Princeton.

———————

From inside Shaker schools, members of the high school faculty were
looking for solutions of their own.

Terry Pollack was about halfway into what would be a legendary
fifty-year career teaching history at Shaker. Pollack's view was that more
Black students needed to be encouraged to take advanced courses, and
they needed more support to do so. He applied for and won a grant from
the Cleveland Foundation for a new idea: Study Circles, targeted tutoring before and after school.

Pollack had seen firsthand—and marveled at—how Shaker parents
voluntarily signed up to bus their children across town at a time when
parents elsewhere were fighting desegregation with all they had. Now, at
a moment of crisis, he wanted to help the next generation of Shaker parents be part of a new solution. The goal was to help Black students build

study skills, but also to develop a sense of community so they would not feel alone if they took these courses. "It's that isolation breeds a sense of failure," he said. "We've created a semi-apartheid system where kids are separated but yet deep down there are kids who are more than capable, and you have to create a snowball effect so those kids can find success."

The program launched in the fall of 2000. At first, Pollack met in families' homes with groups of Black students enrolled in AP classes. He would sit on the floor with them, helping them come together as a group and figure out how to study. Together, they would discuss the interconnections of history, promoting higher-order thinking.

Pollack collected the names of every Black student in honors and AP classes and tracked their progress, with awards at year's end for improved grades. Soon the program expanded to the middle school and then down to the upper elementary school.

English teacher John Morris was enthusiastic and signed up as a tutor. But within a few years, he grew discouraged. The study circles had been targeted to Black students, but white parents learned about them and insisted they be open to all. Soon the sessions were taken over by white students who saw them as another opportunity to get a leg up. "When word got out, suddenly the white kids started to show up," he said, "and the Black kids disappeared."

Pollack saw it, too. "It was incredibly discouraging," he said.

Around this time, the district also promoted a program to help teachers address their own biases, which didn't go over well with at least one teacher. In a letter to colleagues dated April 7, 1997, English teacher Steven Fox lashed out about recent staff meetings and activities that were meant to help teachers examine how they were treating Black students. "I am angry at the repeated charge that because I am white I do not treat my non-white students fairly," Fox wrote. Charges of racism as well as sexism, he said, were being "thrown around freely," and the administration had failed to defend teachers by saying they weren't true.

Fox took specific issue with a reading that had been assigned to the faculty that apparently looked at systemic and unconscious bias of some sort, calling it biased and pernicious propaganda. He said the message appeared to be, "Here, read this, and see yourselves in it." Fox wrote that he wished he had had the courage to speak up during the staff meeting but feared he might have said something he would have later regretted.

"We are not a racist staff," he wrote. "I imagine one would have to go far to find a fairer minded body of people than we are. So it is enormously distressing to me to be sat down and expected to participate in exercises that contradict what I know to be true."

And yet, just a few years earlier, around 1989, a bright young woman who would later become a law professor at Case Western Reserve University and a member of the Shaker Heights school board, Ayesha Bell Hardaway, was a student in ninth grade honors English, taught by Fox's wife, Carol Fox. Hardaway remembered being told by Carol Fox that she should drop down a level "because African American students don't do well in honors and AP."

Fox said she did not recall this conversation, but she said that if Ayesha had asked for advice on what course to take, she might have told her that in her experience, African Americans "sometimes struggle a bit" in advanced classes. Asked if it was possible that Ayesha—or any other Black student told such a thing—might have interpreted this as discouragement, Fox said, "She could have read it that way. I don't want to say anybody's lying about anything." She said her memory is that Ayesha was a strong student who did well.

Interviewed in 2022, Fox said that even now, she saw nothing wrong with telling Black students that other Black students struggled in higher-level classes. "I would try to give that student all the information I could with which to make a decision," she said. If she were in the same situation today, she said that she might not say the same thing but only "because I know how hypersensitive people are." She recalled once advising a white student against taking a high-level class but said she did not issue white students blanket warnings that other white students had struggled.

To state the obvious: These are the subtle—or not-so-subtle—messages that drive some students of color away from advanced classes and eat away at their self-esteem. The sort of thing that makes them feel they don't belong.

Steven Fox died in 2012. Carol Fox retired from Shaker schools in 2002, after thirty years of teaching, and later worked at Case law school, where Hardaway was a professor. Asked about her late husband's rant against the diversity training in 1997, Fox said she would not have voiced concerns in the same way, but she expressed dismay with similar trainings that she said she has repeatedly been required to participate in. "The repetitive presentation of these things might be counterproductive if people get angry by being told they're racist when they think they aren't," she said. "It's kind of insulting after a while."

———

Reuben Harris continued work with Caring Communities into the 2010s, well after Aida graduated from Shaker Heights High School in 2001. After more than fifteen years of effort, he started to consider the limits of what he was able to accomplish as a parent. He had contemplated running for the school board in 1999 but decided he could do more good pushing from the outside. Now Caring Communities was winding down, and Harris wondered if he should try from the inside, after all.

Shaker is the National Merit finalist, and Shaker is the student
who struggles to graduate in five years.
—Gregory Hutchings Jr., 2018 State of the Schools address

12

GREGORY HUTCHINGS JR.

Mark Freeman had been superintendent of the Shaker Heights schools for nearly two decades when a collection of parents, Black and white, began agitating for his removal, convinced he wasn't taking the racial achievement gap seriously enough.

Over the years, Freeman had been constantly confronted with the achievement gap, and he felt the district had worked hard to address it. He also knew that despite those efforts, racial academic gaps stubbornly persisted. In a 2017 interview, he sounded like someone who had become a little tired of the question.

"I don't mean it to be flippant," he began. "It is discovered every five years by groups of students and sometimes adults . . . Every so often an article is written, a documentary, a dissertation, student work, or some committee all address this. People think they've discovered the problem, or the accusation is the district is hiding this."

Freeman emphasized that Shaker had achieved far more than many systems. Large numbers of Black students went to college, and students of all races left Shaker schools better prepared to function in a diverse world. "The evidence is overwhelming that Shaker has been a leader as a school district at working at solving these issues," he said. Asked what it would take to actually close the gap, he gave a fast reply: "End poverty and eradicate racism."

To Reuben Harris and others, that diagnosis felt like a cop-out. "His viewpoint gave the system an out—they couldn't do anything," Harris said. "Mark felt the achievement gap could not and would not end until the economic gap was closed. I felt the economic gap could not close until the achievement gap was closed."

Now a new generation of parents was pressuring the district to be more aggressive.

Among them was Mark Joseph, a professor at Case Western Reserve University who moved to Shaker in 2006, drawn by the diversity, and dismayed by the achievement gap and what felt like a lack of urgency in addressing it. He asked to meet with Freeman, and the pair had lunch at Pearl of the Orient, one of Freeman's favorite spots. When Joseph asked to see the district's strategic plan, Freeman replied that he didn't believe in them. He thought that strategic plans did little in and of themselves to accomplish their goals. "They wind up on a shelf," he said. Joseph thought they were important, as much for the process of creating the plan as for the final product itself and was irritated by Freeman's seemingly cavalier dismissal.

Soon he got involved with community groups pressing for systemic change. One was called Parents, Teachers, Students Working Group, led and funded by John Guinness, a wealthy retired white businessman originally from England who produced a steady stream of long memos with advice for the district. Guinness paid out of his own pocket to bring district officials to Harvard, hoping advice from experts would make a difference. He pressed for more oversight by the school board and better data. And he advocated new policies that would bar students from advancing until they had mastered the material, providing them with extra time as needed to achieve these goals.

A second, larger group called itself ONE Shaker and also worked toward systemic change—pressuring the district, for instance, to adopt a strategic plan (which Freeman eventually agreed to), and then working to engage the community, particularly the Black community, in shaping its details. At the same time, the group launched a quiet campaign to move Freeman out. His contract was set to expire in 2010, and in 2009 some in the community made clear they were ready for a change. (Freeman had already officially "retired" and begun to collect his pension, but was rehired by the school board to continue doing the same job, a common maneuver known as double-dipping because taxpayers are funding a pension and a salary at the same time.)

In 2009, the school board held a public meeting to discuss the contract renewal, and opponents turned out in force.

F. Drexel Feeling, the school board president, believed Freeman had been good for the district and that he genuinely wanted to raise Black achievement, but ultimately concluded he wasn't willing to take any risks to do so. "I came to think that if meaningful change were to be made we probably would need to transition to a new superintendent."

As a middle ground, Feeling suggested a three-year renewal, less than the five years Freeman had been given previously—and made clear to Freeman that any extension would depend on making progress for Black students. In September 2012, Freeman read the room and announced he would be stepping down at the end of the school year.

———

The advertisement for schools superintendent in Shaker Heights caught the eye of Gregory Hutchings Jr., an ambitious thirty-five-year-old school administrator in Alexandria, Virginia.

Hutchings, who is Black, had been in a hurry ever since age seven, when his parents divorced, and Greg and his siblings lived with their mom. His grandmother told Greg he was now the man of the house, and he took that responsibility seriously, helping get his little brother, four years younger, out of bed and ready for school. "I would pick out his clothes, pick out my clothes," Hutchings recalled. He'd make sure everyone had breakfast and left on time for school. He'd walk his little brother to school and then head to his own classroom, red canvas briefcase in hand.

In school, he was assertive and talkative, even a bit disruptive. But his teachers taught him how to channel his energy—none more so than his kindergarten teacher, Dorothy Murphy. One day, she pulled him into the hallway for a talk.

"You can take your leadership qualities and your ability and you could be the first Black president," she told him, according to Hutchings. "So I want you to go in there with your chest pushed out and your head high and I want you to lead this class and not disrupt the class." That, he said later, "changed the trajectory of my life because I believed anything was possible."

Greg's grades and test scores were middling, and in high school, he was placed into regular classes, which he said were taught by unmotivated, disengaged teachers. He wanted to enroll in honors. In the regular courses, students would act out, he said, even fight sometimes. "I felt if I was going to be someone, I had to have access to those honors classes."

Greg composed a petition asking for reassignment and persuaded other students to sign it. He presented his case to the principal, who escorted him to the counselor's office, where he was signed up for honors classes on the spot. At that moment, he later said, he realized he had a voice and could use it. He earned Cs but it helped with college applications that he had taken rigorous courses.

"That has become the fuel for my fire," he said later. "When I heard 'no,' in my mind, I was saying, 'Oh yes I will.' So there was some anger there."

After graduating from Old Dominion University (where he dropped his premed plans after twice failing organic chemistry), Hutchings went into teaching himself. He rose from classroom teacher to assistant principal to principal in just a few years, and earned his master's and doctorate degrees. By this point he was back in his hometown district of Alexandria, a suburb of Washington, D.C., as director of Pre-K–12 programs. It was a senior job, but still a couple of rungs below superintendent.

As he read the leadership profile for the job in Shaker Heights, he felt it was describing him. After a trip to Shaker with his wife—where they were both blown away by the beauty of the community—Hutchings submitted his application.

Hutchings made the final cut and was invited to a public interview in March 2013. He made a strong impression. With shaved head and dapper bow tie, he spoke at a clip about how he had tackled tough problems and what he thought was possible in Shaker. He rattled off ideas for closing the achievement gap: Make sure all children can read by grade three. Provide wraparound services that low-income students need, with social workers and counselors ascertaining needs. Raise the bar for everyone. He spoke with a confidence that felt reassuring to many. *Maybe this was the guy who could finally solve the problem.*

He was asked directly: How would you address the "needs and desires of affluent families" who have choices of where to live and where to send their kids to school?

"Stay, stay with us!" Hutchings replied with a laugh. "Your tax dollars are too high for you to go somewhere else. You're paying for this wonderful education." He said it was important to listen to affluent, educated families, but his tone belied a trace of resentment or maybe skepticism. "I call them the Ivy League families, who have really high expectations for their kids," he said. It was a good idea to listen to their suggestions because "believe it or not, some of those solutions, it helps all kids—even kids who are low performing."

The school board selected Hutchings. He arrived with big ambitions and an abundance of confidence. Speaking to a friend for the oral history project StoryCorps soon after accepting the position but before starting it, he said, "I believe we're going to be the exemplar for school districts across the nation, and in 10 to 15 years from now, I'll be called by the president to be the secretary of the U.S. Department of Education."

Some, hearing about these remarks, didn't appreciate the suggestion that Shaker was a stepping-stone. Still, there was a genuine excitement around his arrival.

"I was ecstatic," said John Morris, the English teacher who also was president of the Shaker Heights Teachers Association. Hutchings seemed deeply committed to attacking the problems. "It was what we were look-ing for—someone to aggressively address the achievement gap."

Hutchings started in Shaker in July 2013, and soon after, Reuben Harris Jr. advised him to move fast. "You're the Obama of Shaker and you've got a year of goodwill to make your waves," he told him, "and then the gloves will be off."

———

In February 2014, the large auditorium at the high school was filled with the joyous beat of Kool and the Gang's "Celebration." Commu-nity members, teachers, and students filed in to hear Hutchings deliver his first State of the Schools address, and it was not just a speech but a show. It began with a trumpeter and continued with projected slides as Hutchings outlined his vision—a significant style upgrade from the talk Mark Freeman had given a year earlier in the cafeteria.

Hutchings, wearing a red bow tie, went right at the racial and eco-nomic achievement gaps, and his criticism centered on the teaching staff. Every student deserves an "expert teacher," he said, the implica-tion being that not every existing teacher was an expert. Too many teach-ers, he implied, focused on the high achievers and weren't connected to those who needed more help.

"It's apparent to me that some of our staff members—and I use the word some, I'm not going to say all—but some of our staff members are teaching in our classes with one Shaker student in mind . . . They may not know any different way."

He ended his speech with a poetic evocation of the district's diversity, of what made the community special and what made it challenging. "Shaker is the student who gets up early to study Greek every day, and the student who stays up late to take care of his ailing mother," he said to a hushed room. "Shaker is the winner of a dozen art awards, and Shaker is the child who can barely hold a pencil."

He concluded: "This diversity is one of the beauties of Shaker Heights, and it is also one of our challenges."

This speech was what many would come to see as classic Hutchings: inspiring, blaming, lecturing, enthusiastic, joyous, hopeful—setting high goals, nebulous on how to reach them.

———

The U.S. educational system was emerging from two decades where the focus was on accountability. President George W. Bush had won bipartisan support for the No Child Left Behind Act, which he signed into law in 2001. Education reformers in both parties believed that if academic achievement was measured and disaggregated by race, if high standards were in place everywhere, and if schools and teachers were held accountable for the results, performance would improve. Schools with persistently low test scores would be forced to overhaul operations, or even to close. Unsuccessful teachers would be encouraged to try a different line of work. The best teachers might get a bonus or a pay raise.

The reforms brought a heavy dose of standardized testing in reading and math, which brought forward lots of teaching-to-the-test, which sapped time for arts and science and music and anything else that wasn't being measured. Moreover, there was little evidence that the reforms were leading to widespread improvements. In 2015, President Barack Obama signed an update of the federal education law, which dialed back the No Child Left Behind reforms and gave states far more flexibility in how they measured success.

The punitive elements of the reform movement faded, but the focus on racial disparities did not. In the aftermath, a new theory of the case emerged for how to fix schools, and specifically, how to raise the achievement of Black and Hispanic students, who persistently lagged behind their white and Asian American peers. It was called equity, and the goals were many: Attack systemic racism embedded in school districts that, coast to coast, had resulted in disproportionately few students of color in advanced classes and disproportionately more suspended. Hire more teachers of color. Employ full-time diversity and inclusion officers who would focus persistent attention on these issues. Make sure Black and brown students see themselves in the curriculum through culturally responsive teaching. And above all, perhaps, make sure every child is given what he or she needs to succeed.

Equity was defined differently than equality, to the amens of some and the consternation of others. Equality means everyone gets the same; equity means everyone gets what they need. That means that, under an equity framework, some kids might need more, and get more—a direct challenge to the expectations and privileges of families who were used to getting what they wanted.

———————

In 2017, Hutchings launched an Equity Task Force. "In Shaker, we've been talking about diversity, we've been talking about equity for a very long time," he said in his State of the Schools speech that year. "It's time to take action."

A nineteen-member collection of parents, school officials, and community members set out to create an equity policy that could eventually be approved by the school board. But first members spent months reviewing the history of the Shaker schools and the racial and economic achievement gaps. They worked to get to know one another and develop trust and talked about how they would explain this work to members of the community.

"We're going to have to tussle with numbers and data and history that is not always our proudest moment," Lisa Vahey, the task force cochair, told the group at the start of one November 2017 meeting. "We can use that as a catalyst for what can come next."

On this evening, the task force reviewed state report cards and in-house data on student achievement. Members saw how the gaps are in place even before students start school. For instance: 16 percent of Black students and 25 percent of low-income students entered kindergarten with no early childhood educational experience, versus 4 percent of white students.

Ideally, those gaps would start to close as all students receive a Shaker education. Yet over time, they grew larger. By third grade—when students are eight or nine years old—91 percent of white students were on track in reading, versus only 58 percent of Black students.

I sat in on this session, on the first of many reporting trips back home to Shaker. The conversation was interesting, but I wondered whether anyone inside or outside that room knew how to make things better. As Mark Freeman had said over and over, identifying the problem is the easy part.

The school district began sponsoring equity cohorts, where groups of Black and white residents would meet for months in a deep examination of their racial biases and identities.

The school board, too, had been grappling with the idea of equity. Reuben Harris Jr., after years as an outside agitator, ran for and was elected to the school board in 2011, and soon after Hutchings arrived, he pushed to add the term to the district's mission statement.

The question was, "How do we put that word in there without causing misunderstandings?" said Annette Tucker Sutherland, another school board member at the time. She said she supported the idea of equity but worried how the district would communicate it. "We were all very aware of the parents of the AP kids who tended to think, 'Oh, they are going to have to divert resources away from my AP child.' There was sensitivity to using that word and how best to use it."

Sutherland added that this was a challenge particularly with a Black superintendent in charge. "The same words coming out of his mouth or Dr. Freeman's mouth were heard differently," she said. "You're always in this dilemma of how to do this without scaring parents" who might leave the district.

The board was so paralyzed by this debate that Hutchings brought in a facilitator to help members find a solution. The final compromise left the word "equity" out of the mission statement but adopted the slogan "Excellence, Equity, Exploration." In the end, the slogan became far more visible than the mission statement anyway.

———

For decades, there had been economic divides in Shaker, with white residents far wealthier than Black ones. Over time, those divides have grown wider, and that has made closing academic gaps even harder. Child-

ren in struggling families—those without nutritious food or adult support or enough space for homework or a hundred other disadvantages—
are far more likely to struggle in school. That's true in central cities where
virtually all children are poor; it's also true in Shaker Heights.

Mark Freeman had argued that closing academic gaps required eradicating poverty. In fact, the opposite happened here. Poverty had not
been eradicated; it had grown.

The white population in Shaker Heights had been stable—and
wealthy. But by the time Hutchings arrived, Black residents were, as a
group, earning much less than Black residents once did. That's partly
because new suburbs had become available, comfortable, and attractive
for middle-class and wealthy Black families. (Nearby Solon, for instance,
saw its Black population more than double over two decades to about
12 percent in 2021.) Some upper-income Black families didn't want to
live in Shaker, in part because Black students, as a group, did so poorly.

"I have tried to recruit people to Shaker," said Emmitt Jolly, a Black
father who worked as a biochemist at Case Western Reserve University.
"They don't think Shaker does an effective job of taking care of their
Black children." Some, he said, feared their kids would be "lumped in
with lower-income Black kids."

On the other end of the economic spectrum, Shaker became more
accessible to low-income residents. Some of this was driven by the Great
Recession and foreclosure crisis in 2008 and 2009, city officials said. The
number of foreclosures in the city spiked, peaking at 261 in 2010, city
figures show. In 2010, the number of tenants using a Section 8 housing
voucher to help pay rent reached 348, a high.

Some homes needed significant repairs and some were abandoned
by owners, as the cost of repairs sometimes exceeded the value of the
house. Foreclosure proceedings allowed out-of-town, absentee investors
to scoop up properties all over the country, meaning homes were now
owned by people who were not part of the community, and not picky
about who they rented to.

These investors "have no real stake in the community. They don't
care who moves in as long as you can pay the rent," said Keith Langford,
a school district official who began working with low-income families in
2016 as director of the Family and Community Engagement Center.

All this hit the Moreland neighborhood hardest. Between 2000 and
2010, census data shows, the poverty rate in south Moreland tripled

to almost 38 percent, median income fell by 25 percent, the owner-occupancy rate fell, and the portion of households with married couples plummeted from nearly 40 percent to less than 15 percent. The relationship between race and class—wealthier white residents in some parts of town and poorer Black residents in others—was starker than ever.

In 2007, the house next to Adriann Kennedy in her north Moreland neighborhood sold for $7,500 to a "total slumlord," said Kennedy, who is Black and grew up in Shaker. She still lived on the same street, now with her husband and grandson. The renters next door, she said, were "some of the worst people you've ever seen. You'd be in fear for your life." Their friends would sit on her stoop smoking pot, refusing to move. They'd tip over her trash can and drive on her lawn. "I thought, where did they come from?"

These trends were turbocharged by the foreclosure crisis, but they fit into a long-term trend in Shaker: The white community was wealthy and stayed wealthy; the Black community earned far less, and over time even less. In 1989, the first year for which census data on race and income are available, the typical white household in Shaker earned $127,015 (in inflation-adjusted 2020 dollars). The typical Black household earned 62 percent of that—$78,702.

Over the next thirty years, that gap grew much wider. By 2020, the median white household income would rise to nearly $140,000. But the typical Black income in Shaker fell to just under $50,000—35 percent of what whites earned. (These figures do not include the families who live in the city of Cleveland but are in the Shaker school district.)

There was more poverty. Over these 30 years, the portion of white households in Shaker living in poverty inched up from 1.1 percent to 3.8 percent, according to census figures. But the portion of Black Shaker families in poverty nearly tripled, from 5.2 percent to about 14.7.

So in addition to serving students of wealth, Shaker schools were serving kids who lacked basic needs. "It's hard to wake up and go to school and be ready to learn if you don't have your own bed, if you're sleeping on the floor, in a chair, on a couch, with others," Langford said. Children weren't starving, he said, but maybe a family skipped dinner sometimes. Maybe kids showed up for school and lunch yesterday was the last meal they ate.

As Annette Sutherland predicted, some in Shaker did not appreciate the changes Hutchings was pushing in the name of equity. In 2017, for instance, Hutchings killed a popular hands-on science lab program at Woodbury, the upper elementary school.

For years, younger students had traveled to Woodbury four times each year to explore skeletons and snakes, examine flowers under microscopes, and find out what happens when an egg is dropped into a jar of vinegar. In April 2017, the administration announced it was eliminating the program and promised that hands-on science would be provided more often in each of the five lower elementary schools using science kits instead.

The response from many in the community was sharply negative. Lisa Cremer, the mother of three girls living in the Lomond neighborhood, helped launch an online petition on the Change.org site opposing the move, which garnered 599 signatures. "The science lab is an invaluable resource that many other schools do not or cannot provide," the petition read. "Removing this seems contrary to what we have grown to expect from our district."

Hutchings said his proposal was a step toward equity. Four trips each year to a science lab might be sufficient for children whose parents regularly take them to a science museum on their own. But other kids needed regular exposure to science, he said. He cast opponents as caring only about their own children, not all children.

"I'm in the business for all kids," he said in an interview, summarizing his response. "I'm not in the business just for your kid." Still, it was not clear why the science lab was preventing teachers from also teaching science in their classes, and Hutchings likely wasted valuable political capital on the matter.

Cremer failed to get the decision reversed, though her involvement led her to launch a campaign for school board in 2017.

Under Hutchings, the district also reduced the amount of leveling, mixing students of different abilities in various ways. At the high school, for instance, the district combined some honors classes with regular-level, or "core," classes. The material covered in both levels was the same, officials reasoned, but the classes had become racially segregated. In the combined versions—known officially as "honors/core" and colloquially as "slash classes"—the goal was to desegregate the classroom with teachers differentiating instruction to each student's appropriate level.

English teacher John Morris thought it was an excellent idea. Years before Hutchings arrived, he had begun offering a multidisciplinary class called The American Experience that included both core and honors students. "I'm a true believer," he said.

One spring, for instance, he taught two English courses. His twenty-nine-person honors class had three Black students, he said. His twenty-two-person core/honors class had thirteen Black students, a near-perfect representation of the student body as a whole.

But some parents didn't like this approach. Hutchings was "not interested in the fact that Shaker has a long tradition of being able to handle the very top kids," one angry mom said. She acknowledged that the high school featured, more or less, Black classes and white classes. "No one is going to say that feels comfortable. On the other hand, I've got to look out for my kid."

One result of the "slash classes," some administrators observed, was that some students moved themselves out of honors and into higher-level AP courses, a new kind of "white flight," which served to make both levels more racially segregated.

Hutchings also ended a practice by which parents could request a particular high school guidance counselor, an option some viewed as a good way to get the right match and others saw as another form of privilege, favoring parents who knew enough about the process and the choices to make such requests.

A more popular initiative was called Bridges. It worked to increase and sustain Black student participation in AP classes at the high school by bringing students to school over the summer to get to know one another, learn study skills, and get a jump start on the material. It began with Advanced Placement U.S. History in the tenth grade.

"Saying the classes are open to all, which Shaker has done for a very long time, helps, but not enough," said Sarah Davis, a veteran history teacher who helped create the program. Too often, Black students recruited into advanced courses were capable of the work but lacked peer support once they arrived. "When they looked around, they felt alone."

In 2016, the Bridges program began with sixteen students, growing larger over the next few years, with more students and additional subjects.

On the other end of the academic scale, the district created the Innovation Center for students who were at risk of not graduating and had been sent to an alternative school a half hour away. The center helped boost Shaker's graduation rate and later would expand to serve a swath of students looking for alternatives to the traditional high school.

Hutchings also dropped fees for summer learning, which brought more students into the programs, and began a small pre-K program. His new Family and Community Engagement Center worked to connect with marginalized communities, distributing school supplies, for instance, to students who couldn't afford them and providing an entry point to the district for parents who might have been intimidated by the formal structures.

Other initiatives didn't pan out. Aiming to recruit a more diverse teaching force, Hutchings tried to set up a partnership with Howard University, the prestigious historically Black university in Washington, D.C. Research shows that having a same-race teacher is enormously beneficial to students of color, but the plan fell apart. Hutchings said the dean he was working with stepped down and the initiative was dropped on Howard's end. Morris, the union president, said the union had suggested a partnership with a predominantly Black school in Ohio, but Hutchings wasn't interested. "He wanted the prestige of Howard," he said. Hutchings replied that the Ohio schools did not produce as many teachers as Howard did.

———

The heart of Hutchings's critique centered on the teachers, and, unsurprisingly, his relationship with the faculty, especially at the high school, was strained. Teachers there were accustomed to respect and even deference from the administration. Now they were being blamed for low Black achievement rates.

As Hutchings saw it, too many teachers had low expectations for Black students, even if they didn't realize it, and were failing to help them advance.

"Everyone was blaming kids. Kids. Kids! They don't have control. I used my personal example. I was on reduced lunch," he said, meaning his family's income was low enough to qualify him for federally subsidized lunches. "Thank God my teachers didn't blame me for that . . . We can't blame achievement gap issues on children we are hired to educate."

He also saw bias impacting student successes. He shared one story with the teachers union that he found instructive. A Black high school student in Shaker walked into her AP class during the first week of school. The teacher greeted her by asking if she was in the right class. When the student said yes, the teacher informed her, "This is AP."

"That was the day she felt her spirit was broken because her teacher didn't even believe she was in the right classroom," Hutchings said. The response from some teachers was sadness. Others defended the teacher, suggesting that she didn't mean it that way.

"Sometimes we're biased and you don't even realize you're being biased," he said.

At the high school, the teachers were defensive, and also irritated. It felt like Hutchings was stripping the autonomy they had long enjoyed— the special sauce, they believed, that had made Shaker an outstanding school system for decades.

At one point, Hutchings told a gathering of teachers that a good teacher could teach a hundred students at once, a statement they found both laughable and offensive. Critics saw an inflated ego. He referred to top aides as his "cabinet," prompting one staff member to say, behind his back, "You don't need a cabinet. You're not the president."

Hutchings angered high school journalism teacher Natalie Sekicky by coming down on the high school newspaper, the *Shakerite*, for a story that disclosed that the top candidate for high school principal had faced criminal charges (which were later dropped), a fact that the district was unaware of even though it had employed a search firm and news coverage of the incident was easily found in a Google search. Hutchings berated Sekicky because the student journalists had called the candidate, using the phone number on the résumé provided to the newspaper by the district. Hutchings told the adviser that he "allows" the *Shakerite* significant freedom but said the coverage "has gone far enough" and ordered the paper to stop reporting the story, according to contemporaneous notes Sekicky wrote summarizing their conversations.

Hutchings later replied that the reporting was opening Shaker up to possible lawsuits. He added, "We don't want to be in a situation where we can't find a principal because if you come here we're going to air all your dirty laundry." Sekicky said: "It was the first and only time in my twenty-five years at Shaker that an administrator tried to suppress reporting."

An incident in January 2015 left teachers particularly shaken. At Lomond School, a kindergartner asked to go to his locker and instead walked out of the building. About five minutes later, his teacher, Shaker veteran Cathleen Grieshop, realized he was missing and called the main office, computer lab, lunchroom, and aftercare space, staying with her class as there was no one else to watch the rest of the children. A few minutes later, a neighbor found the boy and called the police.

The little boy was Black and the teacher was white, and some saw the events through the lens of race. Did the district truly care about Black kids and their safety, or not? "I think in my mind it was hard to not think about would this have occurred if the child was not Black," Hutchings said in an interview. Others thought the teacher had done all she could and resented the allegations of racism.

The administration responded to the incident by removing Grieshop from the classroom and putting her on an administrative assignment for the rest of the school year. At one point, the union thought she might be fired, and her colleagues packed a school board meeting in a show of support. Hutchings later said that he was not aiming to punish her. "I know mistakes happen," he said.

═══════

Hutchings encouraged teachers to examine questions of cultural competence, bias, and equity. This was an important process, given the volume of parents and students who complained that teachers were biased or had low expectations for Black students.

Some teachers began thinking more deeply about these issues. William Scanlon, a veteran high school science teacher, clashed with Hutchings at times, but also said he knew teachers have racial biases that impact students, and acknowledged he had likely made mistakes.

"Maybe I've said to a Black kid, 'Why don't you have your homework done?' and maybe to a white kid, 'Get it to me next time,'" he said. Maybe, he said, he's asked a Black student walking through the hallway for his pass, and not asked white students in the same hallway to show theirs. "I have tried really hard not to do that," he said. But he guessed there have been times when he did something along these lines.

Not all teachers were open to this sort of reconsideration. Tiara Sargeant, who would later work for the schools, got to know Hutchings during her senior year at Shaker Heights High School, Hutchings's first year with the district. As a Black student, she had been dismayed by the dearth of Black faculty in Shaker, and she had found white teachers defensive in the face of any criticism.

"Anything he would say or do [prompted] a backlash because it made [teachers] look at who they were," she said. "Not all teachers at Shaker are willing to do that hard work about how their biases and privileges impact them as an educator."

Trainings around implicit and unconscious bias gained popularity with school districts, employers, and others as the country grappled with the impact of systemic racism on people of color in American institutions. Researchers have found that teachers, like others, make negative assumptions about students of color, with broad implications for their education, including expectations for success and decisions about discipline and course placement.

In Shaker, one outgrowth of the Equity Task Force was a new equity training for incoming instructional staff. During one such session in 2019, David Peake, a high school counselor who had co-chaired the task force, met with a small group of teachers and staff members who had recently been hired. He paired participants up and asked them to discuss questions of equity, and as they finished, asked them to thank each other for something that happened between them, and to be specific.

"That's the grace we need to live in as we have hard conversations," he said.

Peake then launched into the heart of the conversation. So many teachers—so many Americans—will say, "I don't see color, kids are kids," he said. And that may sound like the right answer to some, the nonracist way, the welcoming way. But no. He urged them to think of the question differently. "We do think it's important to see the whole person. We do acknowledge race in this district," he said. He added, speaking personally, "Black is my most essential identity."

Each participant was then asked to take an implicit bias test created at Harvard University, using their laptop computers. "We want to discover our unconscious attitudes," Peake said. "We want to be honest. We want this to be an opportunity for growth."

The test showed participants a series of photos of Black and white faces, and pleasant and unpleasant words. Test-takers were asked to sort each image into "good" and "bad" buckets. It measured how easy or hard it was for someone to identify Black and white faces in positive and negative ways.

After everyone had taken the test, Peake shared his results from the first time he took the test, a few years earlier. He was Black, but the results showed he had a bias toward white people. "It made total sense to me," he said. He explained that when he was younger, he had a tendency to reply more quickly to white students than to Black ones. He didn't want anyone to think that just because he was Black, he favored Black students, so he found himself overcompensating. "I would break conversations with Black students to address whites," he told the group. And beyond whatever damage that might have done for Black kids, he said, "I was showing white students they were of greater importance."

Perched on a stool at the front of the classroom, he let that comment settle over the room.

Participants then began disclosing their results. A white woman said the test showed she had a slight preference for African American students. A Black woman's test showed she favored white people. "I think it's just my upbringing," she said.

After receiving his own unsettling results, Peake told the group, he worked hard on correcting his biases. And when he took the test a second time, it showed no bias for either race. "I was actually proud. I mean I really consciously tried. I wanted to work on that."

———

Teachers at the high school had a growing list of grievances about Hutchings. Chief among them: he was widely seen as having pushed out the high school principal, Mike Griffith. Griffith, a Black man who was seventeen years older than Hutchings, had been principal for fifteen years. He was beloved by the teachers, lived in the community, and had sent five children through Shaker schools. Hutchings's supporters said Griffith deferred too much to teachers and to parents, especially privileged parents.

"I think Mike represented too much of what [Hutchings] would call the 'Old Shaker'—what parents want, parents get," John Morris said.

Hutchings recalled walking the halls of the high school with Griffith soon after arriving and asking why an honors class they saw was overwhelmingly white and a regular-level class mostly Black. "He was like, 'Oh, just a lot of our African Americans, that's just the class they sign up for, and a lot of our white students, that's the class they sign up for.'" Hutchings believed it wasn't just the students but the system itself that was pushing those students into those classes. Griffith said he did not recall that visit or this conversation and said he would not have dismissed that concern.

"I worked hard to strike the balance of serving all students," he said.

Griffith said he is confident the school's work made a significant positive difference in the lives of students from all backgrounds. Still, he said, it's true that the racial gaps at the high school did not close during his tenure. "Could we have done more? That would be a valid statement," he said. "We never got there."

In an interview, Hutchings said, "Even though he is a Black man, he did not know how to support some of the Black families." He added: "When I first came along, Mike didn't know how to deal with me. He was intimidated by me. I wanted to learn from him."

Griffith also described a troubled relationship. He said he wanted to work with Hutchings to address the district's problems, that he knew there were students who needed more and was excited to learn new strategies. "I wanted Hutchings to succeed." But he said Hutchings and his team had no appreciation for anything that had been done in the past or the views of teachers and others with significant experience in the district. And he said he was constantly micromanaged by Hutchings and his staff.

During the 2014–15 school year, Griffith said he was told that the administration did not plan to renew his contract for the following year. So when a local private school reached out to see if he was interested in their head of school position, he applied and was offered the job. Griffith said Hutchings offered him a one-year contract after he told him about the job offer, a belated and insulting offer given that principals usually have multiyear contracts. In April 2015, Griffith announced he was resigning, and while he gave all the usual statements about great opportunities and a new journey ahead, he also cried throughout the faculty meeting where he announced his decision. "This is the last thing I wanted to do," he said.

An interim principal, James Reed III, who was Black, took over, and teachers backed him to get the permanent job. But Hutchings instead hired Jonathan Kuehnle, who was white. Now teachers were doubly mad, first losing Griffith, then Reed.

A February 2015 survey of 137 teachers conducted by the high school's Faculty Senate found more than 3 in 4 teachers said staff morale at the high school was bad, with a majority calling it the worst they'd ever seen. Six in 10 said that in the last two years—since Hutchings arrived—the district was heading in the wrong direction; almost no one said Shaker was heading in the right direction.

Comments in the survey were heavily negative. "Change is not bad," wrote one teacher. "Illogical, ineffective and ill-conceived change is the issue." Another wrote: "We are not treated as professional or trusted to make professional decisions." A third said, "Top down management will not work."

In May 2015, the high school members of the Shaker Heights Teachers Association sent an open letter to the administration expressing "significant concerns about the present and future direction of our beloved building and school district."

Jody Podl, an English teacher who led the Faculty Senate, voiced teachers' views to Hutchings and it didn't go well. She said he called her into his office because her "body language" at a community meeting following Griffith's departure was "inappropriate." After the new principal was announced, Podl said she sent Hutchings an email saying the choice wasn't what they had hoped for but teachers would try to make sure there was a smooth transition. She was invited to a meeting after that, and Podl said she must have reacted negatively to something someone said because Hutchings "screamed, 'Don't you roll your eyes at me! That's disrespectful.'" She said he added, "You've disrespected me from the minute I got here!"

"I was a little bit of a marked person" after that, she said. "For Greg, he just wanted people to agree with him, and if you didn't agree with him, you weren't on his side."

Hutchings said he did "speak sternly" to Podl. He said she was putting her head on the table and turning around in her seat. "I told her it was disrespectful and inappropriate for any adult to act like that. You're either going to sit up and pay attention like everyone else or leave . . . I don't accept that kind of behavior."

Hutchings also faced opposition from a group of white parents who feared he was undermining what had made Shaker schools special.

They feared that high-achieving students would lose out if resources were shifted to lower-achieving kids. They also worried that teachers might water down honors and AP classes if students who weren't prepared were pushed into higher levels. They feared the district was easing up on discipline.

Lara Mullen, a white mom of two, was among those with concerns with the equity push Hutchings championed, as well as his abrasive personal style. Once, she said, he had berated her by phone for asking to see the résumé of a finalist for a top district job.

She supported programs to help boost kids who have untapped potential but was irritated at his move to bar parents from requesting certain teachers. She said each year she would talk with the teachers for the next grade up and consider who was the best fit for her two boys. She rejected any suggestion that this system allowed certain parents to get the best teachers. "I don't get all the best teachers. I get the teachers who are right for my kids," she said. Just because some parents don't make requests, she asked, does that mean that nobody should be able to?

Many parents liked the pullout system whereby top students were taken out of the classroom for enriched work, arguing that it enabled kids of all ability levels to get what they needed. Now the enrichment teachers were "pushing in" to the classrooms, and it wasn't the same. At Woodbury, teachers who used to be dedicated to enrichment classes were now teaching all children.

Some parents spoke to me only on condition that they not be named. They uniformly said they valued diversity and wouldn't live in Shaker if they didn't. Some feared their views would sound racist in print and wanted people to know they weren't.

But some made clear there were limits to how much diversity they would accept, particularly economic diversity. One wealthy white father said he loved that his kids had friends of all races but said a "significant portion" of Black students in Shaker are "maybe what you'd call ghetto. That portion, I don't feel any need to have my kids interacting with that culture . . . But the middle-class Black people—who are a sizable portion, and I think that's fantastic—that's the part I want to live with." He also objected to new rules that prevented families from requesting a particular guidance counselor at the high school. "If you can't navigate this system, you don't want to be in this system," he said.

Another white father was openly disdainful of the push to close the achievement gap. He used a basketball analogy to suggest that closing the gap was akin to getting rid of the top performers. "The achievement gap on the Cleveland Cavaliers went down when LeBron left," he said, meaning the distance between the best and worst player was smaller because a superstar was no longer in the mix. "There's no correlation between closing the gap and achieving excellence. Do you really want to chase the best students out of Shaker by not supporting them and providing what they need?" He compared the idea of equity to an unachievable, inadvisable drive to create equal outcomes. "That's called communism. If that's what they're looking for, they're going to destroy the schools in the process."

"Equity means you're picking and choosing who the heck you are focusing on," said Jim Sammon, a white father who had two children in the Shaker schools. "If you're paying a lot of money [in taxes] and you think your kid's not getting the benefit of it, why are you staying?"

A small group of fathers arranged a meeting with Hutchings to express their concern that wealthy families would leave Shaker, and asked him to promote statistics showcasing high achievers. One even suggested Shaker create a separate magnet school for high achievers, something that would exacerbate segregation.

Hutchings remembered the meeting well. "They told me how much they made, what they did, and that they were Harvard graduates. All right. So that's how you introduce yourself, all right, great. I felt, what was the point in all of that? I don't know if it was the intimidation or . . . what they were trying to do. But that's how it started. So I listened to it," he said.

He had little patience for their complaints that the district was more concerned with equity than excellence.

"I started by first telling them that if I only supported poor Black people I wouldn't be supporting my own kids who are in school because we're African American but we are not poor," he said later. "I live on Parkland Drive. I make very good money and my wife and I are very educated. So let me first tell you that that's not my stance."

Hutchings came away from the exchange resolved to stay the course. "I was courageous and relentless enough to keep pushing forward. I told them that they didn't scare me."

For their part, the fathers came away convinced Hutchings would never take their concerns seriously and decided that the better course was politics, so they backed two white women for the school board who they believed to be like-minded. One was Lisa Cremer, who had clashed with Hutchings over the science lab; it's not clear why they favored the second woman. Both candidates were also endorsed by the high school newspaper, and both won.

232 | Dream Town

Earl Leiken had served on the school board for many years, including as its president in 1987, when the board closed four elementary schools and rezoned the remaining buildings to be racially balanced. Now he was the mayor of Shaker Heights and kept his eye on what was happening with the schools.

After Hutchings had been superintendent for a while, parents started coming to Mayor Leiken with concerns. They said enrichment programs were threatened, and they complained that the school discipline had deteriorated, with bad behavior in the classroom too often tolerated. They worried the district was losing good teachers.

The mayor agreed that Shaker had to serve those with the greatest needs, but he also thought it was important to appeal to those with advantages—those who had other options like private school or moving. The drive toward equity was important but had to be balanced with excellence, he felt.

Leiken had a pie chart showing that in 2015, 28 percent of the income tax dollars collected in Shaker were produced by families earning more than $500,000 per year, and nearly half came from those earning more than $300,000. The suggestion was obvious: if those families leave the district, the economics of the entire community collapse.

"We're blessed to have a great deal of wealth in Shaker. And part of our future is continuing to be attractive to people who have some level of affluence and who are well educated," he said. "I just want people to be mindful of that fact."

"I was strongly in favor of serving the whole population," he said.

Leiken took the concerns to Hutchings, who disputed that anything was being taken from high-end students. "Tell me when I said that," he demanded.

In December 2017, Hutchings announced that he was leaving at the end of the school year. He had been offered what he said was his dream job—school superintendent in Alexandria, Virginia, his hometown.

Some had long thought he was using Shaker as a stepping-stone and said the announcement confirmed it. Some were relieved. But others were devastated, fearful that the equity work he had championed would fall away. Reuben Harris had predicted it would take ten years to make real change; now Hutchings was leaving after five, and the job was undone.

During a public farewell interview in the high school auditorium in May 2018, as he prepared to leave, Hutchings said he had learned to "slow my roll" and take time to listen to others, how to "filter" his thoughts, and "bite my tongue" rather than say everything that came to his mind. "I wouldn't have made it five years in Shaker if I said everything I wanted to say." He said he learned that even parents who may seem "pushy" just wanted the best for their children.

Yet the next month, at his final school board meeting, Hutchings delivered an angry rant, lashing out at his critics and urging the board and others to ignore parents who complain. The board had just declined to give one of his top aides, Terri Breeden, a new three-year contract and he was angry about it. He suspected the board was listening to "hearsay" about her from community members and thought this represented a return to a previous culture where loud voices had outsize influence. "Most of my time is spent dealing with the ignorance that comes from adults," he said at the board meeting. "I'm sorry to say, but just because you went to school does not mean you can run and tell educators what to do, period. It's unacceptable. And it's not okay."

He said he did not let the critics affect his work. "I come to work every single day, even with the disrespect, the unapologetic disrespect. I give a hundred percent even when I'm beat down. I never speak negatively about any person publicly . . . I have integrity and believe in myself even when people don't believe in me."

In an interview later, he said his tenure had been a success because in his final year, Shaker had improved on the state report card. In 2016–17, Shaker earned an F for "gap-closing," a measure of how the most vulnerable students performed on state tests. The next year, that jumped to a B. However, the district's data expert said the improvement was chiefly the result of a change in methodology by the state. A check of seven other diverse Ohio districts found they all got F's on "gap-closing" in 2016–17. Four of the seven, like Shaker, improved to B's the next year.

Hutchings said his most important accomplishment was the fact that he was hired—being in the job as a Black man and role model for students. "Representation—it matters so much," he said.

Mark Joseph, the Black father and activist, had helped lay the groundwork for the board to nudge Freeman into retirement, opening the door for Hutchings. As Hutchings left, Joseph described a mixed record. "He was young and early in his leadership career and he absolutely was

234 | Dream Town

polarizing. He often handled things in an impulsive way. More humility would have helped," he said. But he said his tenure also helped move the district forward into a new era that was "unapologetic about equity as a priority."

"We got a big disruption to the status quo," he added. "It kind of shook us up and we'll never be the same, in a good way."

There is little doubt that Hutchings shook things up in Shaker, but it's also true that he would have made far more progress if he had had better people skills, if he had understood that people with different views are not necessarily enemies. Some of what he brought to the district endured long after he left—innovations such as the family engagement center and a movement toward more mixed-ability classrooms. But, as Joseph said, more humility would have set him up for far more success.

Looking back four years after he left, Hutchings said his time in Shaker helped him hone his leadership skills and was invaluable. He said he still loved the community and does not think there is another place like it. "I am grateful and thankful for my opportunity in Shaker," he said. "They took a chance on me and I will forever be grateful."

After five years in Alexandria, in 2022 Hutchings resigned to open a consulting firm focused on racial equity work. He said he no longer aspires to be secretary of education.

———

In early 2019, six months after Hutchings had departed, his Equity Task Force recommended an Educational Equity Policy to the school board.

"All Shaker students deserve to be held to high expectations while being given the resources and supports they need to exceed those expectations," it said. "The Board believes that expanding opportunities for students who have been historically marginalized will enrich the overall development of all students."

It also noted: "Equity does not mean equal. Achieving educational equity will mean that schools and students may receive different resources based on specific needs."

The policy was approved by the board. The vote was unanimous, including yes votes from the two women whom Hutchings's opponents backed in the campaign. It set lofty goals, but how Shaker would reach them was still unclear.

We need people in power who listen to students, teachers and parents—
not just one group at the expense of the others.
—Editorial in the *Shakerite*

13

OLIVIA MCDOWELL AND JODY PODL

Olivia McDowell was feeling sleepy as she left the cafeteria on a drizzly autumn day a few weeks into her junior year, descended the staircase, and headed to room 118 for Advanced Placement English. It was a tough class to have right after lunch. It seemed like she always felt tired. Her teacher, Jody Podl, had admonished her once already about dozing off in class.

Over two decades as a Shaker teacher, Podl had learned to spot warning signs. Olivia had been fiddling with her phone in class. Earlier, she had failed to finish the assigned reading and the study guide about *A Tale of Two Cities*, one of the first novels they were tackling. Podl had pulled her aside and privately talked to her about the missing work. Olivia admitted she hadn't read one of the chapters, and Podl advised her to catch up because a writing assignment was coming up. The next day she asked Olivia if she was all set, and Olivia gave her a thumbs-up.

Nonetheless, Podl had been worried enough that she left a voicemail for Olivia's mom to discuss it. Better to be proactive, she thought. Podl, who is white, was already acquainted with Olivia's mom, Herlinda Bradley, who is Black, from the high school CommUnity Builders group, a project of the Parent Teacher Organization meant to build cross-racial relationships. In her message, Podl shared her concerns and said she'd love to work together to help Olivia to sharpen her focus.

"She is going to have to make some choices if she wants to be success-ful," Podl wrote in an email to Olivia's guidance counselor summarizing the call.

Olivia—Liv to her friends and family—had been excited when she found out Podl would be her English teacher, optimistic her writing would improve with Podl's help. But the year was starting off rough. Now, heading into English on September 24, 2018, she nervously asked other students if they had their assigned outlines done. Some did; a cou-ple did not, but unlike Olivia, they had told Podl ahead of time. Olivia had had a busy weekend, and the assignment slipped her mind.

As class began, the teacher started circling the room, collecting papers. When she got to Olivia's desk, in the front row, Olivia admitted she didn't have the assignment and asked if she could turn it in on Tuesday. There were still four days until the final paper was due at week's end, so she thought it wouldn't be a big deal. But for Podl, this was another sign that things might be heading in the wrong direction for Olivia, and she started asking some questions, trying to understand why she was struggling: *What English class did you take last year? Who was your teacher? What other courses are you in now?* Olivia replied that she had honors English her sophomore year and finished with a B, and that this year she was taking all honors and AP classes.

Olivia recalled that Podl replied with exasperation: *You must be okay getting a D in this class.* She couldn't understand how she was headed for a D. At that point, her grade in this class was a B. Podl recalled say-ing that her expectations were not going to change, and she worried that Olivia might get a D on the assignment.

If there's a group of people prone to embarrassment, it is teenagers, and in this case, Olivia was horrified, humiliated. She thought the conversation was loud enough for other students to hear and saw them putting their earbuds in, pretending not to listen. (Podl thought it was quieter—that maybe two or three kids nearby overheard it.) After it was over, Olivia asked to go to the bathroom, and as she walked the hall-way to the nearest restroom, past the central office and a long wall of plaques celebrating the accomplishments of Shaker students past, she encountered a security officer she knew, who asked why she was so upset. Olivia started crying, and the officer suggested she call her mom. When Olivia got to the bathroom, she did just that, and told her mom what happened. She then returned to class and finished her work. Soon the bell rang, and Olivia headed to precalculus, her next class.

———

Jody Podl's family went back decades in Shaker Heights. In high school, when she was Jody Brown, she earned good grades, with lots of advanced classes, plenty of friends, a spot on varsity volleyball, and a position on the Student Council. High school yearbooks show her smiling, with thick brown hair and standard-issue preppy clothes in one photo, a sweatshirt from a Paris university in another. When she graduated in 1983, she headed to Brown University, another Shaker alum launched into the Ivy League, well prepared for college on the strength of rigorous academic instruction and three-hour final exams.

"I led a charmed life," she said. "When I think back on it now, I was busy, I was happy, I don't remember complaining a lot. I never felt overwhelmed."

She'd always liked working with children. She'd been a counselor at her overnight camp in Maine. In high school, she had tutored students at a Baptist church downtown. At Shaker, students are encouraged to spend the final weeks of their senior year on an out-of-school project, and Jody used hers to tutor an elementary school student who was struggling to read. "He was trying to learn his letters," she remembered. "I would bring in stuffed animals. I had a stuffed hippo to learn H."

She first considered a career in teaching when she met Ted Sizer, one of the nation's leading education reformers, who arrived to chair Brown's education department. He was starting something called the Coalition of Essential Schools, which worked to implement principles such as personalized learning, demonstration of mastery, and depth over breadth. He became a mentor to Jody. She created her own educational studies major, combining education history, philosophy, educational psychology, and literature, later returning to Brown for a master's degree after a stint teaching at a southern California boarding school.

She met her husband, Tod Podl, at her first job, and his admission to medical school in Cleveland brought the couple to Shaker Heights. By 1995, she was back at the high school, this time as an English teacher.

It felt right from the start. Podl remembered thriving in the freedom offered teachers—being told, for instance, there was just one book she

238 | Dream Town

was required to teach and she could pick from a long list for the others. "There was this incredible intellectual freedom and professional respect," she said. "You could walk over to the administration building and see Mark Freeman and say, 'Hey, I have this idea. What do you think?'"

Over the years, she developed a split-screen reputation—inspiring to some and intimidating, even harsh, to others.

To her backers, Jody Podl personified the Shaker tradition of creative teaching combined with academic excellence—pushing students hard to engage in complex material. Students recalled her pushing and pushing, and then, by the end of the year, realizing they had learned how to write. She would work to build community by taking attendance with a question. Instead of replying "here," students would answer questions as varied as "What's your favorite ice cream?" or "What's something you regret?" She looked for books that would resonate in modern ways, like *Just Mercy*, Bryan Stevenson's unsparing look at racism in the criminal justice system.

Carole Kovach, her colleague in the English Department, saw her as an "extraordinary teacher" who was always reading—not just novels but research papers, looking for something new and cutting-edge to bring to her classroom. She thought to herself, "I'll never be as good as Jody Podl."

W hen Olivia McDowell was in third grade, her mom, Herlinda Bradley, Jean and Henry's daughter, moved home to Shaker.

"There's something special about this community," she said. "The architecture—pretty trees and brick houses—and history. The look of the schools on the ovals. There's a sense of pride living in this community. They take pride. Certain things happen—tragedies happen—we come together. Good things happen and we come together."

Bradley, a 1991 Shaker High graduate, had connections in Shaker, and they paid off as Olivia was making her way through the school system. At one point, for instance, friends advised her to request a particular team of teachers for Liv. Bradley sent an email to the principal, and when the class lists were posted, Olivia was on that team. Year after year, Olivia excelled. "They were great teachers," her mom said. She was channeled into advanced classes almost from the start.

Outside class, Olivia loved dancing—jazz routines, ballet, and hip-hop. She danced onstage with a private company, as well as in the high school's Sankofa celebration of Black culture, with its dance club, and as a cheerleader. Around her sophomore year, she found a love of drawing, and then painting. Her works included two large self-portraits, including one with white fingers probing her large Afro with the words DON'T TOUCH MY HAIR painted above. She moved through the school with confidence—her jeans snug, showing off her curves, her fashion choices bold—bell-bottoms even when they weren't in style, large hoop earrings, bright purple and red lipstick. She wore her hair natural—sometimes dyed bright orange, sometimes in little poof ball buns, sometimes in a huge Afro.

Most of her activities were filled with Black students, but she also was part of the integrated Student Group on Race Relations, still going strong more than three decades after it was created. Olivia remembered when the SGORR students visited her fourth grade class at Lomond Elementary School. She remembered how the high schoolers would voice a robust "Yo!" and the younger students would reply "Yes!" and then go silent. She loved a game called the Knot, in which a group of students would stand in a circle and randomly take hold of two other hands, so that everyone's arms were knotted up. The challenge was to work together, silently, to untangle the group without letting go of hands. "It was a different form of teamwork than I was used to," Olivia remembered. "With this exercise, there were no words. One person can't reign on top. It literally takes the work of everyone."

———

After class on that September day, Podl was unnerved by the exchange she had had with Olivia. She immediately called Olivia's mom to apologize, but the call did little to appease her. Bradley was furious, convinced Podl was trying to belittle her daughter, to show she didn't belong in that room. Saying those things to a student of color was even worse and she thought Podl should know better.

The teacher apologized again and mentioned the earlier message she had left voicing concern about Olivia's performance. Bradley said she never got it and thought it was beside the point anyway. Podl asked if it would be okay for her to apologize directly to Olivia. Bradley said yes.

As Olivia's next-period math class was getting underway, Podl appeared in the classroom and asked to speak with her. The pair ducked into an office off the classroom, and the teacher apologized. She said she deeply regretted making Liv feel like she didn't believe in her, and said this was not her intention. "It's okay," Olivia replied, and she accepted her apology. The pair disagree on what the teacher said next. Olivia recalled Podl saying that every year she tells herself she won't do this again to another student, and that every night she goes to sleep hoping she wakes up a better person. That had an impact on Olivia: *Did she really do this every year?*

Podl recalled saying that each night when she went to bed, she reviewed the events of the day and reflected on what happened and how she could do better the next day. She said she would be thinking about Olivia that night.

Podl then asked Liv for permission to explain what she had hoped to convey when she called her out in class. Over the years, Podl said, "I have seen many students have a really hard time junior year and I get worried for them." That's why she asked about the classes and last year's teacher. She was trying, Podl said, to get some "context" and see if Liv was overwhelmed or if her struggles were isolated to this class. At that point, Podl recalled, Olivia burst into tears and said, "Oh, Ms. Podl, it's been some kind of day. There's so much stuff going on; you have no idea." She also said, "I know I haven't been doing what I'm supposed to do in your class."

The conversation, which lasted about nine minutes, ended amicably, Podl thought. She called Bradley back, summarized the conversation, apologized again.

After that, both Olivia and Podl said, things took a turn for the better. The next day, Olivia came to her room for after-school conferences and they worked on the essay due that Friday, which Olivia turned in on time. Podl looked for ways to engage her in class. One day, when they were reading aloud from the novel, Podl intentionally gave Olivia larger roles, and Liv thrived. A few days after the incident, Podl followed up with an email to Olivia's mom.

"I certainly hope the rest of your week has been better than Monday," she wrote. "Again, I want to apologize for causing Liv and you frustration and pain." She asked if there was anything else she could do.

Unbeknownst to Podl, Bradley was growing angrier.

Within a day or two of the incident, Podl had reached out to Lisa Vahey, who had co-chaired the district's Equity Task Force and often shared resources for building equity in schools. Podl told Vahey she had had an unsettling interaction with a Black student and wanted help thinking through how she could have handled it better. Podl didn't identify the student, but as it turns out, Vahey and Olivia's mom were friends, and Vahey had already heard the story from Bradley. She realized Podl was talking about Olivia, and reported the interaction back to Bradley. (Vahey said later she did not remember the conversation with Bradley or why she mentioned it to her.)

When Bradley heard about what Podl said, she was furious. Everyone always tries to deny that things are about race, she thought. Well, she concluded, here the teacher was confirming it was about race. "She was admitting race was a factor."

So Bradley lodged a formal complaint, emailing the principal, Jonathan Kuehnle, who had been hired over the faculty's wishes, with other officials copied in.

The email made clear she had not accepted Podl's apology. She described Podl as having "verbally accosted" her daughter and publicly questioned her capabilities. She reported that Podl had threatened to give Olivia a D in the class, and said Olivia was "humiliated and embarrassed." She put the incident squarely into the context of race.

"For her to embarrass and humiliate my African American daughter is unacceptable," Bradley wrote, estimating there were just a few students of color in the class. "She presented an African American child negatively to her Caucasian classmates and her statements were false." Even if they were true, she added, Olivia did not deserve "public shaming." Podl's apology was private, she wrote, but the shaming was public.

"This is also a failure of the system," she wrote. "Shaker with all its good intentions and words had failed to adequately address the performance gap and racial inequity. Shaker constantly questions, why there are not more students of color in advanced classes? Mrs. Podl's behavior is one example that helps to answer that question."

Then she accused Podl of violating the district's policy against bullying, which barred repeated "harassment, intimidation, or bullying" that causes mental or physical harm, and is "sufficiently severe, persistent or pervasive that it creates an intimidating, threatening or abusive educational environment." She said she was willing to meet about this but that "more needs to be done to address my concerns."

She asked that the complaint be put into Podl's personnel file.

District officials took the complaint seriously from the start. The day after receiving Bradley's email, Principal Kuehnle reported the matter to Marla Robinson, the district's chief of staff. A couple of days later, he called Bradley to discuss her concerns. Olivia's counselor offered to change her class, an idea Bradley rejected. In the call, Bradley asserted that she'd been around Podl and said she frequently carried herself with "a sense of superiority" regarding education. She said she knew of another Black girl who had a similar experience with Podl and would see if the girl's mother wanted to come forward.

On October 9, more than two weeks after the incident, Robinson interviewed Olivia about what happened, and Olivia submitted a written statement. She recounted her version of events and ended by saying she accepted her teacher's apology. "Since then," Olivia wrote, "Ms. Podl has been extremely nice to me, always asks me questions to get involved and just small stuff like that."

Later that day, Podl was called to the administration building, where she was put on paid administrative leave, effective immediately. Her keys and identification were taken, and her email was cut off. She was told not to set foot in the high school. No reason was given for the action. Two days later, Podl was called in again, alongside a union representative, and told what was going on, and warned not to discuss the case with anyone, Podl said.

The district had launched two investigations: Robinson was investigating whether Podl's comments constituted racial discrimination, and Kuehnle, the principal, was investigating whether they constituted bullying. Podl was given a chance to explain what happened with Olivia, and she told her side of the story. She was told there were other complaints as well, though it would be weeks before Podl was given their statements.

One of the complaints came from a Black student who had already graduated. Robinson recalled hearing complaints about Podl from this student, who was now in college, and reached out to see if she wanted to submit a formal statement.

She did. In it, the former student wrote of some upsetting interactions with Podl, who had been her teacher for AP English her junior year. One day during a quiet time, she wrote, she was whispering with another MAC Sister Scholar. "As the class was widely quiet, Mrs. Podl screamed at us affirming that we are a disgrace to the MAC Sister Scholars and really should not be acting how [we] were if we were supposed to be good examples for our community," she wrote. "Implicit in her comments were the ideas that Black people widely did not follow instruction and generally are not capable of being role models or leaders."

Podl later replied that she was trying to help the student be "her best self" and that "others were looking to her to set an example." She also described what she believed to be a positive overall relationship with her former student, saying the student had frequently dropped by her classroom the following year, when Podl was no longer her teacher, and invited her to one of her volleyball games.

Separately, four other current students who had discussed concerns about Podl with another teacher submitted statements with their own complaints, and they became part of the investigation. Each story had its own complexities, but to the district, it looked like a pattern that had to be addressed.

Podl submitted a nine-page formal statement on October 22, defending herself. She wrote of her work to incorporate racial equity themes into her teaching and to bring training to the high school. She again offered her version of the events with Olivia and recounted her repeated apologies. She couldn't respond to most of the other allegations because they had not yet been detailed to her. But in general, she described a push and pull of encouragement combined with high expectations, and she painted her relationships with students as positive and productive. Podl concluded: "I hope that after you read my statement . . . I can return to school."

———

A week after Podl was ordered out of the classroom, the high school principal emailed the entire school to announce that Podl was on leave, without giving any details. Podl remained in her Shaker home, often alone, growing increasingly anxious. Fall parent-teacher conferences came and went, and she wasn't allowed to participate. She was not allowed to communicate with students who needed letters of recommendation for early decision college applications. And with the circumstances around her case so nebulous, she worried that parents and students were assuming scenarios far more troubling, such as sexual improprieties (as there had recently been a case), or some other crime.

Podl felt trapped inside her house, located on the wealthier eastern edge of Shaker, terrified she would run into someone she knew and be forced to talk about it. She didn't know what to say. She timed walking her dog to when she thought there would be nobody outside. Some of her students texted Podl's daughter to ask whether she was sick.

She couldn't eat and couldn't sleep and spent hours walking around her house. Already slim, she lost 15 pounds. She couldn't believe what was happening. She had taught at Shaker for more than two decades, was a Shaker graduate herself and a parent of three graduates. She lived in the community. And this is how they treated her? No benefit of the doubt at all?

"This has been kind of a gut punch to me," she said. "I feel like they did not try to recognize or appreciate who I am as a teacher or as a person."

"If you're a teacher and you're doing your job, there will be kids who complain about you," she said. It was her firm belief that after the first complaint came in, "the principal went on a fishing expedition to see if anyone else was complaining." She wished she had preceded her comments to Olivia with something softer, something like, "I know you can do really good work. Can I ask you a few questions?" She didn't. "That doesn't make me a racist or a bully because I didn't say that."

In a school district struggling with racial equity, she realized: "I'm symbolic of the issues."

<hr/>

Opinions of Podl as a teacher ranged. Some saw her as an outstanding instructor and coach with a true gift for teaching writing. Others found her too tough, or were hurt by comments they found sarcastic or mean. In a statement in conjunction with the investigation, one girl wrote that Podl had yelled at her for not paying attention, and suggested that that's why she didn't do as well as others in the class. Another student said Podl suggested that she reconsider her enrollment in the class after missing work. Podl described these interactions differently, saying she was always happy to help students improve their grades and encouraged all students, including those who complained, to come in for extra help. In many cases, she said, students who struggled at the start of the year turned things around and thanked her for the push.

Other students saw that nurturing side of her. Khalil Abdullah, a MAC scholar who graduated in 2019, recalled being one of the only Black students in her class.

"I loved her. She was always supportive of me," he said. In an interview, he said she supported him during some tough times, including when he had trouble getting access to a computer. "Whenever I had a problem, I would talk to her." He loved the way she took attendance with a question and the speakers she brought to class. "Ms. Podl was just one of the best teachers I've had," he said. As he started to hear about the complaints against her, he grew upset. "I didn't want to believe it because it's not true. She's not that type of person . . . They were trying to demonize her in a way and I didn't accept that."

Just the previous spring, a Shaker mom had emailed Superintendent Hutchings to detail how Podl had repeatedly gone out of her way to help her daughter, who had been struggling in school. As a result, her daughter's confidence had improved, and she had grown intellectually. "It is teachers like Ms. Podl that make a difference in students' lives by building relationships and going the extra mile," the mother said.

On October 24, a full month after the incident with Olivia, Podl was informed in a brief letter that the evidence did not support the complaint of racial discrimination. Marla Robinson's internal report, based on the incident with Olivia and conversations with five other students, was far more stinging. She concluded that Podl had a habit of criticizing students in front of their peers, of being sarcastic and overly critical. "Her approach is often harsh and not conducive to positive relationships or academic achievement," she wrote in a sweeping conclusion based on a small sample of students. (And in fact Podl had yet to see the students' statements or fully respond to their complaints.) In any case, Robinson concluded that these actions were not directed at any one group, so a finding of discrimination was not supported.

The letter told Podl that while the discrimination complaint was dismissed, she was still being investigated by Principal Kuehnle to see if she had violated the bullying policy.

Soon after this, Kuehnle himself was reassigned, and he was later forced out of his job amid unrelated allegations. The investigation was taken over by another administrator, Terri Breeden, and on Monday, November 5, Podl was brought in to meet with her.

As soon as she sat down, Breeden told Podl she was being disciplined, according to Susannah Muskovitz, attorney for the Shaker Heights Teachers Association, and John Morris, the union president, who were both there. Muskovitz complained, "She's never had a chance to tell her side of the story. Ever." Breeden informed them that she had violated the district's bullying policy and was being given a "documented verbal reprimand"—a letter in her personnel file.

"Where's the due process?" the lawyer snapped back. The union had been given the statements of the other students only three days earlier, and the names were redacted. Muskovitz demanded unredacted statements, wanted to know how they were "solicited," and wanted Podl to have a chance to tell her side of the story. The district maintained that Podl had been welcome to tell her story right then and there, but her lawyer had advised against it without first seeing all the evidence against her.

The next day, Podl was sent a formal reprimand. The letter instructed her to "treat students in a professional manner," and to participate in a "restorative practices" session with students and parents who had been part of the investigation. The purpose was to "learn how to best move forward with productive relationships following this situation." Restorative practices had become a popular alternative to discipline that many schools used for students who broke rules. Those harmed are given a chance to explain how they were hurt, and perpetrators are given a chance to apologize, hopefully better understanding the ramifications of their actions. Podl was also warned that the administration would monitor her to make sure she was in compliance with district policies, including the antibullying rules. She was told to report to the administration office on Wednesday, November 7, for the session. After that, the letter instructed, "you will return to the classroom."

The next day, two things happened: Breeden sent letters to parents of the other students involved in the investigation, telling them Podl had been found in violation of the bullying policy, and giving them the chance to participate in restorative sessions. And the Shaker Heights Teachers Association filed a formal grievance on Podl's behalf.

Podl did not return to work the next day as she had been instructed. She said she was traumatized by the events and how they unfolded and confused over who was angry with her and why. She felt she could not function in the classroom—didn't know where the lines were or when she might cross them. She took a medical leave, and began draining her significant accumulated sick time.

———————

The controversy around Podl was not the only drama at Shaker Heights High School in the fall of 2018. A football coach was dismissed for hiring someone with a felony record. The cheerleading adviser resigned after allegedly fat-shaming a girl on the squad. And, most significantly, Kuehnle had been put on administrative leave, though no one was certain why. Later, allegations would swirl that he had been under the influence of alcohol at school events. (In an interview, he denied any wrongdoing and said the allegations involving drinking were "absolutely untrue.")

The interim principal was David Glasner, a white man who had been hired by Hutchings to lead the middle school and was quickly climbing the administrative ranks. On Thursday, November 8, just two days after Podl was officially reprimanded, the district planned an assembly to introduce Glasner to the community.

The teachers union wasn't thinking much about David Glasner and his introduction. They were furious about how Jody Podl had been treated. The day before the meeting, Morris sent high school union members an email laying out how the entire Podl case had unfolded, with a detailed timeline that painted the investigation as both unfair and overblown.

"In all my years in Shaker, I have never seen a teacher so mistreated—especially in response to allegations by students that were directly related to course assignments, grading, and academic expectations," Morris wrote to the teaching staff. "What happened to Jody (and is still happening to Jody) could happen to any one of you."

He then pointed to the meeting scheduled for the following night to introduce Glasner. "If you are so inclined, I encourage you to attend tomorrow's meeting at 6:30 at the High School Large Auditorium to ask leadership why we are treating our teachers this way. I hope to see you there."

His hopes were realized. The next evening, teachers turned out in huge numbers, wearing their red union T-shirts. The auditorium was packed with more than nine hundred students, parents, and community members. With so much turmoil in an otherwise stable district, local TV news crews were on-site to document the event.

As Herlinda Bradley and her daughter traveled to the high school that evening, they both suspected the conflict with Podl would come up. Few people knew Olivia was the student at the center of it, and Bradley wanted to keep it that way. But on her way to the school, Olivia was thinking about what she might say, how she might need to defend herself, remembering rumors about another student that had once spiraled in the absence of facts. She thought about how her mom always told her, ever since she was a little girl, to use her words.

Bradley tried to cut off that sort of thinking at the pass. She instructed her daughter to keep her mouth shut: "You will sit there."

On the way in, the pair overheard two white girls talking about how Jody Podl had been treated so badly. Once inside the auditorium, they saw a huge show of support for the teacher. JUSTICE FOR JODY, read the signs. Mother and daughter took seats near the front center section, Olivia growing more anxious by the minute.

The meeting started badly and grew exponentially worse. Scott Stephens, the district's communications chief, stood at a lectern. The stage beside him was empty except for two men in chairs to his left. One was Glasner, the new interim principal, who is white; the other was Stephen Wilkins, the interim superintendent, who is Black. The lush red velvet curtain hung behind them, and nearly every seat in the audience was taken, with some standing in the side aisles.

Stephens began with an unpopular announcement: people were to write their questions on index cards and he would read them aloud.

"No! No!" a woman yelled, walking down the aisle toward the stage. "You will not sanitize our questions!"

Others began yelling, too. Someone barked "Shut up!" The meeting had barely begun and Stephens was already pedaling backward.

"You're going to lose control before it begins!" someone shouted.

"Yeah," Stephens replied. "Yeah, thanks for your help."

He then addressed the elephants in the room, sort of. He mentioned the principal's administrative leave but without telling anyone what had happened, trying to reassure the audience that his actions didn't involve police or put students in danger. Then he referred to the Podl case, saying the district was confident everything would be resolved.

"We're not interested in being kind of back and forth about that tonight," he said, an optimistic—or perhaps delusional—pronouncement given that many in the room came to discuss just that.

Stephens added that they could not talk about personnel issues but said they wanted "this particular teacher" back in the classroom. "She has tremendous talent and she's a benefit to our students," the spokesman added, which may have been the nicest thing any Shaker administrator had said to or about Podl since the entire episode began.

Once questions began, it was one after the next about the investigations and their aftermath, with officials replying that they could not discuss personnel matters, leading to more shouting from the audience. When Stephens read the question, "Why was Ms. Podl not given an opportunity to defend herself in these accusations?" many in the audience erupted into applause, with some yelling at the stage. Stephens stared down at his stack of cards, and a chant of "We want answers!" broke out. No one even attempted to answer the question.

The room was white hot, but the three men onstage were cold and quiet. Stephens tried to talk over the noisy crowd. Glasner and Wilkins slumped in their seats, stone-faced and looking as if they wished to be anywhere else.

The audience stirred again when Stephens read another question that clearly was about Podl: "How can a teacher initiate a conversation regarding a student's academic activities and performance if there's any fear that the conversation can be labeled as bullying?" Glasner replied that high expectations were important, and students were always capable of learning and growing. Teachers who approach students with a fair-minded, supportive mentality, he said, get good results. The message might have been the right one, but it was delivered with an emotionless matter-of-factness completely out of step with the passion in the room.

And then, just when it seemed that the administrators would be shouted down by angry teachers, things started to shift, and it seemed they would be shouted down by angry parents. One questioner expressed concern with the union's letter to the teachers and its "dismissive and belittling tone toward the student and parent concerns." This person asked how the district could ensure that student and family concerns were taken seriously. Both men replied with versions of "we're working on this."

Grousing and heckling from the seats continued. There was a palpable longing in the room for one of the men onstage to stand up and say something, anything, even moderately unifying.

Instead, anger continued to rise, and more index cards with questions piled up for Scott Stephens. About a half hour into the conversation, an elementary school teacher walked up to the front of the room and spoke her question to the stage.

"What about the emotional damage that's already been done to Ms. Podl?" the teacher said. It was Cathleen Grieshop, the teacher who had been temporarily removed from the classroom after one of her kindergartners wandered out of the building. "And what's going to happen to make sure that doesn't happen to a teacher again?"

Olivia watched all of this from her center-front seat, keeping quiet as her mom instructed. But when she heard that comment, her legs began shaking, and she felt adrenaline coursing. There was something about that question, about the concern expressed for damage done to Podl, that set her off. She wanted to know: *What about the damage done to the student?* Finally she stood up and walked right up onto the stage and outed herself as the girl at the center of the controversy, the Black girl in AP English who didn't have her outline that day.

"Excuse me! Hi, everyone!" she said with a high wave from the stage. She stood right next to Glasner, who stared at the floor. "I'm Olivia McDowell. I'm a junior and I'm the student that they're referring to in that [teachers union] letter." Many in the audience broke into applause, with some on their feet, and her mom standing at the front beside the stage, as if positioned to catch her should Olivia fall. Liv started to speak again but couldn't be heard. Someone yelled that she should "grab a mic," and Olivia turned to face Glasner, who, seated and silent, handed her his microphone.

"I don't want to get emotional, but I care about my education," she said. "Why is it about the teacher's feelings? What about the students?" She turned to face Glasner. "Y'all say you all care about us so much? But time and time again all our questions are still unanswered. Y'all sweep stuff under the rug and act like it just doesn't matter, act like it's not going on. I don't get it."

Later, she would say that she never meant to make the controversy about race, but from the stage at this moment, Olivia very much put race on the table. "What about the damage to a student when they're, what, one of three, one of five Black kids in their class because of the whole education gap that y'all have?"

Staring directly at Glasner and Wilkins, Olivia demanded: "What are you all going to do about this? Because I've been in Shaker since third grade and nothing has changed." Referring to Podl without naming her, she said the problems stretched well beyond one student and one teacher. "Plenty of other teachers that are in this room right now, I've heard countless things about," she said. She said teachers may be capable of teaching their subjects, but "where are the people skills? You're supposed to teach children, you're supposed to build them up, not tear them down each chance that you get. Period."

With that, she handed the microphone back to Glasner and walked off the stage.

It was, by any measure, a stunning moment. A student telling the world that she was behind a spiraling controversy with a teacher whom the entire faculty was currently rallying around. A teenager directly challenging top administrators in front of hundreds of people. It called for a response, and a strong, empathetic one that could somehow recognize all the conflicting pressures and interests in the room. One longed for someone, anyone, to stand up and articulate the community's very real shared values.

As she walked off the stage, Glasner simply said, "Thank you, Olivia." He didn't address what she had just said. And Scott Stephens, who was sorting through more index cards as Olivia spoke, recorded what might have been the most tone-deaf moment of the evening as he immediately began to read the next question. "What is the time frame for investigating the . . ."

Voices from the audience shouted him down. And standing at her seat now, Olivia yelled, "Everything is always swept under the rug at this school. I need answers! . . . It's my education! My education . . . Just answer the question!" A Black father named Nate Phillips stood and pleaded from his seat in the back of the auditorium for the district to engage with what Olivia had just said. "That little girl is screaming out. She's a good student. You have to address those things."

"Thank you, Olivia, for speaking out," Glasner replied, trying again with a tiny bit more emotion. "I really appreciate it."

Phillips continued. He had graduated in 1988, and the issues are still the same, he said. He wanted more. He wanted the administrators to address what Olivia had just said. "You've got all these parents here—Black and white— that understand Shaker. Appreciate Shaker. Want to do what we can for Shaker! . . . But when the real conversation gets on the table, it won't be addressed!"

As the top administrator in the room, it fell to Wilkins to say something, and he answered the call with a halting, unsatisfactory response. He spoke vaguely about lessons learned from the investigation and said Shaker wanted the student experience to be "positive and supported."

In the midst of all this, a white father near the front stood, faced the crowd, and registered a complaint on a different matter altogether. He said his son had been in classrooms where students misbehaved, fought, and disrespected teachers, where teachers could not control the classroom. "My son has witnessed kids walking up and grabbing stuff off the teachers' desks."

Given that the subject on the table was race, many in the room suspected he was laying the disruption on Black students. Other parents and students started yelling, "Who are 'they'?! Who are 'they'?!"

"Look guys, look," the white dad said, trying to regroup.

"You're privileged!" someone yelled. "Your privilege is very loud and it stinks."

The white dad kept trying to recover, tried to say it wasn't about race. "Stop assuming stuff is always about race," he said.

The back-and-forth continued with the white dad saying his son just didn't want to be around fights and other parents in the room challenging him to say who exactly he was accusing of fighting. Others wondered, quietly, why this white dad chose this moment, when the concerns of Black students were front and center, to change the subject to the concerns of his white child.

Finally, the district's head of security persuaded him to sit back down. "You're not gonna win this," he told the dad.

As the meeting unfolded, the school board president, Jeffrey Isaacs, sitting near the front, wondered if he should grab the microphone himself and try to lead a civil conversation.

"Should I get up?" he asked Ayesha Bell Hardaway, his colleague on the school board, who was sitting next to him.

"Don't do it," he recalled her saying. "You can't make it better."

"It was one of the most painful hours of my life," Isaacs said later. "People were angry but not angry about the same thing."

The meeting had not just gone off the rails. It had left the rails somewhere back in the distance. The back and forth, accusations, and attempts at replies, the calls for leadership all continued for a while longer until, mercifully, the one hour promised for the session was up, and Stephens declared that the meeting was over.

David Glasner sat through the vast majority of the meeting with a deer-in-the-headlights expression and still seemed scarred by it months later. "I relive that moment frequently," he said later. The event was not set up for success, he said, and never should have been scheduled. "It's important that we are able to air out issues. That meeting was not set up to be a constructive conversation. I was out there and was not able to talk about what everyone was there to talk about."

After the meeting was over, Olivia felt a sense of relief but also trepidation. "Oh no," she thought, "I just opened up a can of worms because I'm putting a face to an anonymous face." But rather than eliciting scorn, her public outing drew support. After the meeting, a school board member came to check on her. Keith Langford, a Black father who did community engagement work for the district, asked her how this situation might be prevented in the future. When she went back to school, security guards in the hallways called out, "That was you onstage? Wow!"

One of Olivia's former science teachers, William Scanlon, had a conflicting meeting at the same time in the school, so he missed the conflagration. On his way out, he saw teachers emerging from the auditorium looking as though they'd seen a ghost. He watched the meeting online that weekend and found himself close to tears thinking about Olivia. He imagined her walking the hallways with all eyes on her. "Listen I just want you to know that this was not your fault," he wrote in a message to Olivia. "It was not your fault that this whole thing's happened, that you're in the middle of. It's the fault of the adults who didn't handle it properly." He told her that if she ever needed anything, she could stop by his room.

Herlinda Bradley also felt a sense of relief. Now people could see for themselves. This Black student was not someone who didn't deserve to be in AP English. She was a bright young woman.

"I was proud she had her voice and wasn't afraid," she said.

Still, the stress of the situation, the knowing everyone was looking at her and judging, combined with other stresses in her life, prompted Olivia to seek counseling. Shaker offered to let her do her schoolwork from home, which she declined. Eventually, her life began to return to normal.

But while things ultimately landed fine for Olivia, nothing had resolved for Podl. She remained angry and puzzled about how she had been treated, and felt it would be impossible to teach again knowing any misstep could lead to disaster, with no confidence her bosses would back her up in a dispute.

A few days after the meeting from hell, Wilkins seemed to finally understand just how badly his team had screwed up. He issued a statement apologizing both to Podl and to the families involved in the investigation for not completing the review process around the complaint more quickly.

The apology to Podl wasn't much of an apology, as apologies go. The part about her was exactly one sentence: "I want to apologize to longtime High School English teacher Ms. Jody Podl." The rest was about mistakes in the district's process. But even that set off Herlinda Bradley. In an email that day to Wilkins, she wrote that his apology sent the message that teachers matter more than students and complained that the apology to Podl came before the apology to the family.

"You presented her as if she is teacher of the year. Thanking her for her years of service," Bradley wrote, evidently interpreting the word "longtime" as a thank-you for her service. "She was disrespectful, inappropriate and hurtful to students and Shaker knows it! . . . I'm sure next you will all reverse the decision that the teacher was in violation of the bullying policy . . . shameful!"

The same day the apology was released, Podl published an open letter to her students in the *Shakerite*, her first public comments since she was removed from the classroom. She explained that she had taken a medical leave. "I recognize that the last weeks have not been easy ones for any of you or for the community," she wrote. "They have also not been easy ones for me. I very much wish that events had unfolded differently. We all have suffered. There is a lot of work ahead of us as we reflect on how to handle conflict, how to work together instead of against each other, and how to lead effectively."

She wrote about her love of teaching, her passion for her students. She wrote about the joy she took reading students' work, discussing literature with them, seeing them make connections and building relationships.

"It is my sincere hope that some good can come from what has been a very disruptive and destructive situation," she concluded. "Please know that I am pulling hard for Shaker to find its way."

In the aftermath of the community meeting, the district seemed paralyzed, unable to find a way forward or to promote healing. With the union grievance still pending, officials felt constrained in what they could say.

It fell to the Student Group on Race Relations, now in its thirty-fifth year, to try to repair the damage. With the administration's blessing, SGORR invited the entire high school faculty to a meeting in the upper cafeteria of the high school. Teachers were separated into small groups with SGORR leaders around each round table to lead conversations about implicit bias, race, and teaching. They put a few questions on the table: *What types of biases might you bring to the classroom? What does an inclusive classroom look like, feel like, sound like?*

All sorts of frustrations and fears poured out. Teachers talked about feeling "almost threatened," terrified they would be accused of racism if they admonished students in any way. A librarian said Black students tend to be louder, and she wondered if she'd get in trouble for telling them to be quiet. They discussed the lack of diversity on the faculty, and whether white teachers were able to relate to Black students as they should.

SGORR members themselves felt frustrated, too.

"This district preaches restorative practices, and the one time they needed it, they didn't use it," said Abe Arenberg, who was a junior at the time. Arenberg had been in Podl's class, one of the students who had no idea why she had disappeared from the classroom so abruptly. "No one told us anything for a week."

It's remarkable that SGORR was able to take on this role, and a testament to the group's power and respect. Still, it's telling that students were the only ones leading conversations about the difficult questions that were again out in the open.

An arbitration hearing to consider Podl's case was scheduled for a Tuesday morning in February 2019 in a room at the Shaker Heights Fire Department. At nine o'clock, Podl, Morris, and Muskovitz, the union attorney, were ready to go. The arbitrator was present. But no one from the school district was there.

The day before, Wilkins had emailed the community that the district had decided to remove the discipline letter from Podl's file. "There is a consensus that we, as a community, want to move forward and turn our collective focus toward healing and learning," he wrote. Reached by phone just as the hearing was beginning the next morning, Shaker's attorney, Fredrick Englehart, said there was no reason for him to attend. Rather than try to prove its case, after months of insisting that Podl was guilty of bullying, the district was simply conceding.

The union was demanding more. It wanted an apology to Podl and an affirmative statement of exoneration. It wanted the district to tell the families involved—who all had received letters about Podl's original discipline—that she had not violated district policy. Podl didn't just want a white flag; she wanted her name cleared. She wanted proof of innocence, something she could talk about or just know about as she shopped at Heinen's grocery store, terrified of running into people she knew. Maybe, with an exoneration, she could stop darting down alternate aisles when she saw acquaintances approaching.

"Pulling discipline is not the same as exonerating Ms. Podl," Muskovitz said.

Englehart was indignant, too. He said the district had received serious allegations and properly investigated them. "So for Ms. Muskovitz to try to paint this teacher as an innocent who is being crucified by the district is simply not true," he said. He added that the arbitrator had no authority to order anyone to apologize.

The district would not admit to a mistake, but also would not defend its actions, all while absolving itself of the need to scrutinize its handling of the case. Eventually, Englehart agreed to show up at the fire station in person, and the two attorneys each presented their versions of what happened for the record.

Muskovitz argued that when it gets a complaint, the district is required to set up a meeting with the teacher and the parents and students involved and try to talk it through.

So why didn't the district do that? Most people would hope that if a complaint were leveled against them at work, their boss would talk to them, hear their side, and if possible try to resolve it before cutting off their email, banishing them from the building, and putting them on leave. Podl had a reputation as a tough teacher, but there was no record of formal complaints against her. Then again, the allegations were serious—bullying and racism.

Part of the problem may have been poor management on the part of Jonathan Kuehnle and Terri Breeden, two administrators who would both be pushed out of the district within months. Perhaps administrators remembered Podl's negative interactions with Greg Hutchings, her eye-rolling during a meeting, and were disinclined to cut her a break—or even looking to stick it to her when given the chance.

No doubt race played a big role. Shaker had been trying to instill an equity mindset throughout its schools. It wanted more Black students to take advanced classes, and here was a student doing just that, and being admonished in front of her peers. Black students have said for years that they felt lonely and isolated in Shaker's top courses, and this seemed exhibit A for how to make that problem worse. How is a Black student going to feel she belongs in that room after a teacher calls her out in earshot of others? So if administrators had simply talked to Podl, tried to work it out quietly, what sort of message would that send?

Still, in the end, the district used a hatchet where a scalpel was required, and took its time lowering the blade. Focusing on equity and taking complaints seriously does not absolve you from treating employees right. It's entirely plausible that Podl needed to change how she interacted with her students. Perhaps she did have that magic sauce that helped many students learn how to put their mixed-up thoughts into cohesive paragraphs on the page. But there's evidence that at least occasionally she lacked the discipline or understanding to know that criticism should be delivered quietly and in private.

Yet there are far better ways to help a teacher improve, to help a student succeed, to manage a conflict, to help a district move to a more equitable place.

That spring, David Glasner was named the next superintendent of schools. Soon after, I asked him about the case. He noted that some of the administrative personnel who handled the case had been replaced. He said he was reviewing the district's procedures around staff discipline. As for what happened, he was vague, saying only, "There was a failure of leadership." He said it more than once, like a mantra—or, perhaps more accurately, a settled-upon talking point. Either way, it seemed entirely accurate.

———————

In April, the arbitrator issued his decision. He said Podl had been wrongly disciplined, which was kind of a given in that the district declined to contest the point. He concluded she had not violated any policy, giving her the affirmative statement she was seeking. But he said it was not within his authority to order the district to apologize to anyone.

John Morris cast the decision as a victory. "Jody Podl has been completely exonerated of any wrongdoing," he wrote in an email to union members.

Stephens, the district spokesman, issued a short statement: "We are aware of the decision and are looking forward to moving forward." Some speculated administrators were unwilling to say more for fear that Podl was preparing to sue the district, something she did not overtly threaten but also did not disavow. People she ran into tended to ask if she was going back, and if she planned to sue, and she chose not to answer either question.

The district had to tread carefully also because, while the arbitrator's decision was welcome news to teachers, it was painful and upsetting to those who thought Podl was out of line, particularly Black parents who saw her actions through a racial lens.

In June, Podl returned to Shaker Heights High School for the first time since being put on leave eight months earlier, to deliver remarks at the retirement breakfast of a friend. Anxiety overpowered her. She hadn't slept for three nights ahead of the event. Several friends offered to walk in with her. On the day of the event, she timed it so she arrived just before it was her turn to speak, avoiding most of the small talk she was dreading. Shaking, she delivered her first public remarks about the debacle.

"Over the course of this year, I've been defined by so many others," she said. "So let me just tell you now that I'm not a hero, I'm not a victim. I'm not a snowflake, and I'm not a villain. At the end of the day, just like everyone in the room, I'm a human being. Just an imperfect, good-intentioned, hardworking human being."

She said that Shaker can't just pretend everything is fine. "Moving forward doesn't just happen because you say so; like hope, it is a process that also requires hard, hard work."

Teachers in the room delivered a standing ovation, and Podl departed soon after.

Morris, the union leader, was hopeful Podl would return for the next school year. In July, Glasner and Eric Juli, the new high school principal, met with Podl and Morris in the high school library. Neither Glasner nor Juli, both white men, had been involved in the investigation. They were looking to start fresh. "I'm sorry for what happened to you," Glasner began, an apology for sure, though the English teacher recalled it was delivered in the passive voice. "I wanted the chance to meet you in person and hopefully get you back teaching."

Within five minutes, Podl told them she was not emotionally ready to return to the classroom. At one point, Podl broke down crying, and said she wanted a happy ending to this story. But she suggested that one precondition for her return would be the district grappling with what happened in the case of Olivia—talking through what went wrong and how teachers and students can handle similar conflicts in the future.

"You haven't addressed any of this, and you can't just go on and think that's going to be okay," she said. Glasner promised to review policies but made no specific promises for action, Podl said. She said Juli indicated he'd prefer to deal with cases as they arise.

After about forty minutes, they parted ways.

"We are hoping that she returns, and that's right now up to her," Glasner told me soon after the meeting. He also met with Herlinda Bradley and apologized to her for what her family went through the year before.

It's very possible, even probable, that Glasner did want Podl to return. But he was unwilling to lay out the sort of guideposts or policies that Podl sought to help avoid similar conflicts in the future. Shaker was right to take allegations of racism seriously, but if the district wanted teachers to pay closer attention to their teaching, to guard against bias, they needed to help them do the hard work of recognizing and challenging their own practices. This case simply taught them to be scared.

Podl began to venture into the community, with baby steps, but often felt a cold wind. She ran into Isaacs, the school board president, at a breakfast. "He looked away and never said a word to me," she said. "I've had this person to my house." (For his part, Isaacs read her expression as an icy "don't come near me," so he steered clear.)

Nonetheless she kept hoping for some sort of sign that the district had learned some sort of lesson. She found herself still clipping articles and other material she might want to use in teaching, not quite giving up the idea that she might go back.

In August, she tried once more, appearing before the school board to deliver a long, stinging indictment of how her case was handled, with a string of "what ifs" lamenting how badly she wished it could have been different.

"We teach our children and students that when you make a mistake, you need to own up to it. What if the district had the wherewithal to do the same?" she asked. She said she wished that after the arbitration had concluded, Shaker had brought people together to learn from the experience. Instead, she said, "you basically said nothing and you did nothing."

School board members do not typically respond to speakers during the public comment portion of their meetings. In this case, Isaacs made an exception.

"I want to say that we all wish you well," he said. "And I'm sorry for all the agonizing moments that have come in between last fall and the present moment, and I hope we will find a way forward. I guarantee the high school staff would be willing to work with you on a mediated conversation."

For Podl, that was too little, too late. She began to rebuild her life. She started venturing into the community. A ritzy new shopping and dining development called the Van Aken District had opened in Shaker Heights in early 2019, and it took her months to visit. But in September she finally did, and she ran into the parent of a former student. "She said, 'Oh, you were such a good teacher.'"

Podl did not return to the classroom. She began tutoring teenagers as well as functionally illiterate adults, and did some writing. In 2021, she officially retired at age fifty-five. At the end of the school year, she attended a teacher breakfast for retirees at the high school and praised her former colleagues, now teaching in the middle of the coronavirus pandemic, for all they do. Nice words were spoken about her, and most teachers rose for a standing ovation.

When I met with her that summer, her hair was longer and light from the sun, her skin a golden tan from swimming outdoors. She described herself as at peace, though she observed, "It took a long time to get there." The retirement breakfast had provided a modicum of closure. "It was a nice ending, how's that? It was an ending."

I spent months reporting this story for the *Washington Post* in 2019, and I found myself longing for a happy ending, too. I wanted someone at the district to pull the parties together, have an honest conversation, chart a way forward. I pictured the final scene of my story, a fairy tale perhaps, where Olivia begins her senior year feeling supported and cared for, and Podl walks back into room 118 to take attendance by asking a question.

Interviewing Herlinda Bradley and Jody Podl separately, I became convinced that they were both open to talking to each other, but too scared to make the call. Bradley insisted, in fact, that she had not been trying to get Podl removed from the classroom in the first place. She was sharply critical of the district, saying it "failed the students and the teachers" and did not have basis to suspend her. Podl, over several years of discussion about this subject, remained gracious and supportive of Olivia, if from afar, and angry at the school district that had been her personal and professional home for so many years. The administrators involved were surely driven by an imperative to take allegations of racism seriously. That does not excuse its many failures along the way. After talking to dozens of people about these events, I'm convinced that the district's handling of this case was not just poor but harmful to the entire community.

Looking back on the saga four years later, Bradley recognized how upset and angry she, too, was during this entire period, but she also said she understood that someone can have a bad day, and maybe Podl just had a bad day. "I would never want to be defined by my worst day." When I pointed out that Podl had apologized—immediately and repeatedly— Bradley realized this was true, but said she never really heard it, maybe because at the time she doubted it was sincere. "I need to check myself and reflect back on it. I need to really think about it."

We didn't get our happy ending. The *Post* story ran in November 2019, during Olivia's senior year of high school. Many of the online comments were harshly critical of Olivia, asking why she expected to get away with not doing her work. Friends warned her about them. Like the smart young woman I had grown to know, Liv chose not to read the comments, which, given the fractious and angry nature of contemporary online discourse, is generally a sound policy.

Soon after, she was participating in a community service project with students from other schools when a teacher from Hathaway Brown, a local private school, heard her name was Olivia and that she went to Shaker. The teacher asked if she had heard about the *Washington Post* story. "Oh, that's me," Liv said. The teacher told her they had held seminars at her school, inspired by her story.

"Knowing that could start a conversation was amazing for me," Olivia said.

When it came time to apply for college, four of the five applications Liv submitted were to historically Black colleges and universities. She was admitted to her first choice, the storied and prestigious all-women's Spelman College in Atlanta, and enrolled there in the fall of 2020. She was looking for a place where she would be steeped in Black culture, where the dances and the food would feel like home, where she wouldn't always be a minority in her classrooms.

Spelman, she said, "just seemed almost like a dream land, a land filled with intelligent Black people, oh my gosh . . . That sense of aloneness I felt in high school in some of those classes. I wouldn't want to put myself through that if I didn't have to." She was tired of hearing ignorant comments about race from white classmates, of having to represent all Black people in discussions.

Now, in college, during a class called African Diaspora in the World, a required course, she would see the handful of white and Asian American students who were now the minority, who had to calibrate what they said.

Still, when asked whether she got a good education at Shaker, Olivia did not hesitate. "Absolutely," she said. "I'm not super overwhelmed by the workload [in college] because of all the stressful nights I had in high school. I'm kind of used to it . . . I pulled something out of all the teachers I had, from third 'til twelfth grade."

> You never want a serious crisis to go to waste.
> —Rahm Emanuel

14

DAVID GLASNER

It was summer 2020 and the coronavirus pandemic was stalking every school district in America. That spring, schools had abruptly moved online in hopes of preventing spread of the deadly virus. Now districts across the country, including Shaker, were trying to figure out whether they could operate in person that fall and how to make remote classes work in the meantime.

The online schedule was enormously complicated, and administrators in Shaker Heights realized there was a way to simplify things: they could eliminate much of the leveling, the grouping of students by ability (or perceived ability) that Shaker schools had embraced—and defended—for decades.

It was, in some respects, the worst possible time for a change like this. Teaching (and learning) online was already impossibly stressful for teachers and students, and there was no time for training. And yet, politically, it was tempting, the chance to implement a policy in one fell swoop that administrators saw as key to creating a more equitable system.

When he was President Obama's White House chief of staff, Rahm Emanuel famously said one should never let a crisis go to waste: "It's an opportunity to do things that you think you could not do before."

The pandemic was a mammoth crisis, and detracking would be the thing they could not do before.

———————

Managing the crisis for the Shaker schools was David Glasner, new to the job of superintendent. While he was in his early forties, he had the fresh-faced look of someone early in his career, and a full head of curly brown hair. If it weren't for the suits he typically wore to work, he might have been mistaken for a new teacher. From the start of his tenure, he confronted complex issues of race. Now he was grappling with a global pandemic, too.

As a kid growing up in Montgomery County, Maryland, outside Washington, D.C., Glasner had not been exposed much to people of other races. He attended a private Jewish day school through eighth grade, filled with not just white people but Jewish white people. He moved to a diverse public high school, but he took high-level classes that included few Black or Hispanic students. He noticed that his classes were mostly white but didn't think too deeply about it.

His world opened up as he moved on to the University of Pennsylvania, collecting a pair of history degrees and spending a semester studying in Senegal. After working at schools in Israel and Paris, he earned his master's degree in social studies education and set out to work as a teacher, a job he'd been eyeing since the seventh grade.

Once he started teaching, Glasner sought out diverse schools. He had a chance to work at the elite Stuyvesant High School in New York City, which required an admissions test and was overwhelmingly Asian American and white. He opted instead for a school in East Harlem.

In graduate school, he had thought he'd want to be in the classroom forever, but soon Glasner found himself drawn to administration. At his first job, the politics were ugly, or as Glasner put it in his typically understated way, "challenging." The teachers union was in direct conflict with the principal, and Glasner found himself more sympathetic to the school's leader. He soon earned his administration license, and by 2008 got a job as assistant principal at a school on New York's Lower East Side and, a year later, principal. It was, by any measure, a rapid rise.

Around this time, he and his wife, Elana, were living in a one-bedroom apartment in Park Slope in Brooklyn with one baby and Elana pregnant with their second. She wanted to be closer to her family, who lived in Beachwood, Ohio, next door to Shaker Heights.

Glasner remembered seeing the posting for the position of prin-cipal at Shaker Heights Middle School and thinking it was his dream job. Shaker had adopted the International Baccalaureate program, a curriculum he had participated in himself, earning an IB high school diploma. It was a racially diverse community with a progressive tradition. "I didn't want to work in a Stuyvesant," a place where all the students were academic superstars, he said.

Superintendent Greg Hutchings hired him, and he almost immedi-ately began grappling with the question of tracking and the levels system. Students were sorted into academic buckets in elementary school, setting their course for middle school. Middle school, in turn, set the course for high school. If a student wasn't in advanced English in seventh and eighth grade, the chance of joining those classes in high school was slim. In math, it was all but impossible. If you didn't take Pre-Algebra in seventh grade you couldn't enroll in Algebra 1 in eighth grade and then you couldn't take Geometry in ninth grade and so on. So decisions about math placement made when students were eleven or twelve years old, or even younger, determined whether they could reach calculus by their senior year of high school, a sign of academic rigor that college admis-sions officers value—though only the savviest parents and students are thinking about that when kids are still romping on playgrounds.

It wasn't just that some students received more challenging work in elementary school than others. It's that they had been given a message. The message was either you are smart and good at school or you aren't. Some were told they belonged at the top. Others weren't.

The leveled classes showed the predictable racial patterns, with white students dominating the top classes and Black students filling the bottom ones. The problem was twofold: Black students were not encouraged to take upper-level classes, despite an open enrollment program aimed at making sure they had equal access to challenging courses. Meantime, white par-ents actively pushed to get their children into these classes, and the open enrollment program facilitated those efforts.

"Every white person wanted their kid in advanced and open enroll-ment allowed it," Glasner said. Many pushed for it, and then helped their kids get through with private tutoring and other help.

Glasner went back to school himself for his doctorate in urban educa-tion at Cleveland State University, studying under Mark Freeman, the for-mer Shaker superintendent nudged out for failing to adequately address the achievement gap. For his dissertation, Glasner studied math education in middle school. He found students with average ability levels did better when they were placed in higher-level classes, especially Black students.

———

In Shaker, Glasner continued to climb the rungs. In summer 2018, he was promoted to executive director of curriculum and instruction, and, soon after that, installed as interim principal at the high school (filling in after Jonathan Kuehnle was removed). After Greg Hutchings left the district, he applied for the superintendent's job.

In his public interview for the job, Glasner signaled that he would keep Shaker pointed toward equity. Asked how he would assure that all students are pushed to reach higher academically, he said he would "set universal expectations . . . and then provide targeted supports and enrichments for everyone to meet those goals." He wasn't particularly specific as to how.

The other finalist was a Black woman from the Chicago Public Schools, Elizabeth Kirby. Kirby was a dynamic, experienced candidate, seen as a tested leader with an easy manner with the community and a glowing reputation. She was the school board's first choice, though members were enthusiastic about both candidates, according to two people familiar with the board conversations. Glasner was seen as having done a good job in Shaker, had established relationships, and could hit the ground running.

In March 2019, hours before Shaker was to announce its pick, Kirby accepted the superintendency at neighboring Cleveland Heights–University Heights School District, leaving Shaker with one choice. Glasner was hired, capping a rapid rise to the top. He was forty years old.

School board member Lisa Cremer, who had clashed with Hutchings as a parent, hoped Glasner would be able to work more constructively with the teachers than Hutchings had. Cremer was close with teachers in general, friendly with Jody Podl in particular, and concerned that, in the aftermath of the Podl controversy, many on the faculty feared for their jobs if they made any misstep.

"Whatever equity work we want to do, it's not going to happen until we repair the relationships with the teachers," she said. She understood that in Shaker, as in the entire country, people harbor implicit biases. Given that, she thought Glasner might have more success because, "to be purely blunt, he's a white guy." His race made no difference to her, she made clear, but it might ease the way for him with others.

Glasner's philosophy did not deviate in any significant way from that of Greg Hutchings, but their personal styles could not have come across more differently. Where Hutchings could be bombastic, Glasner came off as quiet and deliberative, even boring. Where Hutchings was excitable, Glasner was measured; where Hutchings embraced the drama, Glasner seemed to embrace the calm. Hutchings used the enthusiastic language of inspiration; Glasner used the dry language of educators and academics. And while Hutchings seemed to view opposition as proof he was doing the right thing, Glasner indicated that he wanted to hear from all sides.

In March 2019, soon after Glasner was named superintendent, he said he was unsettled and unsatisfied with the tracking system. But in an interview, he suggested he would go slow in changing that, perhaps starting with the youngest students.

"We want to be sure the change we develop is successful. One thing I've learned is it's really important to bring people along with this change. Making clear why we're doing the things we're doing," he said. "There are times for drastic change and times for incremental change . . . We need to think about how to promote incremental change . . . We need to see what works."

Six months later, in September, he reiterated that go-slow approach. "In order to take on this kind of work we are going to need champions and advocates in our community," he said in an interview.

So it was something of a surprise, even for those paying close attention, when four months later, Glasner signaled that a sweeping overhaul of tracking was coming.

═══════

This academic revolution was spurred in part by a short trip Glasner took from the administration building to Woodbury, the upper elementary school, set on the other side of a ball field. Glasner had just started in the top job, and he and a couple of aides wanted to observe how fifth and sixth grade students were using computer devices that had been bought for the school. Woodbury was where the tracking in Shaker formally began. For years, advanced students were sent to the basement for enriched English language arts and enriched math with teachers who were seen, rightly or not, as the best. This was not just for the very top students—it was about half the grade. The other half stayed in regular classrooms.

On this day, Glasner popped his head into a fifth grade classroom and saw that all but one student were Black. A colleague asked a child sitting in the corner, "Where are the white students?" And the student replied, "The white kids—they're enriched."

He didn't say the white kids were *getting enrichment*. They *were enriched*. In this formulation, it wasn't just a question of classrooms, but actual identity. White kids were enriched, and Black kids weren't.

"It really hit home what we have put in place in Shaker," Glasner said later. "That student has internalized that idea that those white kids are better than him . . . That one incident was a punch to the gut."

That January 2020, Glasner participated in a Facebook Live event. He took questions, and the first one he picked was whether he was looking at detracking. It was clear the question was a setup, and this time, his response did not signal a go-slow mentality. He described how in the current system, Shaker begins informal tracking as young as third or fourth grade, if not earlier, and that once students are put onto a track, they pretty much stay there. Those tracks are racially divided, he said, with white classes and Black classes. "That's a pretty powerful thing to realize, that we're locking students into specific pathways."

He talked about Shaker's history, and how people move here because they want to be part of a diverse community. In the classroom, that's not happening, he said. And he offered a harsh interpretation of Shaker's history.

"White families wanted to create different course levels so that classes can remain segregated," Glasner said. "We cannot ignore the fact that tracking is really part of a system of institutional racism that we need to address directly."

Indeed, at that very moment, sitting in bound red library volumes at the Shaker Heights Public Library were old School Reviews. Those newsletters document how tracking in Shaker increased as schools desegregated, with school officials reassuring parents that standards were not falling. (There was not evidence, though, that white families' goal was segregation.)

Glasner didn't specify his exact plans, but said the enrichment that some kids get—working in teams to solve real-world problems using a robust and rigorous curriculum—should be offered to all.

A group of equity-minded parents was watching the Facebook Live event together, and a cheer went up after Glasner said that tracking relates to historic and systemic racism. Among them was Joanie Berger, a white 1986 Shaker graduate who returned to the community after she had children of her own.

"That's something Greg Hutchings would not have gotten away with saying," she said. As a white man, she observed, Glasner could say things that would have prompted waves of judgment and controversy had Hutchings said the same.

———

Academic tracking was introduced in America in response to the influx of immigrants in the early 1900s, and used to sort students into rigid educational pathways. Certain students were groomed for college and others for trades such as plumbing or secretarial work. By midcentury most high schools used some form of tracking, but the extreme original version had faded by the 1970s, as policy makers emphasized the importance of all students having access to academically rigorous courses.

Not long after that, school districts began experimenting with more aggressive detracking, spurred by the racial inequities in the advanced classes, with white and Asian students enrolled at far greater rates than Black and Hispanic students. In 1985, the book *Keeping Track*, by Jeannie Oakes, argued that tracking reflected and helped perpetuate class and racial inequities, and that it boosted already advantaged students at the expense of students in lower tracks and students of color. Several studies showed that mixing students of varying ability levels helped lower-level students and didn't hurt high achievers, though the evidence was not universal.

To make it work, teachers must work with students at multiple levels at the same time, a technique called differentiation. That's not easy.

One strategy, known as "high-ceiling, low-floor," gives students multiple options for completing the same assignment. Some might write multipage essays while others write multiple paragraphs, but they are all writing on the same topic. Maybe some students show their understanding better through verbal expression, so the class might have a choice to write a paper or record a podcast. A Shaker Middle School teacher, Kevin Thomas, described a math problem he offers: There are thirty animals—some chickens, some cows—with a total of seventy-four legs. How many chickens and how many cows are there? This problem can be solved through an algebraic equation, or by drawing pictures. "You still get to the same place at the end," he said.

Most detracking initiatives are driven by the same forces at work in Shaker Heights: a frustration with racially segregated classes. Federal data shows that for 22 percent of white students, calculus is the highest-level math class taken in high school. But the same is true for just 11 percent of

Black students and 14 percent of Hispanics. (Asian American and Pacific Islanders top all other races, with nearly half reaching calculus.)

Yet research suggests that high-level courses are better for students of all abilities, said Halley Potter, a senior fellow at the Century Foundation, which promotes school integration strategies. Students who start out with similar lower test scores do better when placed in higher-level courses than those funneled into lower-level courses, she said, echoing the findings of Glasner's dissertation. "Grouping all the low-performing students into one class is not an effective way to help struggling kids catch up."

"We just had tremendous success with it," said Carol Corbett Burris, who detracked courses at South Side High School in suburban Rockville Centre, New York, when she was principal two decades ago and now runs the Network for Public Education, an advocacy group. Research published in 2019 from South Side High found detracking led more students to take advanced courses later in high school, with overall scores in those classes rising or staying flat.

But critics argue that mixed-ability courses don't challenge higher-achieving children and put unreasonable burdens on teachers. The fear is that the excitement of being pushed to think deeper, a dynamic made possible when all the students have mastered the basics, goes away when many in the room are not ready for that level of analysis. When the State of California considered a new math framework that called for mixed-ability classrooms through tenth grade, parental complaints rained down. At a public hearing, one father said his son never fit in at school until he found the advanced math program. "Stop the assault on excellence," he said. "You don't lift people by bringing other people down."

"I don't think that all students should be taught in the same way," said another critic, Angela Hasan, a professor of clinical education at the Rossier School of Education at the University of Southern California, which sponsors a certification program for gifted education. "That doesn't make sense, especially if you have a child in that class and you know that child thinks differently or is more advanced than other students."

Ron Ferguson, the Harvard professor who advised Shaker for years and became a nationally known expert in achievement gap issues, was also a skeptic. In his view, the problem wasn't too few students in advanced classes, but too many—mirroring Glasner's initial conclusions. "It's not that Black kids are underenrolled. It's that white kids are overenrolled," he told me. "There are a lot of average white kids in advanced classes because their parents pushed to have them there." John Morris, the teachers union president in Shaker, said that at least 20 percent of the white students in an honors English class he taught around this time didn't belong there and would have been better off in a different sort of course.

"Why aren't the regular classes also excellent?" Ferguson asked. "The better approach would be to make the regular classes so good that the parents of the average white kids want their kids in those classes."

Nonetheless, the unsettling race data has prompted districts across the country—from small rural districts to middle schools in New York City—to reduce or eliminate tracking.

Evanston Township High School District 202, just outside Chicago, began detracking in 2010 with freshman English and history, moving from five levels to one. Students of all abilities study in the same class-rooms, though they can earn honors credit through strong performance.

The result has been racial integration of classrooms in a district where nearly half of students are white, 25 percent are Black, and 20 percent are Latino. District data shows a rise in Black and Latino student par-ticipation in Advanced Placement classes in the upper grades, and more students passing AP tests. In 2019, the school detracked Geometry, the math class most ninth graders take.

There were strong objections at first, said Pete Bavis, assistant super-intendent for curriculum and instruction. He recalled one parent warning of "bright flight," a term that struck him as "about as racially coded as you can get." But he said complaints fell away once the program was underway.

"Once we proved we could implement this, we were off and running," he said.

It took significant teacher training. In math, the district shifted its approach from explaining how to do a problem and having students rep-licate the work to more open-ended questions that let students engage on multiple levels—the high-ceiling, low-floor approach.

So a teacher might tell the class that she has a bucket filled with water and ask students what they are wondering about the situation, said Dale Leibforth, who chaired the school's math department. Some students might want to calculate how much water is in the bucket based on its dimensions, a fairly straightforward problem. Others, though, might explore what happens if there's a leak and water is draining as the bucket is being filled. That could involve calculating the rate of change, which has an element of calculus in it.

"It's redefining what the math class looks like," Leibforth said.

———

Nationally, the academic gaps between students of color and white students have narrowed significantly over time, with progress through the 1970s and early '80s, as scores for Black and Hispanic students rose faster than those of white students—during the same span in which racial integration in schools was at its peak. After that, progress stalled, and in some cases the gaps grew larger. There were further declines in the 1990s, but even so, the racial gap remained significant.

In Shaker Heights, large racial gaps were apparent when Black and white student groups were compared to each other, and also compared to other schools in the state. Data from Ohio's 2021–22 state report cards shows that white students in Shaker consistently scored higher than white students in other racially diverse districts in the state. But while Black Shaker students outperformed Black students in high-poverty urban districts such as Cleveland and Canton, their scores were about equal to or lower than those of Black students in other suburbs.

In 1999, under Mark Freeman, Shaker had become a founding member of the Minority Student Achievement Network (later called simply the MSAN Network), dedicated to helping racially diverse school districts raise the achievement of students of color. The group included school systems in Evanston, Illinois; Ann Arbor, Michigan; and Chapel Hill, North Carolina, in addition to Cleveland Heights–University Heights, right next door. This was the network Ron Ferguson had worked with early in his research, and it had spent two decades supporting and researching various approaches.

Madeline Hafner, who ran MSAN for fifteen years, said that across the districts there has been little if any evidence of success of some of the most popular ideas, including one-off implicit bias or diversity trainings and intensive efforts to move more students of color into AP classes. She questioned the notion, embraced in Shaker and elsewhere, that AP enrollment is the holy grail. The real question, she said, was whether a school has "created an environment where Black kids feel like they can thrive and experience joy in their lives."

The most important ideas went all the way back to Ferguson's work in the early 2000s: strong relationships between students and teachers that foster a sense of belonging. Teachers with empathic, supportive mindsets, with high expectations for all, saw far more success than those with punitive approaches, Hafner said.

Students of color "thrive when they have a teacher who believes in their intellect and engages them," she said. "It's not necessarily in AP. It may be somewhere else."

Schools also found success with other strategies aimed at belonging, including employing a racially diverse faculty and working to assure that students of color saw themselves reflected in the curriculum. Smaller things also mattered, like making sure the school trophy case and art on the walls reflect the achievements and experiences of all students.

Detracking, she said, was a potentially effective strategy, too, but it had to be done carefully and with training. "It's incredible to watch a teacher in a detracked classroom, but that's a really complex skill."

———

In the summer of 2020, the principals of the schools serving older children in Shaker Heights recommended to Glasner that the district detrack most classes. The official reasoning was it would make pandemic scheduling easier. To minimize the spread of Covid-19, the district was trying to keep students in cohorts that didn't mix with other cohorts. If tracking remained in place, most students would spend all day with others of their race not just for certain academic subjects but for everything else, too. The classroom-level segregation would expand into a kind of hypersegregation, and Glasner didn't want that.

Glasner said that the changes would be put in place for only one year and a decision on whether to make them permanent would come later. In his mind, though, he suspected—and hoped—that they were never going back. His original cautions about the necessity of bringing people along with major change were set aside.

The announcement came at the end of a long discussion of Covid-related protocols. In an eight-page statement ahead of the start of the school year, the detracking explanation began on page six.

AP and IB courses would still be stand-alone offerings in the upper grades of high school, but most classes between fifth and ninth grades would collapse, with honors and regular level students mixed together, by far the most sweeping contraction of the levels system ever implemented in the district.

It was a rip-off-the-Band-Aid moment, and Glasner later said he never would have done it this way absent the pandemic. Then again, many districts in America managed their way through the pandemic with tracking in place. This was, in the end, a choice, with positive and negative consequences. Among them: teachers had to figure out how to teach online to a group of students they had never met, and how to teach a class with the full range of academic abilities, all without any training to speak of and all at once. It was the opposite of incremental change.

"I certainly have come to appreciate the need for acting with urgency in order to meet the needs of our students," Glasner said in an October 2020 interview.

In retrospect, even many supporters of detracking said it was a mistake to make such a huge move in the middle of a pandemic, when schools, teachers, and students were under so much stress already. Even if you agree that tracking is a racist practice that needed unraveling ASAP, it had persisted in Shaker for decades. Waiting another year or two, or phasing the changes in, would have given the district time to train teachers and develop a communications plan to help families understand the new system. And even if the cohorts had been hypersegregated during one pandemic year, that might not have been the worst-case scenario on the table.

As it was, while Glasner had the conviction of a convert, he lacked the savvy of a salesman, and he did little to recruit allies in the community who might have helped sell what was a major change for Shaker. He did not give the district's Parent Teacher Organization a heads-up that the change was coming, or ask for help explaining or advocating for it. There was no Q&A document posted on the district website, and there was a lot of misunderstanding about the new policy. For instance, many wrongly concluded that AP and IB classes at the high school were disappearing or changing, which they were not.

"The district's philosophy on communication with families? I don't know," said Stacey Hren, a white mom who was co-president of the PTO Council, a federation of all the building PTOs. "We advocated early and often for dialogue."

The district communicated mostly through a series of one-way videos, most just a few minutes long, with teachers, administrators, and community members pressing the philosophical case for detracking with scant details about how it would actually be accomplished. (One parent featured in the district's own video actually said that "greater transparency" would help to address community concerns.)

"People were like, 'We get the why. We want to understand the how,'" said Sarah Divakarla, the other PTO co-president, who is also white.

The combination of online learning and detracking delivered a double serving of anxiety. Hren heard families complain that classes were too slow and no longer assigned homework. She personally knew of five families who left the district with generic explanations like, "This is just a better fit for us," which Hren read as "coded white privilege language."

When asked about families who left, Glasner flipped the question around. What about all the families the old system was failing? He said he was on a call with parents in the spring of 2021 during which a white parent voiced frustration that her child wasn't being challenged. But on the same call, he said, a Black parent said, "It's about time we made a change."

The district didn't fully know how the changes were going over with lower-income Black families who stood to benefit most from the new system, partly because these families were the least engaged with the district and hardest to reach. Interviews suggest many Black parents in Shaker did not know about the change. When told about it, many were skeptical.

"I don't think it's fair to have the honors kids in with the, we'll call them regular kids," said Adriann Kennedy, who graduated from Shaker schools, sent three children through Shaker, and now was a primary caregiver for a grandson in elementary school. "Are you really going to be gearing your teaching to those kids? The honors kids will be bored or the regular kids left behind."

But she said the class assignment needed to be fair. "Keep people out (of honors) if they don't belong," she said. "And keep the honors kids out of the regular classes."

Most of her complaints, though, had nothing to do with tracking. She was upset about teachers who she felt underestimated or unfairly picked on her children and grandson. Her daughter, she said, had missed out on a class that gave college credit in high school because no one had asked if she wanted to apply for it. She felt teachers had low expectations for her grandson, based solely on his race.

Among the white families who filled the upper-level classes, the reactions ranged, as well. Some said they thought the changes were worthwhile. Others weren't happy but were willing to give it some time. Some parents griped that Glasner himself did not send his own three children to Shaker schools. (They went to a Jewish day school, something that was important to him and his wife, which he said he discussed with the school board during his interview for the job.) Some families left the district because they did not think their children were being challenged.

"By forcing those kids together when they don't learn at the same level, you're force-feeding to the kids like my daughter that you're just going to be put aside for someone else," said Daniel Raymond, a surgeon in Cleveland who is white.

He said he was willing to give detracking a chance, but he ultimately moved his daughter from Shaker High School to Hawken, a private school, for her junior year after a distressing experience in her detracked tenth grade English class. He said she was seated in the back of the room and told to do whatever she wanted because the teacher needed to focus on students with greater needs. Sometimes the class even watched Disney movies. "The problem is they stopped being educated," he said.

The message to his daughter, he added, was: "You have all the privilege in the world so it's okay if you sit in the back of the classroom because we're righting social norms."

The fact that he was paying $30,000 in annual school property taxes on his eight-bedroom home made it even worse. He said he and his wife had chosen Shaker because they valued diversity and they understood that high taxes were the cost of cross-subsidizing lower-income children, but "you can only stomach that so far" when his own child was losing out. He said there were other factors as well, including that his daughter wanted to change schools. When the timing was right with the housing market, he hoped to sell his house and move to a community with lower taxes.

Some students who remained at Shaker voiced similar concerns. Andrew Farkus, who is white, was a high school sophomore in the 2020–21 school year. He had been on the enriched and advanced track of study since third grade. Now, in tenth grade, his detracked class was still labeled honors but felt very different.

"There were kids who were just learning at such a different speed than I learned," he said. In ninth grade, he said, students would be assigned to read thirty pages per night. Now the teacher had students reading the texts aloud during class. He went from thirty to sixty minutes of homework per night to maybe ten. In ninth grade, his essays would be returned marked up with red pen, and he could see where he'd made mistakes. "Now you just get a score. Oh, 95, great, cool, I guess."

He considered whether he should talk to his teacher, John Morris, and ask for more challenging work. He also understood that Morris was trying to balance the students who appeared to do no work with those who found the assignments too easy. "I'm pretty vocal in my opinions against deleveling," Andrew said. "They're bringing down expectations instead of bringing up expectations."

His mother, Toni Farkus, said deleveling was never explained very well and she didn't think it made sense to implement while teachers were also teaching remotely. She feared students who weren't getting sufficient rigor in honors classes would push up to Advanced Placement, "and that doesn't solve the problem," or they would go to another school.

Morris, who taught Andrew's tenth grade English class, understood Andrew's frustration. He said some of this related to the pandemic year. For instance, among other challenges, families could opt for continued remote learning or in-person classes, so teachers had to teach some students who were in the classroom and others via computer at the same time.

But even the following spring, in 2022, when everyone was back in school, Morris's tenth grade literature class was reading portions of *The Great Gatsby* aloud in class and watching parts of the movie. The high school schedule allowed for longer class sessions, so students had time to do their homework during school hours, and very little was assigned to complete at home.

Morris supported the detracking plan, but he also knew that Andrew's concerns were shared by some teachers. "When you're teaching an AP composition or literature class, or an honors class with students who are motivated and gifted, you can take students places that are extraordinary," he said. "You can almost step back as a teacher and watch amazing things happen. I've seen it. I've had those students. Teachers who are used to that environment, once they are exposed to students who need more, they feel that their instruction doesn't reach those kinds of heights. There's this human sense of a deficit. I think those teachers feel a loss."

And some teachers said they simply did not know how to teach students with such a wide range of abilities at the same time, even though they supported the idea philosophically.

William Scanlon, the high school science teacher, thought the detracking plan was a bold effort with potential to address the achievement gap in a serious way. But in practice, he found it next to impossible to teach science as it should be taught. The idea, he said, that these classes would be taught at a true honors level was "a joke."

In ninth grade honors physical science classes, he said, he used to do complicated problems that required advanced math skills and talk about "the quantum theory of the models of the atoms." Every year, he'd teach something called stoichiometry, where, for instance, students have to calculate how much of each ingredient is needed to produce a certain quantity of product and involved writing out chemical equations, balancing them, and then calculating the quantities. "There is no chance I could teach that this year," he said.

He said teachers got little if any training on how to differentiate their teaching and hoped that eventually they would. If they did, he saw a chance to make the new system work.

The early going was smoother for Erin Mauch, a white English teacher, who worked to create assignments that could be completed in multiple ways. For a unit on graphic novels, for instance, students could choose the more challenging task of creating their own graphic novel, including identifying the elements that make up the format, or they could analyze an existing panel. Both assignments required understanding graphic novels, but one was more ambitious.

Over the course of the year, she heard complaints from two students, both white males, who said the course wasn't challenging enough. One was disappointed that the class did not read *The Crucible*, as had been the case in past years, and the other felt like they should have been writing more essays.

As the year came to an end, she noticed that more of her sophomores were opting to take the advanced course offered in eleventh grade than was normally the case. "I'm cautiously optimistic," she said.

Jayce Bailey, a Black math teacher, called detracking "truly the right thing to do." He said it was challenging as a teacher, but noted that his classes had always had a mix of students because they were not properly assigned under the old system.

And Chuck Kelly, a veteran English teacher, who is white, recalled times when a student who would not normally be in an honors class contributed something unexpected to a discussion. "There is a dynamic created from detracking that is interesting to me, and good," he said. "It's a wonderful thing what a desegregated class can offer, and desegregated in all kinds of ways."

John Morris saw the demographic impact immediately. When classes were leveled, his honors English class had twenty-four students, two of them Black. After the change, eleven of his twenty-one students in the same honors English class were Black. And he had long offered his multidisciplinary American Experience course with honors and core students mixed together.

In his American Experience class on a Monday afternoon in the spring of 2022, racially diverse groups of sophomores spread across the high school library, researching figures and topics from various decades. At one table, the 1960s group was puzzling over Beatlemania, while over at the '90s table, they were considering Bill Clinton and the advent of email. "Who is Bob Dole?" someone asked. No one seemed to know, but they were looking him up. Every group was engaged in conversation, laughing and having fun together. It was a class that looked like Shaker.

"It's just super fun. Everyone's friends with everyone," said Grace Sheets, a white girl. "All of us are friends." They weren't friends before the class, she said. "Now we are." She had transferred in from a private school in Shaker, Hathaway Brown. "At my old school there wasn't much diversity at all."

———

The one group of teachers who got some formal training on detracking (albeit after the new system began) were middle school math teachers, and they arguably faced the toughest challenge. Seventh graders were enrolled in Pre-Algebra—normally an eighth grade class for students on the standard track—even though some had never taken math previously taught in seventh grade and might have done poorly in sixth grade math. Eighth graders were in Algebra 1 without ever taking Pre-Algebra. And that first year, all students began online, and many stayed online all year.

Shaker did not go cold turkey on math tracking. It still allowed for "acceleration," so some seventh graders who were ready for algebra joined eighth grade Algebra 1 classes. Eighth graders who were ready for geometry were offered it in eighth grade instead of ninth. But the vast majority of classes now had a mix of students—a mix of abilities and a racial mix, too.

"We weren't provided training up front," said Kevin Thomas, the seventh grade math teacher. "We were told there's no magic bullet. You have to figure it out."

Their mandate was to collapse a year and a half of math into one year, first in seventh and then in eighth grade, to prepare all students for the advanced track in high school.

To help, the district hired a consulting firm, West Wind Education Policy, though teachers said sessions dealt more with the underlying philosophy and moral urgency of detracking and less with the nuts and bolts of teaching a diverse classroom. Thomas said the chickens and cows problem was a West Wind suggestion, but there were not enough of those. Another math teacher rolled her eyes when asked if West Wind had been helpful.

Asked if teachers were properly prepared for this moment, Glasner ducked the question. "I'm not sure there's any amount of preparation that would make every teacher feel prepared," he said. "We could have spent fifteen years and there would be teachers who feel unprepared." That's likely true, but it's also true that some preparation would have been better than almost none at all.

One question was whether the changes would drive some families away. Data from February 2021 showed that enrollment had fallen more than in the previous years and more than projected. The most common reason for leaving was home schooling, but there also was a small jump in students departing for private schools in town. The following few years saw small declines in enrollment, in line with long-term demographic trends.

Still, even some district leaders were concerned. Emmitt Jolly, a Black father elected to the school board in 2019, was initially skeptical about deleveling but wanted to give it a chance. By mid-2022, he declared flatly, "Deleveling has not worked." He added: "Done well it can be transformative but it hasn't been done well." Lawrence Burnley, a Black man who joined the Shaker school district in 2022 as chief diversity, equity, and inclusion officer, said the intention was well-meaning but the implementation was a mess. "There were parents who value a detracked system but they need it to be done well," he said. "It was a disaster." But in 2021, three school board seats were on the ballot, providing an opportunity for a detracking opponent to run on the issue. Nobody did.

———

Teachers were trying their best to manage deleveled classes with the tools they had.

One morning in the spring of 2022, almost two years into the detracking initiative, seventh grade math teacher Karlee Robinson, a young white woman with a deep reserve of energy, greeted her students with the enthusiasm of a coach on the eve of a big game. "You ready to rock and roll? You got everything you need?" she asked as students filed into room 321 of Shaker Middle School. AMAZING THINGS HAPPEN HERE, read a sign on her door.

She asked students to close their eyes and give a thumbs-up or down as to whether they understood the lesson from yesterday. It was a way of checking in without embarrassing anyone, and most of the thumbs pointed up. For the next fifty minutes, she walked a line, pushing certain students to deepen their knowledge while helping others keep up.

Their first task was to list on a piece of paper every topic they could remember learning from the year. One white girl quickly ran out of space: probability, exponents, integers, order of operations, volume, decimals, and on and on. A Black boy sitting next to her stared out the window, having written nothing on his page. "You didn't write anything?" the girl said to him, glancing at his page. "Wow." And that prompted him to start writing.

When they were done writing, Robinson rapid-fired her way through a bunch of topics covered.

"When we redistribute, what operation do we use?"

"What's a fun fact about vertical angles?"

"What number do we use to approximate pi?" When a student replied "3.14," Robinson enthused, "There you go dude!" And when a student seemed to be spacing out, she called his name and asked, "You with me?"

She then divided the class into stations, each of which offered a different type of review. At one of the stations, students could pick among three worksheets. They were all mazes that required solving a problem to move to the next step, but they could choose worksheets with one-step, two-step, or multistep problems.

"At the beginning of the year, remember how we talked about a growth mindset? We challenge our brains," Robinson told the group seated around a circular table in the corner, a couple of students perched on the adjacent window ledge. She said the choice of worksheets required "some honest self-reflection" for each student about what they needed on this day. Most kids took the hardest worksheet, the multistep version. One girl took the two-step option and slowly but steadily worked her way through it. Another student, clearly less engaged, kept tipping back his chair and staring at nothing in particular. He took the one-step sheet and worked on it a bit, with the teacher offering help in exactly the same tone as she used for every other student in the group.

It was an example of the type of high-ceiling, low-floor exercises that are critical to mixing kids in a class. The boy doing the one-step problems seemed miles away from what anyone would consider honors math work. But that didn't stop others in his group from doing more challenging problems. And maybe he picked up something from being around more engaged students that he wouldn't have otherwise. And this small group had something that traditional honors courses have not had. It looked a lot like Shaker: two white girls, one white boy, three Black boys, and one Black girl.

The potential of detracking was also on display in an eighth grade classroom where students were learning about the difference between correlation and causation: *If ice cream sales rise and so do sunburns, does that mean ice cream causes sunburns?* The class was racially mixed, though most of the white students in the room were seventh graders accelerated into eighth grade math. Tasked with filling out a worksheet matching various formulas to graphs, one Black girl in eighth grade was struggling. The girl next to her, a white seventh grader named Ellie, stepped in to gently explain it, patiently walking her through the problems.

"Which one is positive?" Ellie said, pointing to the options. "What one is negative? . . . Yeah, there you go. Perfect . . . It's positive and there's only one positive left . . . Yeah, that's right."

The older girl said that she understood it better after the one-on-one help. "I'm not so good at math, to be honest. It's not really my thing." Ellie said she liked helping someone else to understand. "When explaining it, it gets that imprint in your head. You can help others but also yourself," she said.

The two met in class, and while they don't hang out or eat lunch together, they both described the other as a friend.

In October 2023, more than three years after the detracking initiative began in Shaker Heights, the school district finally hosted a public session to discuss the new system. Glasner, moderating a panel discussion in the high school auditorium, allowed it to stretch for more than two and a half hours, taking every question from the audience. Two sessions simulating detracked classes for parents to experience would follow later that fall.

District officials focused the discussion more on the "how" than the "why" of detracking. They explained how teachers sorted children into small groups within the classroom. They said extra instructors were often added to help, so there were two adults circulating the room. They said teachers had realized that top learners were not always being challenged, so now, instead of letting them choose, teachers were pushing these students to take on the more challenging assignments.

But the struggles were also on display that evening. One of the panelists, B'Lise Bradley, a Black girl in eleventh grade who had long been on the honors track, said the new system was difficult for students of all levels.

"For a lot of the people who were on the higher-level track, they're like, 'Oh, this is just busy work.' They don't feel like they're getting the same enrichment that they had when they were younger," she said. "And then on the flip side you have the people who were in the lower-level track, and they're really struggling."

In a series of thoughtful turns at the microphone, parents voiced both skepticism and hope. One woman, a white 1997 Shaker graduate, said she had been in all advanced classes as a student and saw the inequities around her. "Since I was a kid, I've been convinced that Shaker is a place that talks the talk and doesn't always walk the walk," she said. "I came here tonight to be persuaded that this is part of walking the walk."

Yet now, as the mother of two, she said she was concerned about how Shaker's detracking program had been rolled out, and worried that her elementary school–aged children were not being challenged in math without the sort of pull-out classes that had benefited her.

Curriculum director John Moore, who also is white, replied that if her children weren't being challenged, something was wrong and those teachers should address the situation. Still, Moore was candid about his own concerns, and he admitted that evening that the district had not yet successfully made its case to the community. "I think we have a ways to go on earning trust that we are making good decisions that are not just ethical but are academic for all the young people," he said.

He knew that a big part of that process was having data to measure the impact of detracking. But that was challenging partly because test scores—nationally and in Shaker Heights—fell, sometimes dramatically, during the pandemic. It was nearly impossible in the first couple of years to untangle the impact of Covid versus detracking.

By fall 2023, though, the district had some data that Moore found promising. Specifically, he was buoyed by the results of eighth-grade math scores.

Before the change, very few Black students took Algebra 1 in eighth grade; afterward, almost everyone did. In testing during spring and summer 2021, after the first year of detracking, 40 percent of Black students demonstrated competency in algebra, a requirement for high school graduation. Two years later, in spring and summer 2023, that rose to 44 percent. It still was less than half the students, but, under the old system, most of them would never have even been in the class or taken the test in eighth grade.

District data also showed that the number of students of all races taking Advanced Placement classes in high school had risen. The number of Black students completing at least one AP course nearly doubled, from 53 in 2018–19 to 98 in 2022–23, and Black student enrollment rose again in fall 2023. Moore allowed that it was too soon to credit detracking, but he did cite a renewed push at the high school to encourage more Black students to try these classes.

In the high school auditorium that October evening, Moore admitted how unsettling the current situation was to him.

"Sometimes I get fearful, in the middle of the night. You want to know this is working," he said. His training was in biology, he explained. "My safety blanket is data. I claw for data. I claw for research. I want to know that this is working, and I want to know now."

Many in the community wanted that, too. They all would have to wait.

> They tried to bury us. They didn't know we were seeds.
> —Poster on Principal Eric Juli's office wall

15

ERIC JULI

During his first meeting with the high school faculty, Eric Juli, the new principal, asked teachers to take a piece of paper and write down their burdens. There were a lot to choose from.

It was August 2019, and the group was gathered in the high school auditorium ahead of the new school year. Juli, a white man with a flair for the dramatic and a good dose of confidence, was well aware of the trauma of the year past, including not just the Jody Podl saga and the departure of the previous principal but the previous years under Greg Hutchings, who had constantly clashed with high school teachers.

Juli came into the job eyes wide open. He had lived in Shaker Heights since 2011, when he moved to the area to take a principal's job at a high-poverty school in the city of Cleveland. His two sons attended Shaker schools. He first considered applying for the job after watching a video of the November 8 community meeting and observing how poorly it had been handled.

"I thought if this place needs anything, it's strong leadership," he said. "I thought to myself, I know how to stand in the middle of a city block with two rival gangs pressing down on each other and de-escalate it. I could be on that stage. Maybe they need a leader who is cut from a different cloth."

Before school began each August, the district scheduled several days of professional learning for teachers. Juli, inspired by a book he had read on leadership, compared the coming year to a driver behind the wheel.

The driver can't ignore the rearview mirror, but if he doesn't look ahead, he might crash. "We are impacted by our past and influenced by our past, but we're not focused on our past," he said.

Juli then asked each teacher to write down what they wanted to let go of from the previous year. John Morris, the union leader who had walked side by side with Podl, wrote a note about that whole ordeal and about what felt like a deprofessionalization of teaching at the school. Carole Kovach, the English teacher who was close to Podl, also wrote about that agonizing time, about distrust and lack of support. "The trauma of the last five years," wrote Natalie Sekicky, the journalism teacher.

After several minutes, Juli asked the staff to stop writing and follow him outside. The group walked from the auditorium up the central hallway, its floors always gleaming. The group turned left and passed the main office and the security guard station where Olivia McDowell had broken down in tears after escaping her classroom that previous fall. They pushed out the front doors of the school to the lawn, where Juli had set up a half dozen fire pits, campfires roaring as the staff arrived. Juli told the teachers he couldn't take away the past, or pretend it didn't happen. But he asked them to put their papers into the fires as a way to mark a fresh start. "Let's take some tentative steps forward."

Some teachers broke down crying as they symbolically set fire to their burdens. Then Juli brought out marshmallows and graham crackers and chocolate bars and the staff made sweet gooey s'mores.

Sekicky said it was "like visiting a therapist." "It's a mass catharsis. It really is," said Morris. "I can't think of a better beginning to an administration. I really can't." Juli had assured the staff that, when problems arose, he would handle them privately, unlike the public humiliation Podl suffered. As Morris tossed his paper into the fire, "I let it go. I feel at that moment I did let it go."

———

Eric Juli had a blunt and straightforward way about him, happy to answer just about any question and not particularly worried if the answer was popular or not. He was raised in southeastern Connecticut, where he said his education was entirely ordinary. "I was absolutely willing to do the minimum to get by," he said. He described himself as "teacher proof," meaning he'd be successful no matter who his instructors were or what they did. Like Glasner, he went to a Jewish day school for elementary years, then public school and on to Syracuse University. He worked as a teacher, then principal, in a series of mostly high-poverty schools, chosen intentionally, most recently in Cleveland. Arriving to the area, he and his wife fell for Shaker and moved in.

It didn't take long for Juli to observe some of the unsettling racial dynamics at work. At Fernway Elementary, his neighborhood school, the lion's share of the students who rode buses were Black. After school, neighborhood moms, most of them white, gathered as their kids continued to play. They traded notes about the school and set up play dates for the future, while the Black students boarded the bus and went home, their parents likely unaware of the after-school scene.

Juli wasn't particularly enthralled with the academic rigor that so many touted about Shaker Heights High School. At a Christmas party, he heard a neighbor's son proudly declare he had taken 18 AP courses, which Juli found appallingly high. "That's the narrative—'AP is best,'" he said. He would have preferred if this bright student were out in the community, applying his knowledge to problem solving.

In 2015, when the high school was searching for a new principal, Juli attended a meeting for community members to offer opinions. He recalled a group of parents insisting that the school continue to offer an early morning Greek class. Juli stood up to suggest that maybe the high school should change "so it would look and feel different," without specifying what might change. The response, he said, "was like I shot someone. The rest of the parents wanted it to stay the same."

He wasn't seriously considering applying for the job but after the meeting, a few neighbors approached him and remarked, "Well, if you were interested in the job before, I bet you're not now."

Four years later, after the Podl controversy exploded, the principal's position opened again, and this time Juli applied and was hired for the 2019–20 school year.

―――――

On May 30, 2020, five days after George Floyd was pinned to the ground and murdered by Minneapolis police in broad daylight, someone took a can of spray paint to the red brick walls of Shaker Heights High School and unleashed a string of antipolice, anti–Donald Trump statements. The graffiti referred to "Amerikkka," with three k's. It was one in a flood of emotional protests that exploded in the days following

Floyd's killing, the siren of a nation confronting systemic racism in raw and wrenching terms.

Eric Juli responded with a long and searing letter to the community. The high school could not just be a nonracist place, he said, echoing ideas popularized by historian Ibram X. Kendi. It had to be an antiracist place—a place actively working to combat racism and promote policies that produce or sustain racial equity.

Juli began with a discussion of his own white privilege, contrasting the safe and carefree childhood his children were enjoying against news that a second one of his former Cleveland students had been murdered since the start of the pandemic, and the warnings about the life-and-death consequences of compliance with police that Black parents must deliver to their children.

"It's a talk that I will never have to give to my boys," he wrote.

Shaker, he said, was filled with passionate teachers and amazing students. But the problems so easily identified in central cities existed here, too. "We have Black classes and White classes," he wrote. "We have lots of struggling students in far too many segregated classrooms."

He blamed himself for not leading by example as an antiracist. He said he should have spoken out around other high-profile Black deaths. If he had been "publicly and explicitly anti-racist," he said, maybe the school would not have been spray-painted. "I need to leverage my power and privilege to stand up for racial justice," he wrote. "I know that I can do better."

The letter won Juli some national publicity and an invitation the following January to give a talk sponsored by Case Western Reserve University on racism in the Shaker schools. In his talk, he said Shaker High was "two schools in one." The first, mostly white school was high achieving, dynamic, exciting. The second was made up of almost entirely Black students and was "only a little better than the inner city high school I left in Cleveland."

"I intend to make a third school, better than the two," he said, "grounded in antiracism, equity, and the application of learning."

―――――――――――

Juli brought a fundamentally new view of the very purpose of a high school education. For as long as anyone could remember, Shaker focused on helping students master sophisticated material, show their work on tests and quizzes, write long papers, solve tough math problems, and understand what happens when two chemicals are combined. Some students did it brilliantly; others struggled or outright failed.

From Juli's vantage point, the entire system was pointed in the wrong direction. The levels system that he and Glasner were intent on dismantling made sense when school was about mastering increasingly complex material. But he didn't see that as the goal.

"If we're starting with the premise that the most important thing is to learn about the Battle of Gettysburg and the Pythagorean theorem and you know, how to solve for X and photosynthesis — distinct and discrete pieces of content—then it's easier to argue that some kids can learn faster than others . . . and that's an argument for levels," he said. An alternative vision posits: "You can Google when the Battle of Gettysburg was and who were the major players in it, and solving for X matters in an Algebra 2 class but Algebra 2 doesn't exist on Planet Earth outside of an American high school, and the Pythagorean theorem, it's nice if you know it, but also when was the last time either of us used it in our lives?" He said schools should really care about students' ability to write and speak persuasively and collaborate with one another, with content taking a secondary role to skill development.

If the goal was learning to speak or write or work together, then students of mixed abilities could more easily learn in the same space. So while many parents and students worried that detracking translated to less rigor, Juli wasn't concerned—though he was quick to point out that he had not reduced any AP or IB course offerings. In fact, he added an AP course—Calculus 3, because there was a cohort of students ready for it.

Juli's vision for school centered on project-based lessons, where students learn by doing, where they are given a problem and have to solve it. So instead of simply studying physics on paper, students might learn how to build and fire a rocket. Maybe students would lobby City Council for some sort of policy change rather than just write papers. He was thrilled, for example, when students in a German-language class had the chance to translate documents given to them by a local man whose father survived the Holocaust. Ultimately, they hoped, the translations would end up at the U.S. Holocaust Memorial Museum in Washington.

Another example: During the pandemic, some students didn't have desks at home for remote school, so a group of students built desks. It was part community service, but also budgeting, woodworking, and engineering. That program was not for class credit, but Juli envisioned that someday something like it might be.

Asked if there was value to traditional learning—say, the ability to read a novel, identify themes, understand character development, and then put those thoughts on paper, Juli replied, "Absolutely. Just not every semester, all four years."

With this philosophy in mind, in the spring of 2022, Juli started looking around the building for a spot to put a makerspace where students could, for instance, create podcasts, rebuild motorcycles, or use a 3D printer. The school had a motorcycle program, but it was hidden in the basement, inside a room once used as a shooting range. He wanted it front and center for all to see. He settled on repurposing part of the school library and sent operations staff over to take some measurements. That's how the librarian found out her principal was considering taking over part of her library, and she was livid.

Juli said she had every right to be angry but also argued that the library should balance the value of books against other needs. "Why can't it be an 'and'?" he asked. Despite her protests, that summer, crews pulled up carpet in the back of the library to create the makerspace. They found room for the books on shelves along the perimeter.

His hope was that project-based learning would excite disengaged students in a new way and appeal to high-achieving students as well. The classes would work, he believed, by drawing a mix of students together who wanted to do cool things. Maybe building a rocket would prove more attractive than AP Physics.

He also pushed the faculty to change how they measured success. Traditionally, he said, teachers valued compliance: completing work as instructed and turning assignments in on time. That prepared students well for college—the goal for many Shaker students and their parents—but not particularly well for the real world, he said.

So when the pandemic hit, Juli's instinct was to undo the policies he found problematic and punitive in the first place. In addition to the detracking, he discouraged homework because students were already spending too much time online. He reduced the number of tests and quizzes, because teachers were having trouble getting through all the material, and what's the point anyway if students are at home and can easily look up the answers? He mandated that the lowest grade possible on an assignment would be 45 percent, because if a student gets too many zeros, he will fall into a hole almost impossible to climb out of. He required teachers to allow students to make up any missing assignment without penalty, because what matters is *whether* the material is learned, not *when* it is learned. He noted that it doesn't say on your driver's license how many times you had to take the test. It just says you passed. "It's only in high school that it matters when you learn it."

Like detracking, many of the changes were retained once school resumed in person, as they were consistent with Juli's overall educational philosophy. He ended the traditional finals week and made final exams optional for teachers, saying those who wanted to give finals could do so during regular class periods.

To understand how radical all this was, consider a scene from the late 1990s in the documentary *Shaker Heights: The Struggle for Integration*. The principal of Shaker Heights High School, Jack Rumbaugh, is meeting with a family considering moving to the community.

Rumbaugh, seated behind his desk in the same office Juli now occupied, leans back in his chair confidently to address the ninth grader in front of him. "How many hours do you spend on homework every night?" he asks her.

"If I average everything out," she says, "it would be like an hour each night or two hours each night."

"I hope that changes," Rumbaugh says.

"More, or less?" the girl replies sheepishly.

"More. I'd like to see three or four hours a night."

Juli's philosophy was a direct challenge to the Shaker of old, which valued academic rigor, three-hour final exams, and homework to reinforce lessons from class. Juli spoke with enormous confidence about his approach. If the school didn't want big change, he said flatly, then someone else should be principal.

———

The changes Juli championed in Shaker were part of a heightened embrace of racial equity already underway in education, strengthened now in response to both the pandemic and the murder of George Floyd. School districts nationwide, including Shaker, hired diversity and inclusion officers, and many commissioned audits of their data, which exposed widespread disparities by race. Like Shaker, districts wrote strategic plans that centered equity, which typically included taking a deep look at racial and other patterns in academics, discipline, and other metrics, and sought to deliver to students and schools needed resources. Many changed their policies in an effort to correct injustices and beefed up conversation about race in the classroom.

In Evanston, Illinois, students from marginalized groups were given first priority for in-person classes during the pandemic, based on the fact that they were more likely to be struggling with remote school. In San Francisco, the school board voted to change admissions to the city's elite Lowell High School from an exam to a lottery, hoping to increase the number of Black and Latino students, who were under-represented. Similar changes were enacted at elite magnet schools in Boston and in Fairfax, Virginia, for similar reasons. In New York City, the nation's largest school district stopped allowing middle schools to use academic criteria to admit the best students, a practice that drove segregation.

Changes to how grades were administered were already underway in some districts but took on new momentum during the pandemic, as educators became more attuned to disparities in children's ability to complete homework. Remote school was far more manageable for students from two-parent families and peaceful home lives than for those who had to hunt for a quiet place to study, who may not have had a parent available who could help, who might be responsible for younger siblings even as they tried to do their own schoolwork.

Los Angeles and San Diego Unified, California's largest school districts, told teachers to stop penalizing students for misbehavior and missed deadlines and instead to base grades on whether they learned what was expected. They were encouraged to let students revise assignments and retake tests to show they had mastered the material, regardless of the deadlines. There might still be consequences for behavior problems, but it was not part of their academic grade.

Joshua Moreno, a world languages teacher at Alhambra High School in southern California, told the *Los Angeles Times* that he had grown frustrated with his own grading system, which gave points for various tasks. Some students quickly earned lots of points and knew they didn't need to do any more work to still get an A, where others—typically those who had to juggle work or care for family during school—would fall behind fast and then give up.

"It was literally inequitable," he said. "As a teacher you get frustrated because what you signed up for was for students to learn. And it just ended up being a conversation about points all the time."

He decided to do away with homework and instead give students multiple chances to improve essays and classwork, with grades based on how much of the material they eventually mastered.

One of the people driving the change nationally was Joe Feldman, whose 2018 book *Grading for Equity: What It Is, Why It Matters, and How It Can Transform Schools and Classrooms* served as a handbook for schools to revise their policies. Feldman found vast inconsistency in how grades were assigned. And he concluded that many systems did not work. Threatening to fail a student, he said, does nothing to help the vast majority of students avoid failure, because it does not address their lack of confidence and dearth of experience with academic success. "Clearly, we don't want to grade students based on their environment or situations beyond their control," he wrote, "but unfortunately, when we use grading practices such as penalizing students for late work, that is often what we do."

In much of the country, these changes, along with efforts to address race in the curriculum, sparked a political backlash, with conservatives charging that schools were overly focused on race and indoctrinating students with liberal ideologies. School board meetings grew angry and even violent, and candidates for school boards ran on platforms of eradicating "critical race theory" in the classroom, using a previously obscure academic term that came to stand in for an entire basket of conversations and policies that addressed systemic racism, including the sort of work underway in Shaker. Some of the changes—such as the admissions policies for sought-after public schools in New York and San Francisco—were later reversed after elections produced leaders who saw rewarding merit as more important than fostering diversity.

Politically, Shaker Heights is overwhelmingly Democratic and didn't experience anything approaching the vitriol that divided many communities. But that doesn't mean there wasn't resistance, and it doesn't mean there weren't people in Shaker who thought the schools were overly focused on race.

———

Juli was determined to be a visible presence at Shaker Heights High School and ran himself hard trying to do just that. He began most days standing in front of the building as parents navigated the drive-through lane to drop their kids off at the front door, greeting students by name and being present for parents who might have questions. He personally delivered the morning announcements, reading an inspirational message from a compendium of inspirational messages and always ending with, "Make it a great day, or not. The choice is yours."

In between class periods, he darted from his office to a narrow hallway outside the guidance counselors' offices to play songs from his phone over the PA system, filling the hallways with music—pop, classic rock, instrumental—as students made their way between classes. If there was a fight, the next day he always played "Why Can't We Be Friends?" by the funk band War, and wondered whether anyone noticed.

Not everyone appreciated his style. Carole Kovach, chair of the school's morale committee, loved to plan fun treats for teachers. But under Juli, she felt pushed aside and rarely appreciated. He told her he had his own ideas, she said. "They call it the Eric Juli show. He's the star, and if it's not about him, it's not important."

Juli often neglected to eat lunch himself, but he almost always made his way to the cafeteria during student lunch periods, where the smells and residue of pizza and French fries filled the large open space. He would find a garbage can on wheels and push it from table to table, collecting the empty ketchup packets and disposable plates and candy wrappers. It helped tidy things up, but the real point was to show his face.

"Who's got trash?" he said as he rolled by each table one spring day in 2022.

"What's up, Juli?" a girl said as he approached with the trash can.

"You writing your thing yet?" he replied. "I'm telling you, it will be good."

She enthusiastically agreed. "It'll be great, actually!"

He approached another student, who had collapsed several times in recent weeks. "What did you eat?" he inquired. "Enough water?"

On another day, a student approached him. "When can we talk about doing the announcements? We're serious about it." Juli told him to come up with a plan and bring it to him.

Juli hoped the trash-and-chat lunch periods would set a tone. "Everybody needs to see me, to see there's not a job in this building I'm not willing to do," he said. A day earlier, the security team saw him restraining a student who was fighting. "It's about the kind of culture I want to build, and it takes time."

Juli spent a fair bit of his time in the 2021–22 school year dealing with fights. Coming out of remote school, districts across the country saw spikes in violence, shootings, fighting, and general misbehavior. Shaker was no exception. Students had forgotten how to relate to one another, it seemed, and schools reported a huge increase in demand for mental health services.

At the high school, Juli approached the challenge with the mentality of hand-to-hand combat, sometimes literally. One day, he restrained a student who had been pulled into a back office and was trashing the room. (Based on the student's behavior and history, Juli suspected he was using drugs.) That evening, the school's monitoring system picked up notes between two students about suicide, and he arranged for intervention with someone on the mental health team. The following day, he interrogated two girls who had almost fought the previous day and who he feared were ready to go at it now. Their dispute, whatever it was, went back to eighth grade.

"Resolve it," Juli told the first girl, who was seated across the desk in his office.

"There ain't nothing to resolve," she replied.

"I'm not having a fight here today," Juli told her. He noticed she was wearing sweatpants, a sign to him that she was expecting a brawl. "We have to figure out a way to end this." He called her mom and sent her home. "We'll try again tomorrow."

Then he brought the second girl into his office. She really didn't want to fight, but she admitted she would not hold back if the first girl or one of her friends came at her. She pulled out her phone, toggled to Instagram, and showed Juli a post from the first girl showing off her sweats with the caption, "We dress this way to fight." Turns out he had been right about the sweatpants.

"I just have anger built up inside me," the second girl told Juli. "I've been not saying anything about her and keeping my cool for two long years and I'm angry. What am I supposed to do?" Juli promised to sit them down and help them work it out. For the moment, though, he sent her home, too.

It was all exhausting. "We are all wishing this year was normal, but it is not normal," he said.

———

On a Wednesday morning in the fall of 2021, one of the first things to cross Juli's desk was an email from a parent demanding to know why the AP Physics teacher had asked her Black son to remove his do-rag, a tight scarf that covers the skull, sometimes worn by Black males. Juli called the teacher and the science department chairman into his office to ask about it.

"We do have that rule," the teacher said, referring to the dress code that does not allow do-rags.

"Here's the thing," Juli replied. "We're not enforcing this rule. The reality is our dress code is not something we enforce. It's common to see mostly naked white girls walking around."

The teacher stood his ground. He remembered one of the assistant principals explaining the rules: no hats, scarves, or hoodies.

"I'm not saying she didn't say it," Juli said. "We don't want it to be just one teacher enforcing it." He said the optics here were that the rule was being applied to one Black boy.

The teacher wondered aloud what might be next if they allowed this. Do-rags do not cover the ears, but if hoodies were allowed, then kids could easily use earbuds undetected. "Is that where we're heading?"

Juli agreed that listening to music in class was not okay but said the staff simply had not agreed among themselves to consistently enforce the dress code and that no one had the bandwidth right then to start.

He told the teacher he understood that he was not singling out this student because of his race. "But these are the optics," he said. He said the truth of the matter is that student dress is looked at differently based on race. A skinny white girl wearing a tight cropped shirt, showing skin, might be ignored while a heavyset Black girl wearing the same thing might be told to go change.

With that, something appeared to click for the teacher, or maybe he concluded he wasn't going to win this one. "That logic," he said, "I can latch onto." Juli later reported the results back to the parent who had complained about the physics teacher's treatment of her son.

Left unsaid were the broader implications of a moment like this. If teachers were selectively enforcing the dress code, were they selectively enforcing other school rules? Did this help explain why in Shaker, as in most other diverse districts, discipline rates for students of color were higher than for white students? And how did this mindset affect teaching? Were white and Black students getting the same breaks, the same benefits of the doubt, the same high expectations? And if some students' outfits were being picked apart, would they feel like they really belonged?

That's not to say this particular teacher was guilty of any of this. But these were the big issues facing the school district. For today, though, Juli had resolved a small issue, a sticky question about the dress code, recognizing that the complaint went far deeper than one simple covering on one student's head.

———

J uli was not the only person in the high school rethinking how things were done.

In the English Department, many teachers began reconsidering the types of books they assigned. Maybe it was time for new novels, where students might more easily see their own lives. Some teachers had long worked to bring in modern novels, but they also believed books like *The Great Gatsby* and *Of Mice and Men* were classics for a reason.

"In the past, I would have said, 'Don't let go of the classics,'" said English teacher Chuck Kelly, who is white. Sure, Hemingway used offensive language, but Kelly would explain that simply reflected his time. Now he saw how offensive that could be to students. He noticed, for instance, when the class was reading the play *A Streetcar Named Desire* aloud in class, a Black student handling a character identified in the text as "Negro woman" changed it to "Black woman" as she read.

"I am so impressed," Kelly said. "I thought, should I even be doing this work? . . . Kids have just had enough. I don't want to give one more excuse for one more author from fifty years ago. There's something bigger at stake now than reading 'great' literature."

———

S haker's Parent Teacher Organizations—each school had one—had for years been dominated by white moms. Increasingly, this felt not okay, and the PTOs tried to recruit a more diverse leadership, with mixed success.

The stakes were apparent one evening in early 2019 at Onaway Elementary School. The school's PTO hosted a program featuring John Moore, who then directed the prestigious and rigorous International Baccalaureate diploma program at the high school. Moore had worked hard to diversify the IB diploma program, and on this evening, he brought two white and two Black students for the presentation.

Moore, with his trim beard, blazer, and oxford cloth shirt, looked the professorial part as he and his students divided parents into small groups to consider a question: Should school begin later in the day? Participants were assigned to look at it from the perspectives of employers, coaches, students, and parents, and it became apparent that one person's "of course you should start later" was a ridiculous notion for someone else. The big question on the table: "To what extent does perspective shape truth?"

It was a cool presentation, one that would excite parents for the opportunities for interesting discussions in the high school IB program. But out of more than two dozen Onaway parents in attendance, not one was Black.

In the summer of 2021, Randi Gross Nathenson, who is white, took office as co-president of the PTO Council, which dealt with district-wide matters. She had another idea for how to create a more equitable system.

Her family's first house in Shaker was in the Lomond neighborhood, an integrated community of middle-class homes. Nathenson remembered working on the PTO's Pumpkin Affair, a carnival fundraiser, and being thrilled that they raised $2,000 for the school toward an annual haul that typically hit about $5,000. She later learned that another Shaker elementary school, Mercer, set in a wealthier neighborhood, usually raised some $25,000 per year. "I couldn't even fathom it," she said. "All the other schools had more than Lomond. It was sort of shocking."

So when she became co-president of the PTO Council, she and her co-president pitched the schools on a combined fundraising effort. The money would be pooled and equalized. "You may not get everything you always get, but what do you need?" she said in summer 2021, rehearsing her pitch.

At the start of the year, the pair met with all the PTO building presidents. "We talked about inequity and also maintaining each school's individuality," Nathenson said. "There was a lot of pushback on sharing that kind of resource." She declined to identify the school or schools that objected but said their leaders "felt that essentially, 'This is our school, the money should stay in our neighborhood.'" She said there were also logistical concerns about tracking and managing the money. Either way, the proposal was not adopted.

Still, Nathenson felt like it was useful to put the question on the table. "It started the conversation."

———

After school one afternoon in the spring of 2022, Juli gathered with the teaching staff in the upper cafeteria to discuss one of the most intense issues facing the school: the schedule. To Juli, the schedule was a statement of a school's values, and he intended to use it to drive change. He had already changed the rules so that students would be required to take health class in person; when online was an option, white students tended to take the online class and Black students did not, resulting in segregation where there didn't need to be any. He'd eliminated "zero period," the slot before school started when some students took classes such as Greek and yoga, because not everyone was able to get to school early.

Another early target was the marching band. For as long as anyone could remember, the huge band met together during first period. It was one of the most diverse groups in the school, with a racial makeup that reflected Shaker. But oddly enough, the band was driving segregation in other classes throughout the day, Juli noticed. That's because a large group of white students who were in the band were also in several advanced courses that, like band, each have only one section. The result was that their schedules wound up almost identical and disproportionately white. They would be together not just for band and calculus but also physical education and art.

So Juli broke band class into two sections, prompting a mini-controversy among people upset that the musicians would not be able to practice all together.

He also switched the high school from a traditional schedule, with every class meeting every day, to a block schedule, with classes meeting less frequently but for longer. The change was initially driven by the pandemic, but he stuck with it because he hoped it would give teachers the time they needed to provide everyone in the class with personalized teaching, particularly in mixed-ability classes. He also wanted to prevent teachers from lecturing all class long. Instead, he wanted teaching that was more engaging to students—more discussion and sharing and not just listening. He reasoned that no teacher would lecture for an hour and a half.

Heading into the next year, Juli also wanted a block schedule in order to build flextime into the week. He saw that time being used for teacher collaboration and meetings, extra practice for the marching band, and, perhaps most urgent, academic interventions—extra help for struggling students.

Yet math and science teachers didn't like meeting every other day. They were trying to drive complicated concepts into students' brains. For them, shorter but more frequent classes were far preferable.

On that spring afternoon, the cafeteria was buzzing as teachers gathered at the round tables to give feedback on two options Juli and a scheduling committee had come up with.

At table two, science teacher James Schmidt, a leader in the teachers union, was tasked with facilitating the conversation and taking notes, and he toggled between explaining Juli's vision and stoking teacher skepticism about it. When history teacher Sarah Davis complained that there wasn't enough time for her to go to the bathroom in between classes, Schmidt replied that Juli "doesn't really care if we can go to the bathroom or not." Arguing that things used to be better, Davis offered to look up her own student schedule from 1989, something Schmidt said would not be necessary. And when another teacher suggested that the schedule appeared to change year to year, he quipped, "Yeah, until we get a new principal."

In the end, a solid majority of teachers favored the schedule Juli wanted, with all classes meeting on Mondays and the longer blocks every other day. He would get his flextime twice a week.

———

For years, Shaker had talked about the importance of moving more Black students into advanced classes. All sorts of programs were tried. Juli didn't oppose them, but this wasn't his priority. He wanted to focus on rethinking how high school was organized in order to better serve students, particularly lower achieving students. He wasn't against rigorous coursework, but he didn't see it as the North Star in the same way as his predecessors did.

So Juli wasn't particularly sympathetic when he heard that Sarah Davis, the history teacher who helped create the summer Bridges program, was pressuring her high-achieving students to attend the after-school conference period, a block of time at the end of the day when all teachers were available to meet with students and offer extra help. He met with the History Department chair to figure out how to get this message to Davis. It had to end, Juli said. Parents were complaining, and it was putting too much pressure on students.

"My concern is she won't be receptive and will take it out on the kids," the chairwoman replied.

The problem, she said, was that Davis believed deeply that the most important thing was for her students to absorb the complicated material she was teaching, in this case, in an advanced course about Eurasian history. "Her passion for the content trumps everything else . . . She's holding on to the Shaker of the 1990s and refuses to adapt because I think she believes her approach is the only approach."

The pair contemplated how to manage the situation, how to get Davis to ease off, and whether Davis would try to figure out which students complained and punish them for it.

The conversation ended with Juli saying he would talk to Davis.

"Good luck!" the chairwoman said sarcastically.

"Ultimately, I'll be the bad guy," Juli replied.

That week, in Davis's IB EurAsia history course, a group of about twenty students was debating the origins of the Cold War, with each of four groups defending a particular argument. Among the students, seven were people of color, including two Black students, demographics that were unsurprisingly unrepresentative of the school.

Each group made its case. Group one argued that traditional world powers had declined, leaving a power vacuum filled by the United States and the Soviet Union. Another group said it was the United States' dropping of the atomic bomb, seen as a threat to the Soviets, that spurred the arms race. Perhaps it was ideological, another said, the Communist drive for power. No, argued group four, it was Stalin, and the concessions made to a man who could not be appeased.

The groups debated their points and then Davis walked the class through each one, citing historians and facts that bolstered or undercut each argument.

"This is where we have a public advocacy campaign by MacArthur to use the bomb," she said. "Truman has to fire him because Truman is not going to use the nuclear weapon. Why?"

This was, without doubt, academic rigor for some of the school's most advanced students. And Davis worried this level of education was slipping away from the school she had graduated from in 1990 and taught at since 1996.

To Davis, the answer to the achievement gap was found in programs such as Bridges, the conference periods after school, and Study Circles, which met after conferences—opportunities to deliver the best of what Shaker offered to a more diverse group of students. She watched as the number of Black students in AP U.S. History rose after Bridges got going. She saw the number of Black students in the IB diploma program rise, too, with hard work and recruitment.

Now, with detracking, she feared students would be less prepared for rigorous classes like the ones she taught. "We've received a lot of mixed messages as a staff about rigor and expectations," she said. For instance, all students were supposed to be taught at the honors level in detracked classes, but literature must be read aloud in class instead of assigned as homework, and some teachers had been told they were assigning too much writing. There were students, she said, who still didn't understand how to write a paragraph.

Indeed, many teachers used the longer class periods offered by the block schedule Juli created to let students finish homework in class. That was helpful for students who might not have done it otherwise, or who benefited from having the teacher right there when they had questions. But it meant less total teaching time for students who would have done the homework at home.

Some Shaker students, Davis said, had parents with multiple post-graduate degrees and were taught early how to "play school," and were now being denied the chance to move faster than their peers. "You have this group of families who are so good at doing school, generations of families, Black and white," she said. "That's why people move to Shaker, right? Because they really value school and they teach that to their kids. Others are coming from very different family stories . . . In Shaker, the difference between the kids can be very large and that's not the fault of the school but it's often phrased like that.

"It's very difficult to have conversations," Davis added. "People feel if you come out against detracking, you're a racist or will be called one."

As for the allegation that she had been requiring students to attend after-school conferences, Davis said conferences were a critical tool for helping students improve and that she told students who wanted to improve their grades that they needed to attend. She also encouraged others, she said. "Why would we be upset about a kid feeling like they should go to conferences?" But she said she never issued a blanket requirement that students attend.

Months later, after they had a conversation, Juli said Davis loosened up on pushing students to attend conference periods. "It's been a push and pull and dance all year long," he said, and though he was referring to Davis, the same sentiment applied throughout the school.

> Not long ago, if someone had called me a racist, I would have
> kicked and screamed in protest.
> —Debby Irving, *Waking Up White*

16

KATHLEEN FITZSIMONS

Kathleen FitzSimons logged off her antiracism book club feeling despair. She was also confused.

That day, a mob of Donald Trump supporters had stormed the U.S. Capitol in a deadly and terrifying attempt to overturn the results of the 2020 presidential election. So FitzSimons, who is white, was already shaken when she joined the Zoom call that evening to discuss another gutting topic. The group, co-led by her daughter Molly, was discussing *The New Jim Crow*, by Michelle Alexander, about the devastating impact of the criminal justice system on Black men.

During the conversation, Molly recalled one of their Black neighbors from when she was growing up in the Lomond neighborhood of Shaker Heights and his later experience with police. Kathleen couldn't remember what her daughter was talking about, and it bothered her. She went to sleep and then, in the middle of the night, woke up suddenly and started remembering.

Kathleen had tuned in to the conversation about race in America, about Black Lives Matter, about antiracism. She was trying to figure out what it meant to be an antiracist, and how that was different from simply not being racist. For her, this book club was helping in her hunt for answers. The idea for the book club had come to Molly when she was helping her mom clean out her apartment and found notes from conversations on race Kathleen had held with friends in the 1970s, after moving to Shaker Heights. "It was very moving to me to see she had been making that effort way back then and we were still in the same spot," Molly said.

Indeed, for decades, Kathleen had considered herself a small part of the solution to America's troubling relationship with race. Now she wondered if it was enough.

Similar antiracism groups had been organized all over Shaker Heights, all over progressive America, really. Lisa Vahey, who had co-chaired the Equity Task Force under Greg Hutchings, began a series of *Waking Up White* discussion groups in Shaker. She kept a public Google document updated with racial equity events and opportunities in and around the community. She regularly emailed several hundred people with information about pending legislation and community-building events around town. She helped distribute 550 Black Lives Matter yard signs, and with each sign, she signed up the recipient for a weekly email guiding them on "how to learn and act."

"I continued to notice not enough white women were striving to be actively antiracist," Vahey said. Too many, she said, "had bought into the promise of Shaker" and thought that it was all good because their kid had a Black friend in the fourth grade.

Kathleen and Dan FitzSimons very much bought into the promise of Shaker. She had been raised on the west side of Cleveland, which was almost entirely white and Christian, to parents who cared about social justice, though race was rarely mentioned. After college, Kathleen worked as a probation officer for the juvenile court and saw racial issues up close. Together, she and her husband were drawn to the idea of a racially diverse community. They bought a home in the Lomond neighborhood in the midst of Lomond's push to recruit white buyers and preserve racial balance.

Several years later, she and her husband divorced, and Kathleen became the primary caregiver for their three children—Danny, the oldest; Caitlin, who was in my class at Shaker; and Molly, who was close friends with my sister, Amy. (Amy, in fact, co-led the antiracism book group with Molly.)

In the middle of the night after that January 6, 2021, book club meeting, FitzSimons woke up recalling the incident her daughter had referred to involving their neighbor and the police and found herself overcome with memories about her relationships with her Black neighbors. Suddenly, she saw her decades in Shaker in a completely different light. In an email to the book group the next morning, she detailed her newly remembered experience.

Across the street lived a young Black boy, just a little younger than Molly. FitzSimons remembered, as her daughter had said, that he would later be caught up in the criminal justice system. (In fact, he'd been sentenced to ten years in prison after pleading guilty to voluntary manslaughter, though she didn't know that.)

Other stories that filled FitzSimons's mind that night weren't about crime. They were about everyday life. Living next door was another Black family, the Rushins. The mom was a teacher, and FitzSimons remembered that she had had to fight with teachers at Lomond because they kept putting her sons into the lowest-level learning groups. Yet all three of FitzSimons's kids had been placed in upper-level groups without her having to ask.

"She had a hell of a time convincing the school that her boys deserved better, and was ultimately unsuccessful," she wrote in her email. It never occurred to FitzSimons to advocate on her behalf, to say to the school, "What are we doing here?"

One of these boys struggled as he went on in school, a situation FitzSimons attributed to how he was treated at Lomond.

Down the street was her babysitter. She was bright and caring and had such a hard time. Her dad was in jail and she had to give her babysitting money to her mom, who was ill and struggling to keep the household together.

"I am flooded with shame when I think now of how little I did to support these families," FitzSimons wrote on the morning of January 7. "Not that I was so sophisticated or had it all together myself, but what is clear to me now is how little recourse or few resources they had to effectively navigate within the system. Ingrained attitudes, assumptions, and biases among teachers, community members and all the rest of us well-intentioned liberals, made up the invisible barriers that actually prevented their full inclusion."

It's not that FitzSimons had it easy. She was a single mom with stretched finances. But looking back, she saw that she was better situated than these neighbors, simply because she was white.

It wasn't just about money. She had been friendly "across the fence," but never thought to include these neighbors in her wide social circle based on Lomond Boulevard and nearby streets. "We were committed to integration. We thought that was enough," she said later. "It didn't occur to me you have to go the next step, you have to invite them over."

She remembered one experience more fondly. One day she went next door to Janice Rushin's house to see some new furniture she had just bought. Rushin asked FitzSimons if she had ever heard the Black national anthem. She hadn't. So Rushin sat down at her piano and played "Lift Every Voice and Sing." The pair sat together, tears streaming. The music was beautiful, hauntingly so. "It makes me cry to imagine what maybe we could have done together," FitzSimons said, decades later. "I didn't know how to go further."

———

Janice Rushin died in 2017. Her two sons confirmed most of the basic facts of FitzSimons's memories, and yet they saw things in a different light.

Michael Rushin, the younger of the two, said he was put into lower-level reading classes because that's where he belonged. He didn't love academics and didn't want to do homework. It wasn't until he was older that he found his calling: flying. His mom paid for flight lessons, the one thing he wanted to learn. And after college, he became a pilot.

The story was different for his older brother, Mark, who was also placed into the lowest group in kindergarten even though he was academically advanced. The teacher, he said, "had all the Black kids in the lowest group." His mom had to fight to get him into the middle-level group, and then fight again to get him into the top group, he said.

As he made his way through the Shaker schools, he encountered racism periodically—like the time he took a typing class in summer school and ran into the vice principal, who delivered a lecture about how this was his chance to make up for his bad performance during the year. The vice principal had clearly assumed that Mark had failed a class, even though he had never come close to failing a class. "I said to him, 'Umm, I'm here taking typing. I don't need that speech.'"

But both Rushin kids had warm memories of Kathleen FitzSimons and her children.

Mark remembered a big party she hosted for all the neighborhood kids. He and Danny FitzSimons played together all the time. Once, he said, her ex-husband, who was in advertising, took them to an event where they met Mike Phipps, the starting quarterback for the Cleveland Browns.

Mark also remembered a time when he was in about fourth grade and had to leave school because he was sick with the stomach flu. Fitz-Simons picked him up and took him home with her, where he proceeded to puke all over her bed. "She can't say she never did anything [to help]!" Mark said.

Michael said his mom thought of Kathleen FitzSimons as a friend. "My mother loved her," he said.

Without doubt, Shaker launched both Rushins successfully into the world. Their mom's battle to get Mark onto a higher academic track paid off. He graduated from Duke University, then the University of Michigan law school.

Michael, a successful pilot, looks back on his time in Shaker as a sort of bubble, in a good way. "Other places are so segregated," he said. "That's the gift Shaker Heights gave me—that diversity. It kind of spoiled me." Now he is comfortable around other cultures. "I know the Jewish holidays. I know a good corned beef sandwich when I see one," he said. "I wouldn't want to have grown up anyplace else."

Their mother died after years of living with Alzheimer's disease. At the end, Michael said, when she could no longer remember anyone around her, she still played the piano.

———

FitzSimons's older daughter, Caitlin, had grown up witnessing Shaker's joys and its limitations. Her friend group was racially diverse in elementary school, becoming mostly white as she moved to junior high. Her classes grew segregated, too. Still, she said, "it felt because we were in Shaker and it was mixed we were on the right side of history."

It wasn't until years later, when she was a mom herself raising two children in New York City, that she started to become aware of her own white privilege and how that connected to education. In Brooklyn, her kids went to a giant elementary school filled with immigrant children, but they were pulled into a small gifted class that was disproportionately white. She suspected the class was created to draw and keep families like hers, which was uncomfortable—and yet she benefited from it, and she liked those benefits. It seemed that the best teachers were teaching her kids' classes, and her kids were thriving. Her daughter attended this school, and this special class, from pre-K through fifth grade, as did her son, from pre-K through third.

After years of struggling to afford New York, Caitlin and her husband had a new idea: Why not move to Shaker, where they could put their kids into excellent schools and afford more than a one-bedroom apartment? They moved back to Lomond in 2017.

She was just as happy with the schools as a parent as she had been as a student. But now it seemed questions of race and racism were much more in the forefront than she recalled from her childhood. She noticed far more poverty than she was aware of as a teenager—partly because there was more and partly because she was more attuned to it. She was surprised to learn that her school PTO raised money and donations to help families in need living right in Lomond. She was unsettled when a proposal for the elementary school PTOs to share fundraising was rejected by wealthier schools.

She attended a vigil for racial justice at a local park and was shaken to hear stories of how academic tracking, which she had benefited from, hurt Black students. She joined one of Lisa Vahey's *Waking Up White* book groups. When she heard about the detracking initiative, she thought it was a good idea.

"I thought I was coming back to the Shaker utopia," she said. It wasn't utopia—not the version put forward by the original Shakers or the Van Sweringen brothers or the Ludlow Community Association. "I felt like I was learning something, learning how much we have benefited from being white."

And yet she still saw that Shaker magic when she looked at her daughter's group of friends—Black, white, gay, straight, trans. Their teachers were fantastic. At Thornton Pool in the summer, Black and white kids and their parents shared space joyfully.

When the Van Aken District opened in 2019, she worried it would be a place where only wealthy white people felt comfortable. It featured an open and airy food court and retailers including a salon, an art gallery, and a Shinola store, where watches started at around $400.

But in fact it felt more like a community gathering space, with mixed crowds. On summer evenings, all sorts of people gathered around Mitchell's Ice Cream, next to an open, grassy area where kids could play.

And Black and white families continued to move onto her street, an integrated area that remains integrated more than fifty years after the first Black families arrived. "People still want to come here because of what it stands for."

No, Shaker wasn't utopia, nothing was, certainly not in America and certainly not when it comes to race. The mantra in Shaker, for decades, was that if any place in America can close the achievement gap or bring together the races or deliver on Dr. King's version of the American dream, it was Shaker Heights. Maybe no place can. But Shaker was still trying in its imperfect, inadequate way.

Diversity, Equity, and Inclusion are among the deepest
core values of the Shaker community.
—Forward Together Educational Visioning document

17

KIM HARRIS

It had taken Kim Harris years to figure out Shaker Heights. She arrived in 1994 as a Black single mom, twenty-four years old, barely able to pay her bills, struggling day to day with her young son. Now she knew more, and she worked to pass that knowledge on to her neighbors in Moreland, where many struggled just as she once had. Much of her free time was devoted to the support and advocacy group she founded: Shaker African American Moms, or SAMS. Always, she tried to tell them something she had never heard as a young mother: Your voice matters.

Hoping to see Shaker Heights through Harris's eyes, I asked her to take me on a tour of Shaker as she knew it. From her house in Moreland, Harris, sporting braids, stretchy workout pants, and sneakers, navigated her white Kia Optima with the vanity license plate CUTE KIM out of the neighborhood and across Van Aken Boulevard. A few minutes later, we pulled up alongside Fernway Elementary School.

"So here's pretty Fernway," she said. "It's brand new."

In July 2018, a fire had destroyed the ninety-one-year-old school, an accident caused during work on the roof. It was a massive conflagration, smoke visible for miles, residents falling to the sidewalk in tears in front of the burning building.

After the fire, the devastated Fernway community organized itself, tapping into the emotional pain of the destruction as they pressured the district to rebuild. Enrollment in the district overall was on a slow but steady decline thanks mostly to regional demographic trends, and leaders knew there was a conversation coming about possible consolidation, including school closings. The Fernway neighborhood, filled with lovely colonials and Tudors, was home to many politically active white professionals. They rallied around the slogan #FernwayForever, and within days, a huge FERNWAY FOREVER sign was erected on the school lawn. Yard signs and T-shirts sprouted in the neighborhood. Soon the Shaker schools' social media accounts had adopted the #FernwayForever hashtag.

"I couldn't imagine not rebuilding my elementary. It was unthinkable to me," said Fred Hart, who attended the school as a child and now lived a block away. He had FERNWAY FOREVER T-shirts made and sold them for $10 apiece. His children had already gone through Fernway, but he worried that if the school was not rebuilt, "my property value is going to take a serious hit."

The campaign was successful and Fernway was rebuilt into a beautiful facility, reopening in 2020. Private donations paid for the new playground and park, with a climbing structure that looked as though it were constructed with giant Lincoln Logs and a slide built into a small hill. The district spent $400,000 to add air conditioning because it was far cheaper to include during the rebuild than it would have been after the fact, though no other Shaker schools had air conditioning. A few years later, a #FernwayForever sign still welcomed visitors at the front door.

In an article about Fernway in *Shaker Life* magazine, Scott Stephens, chief communications officer for the schools, affirmed the importance of neighborhood schools, writing that real estate agents saw having a school within walking distance of a home to be "a crucial selling point."

"In that sense," he wrote, "eliminating the school would have been catastrophic for the neighborhood."

Now, sitting in her car looking at the beautiful school—classic red brick on the outside, state-of-the-art renovations on the inside—Kim Harris was not angry. She was jealous.

"They lifted their voices in a big way," she said. "They made it a thing—#FernwayForever. They did not wait to hear what they'll be given, but decided what they'll be given. They had the confidence to say, 'We will not go without a school in our neighborhood.'"

She saw none of that in Moreland, barely a mile away. Moreland had long been the Shaker neighborhood most heavily populated with Black residents. In Moreland, nearly 18 percent of people lived in poverty, and the median income was about $44,000 in 2020—figures that had improved since the depth of the recession but were still far below the rest of the city.

In 1987, Moreland lost its elementary school and ever since, most Moreland kids had been bused across town to Mercer Elementary School, about four miles away. This was done in order to racially integrate the elementary schools. But it meant that many of the children facing the toughest life circumstances also faced the longest commute. Harris found this patently unfair.

Harris was also irritated about the new Van Aken District, a project championed by the city. What bothered her was that people had started calling it Shaker's "downtown." *No, no, no,* she thought. The downtown was around the corner from Moreland, where City Hall and the police station and the public library were. Was Moreland losing that, too? Harris was putting her finger on one of Shaker's most significant challenges: a gulf between the city's wealthier, more politically savvy, and mostly white population, and the poorer, mostly Black residents who have much greater needs and less capacity to advocate for themselves. Decades earlier, Shaker Heights had met the challenge of racial diversity. Now, on top of the question of race, the community was reckoning with significant economic diversity.

———

Less than a year after Fernway burned, Shaker Heights began serious conversations about a long-term facilities plan. Originally intended to look broadly at schools, recreation, libraries, and other structures in Shaker, it soon evolved mostly into a discussion of how to use, renovate, shutter or replace school buildings.

The century-old brick school buildings were cherished by residents, with their iconic bell towers and sturdy foundations, but they were beset by maintenance problems and, by any definition, old. Adding urgency: a state program would subsidize 36 percent of construction costs if they came up with a plan by September 2022, a subsidy officials feared might drop in the future.

The effort was called Forward Together, and officials said they were determined to hear from every corner of Shaker Heights. From the start, white residents were far more likely than Black ones to respond to surveys and give feedback. Superintendent David Glasner worked to set up living room meetings and other gatherings across the district but at every turn, the lowest-income residents were the least represented.

Kim Harris was encouraged by the commitment to equity and tried to help. "The old Shaker would move ahead anyway," she said in a February 2022 interview. "Now I see them saying, 'We're not getting diverse feedback.'"

School leaders looked back with some disdain on the 1987 school closures, when the district shuttered two of the district's three majority Black schools, Moreland and Ludlow. Glasner and members of the school board saw the process now underway as an opportunity to right a wrong.

In early 2022, Forward Together offered two concepts for the schools. The more controversial one featured a centralized elementary school to replace the five existing K–4 buildings. It was a radical idea for Shaker, where neighborhoods had been built around elementary schools since the very beginning. District leaders were officially neutral but made a vigorous case for this plan, partly because it would be more equitable. As it was, some families had schools in their neighborhoods and others did not. Black students were more likely to qualify for busing than white students, meaning they were most likely to live outside the immediate area around their school.

Resistance to a centralized elementary was strong and swift. Some worried young children would get lost in a huge school and argued that developing the same sense of community that small schools offer would be difficult. And people with neighborhood schools didn't want to lose them.

At a joint meeting of the City Council, school and library boards, City Councilman Tres Roeder made a lengthy speech in defense of neighborhood schools.

"We were founded on it. Many of you moved into your neighborhoods because of that neighborhood school," he said. Roeder, who is white and lived in the Malvern neighborhood, said he personally did not have a neighborhood school. "But I appreciate, as many of us do, that this is something that's very important to the fabric of Shaker Heights."

Glasner was somewhat unsympathetic to these arguments. He heard white people suggesting that those without neighborhood schools were welcome in their communities. "That is a very white privileged perspective. 'It's okay to have diversity, as long as it's the Black kids, as long as that responsibility falls on the shoulders of Black students,'" he said.

Glasner and the district also drew fire because the district appeared to favor replacing old buildings with new ones rather than renovating, a notion that offended a deep appreciation for the historic architecture that ran through the city.

Sensitive politics hung over the debate. Any plan would require a large tax increase to be approved at the ballot box, so the district would have to sell it to the community. Eliminating neighborhood schools would generate a lot of "no" votes, as would demolition. How do you get people to pay for something that they wouldn't want even if it were free?

Opposition ran deep among many of the most privileged people in town, though it was hard to separate anger around losing neighborhood schools from concerns about replacing historic buildings.

It was less clear what the more marginalized families wanted. In October, Kim Harris helped set up a Zoom meeting with members of SAMS and Forward Together officials. No one voiced support for a centralized school. To the contrary, they wanted more neighborhood schools in their own neighborhoods. They wanted a school in Moreland. For some in town—Black and white—that seemed more important than integration. But there was never serious consideration of creating a school in Moreland. For starters, a key goal of the planning was to reduce the number of buildings. More fundamentally, Glasner was convinced of the value of integration. Shaker had been focused on school integration since 1970 and all-in since 1987, and that was not about to change.

———

Kim Harris was born and raised in Warrensville Heights, the suburb immediately south of Shaker Heights. The street was almost entirely white when her parents bought their house in 1969, then rapidly flipped to virtually all-Black, as did the suburb. It was a counterexample of what could have happened in Shaker Heights.

In high school, Harris was in church when she met a cute boy from Shaker with huge, gorgeous eyes. They started dating, vowing to stay together as they each went off to historically Black universities—he to Florida A&M in Tallahassee, and she to Wilberforce in southern Ohio.

Soon Harris learned she was pregnant, and in 1991, at the tail end of her pregnancy, she moved to Florida, joining her boyfriend in a roach-infested apartment and giving birth to a boy, Jonathan. The relationship wasn't stable, and Harris had to scramble. For a time, the baby lived with her boyfriend's mother in Shaker Heights while Harris attended college in Savannah, Georgia. But being away from her son was too hard, and she joined him back home in Cleveland.

Harris floated the idea that she would move to Shaker, which her sister scoffed at. That motivated Harris to make it happen, and she moved into an apartment near Shaker Square. Jonathan had the bedroom, and Harris slept on a daybed in the back of the living room.

She worked all the time, sometimes as many as three jobs. She helped market a "horrible nursing home that was hard to market." She worked overnight, from 11 p.m. to 7 a.m., at a residential facility for youth with behavior problems. Often she didn't have money for food, so she would feed Jonathan and eat plain bread herself. She knew little about welfare or food stamps, and anyway was determined to make it without that sort of help.

She did get help from Jonathan's paternal grandmother, Lois Martin, a longtime Shaker resident, who would watch Jonathan when Harris was working. But Harris would only take so much assistance, fearful she might lose control. Martin wished she would have accepted more but was impressed by how Harris managed—catching the bus to work and taking Jonathan to the library for story time. "She did a great job," Martin said.

At one point, Harris was so tired from working nights that when she saw Jonathan put a chair on top of a box and climb up on it, she simply told him to get down. "I was so sleepy. I knew in my mind I had to get him off that box." Then, boom, he fell and cut his chin, requiring a trip to the emergency room and multiple stitches.

"I remember thinking, 'What am I doing?'" she said. "It was a quality of life check. Even when I'm awake I'm really not because I was so exhausted."

Years later, she would think back to that experience when she heard laments about how some parents never show up at PTO meetings or school events and how some parents don't understand how the schools work.

Harris knew nothing. She always made it to parent-teacher conferences but was selective about other school events. If Jonathan was performing, she'd try hard to be there. But a family fun night? Sorry but no.

"I was so out of the loop, I didn't even know I was out of the loop," she said.

Slowly, things got easier, as she found better jobs with better pay and started to figure out how to navigate motherhood and life. Once Jonathan was school-aged, she'd moved to a two-family house in Moreland. She was working just one job now. She was able to sleep at night.

When Jonathan was about ten, after an on-and-off relationship, she broke up for good with his dad. A few years later, she was working at

National City Bank when, during a training, she couldn't stop staring at the good-looking man running the session. She handed him a note. He called her.

A volatile relationship began, made difficult by his violent temper, she said. She saw the danger signs early, but then she discovered she was pregnant. She was determined not to be a single mom again, so she stuck with the relationship. They never married, but they lived together, eventually in a house in Lomond. They had one boy, then another. He made decent money, allowing Harris to stay home with their kids for five years.

It was not idyllic, but it was much more stable than her experience as a single mom when Jonathan was young. She started to understand how things worked in Shaker, and her eyes began to open in both good and troubling ways.

Jonathan, for instance, was now old enough for sports, and he played hockey, sometimes the only Black kid on the team.

"Hockey was so extremely expensive," she said. She could barely afford the equipment he needed. And yet she saw how the other families lived. "A lot of those hockey parents seemed to have everything. Fancy cars and houses." She was determined to keep him playing, but she felt a chill.

One of the coaches suggested she think hard before letting Jonathan play because "it is a commitment." Her interpretation of that was "where would I buy these expensive skates?" Not only were they expensive, Jonathan's feet were growing so fast that he kept needing bigger sizes. She bought him skates at a secondhand sports store. Where other players had expensive bags to carry their gear, Jonathan shoved his into a duffel bag she already owned.

"I remember being looked at, that side-eye look. A lot of the parents were not welcoming," she said. "I felt like they're waiting for me to fall off."

And yet, Jonathan said he felt none of that animosity. He loved the game and his teammates. He never felt singled out because of his race even though he was one of just two Black players. "We were wholeheartedly accepted," he said. "I grew up around white people all the time in Shaker. I didn't think, 'Oh, what do I do?' It barely crossed my mind."

He remembered a few run-ins with opposition players. "My team would stick up for me," he said. Once, in particular, a big kid was "all over me the whole game, he was trying to rough me up." The opponent rammed Jonathan into the boards and called him the n-word, he said, the first time that had ever happened. He never told his mom, knowing how upset it would make her. But his teammates backed him up. "A forward came back and was like, 'Yo, back off!' The team supported me."

He was aware that other players had a lot more money than his family did, but he thought they were the outliers. "I thought, 'Oh, they must be really rich.' I thought what we had was the norm. Everyone I knew rented. No one I knew owned a house," he said. He added: "I got everything I wanted for Christmas. I knew I wasn't poor." Looking back later, he realized that the only way his mom could afford Christmas presents was to, at times, hold down three jobs. "She had to work so hard for us to have normal."

Jonathan said he learned to navigate his different worlds he found in Shaker. When he was younger, he said, if he spoke standard English, his Black friends might make fun of him, accuse him of "speaking white." "If I said 'aren't' that would be noticeable for some people," he said. "So I would switch to 'ain't' really quickly."

That got better as he moved to high school in 2005.

"In middle school, I was trying to figure out the right way to be," he said. "In high school, I was pretty much myself." He had Black and white friends. In the cafeteria, he felt at home at tables of white and Black kids. "It was not until I got a little older that I realized that most people don't feel that way."

Academically, he did fine but not great. He was in regular classes and good with that. "It just wasn't on my map to ask for it," Jonathan said. "I didn't like homework." He recalled graduating with a grade point average of about 2.7—a B−.

———

The Moreland neighborhood seemed to be the perpetual stepchild of the Shaker school system, but the City of Shaker Heights had begun to think more creatively about how it could boost the area, which was hard hit by the 2008 recession and housing crisis, with rising poverty, a spike in absentee landlords, and some houses in terrible shape.

In response, the city began an aggressive demolition program of houses that had fallen into foreclosure and were uninhabitable. Between 2008 and 2022, 264 properties were demolished, mostly by the city, nearly half of them in south Moreland, on the border with Cleveland. Shaker then landscaped the lots and maintained them—replacing dilapidated properties with manicured patches of grass. They also made the lots available to neighbors or developers, and to the surprise of some, developers came calling.

As of August 2022, twenty-nine of the lots had been sold or were under contract with developers, including twenty-five in south Moreland. It was solid evidence that concentrated public policy can influence the trajectory of a neighborhood. Instead of homes falling down, owned by out-of-towners, rented for almost nothing to people who couldn't afford anything better, the neighborhood had new houses on the way to ownership by middle-class families.

On one road in Moreland, called Ludgate, three brand-new homes were built on those vacant lots, and each sold in the $300,000 range— more than triple the median sales price in the neighborhood. More houses went under construction, with asking prices pushing $400,000, a jaw-dropping figure for this neighborhood.

Not everyone appreciated this development, fearing negative impacts of gentrification. At a meet-and-greet with Shaker's mayor on a Saturday morning in August 2022, Sophronia Hairston, a thirty-four-year resident of Ludgate, complained that the new houses didn't match existing homes. "The houses are overpowering the rest of us," she said. And dotted through this part of Shaker were families living in poverty, fearful they would soon be priced out and forced to move.

Other economic indicators in Moreland were also heading upward as the economy recovered. Median income bounced back to its pre-recession level. The poverty rate fell to about 18 percent, less than half of its peak (though still higher than in 2000). The median sale price for single-family homes in south Moreland rose to $140,000 in 2022, up from $43,450 in 2015. And the number of residents using Section 8 vouchers fell from 348 to 175. In north Moreland, the next neighborhood over, the house next to Adriann Kennedy that had sold for $7,500 in 2007 sold for $121,000 in 2022.

Further, decades after Shaker concluded that white people simply would not move into Moreland, the portion of white residents had inched up. Black people still represented about 91 percent of the area in 2020, but ten years earlier it had been 96 percent. Anecdotally, residents said they noticed more white neighbors as well.

It wasn't only about economics. In 2015, the city launched an initiative called Moreland Rising, focused in part on developing a sense of community. Programs were created to celebrate the neighborhood's history. A play was staged. Neighbor nights gathered folks together. The city also offered help with tax preparation and other financial matters. "Anything we could think of to connect people with resources or solutions to immediate problems," said Kamla Lewis, who headed the effort for the city.

Now the city had its eye on another Moreland project: Lee Road, a major north-south thoroughfare that divided Moreland from Lomond. Decades earlier it had been home to car dealerships with their garish signage. The school bus depot sat on Lee Road, blocking views of a neighborhood park. It was in sore need of the kind of magic dust sprinkled on the Van Aken District.

"The city has not done as much as it could in that area," said councilman Sean Malone, who championed the project. In 2022, the city launched a full-scale visioning exercise and study of how the area might be transformed into a commercially vibrant and aesthetically attractive area. Ideas included an expanded public park, public art, new sidewalks and seating, better lighting. The hope was that if better conditions and infrastructure were created, businesses would follow. Perhaps, given the facilities conversation underway, the ugly bus depot could go somewhere else.

Donna Whyte, a longtime resident of Moreland, was excited about the possibilities. Maybe, she thought, they could get a decent restaurant in the area. "Anything that happens to Lee Road, anything, will be an improvement," she said. "There's really an opportunity to think about what could happen on this side of town."

———

Harris had moved from poverty into the middle class, and with her two younger sons, she was determined things would be different. She was a different kind of mom now. She knew where the loop was. She resolved not to allow herself to feel "less than."

"I started really fully living the experience of being a mom in Shaker," she said.

She found a job working for the school district, first as a substitute teacher's aide and eventually full-time as a library tech at Woodbury Elementary School.

In 2017, Harris bought a three-story, three-bedroom house in the Moreland neighborhood for about $70,000 on her own—not her dream house, but what she could afford. In 2018, the father of her younger children died, ending years of stress but also making her a single mom again.

She started noticing that the city was full of Kims—ones like the old Kim Harris—the ones who looked lost, the ones who could barely scrape by.

"That's a mom with her head down," she'd realize, "and she's just trying to eat."

In 2014, she had melded her new life with her old life and created SAMS. It began as a collection of moms gathering once a month to discuss various topics, with sessions often morphing into venting and advice swaps about life. Official topics would include how to navigate particular parts of the schools, such as special education support. Around 2017, near the end of Greg Hutchings's tenure, she said, the group membership peaked, with close to thirty women turning out for meetings.

But turnout dropped off, and Harris thought maybe there were too many meetings. So she began executing projects on her own with help from anyone who wanted to help. She collected gloves in the winter and dropped them off at schools. She scheduled SAMS "walk and talks," where moms could meet and walk together—to Horseshoe Lake, for instance, or once to the Van Aken District, where she persuaded a vendor to provide drinks for the group. "Black women were like, 'I'm not shopping there, it's too expensive,'" she said. "I asked them [the vendors], 'Is there a way to lure Black women to Van Aken and let them know it's okay?'"

During the pandemic, she took a hands-on approach to helping women who needed it. Through an appeal on social media, she raised $10,000 from others in Shaker. She met moms in parking lots or at their jobs, handing out emergency funds for child care, rent, and car payments—putting out life fires.

SAMS also sponsored an art installation for Black History Month at the Van Aken District and set up conversations between the Black community and the Shaker Heights police, including one on racial profiling and another on bias. An event where single moms put their experiences into spoken word and poetry, art, and photographs was staged in 2021 at the Shaker Historical Society. With time, Harris became one of the go-to people for official Shaker as certain leaders sought to reach out to a part of the community long ignored. She found herself asked to serve on all sorts of commissions and boards: the Shaker Arts Council, the city's public works committee, and the city's diversity, equity, and inclusion committee. She also was nominating chair for the high school PTO, responsible for recruiting other parents.

"Whatever I do, I touch it with the twenty-year-old Kim in mind," Harris said.

But eventually she grew concerned these events were taking her away from what she saw as her core mission: helping moms who needed it. She was stretched thin. Some moms, in fact, grew frustrated with her. They needed more help than she was providing.

"I expected [SAMS] to be advocates for the parents," said Melissa Breckenridge, a single Black mom who reached out to Harris in the spring of 2022 and hoped she would accompany her to a meeting with the principal of her daughter's school. Harris wound up inviting Breckenridge to some events but not providing the sort of support she wanted. "I think she had her hands in so many other different organizations and groups that she let SAMS fall to the wayside," Breckenridge said. "It wasn't consistent."

———

By 2021, the enrichment pullouts that teachers and others found so racially biased at Mercer Elementary School had ended. Instead, the district sent literacy specialists to work with children who needed extra help in the classroom, most of them kids who rode the bus from Moreland.

One afternoon that fall, students in fourth grade teacher Cathy Richards's classroom were conducting research and putting their findings on PowerPoint slides. In the back corner of the room, specialist Laurie Sullivan was huddled with a boy who was far behind on his earthquake project. He was still filling out his planning sheet while most others were completing their slides.

Sullivan showed him how to type "when was the first earthquake in the United States" into a search engine. Then she guided him through his writing. He began writing, "1964, March 28 . . ."

"How do we start a sentence? You know that," Sullivan said.

He added an "In" at the start of his sentence, which he now began, "In 1964, March 28, in alaska . . ." Sullivan asked him to tell her what he wanted to say next, and he finished the thought, ". . . was the biggest earthquake in the United States."

"That's a great first sentence!" she said.

From there, she guided him toward adding details, gathering more earthquake examples and moving the information from the internet to his brain to the page.

Soon it was three o'clock and class was over. The announcements began over the loudspeaker, calling kids to their buses.

At Mercer, many white children rode buses, but the Black students coming from Moreland were on the bus longer. Richards had noticed that kids with long rides often arrived at school already unsettled after fights or behavior flare-ups on the way. "There would be days as the kids were coming in, you could see immediately who has already gotten written up from behavior on the bus, or the bus driver yelled at them," she said. "Then we expect them to get it together and have a great, successful day at school."

Moreland resident Ronda Wright experienced other disadvantages after her twin boys started being bused to Mercer in second grade in 2019.

Wright was happy with the education but found herself removed from the life of the school. She didn't have a car, so attending PTO meetings and family events at school was hard. She took a bus to work, but trips to Mercer required an Uber or Lyft. Her kids would beg to go to an after-hours family movie night, for instance, but she said no. It was too expensive. She would go to the school only for the most important things, such as parent-teacher conferences. "My kids just felt like they were left out."

Beyond movie nights, what happens when a parent misses something more important, like back-to-school night or a teacher meeting? When parents simply cannot get themselves to the school, it's easy for teachers or other parents to conclude that these parents just don't care, creating and reinforcing stereotypes that might have more to do with whether a car is available than with the value placed on education.

———

The Shaker schools saw engaging families and aiding those on the economic edge as part of its mission, and they employed Keith Langford, a six-foot-two-inch Black man with a shaved head, bodybuilder biceps, and a bushy graying beard to execute it. His office was in the Shaker library, an effort to bring his services into the community. This was no small matter: the portion of Shaker families poor enough to qualify for free or reduced-price lunches in the schools had hovered around 30 percent for the last decade, and some were barely getting by. Among Langford's duties: keeping track of the dozens of Shaker school families without permanent housing and helping put out fires for those whose lives always seemed to be ablaze.

One afternoon during the summer of 2022, Langford was leaving the library when he ran into Tasha Hooker, a woman in her midforties whom, a couple years earlier, he had helped acquire furniture for her house, clothing for her kids, and other necessities. She greeted him with a big hug, and he soon learned that since they had last spoken, her family had found itself in flames again.

Hooker's journey to Shaker Heights had been long and painful and stood in sharp contrast to the many families here born in comfort and privilege. To understand how deep the economic divides in town were, and to understand the challenges the school system faced in educating children with such a wide range of preparation, it helps to hear her story—her sad, frustrating, infuriating story.

Her life was marked by trauma, abuse, and self-defeating choices. She was nearly drowned as a baby and was taken away from her mother. She dropped out of high school at age sixteen and spent the next thirty years trying to create a family of her own, entering relationships with unreliable, sometimes violent men, having children, finding new men—disappointing men, men who cheated on her, brought home STDs, refused to go to work, and left her feeling betrayed. Twice she married, and twice she divorced.

Over a fifteen-year span, she had eight children (one the product of rape) with four different men, only one of whom paid child support. With new relationships, she wanted more children. "I kept longing for a partner, a family," she said.

After bouncing among Wisconsin, Cleveland, and Miami, Hooker returned to Cleveland. Around 2018, she was living on the west side of the city when her children were caught stealing neighbors' packages and selling them. The family was kicked out, and that's when they landed in Shaker Heights.

She and five of her children (the other three were adults on their own by then) lived in the Moreland neighborhood, in a house that seemed to be collapsing in on itself. The front stoop was broken and shaky. Flies and other insects flew around inside. The kitchen ceiling fell through, feces and urine from the upstairs toilet landing near the stove. They stopped using that toilet, but it was hard for Hooker to complain. Her landlord—"some African guy"—lived out of town, and she was so far behind on the rent that she didn't think she could make any requests, much less demands. She would have been even deeper in arrears were it not for housing aid organizations that helped clear $15,000 of back rent payments.

The rent was $1,500 a month for the five-bedroom house (six if you counted the basement, where Hooker slept), and she didn't earn enough in her job making deliveries for a catering company to pay it. She had just qualified for a Section 8 housing voucher, but the program authorized only up to $1,100 in rent (of which she would have to pay $200). If she wanted to use her voucher, she would have to move. A bigger problem: She was $5,000 behind in rent and facing possible eviction. Hooker wanted to stay in the Shaker school district, and needed to find a house she could afford.

Hooker loved the Shaker schools, but at least three of her four school-aged children were struggling, their problems heightened by a pandemic that exacerbated educational inequities nationally and locally. Her youngest, age eleven, was constantly getting in trouble for speaking disrespectfully to students and teachers and for fighting. She was headed for fifth grade in the fall, and her mom's advice was to refrain from starting fights but to defend herself if need be. ("She shouldn't have to get pulverized because [her] parent said don't hit back.") Her second-youngest, a boy, seemed the happiest in the family. He had always done well in school, though his grades fell off during the pandemic, when classes were remote, and hadn't recovered. Now he was heading to middle school, and excited for it.

Her eighteen-year-old and the fifteen-year-old both attended a mostly online charter school in 2021–22, and heading into fall 2022, both wanted to drop out. Hooker was particularly worried about her fifteen-year-old daughter, who went by the nickname Butter. She was too young to leave school, her mom felt. In middle school, Butter was constantly skipping classes. Then came the pandemic. She hardly ever logged on to remote classes. Hooker said she left it to the kids to decide whether to participate, seeing her responsibility as keeping the internet service available, though looking back, she thought maybe she should have done more. She also hadn't attended any parent-teacher conferences since the pandemic, though she wasn't sure why, or seen report cards, because they were online and she could not find her log-in information.

Now Butter was determined to leave school and start work.

"I'm tired of school," she said. "I just want to do other stuff, have fun with my friends."

Her mom said Butter seemed to just feel out of place in school. "It kind of reminds me of myself. That's how I felt," she said.

It was about a week or so before classes were to begin that Keith Langford ran into Hooker at the library. Soon after that, he stopped by the house and greeted the kids with hugs. "I told your mom I'm back," he told them. "You're going to be seeing a lot more of me."

That evening, he dropped off fresh fruit, chicken wings, and pizza. And he asked Butter to consider enrolling in Shaker's Innovative Center for Personalized Learning, located close to their house, an alternative high school for students who didn't do well in traditional classes. He told her he would personally take her there to check it out, and he looked right at her: "I want you back in school."

Back in the summer of 2021, Kim Harris was getting ready for what she hoped would be a big event she was calling the Hildana Hug, a neighborhood party with music, snacks, and games that was to end with a big circle representing a hug. It was taking place at Hildana Park in the Moreland neighborhood, where SAMS had hosted a successful neighborhood event before the pandemic. Now people were starting to venture out and socialize again. Harris had invited school board members and city officials and high school sports teams and just about anyone else she could think of, hoping for a good turnout on this beautiful July day.

She began the morning distributing the new issue of the weekly Moreland newsletter, *Neighbor Notes*, to pickup spots across the neighborhood. During the pandemic, Harris had persuaded the city to produce the newsletter, which was filled with announcements and information about food distribution and other resources, but she had to bring copies to the pick-up spots herself each week. At one stop after the next, she slipped the new set of newsletters into weatherproof pouches hanging off the easels around the neighborhood, mostly in front of homes, and collected last week's extras. In most neighborhoods, this sort of communication was handled via email listservs and Facebook groups, but many here didn't have regular access to the internet, so Harris took it upon herself to get out the information old-school.

"It's our way to reach the so-called unreachable," she said.

As she circulated in the neighborhood, she spread word about the event. In truth, she was a little worried that no one would show up. While the event was officially sponsored by SAMS, other moms were unavailable and she was the only one from SAMS doing anything to make it happen. "I hope we have someone to hug with," she said.

She moved on to the next stop, at Chelton Park, a city-owned space with a playground and athletic fields and a bad reputation. As Harris replaced the previous week's newsletters, she explained that the park had attracted teens from Cleveland, which was just a couple of blocks south, and they did "teenage stuff"—fights broke out and police were called.

Harris complained that this trouble was all long ago and yet the city still ignored Chelton Park. Her son played soccer and the teams were often looking for fields, she said, but Chelton was "never in the mix."

"Now it's all overgrown, and it's just not used that way," she said.

It all felt ironic to her. The Shaker soccer association was working to recruit more Black players, starting with little kids, hoping that the high school team would eventually not be so overwhelmingly white. Yet they didn't use the fields right here in Moreland. She hoped Forward Together might address this matter.

Her next stop this Saturday morning was several blocks east, at a "little food pantry" behind Heights Christian Church, where Dr. King had once spoken from the steps. It was one of three in Shaker modeled on the little libraries where neighbors are invited to take or leave books, and it was filled with boxes of pasta, macaroni and cheese, and other nonperishable food items free for the taking. Harris stuffed some newsletters into the box, hoping to reach more disconnected residents. She often dropped off food, too, to the embarrassment of her sons, who feared someone might think she was taking, not giving.

From the pantry, Harris headed to the Van Aken District. It had taken maybe five minutes to drive from the place where pasta was free to hungry Shaker residents to the place where a gift shop sold a set of poodle-shaped salt and pepper shakers for $50.

Harris bought five gift cards from Mitchell's Ice Cream, prizes for the Hildana Hug raffle. After that she worked the crowd, moving from table to table, telling the dad in the polo shirt and the mom wrangling three preschoolers and anyone else she could find about the Hildana Hug later that day.

"Hi, everybody," she said, approaching a group eating ice cream outside Mitchell's. "I just want to interrupt you for a minute and let you know about an event that's going to be at a park nearby."

"We're going to do a big hug," she told the next group. "We're going to try and make a big circle, as big as we can."

The weather was perfect—sunny and in the midseventies—as the event began with a racially diverse turnout. Keith Langford was there, setting up a sound system, filling the park with music. A pair of sisters who had graduated from Shaker arrived to lead a field hockey demonstration, and a group of soccer players from the high school set up cones for kids to practice dribbling. A member of the school board running for reelection, Heather Weingart, was there, as was Lora Cover, who was running for school board as well. Carmella Williams, who served on City Council, arrived. A woman recently hired to be the city's new diversity director was mingling.

"I'm feeling good," Harris said.

Still, the event was underway and there were almost no regular people from the neighborhood there, much less from her rounds at the Van Aken District. Those gathered were having a nice time, enjoying the summer weather. But there still were only a handful of people there apart from those who had official roles.

About forty-five minutes in, it was time for short speeches, and then the drawing of tickets to see who won the Mitchell's gift cards. Harris asked the assembled to stand in a circle, representing a hug.

"We are really resilient, and we can do so much," she said. "This circle really represents that." On the count of three, she asked everyone to say, together, "Shaker family," and all together, everyone did.

———

Throughout the spring and summer of 2022, school district officials worked to develop their school facilities plan, hoping for a decision by September so they could put the question to voters in May 2023. For Superintendent Glasner, one of the chief questions was how to create a more equitable plan, particularly if his idea for one centralized elementary school died.

At a meeting with the high school PTO, Kim Harris asked David Glasner directly about reopening schools in Moreland or Ludlow. In the room that night, Glasner suggested that wasn't likely. But the conversation influenced his thinking. There was no obvious spot for a school in Moreland, but the district still owned the school building in Ludlow.

At a school board work session in the spring of 2022, Glasner put four options on the table. Three of the four maintained neighborhood schools, and all three reopened Ludlow.

Since 1987, Ludlow students had attended either Onaway or Boulevard elementary schools on the other side of Van Aken Boulevard. Under these new plans, Onaway and/or Boulevard would close, and the commute would reverse.

It had been thirty-five years since Carolyn Milter broke down crying in her car after voting to close her cherished Ludlow school, with virtually no discussion of reopening it since. Suddenly Ludlow was in the mix.

"I'm honestly shocked and excited that Ludlow school is being seriously considered in the new plan!" Ludlow resident Lyzz Lake wrote in an email to Glasner after that meeting. "I am cautiously optimistic that this project could actually benefit our community, something I was skeptical about before. Thank you for that!"

By June, the district had officially dropped the idea of a centralized elementary school and in July, Glasner told the school board that he wanted to pursue the version that reopened Ludlow but closed two other schools, with the aim of finalizing a plan by September.

Glasner liked his plan but he was also nervous. Members of the school board, who would have to vote for the plan, encouraged his work but never explicitly endorsed his vision. "Are we really moving forward?" Glasner wondered.

Meantime, there was virtually no broad-based outreach to the community or aggressive effort to sell what was sure to be a controversial plan. There were no open-to-all community meetings to discuss the process. The documents about the planning were buried on the district website. And unlike in previous generations, local media was now a shell of its former self, so there was almost no coverage of the debate. Unless someone had attended a school board meeting or one of the small living room sessions, they may not have known any details at all, even as the plan was barreling toward a school board vote.

And the district made its job more difficult by combining multiple controversial ideas into one package—the plan would demolish beloved buildings and close cherished elementary schools and raise taxes. This required an extraordinary communications plan that never seemed to materialize. It seemed that, as with detracking, the district failed to grasp that if they were going to attempt to advance controversial ideas, if they were going to ask people to give up something they had and liked, they had to make the case persuasively. Instead, they put the ideas out there, and soon opponents filled the void with reasons to say no.

Kim Harris had started out engaged in the facilities conversation but with time, she grew frustrated and decided she was no longer interested in helping the process along. She was unconvinced new buildings were the most important priority for Shaker and grew more concerned with academic achievement, particularly given regression following the period of pandemic-driven remote classes.

So Harris decided she would no longer help the district by gathering Black moms to give feedback on the facilities plan, and she canceled a scheduled SAMS meeting with Glasner. Instead, she worked to change the subject to something she found more urgent: promoting Black excellence, the promise Glasner had made in 2019. She successfully urged other moms to submit comments at school board meetings requesting a shift in emphasis. Soon, she made common cause with others who opposed the facilities plan for other reasons.

"Maybe I have trust issues with Shaker . . . and feel that my priorities as an African American mother are not being met," she vented in a post in a community Facebook group. "Maybe I am just frustrated that the African American community has not stepped into the conversation enough."

It felt useless, she wrote, to fight for Moreland and Ludlow to reopen. Even as the district announced that it might, in fact, reopen Ludlow, she was unwilling to engage.

Harris began cutting back on other volunteer work as well, resolving to leave positions on time-consuming organizations that were outside her core interests, such as the Shaker Arts Council and the public works board.

After five years in Moreland, she moved her family away. She wanted to get away from the constant fighting with her next-door neighbor. But she also struggled with the reality of a neighborhood set so close to the city of Cleveland, where she sometimes heard gunshots and blaring music.

"It's that feeling of a lesser quality of life," she said. When her sons rode bikes, Harris worried a right turn instead of a left could land them in a dangerous area. "For this single mother who has boys, living on this border may be risky," she said.

One of Shaker's big challenges, she added, was that upper-income Black families don't want to live around lower-income Black families. "There is a mindset within the Black community that we are in two categories, and the less successful group is the group that you should separate from," she said. "I am guilty of this myself." While she devoted her free time to helping those struggling the most, she admitted her eagerness to leave Moreland was an example of her own desire to distance herself.

After a few false starts, Harris bought a house just a few blocks from the shiny new Van Aken District. She was now living closer to the $50 salt shakers than the free food pantry at the church.

Lawrence Burnley, the district's chief diversity officer, had asked her to arrange a meeting with SAMS moms, but Harris wouldn't do it. She worried Burnley was simply a mouthpiece for the administration, and she didn't feel like exposing women she knew to what she assumed would be district talking points.

Not surprisingly, this irritated and confused Burnley, who was in fact a potential ally to Harris and her work, even if he did at times voice his boss's talking points.

"Kim is strange to me," he said. "I don't know what her agenda is." He started to question whether SAMS actually existed. "I have to believe people because I've never seen it."

It was all very frustrating to him. "This building," he said from a conference room in the administration headquarters, "it needs pressure from the outside. My work is helped by pressure."

Still, he had his own concerns about the district's facilities plan. He feared the district would wind up with "new buildings with the same systemic issues" and hoped there would be more focus on the "lived experience in these classrooms." Too often white people don't really understand the core issues confronting people of color, he said. "As a Black man, I know about your history and your story, but you know very little about mine. You are a required read. I'm an elective. Both stories need to have equal weight."

———

Emmitt Jolly, the biochemist at Case, was used to solving tricky problems, albeit ones that typically involved managing lab samples of tiny microbes that might someday lead to a cure for tropical diseases. By 2022, he was president of the school board, and he realized he might have a different kind of tricky problem in front of him.

He had wanted to give Glasner space to come up with a facilities plan, so was purposefully hands-off. He compared his approach to how he works with graduate students. "They need the freedom to explore and try things out," he said. "If you intervene too much, you get in the way."

But now opposition to Glasner's plan was gaining steam fast and from many directions all at once.

The Onaway parents didn't want to lose their neighborhood school. The preservationists didn't want to tear buildings down. Fiscal conservatives didn't want to pay more taxes. (Even with state subsidies, the plan was slated to cost more than $220 million.) A study circulated on Facebook showing that property values fell when neighborhood schools were closed. Opponents were lining up to speak at school board meetings.

Then, in July 2022, two days after the school board offered passive approval to Glasner's plan, a group of six or eight white parents met at the Van Aken District to talk about how they might stop what appeared to be a fast-moving train. Some of them had been talking with Kim Harris about the problems they saw in the district's priorities. Now this group was set to launch its own effort to push back.

One of the leaders was Amber Malek, a white mother of five who lived in Fernway, who thought the entire plan was ill-conceived and poorly timed. She volunteered to create a website and a Facebook group called Informed Shaker, and within weeks, the group had nearly nine hundred members. "We are collaborating to send a strong message to the Board of Education that it is time to stop the long-term facilities process," Malek wrote. Within days, she had fronted some $2,800 to buy red yard signs, and, across town, more than two hundred of them popped up on lawns with the word PAUSE in all caps, along with a plea to the school board to VOTE NO. The signs didn't explain what the issue even was, but by now, people knew.

In the meantime, no one spoke up much in favor of reopening Ludlow. "For the most part, it was crickets," Jolly said. It's not that people in the community opposed the idea. In the abstract, many liked it. It's that no strong champions for the plan emerged to pressure the district to keep it.

Jolly realized he could no longer sit back. He called the other four school board members to take their temperatures and concluded the plan on the table would not win unanimous support, which was the board's preferred way of operating. It might not even pass the board, much less a public vote, and defeat at either step would be devastating. That Saturday night, after an evening with out-of-town family at his home, Jolly sat down in his home office and started to study.

Using the work account he normally deployed to review research about microbes and obscure diseases, Jolly began reading academic literature. First he dug into studies about grade bands, and after a couple of hours he concluded that elementary school should go through fifth grade, not fourth, as was the case. That would mean the district needed five elementaries, not four. That meant Shaker could, theoretically, keep all five existing buildings open.

His next conclusion was less academic and more political. He decided the district could not close Onaway. First of all, it might lead to defeat at the ballot box. Even if it passed, he feared Onaway parents simply would not send their children to Ludlow. They might defect to private schools, or leave the city of Shaker Heights altogether. "It's a real fear. It's a real concern," he said. "I grew up in Alabama. I've seen a lot of things. White flight is a real thing." Keeping Onaway meant, among other things, that Ludlow would not reopen.

It was getting close to morning, but Jolly had one more subject to research. He began searching—first via Google and then in the academic literature—for what was the most transformative policy available to promote equity. One answer came through loudly: universal prekindergarten.

It was an idea long on Shaker's wish list, but it was expensive. Jolly concluded this was his answer: a big equity play, a popular program that would benefit all Shaker families, but particularly those who couldn't afford private preschool. It was a win-win, he thought, that people would get behind. It offered something and took away nothing, though with no state or federal funding available, it would be expensive.

The sun came up and Jolly began working the phones after his all-nighter. He checked in with other school board members, who he said all supported this new plan.

"The one piece I did get very excited about, and the entire board is excited about, is the idea of universal pre-K," said Lora Cover, a white school board member. She wasn't enthused about reopening Ludlow in the first place—her first choice was the single elementary school—because she didn't think it would make a huge impact.

She was upset, though, that a group of white parents had managed to get their way and slow the project down by flexing privileged muscles. There was no way that the district could finalize this plan in time to get approval from the state (which was needed to access state dollars) and put it on the ballot in May 2023, as had been the goal. "We are saying we are going to listen to a small, vocal, fairly white, fairly entitled group of people over others," she said. "I am extremely angry at how my neighbors are behaving."

That Monday morning, Jolly went to see Glasner, and together, they worked out a new roadmap. On July 22, not long after the red yard signs opposing Glasner's plan began appearing on Shaker lawns, the district sent an email from Jolly to every parent. It outlined his new approach: All five existing elementary schools, with grades K–5, would remain, and they would likely be renovated, not rebuilt. The iconic Woodbury building would be renovated. And a new pre-K plan would serve all four-year-olds. The families with the loudest voices, the ones who liked the neighborhood school configuration just as it was, had won.

The reaction on the Informed Shaker Facebook group was immediate and giddy. "Everyone should check their email for an email from Dr. Jolly!" one person wrote. Another posted, "Thank you, Dr. Jolly! Today is a good day. Congrats to all on getting our collective voices heard."

But others were deflated. With this new promise to maintain all existing elementary schools, Ludlow's revival appeared to be off the table. A few voices in the Facebook group raised the question: What about Ludlow? "I do hope equity is addressed explicitly at some point," one person wrote. Another posted, "We need to consider which groups are getting what they want." Burnley, the diversity officer, described the development this way: "The most influential voices, the loudest voices, the most privileged voices—that plan responds to that reality." Ludlow, he said, was invisible again. "This decision takes us backwards."

In his short tenure, Glasner had now advanced two controversial initiatives that challenged the privileges certain people in Shaker enjoyed—first detracking and now the facilities plan. Given the circumstances, he said he had no regrets about how he had approached either matter. Asked what he had learned, he gave two answers that he acknowledged were contradictory. He said he needed to develop stronger relationships in the community so people understand what he is trying to do. But he also said he learned not to succumb to "equity detours" that seek to delay the disruption of "historical patterns around privilege and oppression and discrimination."

"If we wait 'til everybody's ready, we'll never be ready," he said.

His approach might have been more successful if it were tempered with a deeper appreciation for the real-world obstacles—beyond opportunity hoarding and white privilege—that important initiatives face. A community must be brought along with big changes through leadership and top-notch communications. Past integration plans had featured big, ugly meetings where people got to ask questions in public, and officials were forced to offer answers. Those sessions are difficult, but if your plan can't survive a public airing, it probably can't survive.

═══════════

After a tense debate, the district now had a plan officials thought the public would support. It would preserve and renovate neighborhood schools to serve children through fifth grade. Woodbury would be renovated and cover grades six through eight. And the middle school, a 1957 building that was beset with maintenance issues, would be demolished. Officials decided to put off a decision on the high school.

Closing any existing elementaries had proven politically untenable. Still, leaving Ludlow out of the plan nagged at Glasner. So when he heard that a private program renting space there would be leaving, it felt like a fresh opportunity. Glasner suggested the district expand its new pre-K program into Ludlow. This idea gained fast traction and was added to the facilities plan that would go before voters in November 2023.

The total cost would be $187 million, with 37 percent of eligible expenses paid by the state of Ohio. It would amount to an annual tax increase of $296 for every $100,000 of property value assessment. That would cover building renovations and also an expansion of the pre-K program, which would grow larger though stop short of serving all four-year-olds.

Supporters formed a citizens group to campaign for the proposal and provided a wealth of information about the plan. Opponents organized, too, with many complaining about the process and some suggesting a "no" vote as a way to express unhappiness with Glasner and the district leadership.

Among the opponents was Kim Harris. Her chief complaint was that the district was set to spend millions of dollars and yet the plan did nothing to alleviate the long commute faced by students in the Moreland neighborhood. Some district officials had said they would consider redrawing boundary lines to address this concern, but that would be a complicated and politically fraught process that might never happen. Harris made her case on a community Facebook group. "Vote NO and don't turn your back on Moreland," she wrote.

Many expected a close result, but the proposal passed with 59 percent of the vote. This was only a little lower than the 63 percent average passage rate of eight other tax proposals that had been approved since 1995.

The plan left some major questions unaddressed, including the boundary lines, future plans for the high school, and full scope of the pre-K expansion. But the pre-K program would expand. And more than thirty-five years after Ludlow Elementary School had been closed, the brick building at the center of the neighborhood that set Shaker Heights on the road to integration was set to serve Shaker children yet again.

We are responsible for our own ignorance or, with time and
openhearted enlightenment, our own wisdom.

—Isabel Wilkerson

18

DREAM TOWN REVISITED

The woman was angry, furious really, at the newly instituted busing
plan for the Shaker schools. She picked up a pen and in a loopy
script, wrote a card to the school board. "I know the enclosed will be
destroyed," she began. "At least I expressed my thoughts."

She wrote those words fifty years before I am writing these words, and
no, her card was not destroyed. It was preserved in the Shaker Heights
Public Library with so much else of this community's rich story.

Shaker Heights is a community that has long been aware of its own
place in history. National media coverage beginning in the 1960s told
people living in Shaker that they were special, that their approach to
race and integration was innovative, progressive, newsworthy. In the
beginning, integration was a day-to-day reality for some and, for many
others, more of a cocktail party conversation, as one writer put it. Slowly
that changed. The city realized it could fight a losing battle to resist integration, or it could remake its own image—to itself and to the world—as
an integration pioneer. It chose the latter.

Academic researchers followed the journalists. Dissertations and
scholarly articles broke new ground and offered new analysis of old
ground. And now here I am, with my take on the Shaker story.

It is, in fact, just that—my take. I'm a white, Jewish, Gen-X woman
who grew up in a family with professional parents with comfortable but
modest incomes. My perspective is shaped by those facts, and by my life

experience ever since—as a journalist, as a parent, as a member of my own community in Washington, D.C. I have tried to be as comprehensive in this telling as I could, to include as many perspectives as possible, to pick this place up and examine it from the back and around the side. I have interviewed more than 250 people—school board members, administrators, parents, experts, teachers, children, and teenagers. I've sat at countless tables alongside students eating lunch in the cafeteria, watched a high school principal juggle a dozen balls at once, and observed expert teachers plying their craft. I have reviewed well over a thousand documents, news clippings, videos, memoirs, memos, and letters, plus a handful of angry postcards. But, of course, this is not the definitive take. No take can be. In particular, a Black author looking at these same events likely would have her own interpretation of what unfolded and what is still unfolding. Shaker Heights offers a fascinating story that many have told, that many will continue to tell, each of us from our own perch, as it should be.

Shaker Heights is far from perfect, as these pages have made plain. But it's also far ahead of most of the country and offers lessons for places and people who want to try to do better. Most neighborhoods and school districts in America are racially and economically homogeneous, and because schools heavily rely on local taxes, the rich benefit from this system every day. Nationally, groups such as EdBuild have highlighted vast funding disparities between predominantly white school districts and districts that mostly educate students of color. The UCLA Civil Rights Project has spent decades arguing that students of color benefit when they attend school with white students and documenting how Black students in particular have become more likely to attend hypersegregated schools. In Shaker, Black and white students occupy the same buildings starting in kindergarten, sharing space in a well-funded system. The Century Foundation, a think tank in Washington, runs a project urging school districts to employ strategies such as redrawing boundary lines to reduce segregation. Shaker did that thirty-five years ago and hasn't backtracked.

That said, the challenges facing Shaker Heights today are enormous, and they are driven by economics as much as by race as well as by the complex intersection of the two. Shaker once was one of the only suburbs available to Black families, and it drew the most educated among them.

The pioneers, people like the Harvard-educated physician Drue King Jr., made middle-class white people like Emilie Barnett feel, as she said, like she was moving up in the world. Today, Shaker faces stiff competition among the suburbs of Cleveland, and many wealthy Black families are choosing to move elsewhere. The racial balance in the community has remained, in part because as upper-income Black residents have left, lower-income Black residents have arrived.

I think some of this comes back to a feeling of belonging, as Hubert McIntyre explained so clearly that summer day in the near-empty high school. I was reminded of his words one afternoon as I watched my older son play Little League baseball, where the lineup of parental cheerleaders included a Black couple who had recently moved back to D.C. from Shaker Heights.

They had lived on one of the loveliest streets in Shaker, in the Malvern neighborhood, a stone's throw from the ultratony Shaker Heights Country Club. The dad, Carlos Jackson, had grown up in the suburb next door, and the family moved back to the area so he could take a job as a top lobbyist for the Cleveland Clinic. But they were disappointed to learn that their neighborhood included few people of color, and when they thought about their young son and daughter growing up, they worried there was almost no one nearby who looked like them. As their kids moved into advanced classes, maybe there would be no one there who looked like them either.

"There weren't very many Black families around us in Shaker," Jackson said. He said his kids "were on that pathway to be that only one." He knew how hard it could be to be the only one—"how lonely it is." And he didn't want that for his kids.

The couple had lived in D.C. before moving to Shaker Heights, and for a range of reasons, they returned. But even though they made wonderful friends, they left Shaker with mixed emotions.

Questions going forward include how Shaker can make itself an attractive place for all kinds of families into the future, and how it can be a place today where families of all races and incomes feel like they belong.

This is not and will not be easy. So far, though, Shaker has shown it can do what seems impossible in so much of America: create and maintain a diverse, shared community.

It can be done—but not without trade-offs, compromises, and commitment, and it's important to understand how it happened.

The work here began with the commitment of a handful of people in Ludlow—Black and white—who saw how race was tearing America apart and wanted something different. Their success encouraged others in Shaker to adopt their attitudes and their techniques. Some were driven by idealism, some by realism, but together they charted a different path, one neighborhood at a time. Ultimately, the people living here created and then embraced an identity that celebrated diversity and integration.

People living in Shaker who didn't care for this tended to move away, while others arrived, precisely because these ideas aligned with their values. So many people in Shaker Heights today will tell you that they chose the community because they value diversity. And these trends have combined to reinforce the community's commitment, to keep it going, one decade after the next.

In trying to understand why Shaker turned out this way when so many other places did not, the stories I found most compelling were of everyday extraordinary people who showed a commitment to their values with their actions. That meant Beverly Mason telling other Black people not to move to Ludlow because it would undermine their integration goals. It meant Emilie Barnett, who had never spoken to a Black man before, crossing the street to say hello to Mr. Price, who was out mowing his lawn. It was white and Black parents who volunteered to bus their children to and from Moreland School because they believed deeply in the promise of integration. It was a school board that redrew boundaries to make every elementary school racially balanced, and Carolyn Milter, who voted to close her beloved Ludlow because that's what was needed to make a larger plan work. It was Reuben Harris Jr. showing up in his daughter's classroom so he could help her succeed in science. It was parents of high- and low-achieving students alike giving Shaker time to try to make an ambitious, albeit poorly implemented, detracking plan work. And that commitment was affirmed every time Shaker voters agreed to pay more taxes for the schools, with some of the richest people in the Cleveland area helping to fund an education for some of the poorest.

At every critical moment there has been resistance, chiefly from privileged white people seeking to protect their privileges. There's an ethos in America that argues parents can justify almost any decision if it is in the best interest of their own children, because who wouldn't want what's best for their kid? I certainly want what's best for my two kids. We all do.

But to create a community where we all belong, we need to also consider the needs and wants of all children. It's a big ask. It's not easy to, say, give up a neighborhood school. This doesn't mean parents should send their kids into any school and simply hope for the best. It does mean these decisions need to be made mindfully.

I think back to a woman from San Francisco I interviewed in 2021. She and her husband went into debt to put their children into private elementary and middle schools because they did not like the public schools where their children were placed under the city's lottery system. The mom described herself as politically center-left, said her dad was a civil rights activist, and volunteered that she had gone to a Black Lives Matter march. But she did not even visit most of the public schools her children were offered, deciding that they were unacceptable based chiefly on test scores, which are heavily correlated with poverty. Her children asked why they couldn't go to a school right in their neighborhood; she had rejected it based on test scores without ever setting foot in the building. She said no to another school because, in addition to low test scores, she "didn't know anyone there, didn't know much about it, not a great neighborhood. None of my friends' kids went there."

"I just felt like I'm not going to experiment on my kid," she said. "When we chose to do independent [school], nearly all my friends were like, 'This school system needs families like you' and 'Your kids will be fine,' but I'm just not sure fine is good enough."

I didn't have much knowledge about the specific schools she mentioned, but I did know a lot about Burton High School, set in a high-poverty part of San Francisco. I had written two long stories about Burton students navigating through the pandemic and had seen some truly excellent teaching and learning. This mom declared, straight up, that her kids "would never go to Burton" and then decried "the whole mess of our system."

She asked me, "Do I sound racist?"

Nobody wants to "experiment" on their kids, but so many of us rely on superficial assessments of educational options without thinking more deeply about our own place in the larger "mess of our system."

When I was back in Shaker during the summer of 2022, I had a long conversation with a white friend who had two children in the Shaker schools. She wanted them there but was anxious. What if her daughter wasn't challenged? In sixth grade, amid the pandemic and the develeling, she had aced every assignment, and my friend worried she might not be getting the academic rigor she needed. Like the mom in San Francisco, she wanted more than "fine." I was confident her daughter will be more than fine because she is a great kid with smart parents who would make sure she gets what she needs. Still, she and her husband had started to talk about something they never had considered before: private school.

Nine months later, I checked in with my friend. The situation at her daughter's school had improved, and her concerns from the prior year had melted away. Her daughter was still in the Shaker schools, and thriving.

Success in places like Shaker Heights depends on families like this one remaining committed to the system and its goals. At the same time, school leaders must understand that parents have high expectations—rightfully so—and that not every complaint is someone seeking to erect an "equity detour." Changes can be made, even changes that challenge the desires of the privileged, but they must be made carefully and thoughtfully.

———

Growing up in a racially integrated community laid the foundation for who I am. I was raised not just with words about racial equality but with actions. There was nothing unusual about being friends, neighbors, classmates with Black people. Being part of a community that was intentionally working toward racial justice helped me develop an innate spark of optimism that this country can rise above its past. In this divided nation, that's saying something.

And yet I realized in the years since then how much I didn't understand as a kid, including the pressures and prejudices that many Black students faced. Of course, I saw that advanced classes were disproportionately white, and I talked about it at the time. What I didn't realize was just how hard it was for Black students trying to navigate the system. The story Ayesha Bell Hardaway told about her English teacher was a case in point. Hardaway recalled her teacher discouraging her from taking advanced courses, saying, "African American students don't do well in honors and AP." As it happens, I had the same teacher for AP English when I was a student, and I loved her class. Hardaway's experience was a sharp reminder of my own privilege. Nobody discouraged me from higher-level classes, even in areas such as math that didn't come naturally to me.

Working on this book, I sometimes vacillated about what my ultimate conclusion would be. Was this a story of the power of white privilege and systemic racism always finding a way to come out on top? Was it a story of economic realities overwhelming good intentions? Or was it something more hopeful, about a community that is still at it, still trying?

Over the course of five years of reporting on Shaker Heights, I saw a lot for the community to be proud of. I sat in on a SGORR visit, where high school students talked to sixth graders about what it means to be a bystander versus an upstander, and had students toss a ball of yarn around a circle, each child offering a compliment to the next in a "validation web." I watched as Black fifth and sixth grade boys were celebrated and prodded to live up to their academic potential. They were young MAC Scholars, the expansion of a program begun back in 1990. "*Who are you going to be?*" the leader asked, and the answer came back, "Men!" "*And what kind of men are you planning on being?*" "Leaders!"

At a PTO meeting at Fernway Elementary School, I watched the group consider a suggestion that students bring flowers to their teachers for teacher appreciation week. The principal immediately noted that communication with Black families at the school, most of whom were bused from a nearby area, was not great. Would they all get the message? "What I don't want," he said, "is all the white kids show up with flowers"—while the Black kids don't. A mom suggested that instead, PTO moms stand outside the school with buckets of flowers, with each kid taking one to bring to the teacher.

And over the last two summers, as my own family lived in the community while I worked on this book, I saw my two children get a dose of that Shaker magic. Every day they played with a racially diverse group of kids on the street where my dad and stepmom live, one backyard connected to the next as they threw baseballs and played hide-and-seek and tried to trap an elusive groundhog that was eating up the gardens.

These are all small moments, and important ones.

———

There were other lessons, too. Communication is essential in doing hard work like this, and that doesn't mean posting a video explaining your point of view, as the district did when it rolled out its detracking plan. It means talking *and* listening. And that goes for everyone—teachers, students, parents, administrators. It's easy for school or city insiders to think that they've had a public conversation because an issue was discussed at a public meeting attended by a handful of people. It takes a lot more than that. And doing hard things, especially tackling sensitive issues around race, requires trust and relationships, which are not created on the fly. I tell young journalists that a breaking news story is not the time to develop sources. It's the same for school leaders. A crisis is not the time to develop relationships. It takes day-in, day-out effort.

For instance, in my interviews with Black parents, I found a lot of concern about making sure teachers were fair to their kids, that they were being given equal opportunities with high expectations. I found very few who wanted mixed-ability classes, and some who opposed the idea altogether. But I heard much more enthusiasm from the district about detracking than about finding ways to address bias. More dramatically, in 1970, Superintendent Jack Lawson—who was by many accounts an inspired leader—was prepared to roll right over the Black community in Moreland and institute a one-way busing plan. He was forced by white people in the community to change course. He wasn't really listening.

On the other hand, the Black community has to do more talking. The district says, time and again, that marginalized communities are hard to reach. Officials need to try harder, but all parents should help them. The barriers are real and often profound. Still, they should show up, as much as possible, to parent-teacher conferences, to back-to-school night, to community meetings.

Support for families to allow that kind of engagement may be as important as support for tutoring or academics. It is undeniably harder for parents who are worried about paying the rent, who are working long hours, who might not have done well in school themselves taking the time needed to patiently sit down and help a confused or upset or resistant child do his homework. Watching Keith Langford jet around town from one distressed family to the next, knowing he sometimes shows up with pizza and sometimes looks a kid in the eye and tells her he expects more was a sight to behold. These are important things. Often they are seen as extras. They are, in fact, essential.

At the same time, Shaker and communities like it cannot write off the privileged families, either. Some of them are self-righteous and demanding. Some are textbook examples of white privilege in action. But school districts like Shaker Heights have to serve them, too. They shouldn't get more than anyone else, even if they think they should. But it's not enough, either, to tell them that their kids will be fine and stop whining. They have expectations—many of them reasonable. They want teachers who are able to properly teach advanced students—whether in a mixed-ability or an AP course.

Doing hard things requires planning, communication, preparation, and savvy. Having lived in Washington for a long time, I'm used to people thinking through political obstacles and how to navigate them. I've also seen people of good will develop true consensus. Both skills are needed for any school district trying to do hard things.

<hr>

And still, this remains a special place. Few communities have tried as hard and as long as Shaker Heights to bring Black and white together into a shared community—a place where people share the same grocery store, the same ice cream shop, the same swimming pool and basketball courts, the same mayor, and the same schools. Even, thanks to the detracking initiative, the same classrooms.

Seven decades of experience show us that creating shared community is hard and takes constant commitment, constant work. The forces of systemic racism and white privilege, the tendency of some in the Black community to disengage, mistakes made by flawed human beings—they are all real. They are forces that have to be fought back against, not just once or twice or for a year or a decade, but over and over and over again. In Shaker, this work has passed like a baton—from the Masons and the Barnetts to Jack Lawson to Carolyn Milter and on to Kim Harris and David Glasner. It has faced ugly moments, and the economic trends have made the work harder. And yet Shaker has achieved what few other places have. The community is still integrated. The schools are still racially balanced. A new plan on the horizon promises to improve on it further, with equity at the forefront.

They are still doing this work, still making progress. But it's an ever-present challenge to the people in the community: *Do you value this enough to . . .*

Do you value this enough to let lower-achieving kids into your honors class? Do you value this enough to show up at a meeting, or a parent-teacher conference? Do you value this enough to give up a neighborhood school? Do you value this enough to pay more taxes to fund pre-K for all?

And so far, the answer has been, more or less, yes. Enough yes. Enough yes to drown out the no.

Shaker isn't making water run uphill, as the sociologist told the Ludlow pioneers. But it is building a sandcastle by the side of the ocean, as Ron Ferguson, the Harvard professor, said. And the waves are lapping it—not just day in and day out, but moment in and moment out. But, as Ferguson says, as long as you have people working to build, sustain, and protect that sandcastle, you are going to have something that looks, more or less, like a sandcastle.

The Shaker sandcastle is not the fairy tale castle I wished it to be, that I wish it to be. Shaker Heights has not made all its dreams come true. I wish that all teachers and counselors had been as encouraging to Black students as they were to me. I wish that Greg Hutchings Jr. had been able to mix his passion for his work with more humility and respect for those who didn't see things his way. I wish that when Herlinda Bradley complained about how Jody Podl had treated her daughter, someone had brought these three women together and talked it out, found a solution.

The sandcastle is missing a turret or two and the water keeps overwhelming the base. But it's still standing. Seventy years after the first Black families moved into Shaker Heights, it's still standing.

A NOTE ON SOURCES

The vast majority of interviews for this book were conducted on the record; in select cases, sources were granted anonymity to speak candidly about sensitive or private matters. I conducted multiple on-the-record conversations with each of the people whose stories anchor each chapter, or, if they were no longer living during my reporting, their children, friends, and associates. The only exception is the Van Sweringen chapter, for which I relied on documents, newspaper and magazine articles, and books. I witnessed many of the scenes in the final chapters of the book. Earlier scenes were reconstructed through use of interviews, documents, and videos. In some cases, for the sake of clarity, I have included notes that mention interviews that I conducted. Much of the rest of the book is also based on interviews I conducted between 2017 and 2022, even though not all the interviews are cited in the notes.

I also relied on interviews conducted by Maurice Klain, a political scientist at what was then called Western Reserve University, and his associates. The Cleveland Area Leadership Studies was a project to identify, describe, and analyze leadership, decision-making, influence, and power in Greater Cleveland, Ohio, during the 1950s and 1960s, and more than seven hundred interviews were conducted of a wide range of community leaders. Under the terms governing the collection, interviewees may be identified only with permission from the person or his or her heirs. In my notes, I have identified people in cases where I obtained permission.

NOTES

Chapter 1: Dream Town

3   **"I had a locker?":** Quote relayed to author by Paul Mason, who met Newman at an event in New York City circa 2005.

7   **a significant study:** Frances Reissman Cousens, *Public Civil Rights Agencies and Full Employment: Promise vs. Performance* (Westport, CT: Praeger, 1969), https://www.google.com/books/edition/Public_Civil_Rights_Agencies_and_Fair_Em/9yc9AAAAIAAJ?hl=en.

8   **the economic divides in Shaker:** Census data from the decennial censuses of 1990 and 2020. Data for 1989 from "1990 Census of Population: Social and Economic Characteristics: Ohio," 1990 CP-2–37. Data on median income: table 186, p. 895; data on poverty: table 187, p. 913. Data for 2020 from online search tool.

9   **Separately, a 2004 study:** Jonathan Guryan, "Desegregation and Black Dropout Rates," *American Economic Review* 94, no. 4 (September 2004), https://www.aeaweb.org/articles?id=10.1257/0002828042002679.

9   **And a 2022 paper:** Garrett Anstreicher, Jason Fletcher, and Owen Thompson, "The Long Run Impacts of Court-Ordered Desegregation" (working paper, NBER Working Papers Series, National Bureau of Economic Research, April 2022), https://www.nber.org/system/files/working_papers/w29926/w29926.pdf.

10   **A 2022 study by Harvard University's Raj Chetty:** Raj Chetty, Matthew O. Jackson, Theresa Kuchler, Johannes Stroebel, et al., "Social Capital I: Measurement and Associations with Economic Mobility," *Nature* 608 (2022): 108–21, https://doi.org/10.1038/s41586-022-04996-4.

10   **And in a study in Montgomery County:** Heather L. Schwartz, "Narrowing the Economic Achievement Gap: The Role of Housing," *The RAND Blog*, January 11, 2012, https://www.rand.org/blog/2012/01/narrowing-the-economic-achievement-gap-the-role-of.html.

11   **at least eighteen laws were enacted:** Hannah Natanson, Clara Ence Morse, Anu Narayanswamy, and Christina Brause, "An Explosion of Culture War Laws Is Changing Schools. Here's How," *Washington Post*, October 18, 2022, https://www.washingtonpost.com/education/2022/10/18/education-laws-culture-war/.

11   **The new laws and heightened scrutiny:** Laura Meckler and Hannah Natanson, "New Critical Race Theory Laws Have Teachers Scared, Confused and Self-Censoring," *Washington*

Post, February 14, 2022, https://www.washingtonpost.com/education/2022/02/14/critical-race-theory-teachers-fear-laws/.

12 **"If you are told in sixth grade":** Laura Meckler, "Can Honors and Regular Students Learn Math Together? A New Approach Argues Yes," *Washington Post*, June 4, 2021, https://www.washingtonpost.com/education/2021/06/04/california-math-class-detrack-race-equity/.

12 **My story about Shaker Heights:** Laura Meckler, "This Trail-Blazing Suburb Has Tried for 60 Years to Tackle Race. What If Trying Isn't Enough?" *Washington Post*, October 11, 2019, https://www.washingtonpost.com/education/2019/10/11/this-trail-blazing-suburb-has-tried-years-tackle-race-what-if-trying-isnt-enough/.

Chapter 2: The Van Sweringen Brothers

15 **"twins by choice":** Joseph G. Blake, "The Van Sweringen Developments in Cleveland: A Senior Thesis on the Van Sweringens" (submitted to the History Department of the University of Notre Dame [Indiana] in partial fulfillment for a Bachelor of Arts degree, 1968), published by *Cleveland Memory* in 2015, https://engagedscholarship.csuohio.edu/clevmembks/29.

15 **Their ancestors:** Ian S. Haberman, *The Van Sweringens of Cleveland: The Biography of an Empire* (Cleveland: Western Reserve Historical Society, 1979), 3–5.

15 **As kids growing up:** Taylor Hampton, "Fabulous Vans: Boyhood of Two Shy Brothers," *Cleveland News*, August 2, 1955, Shaker Historical Society, Shaker Heights, OH.

16 **"We used to sit up":** Louis B. Seltzer, "Van Sweringen Wanted to Run Horse Car but He Couldn't Grow Walrus Mustachios," *Cleveland Press*, May 6, 1925.

16 **In April 1897:** "Letters Written to James Towar Sweringen, Spring and Summer, 1897," Shaker Historical Society, Shaker Heights, OH.

16 **O.P. had determined:** Taylor Hampton, "Cleveland's Fabulous Vans: Lured by Shaker's Farms," *Cleveland News*, August 3, 1955, Shaker Historical Society, Shaker Heights, OH.

17 **They envisioned a world of peace:** Shaker Heights Board of Education, *Shaker Heights: Then and Now* (1938), 3, Local History Collection, Shaker Heights Public Library; David G. Molyneaux and Sue Sackman, eds., *75 Years: An Informal History of Shaker Heights* (Shaker Heights, OH: Shaker Heights Public Library, 1987), 14, https://shakerlibrary.org/wp-content/uploads/75years-cover.pdf.

17 **The group was founded by Ann Lee:** "Lee, Ann (1736–1784)," Shaker Museum (website), https://www.shakermuseum.us/people/?id=392#:~:.

17 **One future site sat in northeast Ohio:** "Native Americans and Early Statehood," Black, White & Beyond: An Interactive History (website), University of Akron, https://learn.uakron.edu/beyond/nativeam_earlystate.htm.

17 **Early settlers here included Jacob Russell:** Description of Jacob and Ralph Russell's roles from "Russell, Ralph," *Encyclopedia of Cleveland History*, Case Western Reserve University, https://case.edu/ech/articles/r/russell-ralph.

17 **"the Valley of God's Pleasure":** When it came time to sign the final covenant committing themselves to Shaker beliefs, Ralph and his family walked away. It's not clear why. Theories include that he was unhappy with Union Village ministry's sending an elder to replace him, and that he did not want to live a celibate life separate from his wife. Email from Brianna Treleven, executive director, Shaker Historical Society, June 15, 2022.

17 **Shakers advocated for the abolition of slavery:** "Black Shakers at North Union, Ohio," *Journal*, Shaker Historical Society, Shaker Heights, OH, Spring 2009.

18 **"Sex," she said:** Molyneaux and Sackman, *75 Years*, 14.

18 **Even their graveyards:** *Shaker Heights: Then and Now*, 7.

18 **"Youth shall ever":** Haberman, *The Van Sweringens of Cleveland*, 8.

18 **The North Union colony disbanded:** Haberman, *The Van Sweringens of Cleveland*, 8–9.

19 **In late 1905:** Haberman, *The Van Sweringens of Cleveland*, 9–10.

19 **"It was a rugged job":** Molyneaux and Sackman, *75 Years*, 37.

19 **"people of the right sort":** Fred C. Kelly, "Two Young Men Who Are Real Estate Marvels," *American Magazine*, January–June 1917, 50.

19   **Their work began during a heady time:** David C. Hammack, "Economy," *Encyclopedia of Cleveland History*, Case Western Reserve University, https://case.edu/ech/articles/e /economy.

20   **One 1923 issue:** "Society," *Cleveland Topics*, June 23, 1923, 19.

21   **As early as 1905, the Shaker Heights Improvement Company:** Cynthia Mills Richter, "Integrating the Suburban Dream: Shaker Heights, Ohio" (dissertation submitted to the University of Minnesota, December 1999), 12.

21   **An ad in April 1923:** Advertisement, *Cleveland Topics*, April 21, 1923, 5, Western Reserve Historical Society, Cleveland, OH.

21   **Shaker promised to protect:** "The Van Sweringen Company: Information for Lot Owners in Shaker Heights in Reference to House Design and Construction," Cleveland Memory Project, https://clevelandmemory.contentdm.oclc.org/digital/collection/shaker/id/819/rec/4.

21   **Written permission was needed:** "Official Price Lists of the Van Sweringen Co.: Shaker Village and Shaker Country Estates Properties," July 1, 1932, Shaker Historical Society, Shaker Heights, OH.

21   **"Shaker Village Standards":** "Shaker Village Standards 1928," Van Sweringen Company, April 1, 1928, Local History Collection, Shaker Heights Public Library, Cleveland Memory Project, https://clevelandmemory.contentdm.oclc.org/digital/collection/shaker/id /821/rec/2.

22   **The rigid planning drew national attention:** Richter, "Integrating the Suburban Dream," 10.

22   **Lord Rothermere:** Taylor Hampton, "Cleveland's Fabulous Vans: Triumph in Shaker," *Cleveland News*, August 11, 1955, Shaker Historical Society, Shaker Heights, OH.

22   **Salmon P. Halle:** Jim Dubelko, "The Salmon Halle Mansion," *Cleveland Historical*, https://clevelandhistorical.org/items/show/424.

23   **Most schools, restaurants, and public spaces were integrated:** "Know Our Heritage: The Great Migration," Cleveland Restoration Society, https://www.clevelandrestoration.org /projects/the-african-american-experience-in-cleveland/the-great-migration; and "Central (Neighborhood)," *Encyclopedia of Cleveland History*, Case Western Reserve University, https://case.edu/ech/articles/c/central-neighborhood. The Central neighborhood's boundaries were roughly Euclid Avenue to the north, East 71st Street to the east, Woodland Avenue to the south, and East 22nd Street to the west.

23   **the Black population was dispersed around town:** Kenneth L. Kusmer, *A Ghetto Takes Shape: Black Cleveland, 1870–1930* (Champaign: University of Illinois Press, 1976), 161–62.

23   **The Black population in Cleveland:** Kusmer, *A Ghetto Takes Shape*, 160–62.

23   ***Cleveland Topics* warned:** "Cleveland and the Negro," *Cleveland Topics*, January 17, 1925, Western Reserve Historical Society, Cleveland, OH. While the editorial warned of the unwelcome arrival of Black migrants, it also encouraged the city to deal with the new reality in practical ways, including urging support for and praising the Phillis Wheatley Association, founded to aid young Black women and girls.

23   **A January 1924 advertisement:** Advertisement, *Cleveland Topics*, January 5, 1924, Western Reserve Historical Society, Cleveland, OH.

24   **subjected to a pressure campaign:** "Two Versions of This Controversy," *Cleveland Gazette*, February 7, 1925; and Blake, "The Van Sweringen Developments in Cleveland," 29. The *Gazette*'s account of Wills being paid to leave Shaker is supported by Blake's 1968 thesis, which reported the brothers "bought out a Negro undertaker for $10,000."

24   **Earlier, in developing a portion of neighboring Cleveland Heights:** Haberman, *The Van Sweringens*, 18–19.

24   **The brothers pushed the railway company:** Haberman, *The Van Sweringens*, 18–19.

24   **Helped along by creative financing:** Haberman, *The Van Sweringens*, 26–30.

25   **"The size of an undertaking":** Kelly, "Two Young Men Who Are Real Estate Marvels," 51.

25   **As the brothers' local and national profile rose:** George E. Condon, *Cleveland: The Best Kept Secret* (New York: Doubleday, 1967), 193–95.

25   **"The Van Sweringen brothers are conveniently regarded":** *Fortune* magazine, quoted in Condon, *Cleveland: The Best Kept Secret*, 185.

26   **and, in a profitable turn:** Herbert H. Harwood Jr., *Trains* magazine, April 1955.

26   **three increasingly urgent letters:** Letters to Helen Luthi on file at the Shaker Historical Society; identification of the location of the property at the corner of Albion and Southington Roads, detailed language of the restriction, and confirmation the lease was returned with the restriction added are in Virginia P. Dawson, "Protection from Undesirable Neighbors: The Use Deed Restrictions in Shaker Heights, Ohio," *Journal of Planning History* 18, no. 2 (May 2019): 4; footnote 5, 27–28, https://shakerlibrary.org/wp-content/uploads/Article-on-restrictions.pdf.

27   **The first private racially restrictive covenants:** "Civil Rights in America: Racial Discrimination in Housing," National Historic Landmarks Program, Cultural Resources, National Park Service, March 2021, 10–11, https://www.nps.gov/subjects/nationalhistoriclandmarks/upload/Civil_Rights_Housing_NHL_Theme_Study_revisedfinal.pdf.

27   **The next year, the National Association of Real Estate Boards:** Michael Jones-Correa, "The Origins and Diffusion of Racial Restrictive Covenants," *Political Science Quarterly* 115, no. 4 (Winter 2000–2001).

27   **A 1928 study of deeds:** Helen C. Monchow, "The Use of Deed Restrictions in Subdivision Development," Institute for Research in Land Economics and Public Utilities, 1928, 50, https://babel.hathitrust.org/cgi/pt?id=mdp.35128000769529.

28   **The National Housing Act of 1934:** Catherine Silva, "Racial Restrictive Covenants History," Seattle Civil Rights and Labor History Project, University of Washington, 2009, https://depts.washington.edu/civilr/covenants_report.htm.

28   **Dr. Edward A. Bailey:** "Dr. Edward Anderson Bailey and Mrs. Bailey Attend the American Medical Association's Annual Meet in San Francisco and Return Thru Southern Canada—Exceptional Experience," *Cleveland Gazette*, July 21, 1923; and "Charging Run Around Dr. Edw. A. Bailey Runs," *Cleveland Gazette*, June 24, 1939.

29   **A few years earlier, the Baileys had bought a home:** "Cleveland Social and Personal," *Cleveland Gazette*, May 15, 1920, 3.

29   **"Their new home is a beautiful one":** No headline, *Cleveland Gazette*, September 19, 1925, 2.

29   **The Baileys' new neighbors:** "Hold the Fort!" *Cleveland Gazette*, October 17, 1925, 2; and a second story, no headline, *Cleveland Gazette*, October 24, 1925.

30   **Before buying the property:** "Negro Home in Wade Park Is Protested," *Daily Times*, New Philadelphia, OH, September 22, 1925; "The Battle Opens in Cleveland! Residential Segregation!" *Cleveland Gazette*, September 26, 1925.

30   **His purchase in the Wade Park Allotment:** Todd M. Michney, *Surrogate Suburbs: Black Upward Mobility and Neighborhood Change in Cleveland, 1900–1980* (Chapel Hill: University of North Carolina Press, 2017), 39–40.

30   **about four hundred residents:** "PROTEST: Not Only Against Our People! About 400 Meet and Effect a Permanent Organization," *Cleveland Gazette*, October 3, 1925, 1.

31   ***Buchanan v. Warley:*** "Buchanan v. Warley," *Oyez*, www.oyez.org/cases/1900–1940/245us60.

31   **listed Mrs. Bailey as a hostess:** Cornelia Curtiss, "Association of Plymouth Has Musicale," *Plain Dealer*, January 21, 1926. One of the hostesses listed is "Mrs. E. A. Bailey"; city directories show no other E. A. Baileys in the Cleveland area.

31   **records show that by January 1927:** *Cleveland City Directory*, 1924, 1925, 1926, and 1927; *Criss Cross Directory*, Criss Cross Agency, 1926; Cuyahoga County Recorder's Office via Cleveland Public Library. The Baileys are listed in the city directory as residing on Huntington in 1926. In January 1927, the property was transferred from the county sheriff to Jennie Palmer; her husband, Carl Palmer, is listed as residing at the address in 1927. It is unclear when or how the property was transferred to the sheriff.

31   **Committee of the Shaker Heights Protective Association:** "Report of Committee, Shaker Heights Protective Association," October 19, 1925, Shaker Historical Society, Shaker Heights, OH.

32   **Newton D. Baker:** Baker's death in 1937 was front page news in the *New York Times*,

which described him as "the mildest, most peaceful, most intellectual and shortest man to exert managerial authority over the armies of the United States." He cofounded the law firm later known as BakerHostetler. "Newton D. Baker Dies in Cleveland; War Secretary in World Conflict Passes at Home amid Family Christmas," *New York Times*, December 26, 1937, https://www.nytimes.com/1937/12/26/archives/newton-d-baker-dies-in -cleveland-war-secretary-in-world-conflict.html. See also BakerHostetler History: https:// www.bakerlaw.com/aboutus/history.

32 **By 1927, three-quarters of Shaker property deeds:** Molyneaux and Sackman, *75 Years*, 20. The book says 75 percent of the deeds had been returned with revisions but does not specify that they had all added Restriction No. 5. Given the effort underway at the time, it seems likely that most if not all of the revisions included this one.

32 **to serve several railroads:** Peter Jedick, "They Called It the Greatest Thing Since the Pyramids," *Cleveland* magazine, February 1975, 56. Shaker Historical Society archives. The terminal project was sorely needed to replace existing shabby stations. The Union Depot, for instance, was such a soot-covered eyesore that a local advertising executive had erected a billboard positioned with a plea to incoming travelers: DON'T JUDGE THIS TOWN BY THIS DEPOT.

32 **a preexisting, competing plan:** Jedick, "They Called It the Greatest Thing Since the Pyramids." The alternative plan for a terminal was called the Group Plan and had already been approved in a 1915 referendum. In a new referendum in 1919, the Van Sweringen plan was approved instead.

32 **not just a grand terminal:** Taylor Hampton, "Fabulous Vans: They Remodel Downtown," *Cleveland News*, August 5, 1955, Shaker Historical Society, Shaker Heights, OH.

33 **The first passenger train:** Dale Cox, "12 Trains Open New Station," *Plain Dealer*, December 2, 1929, 1.

33 **listening in via a special telephone hookup:** Jedick, "They Called It the Greatest Thing Since the Pyramids," 56. The luncheon was on June 28, 1930.

33 **They soon built a rail empire:** Sources on the Van Sweringen railroad empire include "The Current State of Mr. Van Sweringen," *Fortune* magazine, 1936, and "They Changed the Face of Cleveland," *Cleveland Plain Dealer Pictorial Magazine*, January 1, 1950, Shaker Historical Society, Shaker Heights, OH. Railroads acquired included the Clover Leaf, Lake Erie & Western, Chesapeake & Ohio, Erie, Pere Marquette, Wheeling & Lake Erie, and Missouri Pacific.

33 **Separately, in 1934, O.P. was indicted:** Harold E. Hatch, "O. P. Van Sweringen, Nutt, Baldwin Indicted in Bank Probe; Deny Wrong," *Plain Dealer*, April 14, 1934, 1.

33 **In August 1935, M.J. entered Lakeside Hospital:** Taylor Hampton, "Cleveland's Fabulous Vans: Death Ends the Dreams," *Cleveland News*, August 19, 1955, Shaker Historical Society, Shaker Heights, OH.

33 **that November he was embroiled:** Caption on photo, no headline, *Plain Dealer*, November 21, 1935, 24.

Chapter 3: Ted and Beverly Mason

36 **The determination came naturally:** The story of the Masons' arrival in Shaker Heights comes from interviews with Paul Mason, 2020 to 2022.

36 **named for one of Susan's sons:** "Susan M. Johnson," *Cadiz Republican*, September 17, 1908, provided by Paul Mason.

36 **there were two officers' clubs:** Farrell Evans, "How Tuskegee Airmen Fought Military Segregation with Nonviolent Action," History.com, January 20, 2021, https://www.history .com/news/tuskegee-airmen-impact-civil-rights-movement.

38 **a 1966 documentary:** *When Ludlow Stopped Running*, documentary produced by local TV station WKYC-TV, part of a series called "Montage," 1966, Shaker Heights Public Library.

39 **(Ted Mason, in fact, sat on a panel):** "Forum to Discuss Jim Crow Schools," *Call & Post*, February 28, 1953, 7-A.

39   **there had been a few Black families:** Bill Clark, "Model Integration Effort Drives Property Values Up," *Dayton Daily News*, October 23, 1968, 1.

39   **the parcel did not carry the deed restrictions:** *When Ludlow Stopped Running.*

39   **"We were young":** *When Ludlow Stopped Running.*

40   **He made a preliminary inquiry:** Container 8, folder 414, MS 4219, Maurice Klain Research Papers: Cleveland Area Leadership Studies, series I, Western Reserve Historical Society, Cleveland, OH. Interview with Ted Mason was conducted on January 7, 1962.

40   **a Black-owned bank, Quincy Savings and Loan:** Todd M. Michney, *Surrogate Suburbs: Black Upward Mobility and Neighborhood Change in Cleveland, 1900–1980* (Chapel Hill: University of North Carolina Press, 2017), 181–82.

41   **"Before we even moved in":** Clark, "Model Integration Effort Drives Property Values Up."

41   **She was in the hospital:** *When Ludlow Stopped Running.*

41   **Marie J. Chader:** Most news reports identify the group's leader as Mrs. Stanley F. Chader, but Cuyahoga County marriage records and other newspaper clippings confirm her full name was Marie J. Chader.

41   **"This is not a racial matter":** "Home Owners Organizer Denies Racial Motives," *Cleveland Press*, September 24, 1955.

42   **When someone at the meeting noted:** "Klan-Type Meet Fails to Stop Negroes from Building Near Shaker," *Call & Post*, October 1, 1955, 1-A.

42   **One resident who arrived late at the meeting:** Kent Weeks and Karen Weeks, "A Suburb Faces Its Future" (unpublished, circa 1968), Local History Collection, Shaker Heights Public Library, 17.

42   **It called the gathering:** "Klan-Type Meet Fails to Stop Negroes from Building Near Shaker."

42   **And yet there was something different this time:** Account of the pro-integration effort from Weeks and Weeks, "A Suburb Faces," and Cleveland Clearinghouse on Civil Liberties, September 1955 meeting minutes, container 32, folder 6, MS 3520, National Association for the Advancement of Colored People, Cleveland Branch Records, Western Reserve Historical Society, Cleveland, OH.

43   **The school district's odd boundaries:** Virginia P. Dawson, "Shaker Square and the Shaker Schools," Shaker Square website, December 2011, https://www.shakersquare.net/history/square-shaker-schools.htm.

43   **School district boundaries make this sorting possible:** Laura Meckler and Kate Rabinowitz, "The Lines That Divide: School District Boundaries Often Stymie Integration," *Washington Post*, December 16, 2019, https://www.washingtonpost.com/education/2019/12/16/lines-that-divide-school-district-boundaries-often-stymie-integration/.

44   **The Cleveland suburbs grew rapidly:** Susan Kaeser, *Resisting Segregation: Cleveland Heights Activists Shape Their Community, 1964–1976* (University Heights, OH: Cleveland Landmarks Press, 2020), 32–34. Data cited is from the U.S. Census Bureau.

44   **Housing segregation in twentieth-century America:** Richard Rothstein, "Powerful Government Policy Segregated Us; the Same Can Desegregate Us, Says *Color of Law* Author Richard Rothstein," *Working Economics Blog*, Economic Policy Institute, April 14, 2021, https://www.epi.org/blog/powerful-government-policy-segregated-us-the-same-can-desegregate-us-says-color-of-law-author-richard-rothstein/.

45   **"African American pioneers were in a difficult position":** Interview with Andrew Wiese, April 23, 2021.

46   **In a 1960 interview:** Container 10, folder 500, MS 4219, Maurice Klain Research Papers: Cleveland Area Leadership Studies, series I, Western Reserve Historical Society, Cleveland, OH. Interview with John G. Pegg was conducted on January 14, 1960.

47   **A woman phoned the Peggs:** "Small Super Bomb Blasted Pegg House, Police Report," *Plain Dealer*, January 5, 1956, 44; Winfield G. Leathers, "The Ludlow Community Association: A Political Interest Group," May 20, 1964, Ludlow Community Association files,

Local History Collection, Shaker Heights Public Library. First caller cited in newspaper article; second caller cited in Leathers interview with Dorothy Pegg.

48   **But just before ten o'clock:** "Neighbors Heal Scars of Hate," *Plain Dealer*, January 6, 1956, 18-A.

48   **"one of the most significant exemplifications":** "White Neighbors Help Clean Up Pegg Home Bomb Damage," *Call & Post*, 1-A.

48   **A few days after the cleanup:** "Home Is Guarded in Bomb Threat," *Plain Dealer*, January 11, 1956, 17.

48   **Police also provided the Peggs with protection:** Weeks and Weeks, "A Suburb Faces," 20.

Chapter 4· Irv and Emilie Barnett

50   **It was 1956:** Principal sources for the Barnetts' story include two unpublished memoirs: Emilie Barnett, "Crossing the Road and Daring to Do So" (unpublished, ca. 2008); Irv Barnett, "Ludlow Memoir" (unpublished, 1967), both shared with the author by Bill Barnett; as well as interviews with their children: Dan Barnett; Bill Barnett and his wife, Nancy Barnett; and Laura Barnett Webb.

51   **In 1956, For Sale signs were posted:** "Historical Notes," handwritten document, MS 3662, Ludlow Community Association Records, Western Reserve Historical Society, Cleveland, OH.

51   **So Emilie, who had never before spoken with a Black person:** Emilie Barnett, "Crossing the Road and Daring to Do So," 7–8; *Shaker Heights: The Struggle for Integration*, directed and produced by Stuart Math (Independent Television Service, 1997), interview with Emilie Barnett, 7:43 to 8:35, https://youtu.be/FENwJaoeEeo.

52   **A few months after arriving:** Joseph P. Blank, "Ludlow—A Lesson in Integration," *Reader's Digest*, September 1968.

53   **A white couple named Joanne and Joseph E. Finley:** Container 4, folder 194, MS 4219, Maurice Klain Research Papers: Cleveland Area Leadership Studies, series I, Western Reserve Historical Society, Cleveland, OH. Interview with Joanne Finley was conducted on April 4 and 9, 1962.

53   **"It was fine with us":** Elinor Polster, interview with author, December 28, 2020.

54   **The neighborhood meetings began on streets:** "Ludlow Community," handwritten note indicates this early history was written in 1959; container 2, folders 6 and 7, MS 3662, Ludlow Community Association Records, Western Reserve Historical Society, Cleveland, OH.

54   **the group's treasurer, who sold his house:** Carolyn Milter, "Ludlow Community Association: Striving for Integration in a Divided America" (unpublished paper, December 8, 1972), 4.

55   **Integration proponents preferred to tell the story:** Kent Weeks and Karen Weeks, "A Suburb Faces Its Future" (unpublished, circa 1968), Local History Collection, Shaker Heights Public Library, 22.

55   **A community research project:** Ludlow Community Association files, Local History Collection, Shaker Heights Public Library. The Ludlow Community Research Project found the following percentages of white residents in Ludlow: 75 percent in 1958, 68 percent in 1959, 58 percent in 1960, 55 percent in 1961, 52 percent in 1962, and 48 percent in 1963.

55   **the association invited a sociologist:** Irv Barnett, "Ludlow Memoir," 8.

57   **In September 1958, a Gallup poll:** Data provided to author by Gallup, via the Roper Center for Public Opinion Research. Poll conducted by Gallup Organization September 24–29, 1958, and based on personal interviews with a national adult sample of 1,665.

58   **Irv Barnett met with the executive secretary:** Irv Barnett, "Ludlow Memoir," 9.

58   **Another official with the real estate board:** Container 8, folder 374, MS 4219, Maurice Klain Research Papers: Cleveland Area Leadership Studies, series I, Western Reserve Historical Society, Cleveland, OH.

58   **In July 1959, the *Cleveland Press* reported:** "Ludlow Neighbors Given Funds to Aid Model Negro-White Area," *Cleveland Press*, July 21, 1969.

356 | Notes

58   **Funding in hand, the association approached:** Irv Barnett, "Ludlow Memoir," 9.

59   **"We do not want to see the area become a Negro ghetto":** H. L. Samford, "Local Group Asks Support to Prevent Negro Ghetto," *Sun Press*, December 8, 1960, 1, Local History Collection, Shaker Heights Public Library.

59   **had been working behind the scenes:** Container 2, folder 71, MS 4219, Maurice Klain Research Papers: Cleveland Area Leadership Studies, series I, Western Reserve Historical Society, Cleveland, OH. Interview with William Burton was conducted on April 8, 1964.

59   **delivered the main address:** Samford, "Local Group Asks."

59   **Yet the neighborhood continued to draw:** "Colored Children," June 5, 1959, Shaker Heights City School District archives. Chart shows 19 Black children at Ludlow Elementary School in 1955–56. (Two years later, there were 31; the year after that, 84.) "Ludlow School: November 1963," District archives, chart shows 72.4 percent of students at Ludlow were Black.

59   **The mayor, Wilson G. Stapleton:** Irv Barnett, "Ludlow Memoir," 5.

60   **In 1961, he bragged:** "Jump in Tax Values Proves That Shaker Is Worth Its Salt," *Plain Dealer*, October 25, 1961, Shaker Historical Society, Shaker Heights, OH.

60   **Around 1959, there was a spate of crimes:** David G. Molyneaux and Sue Sackman, eds., *75 Years: An Informal History of Shaker Heights* (Shaker Heights, OH: Shaker Heights Public Library, 1987), 60, 71.

60   **Stapleton also spoke out in favor of a plan:** "Shaker Sets Up Street Barriers," *Call & Post*, August 29, 1959, 1-A. The plan would have dead-ended Avalon and Ingleside Roads at Scottsdale Boulevard.

60   **At one point, Stapleton suggested:** Container 10, folder 501, MS 4219, Maurice Klain Research Papers: Cleveland Area Leadership Studies, series I, Western Reserve Historical Society, Cleveland, OH. Interview with A. M. Pennybacker was conducted on April 29, 1964.

60   **Stapleton and members of Shaker's City Council:** Container 2, folder 71, and container 5, folder 226, MS 4219, Maurice Klain Research Papers: Cleveland Area Leadership Studies, series I, Western Reserve Historical Society, Cleveland, OH. Interview with William Burton was conducted on April 8, 1964; interview with Alan Geismer was conducted on May 12, 1964. See also container 4, folder 180.

60   **In 1964, Burton said:** Klain interview with Burton.

61   **In the fall of 1960:** Marc D. Gleisser, "Suit Seeks to Oust Negroes from Home," *Plain Dealer*, October 20, 1960, 18.

61   **the mayor spoke to the Greater Cleveland Ministerial Association:** Richard Wagar, "Clergy Hears Housing Plea by Stapleton," *Plain Dealer*, October 20, 1960, 19.

61   **he reached out to the newspaper:** "Race Stand Is Clarified by Stapleton," *Plain Dealer*, October 21, 1960, 12.

62   **A few days later, he spoke to the Cleveland Real Estate Board:** H. L. Samford, "Shaker Mayor Cites Strong Support for Race Stand," *Sun* newspapers, October 27, 1960, Local History Collection, Shaker Heights Public Library.

62   **And in a letter to the editor:** Joseph E. Finley, "Acceptance for All," *Plain Dealer*, October 28, 1960, 44.

63   **"THERE IS PRESTIGE TODAY":** Weeks and Weeks, "A Suburb Faces," 53.

63   **in a 2004 interview with ABC News:** Interview with Alan Gressel, *20/20*, April 20, 2004, 15–16, 22. Transcript provided by Paul Mason.

64   **In the summer of 1961, the association won:** "Ludlow Granted $5,000 to Assist Integration," *Courier*, July 29, 1961, 2, Local History Collection, Shaker Heights Public Library.

64   **"Ludlow Progress Report":** H. L. Samford, "Ludlow Progress Report: Integration Works, White Families Moving In," *Sun Press*, July 20, 1961, Local History Collection, Shaker Heights Public Library.

64   **feared they would suffer financially:** Container 5, folder 201, MS 4219, Maurice Klain Research Papers: Cleveland Area Leadership Studies, series I, Western Reserve Historical Society, Cleveland, OH.

65   **In 1962, Finley got a call:** Cynthia Mills Richter, "Integrating the Suburban Dream:

Shaker Heights, Ohio," (dissertation submitted to the University of Minnesota, December 1999), 238–39, based on Richter interviews with Lavona and Bush Olmsted.

65 **"It was far from easy":** Blank, "Ludlow—A Lesson in Integration."

65 **considered filing a discrimination suit against the association:** Lee Berton, "Integration on Trial: Area in Cleveland Suburbs Struggles to Keep Racial Balance," *Wall Street Journal*, September 2, 1964, Local History Collection, Shaker Heights Public Library.

65 **In a letter to the community:** William L. Percy, "From the Desk of the President," Ludlow scrapbook, Local History Collection, Shaker Heights Public Library.

66 **It gave voice to critics:** Weeks and Weeks, "A Suburb Faces," 74–75. See also Grover C. Crayton, "Astronaut in Orbit . . . Suburb Bars Negro . . ." *Cleveland Courier*, March 3, 1962, 2, Local History Collection, Shaker Heights Public Library. The full headline of the article was cut off in clip included in files.

66 **To address the critics:** Weeks and Weeks, "A Suburb Faces," 75–76.

66 **and perhaps their own guilt:** Gressel interview, 57.

66 **In February 1962, two hundred people showed up:** Eugene Segal, "Ludlow Open House Draws 200 Visitors," *Plain Dealer*, February 18, 1962, Local History Collection, Shaker Heights Public Library.

66 **In the group's November 1962 newsletter:** *Ludlow Notes, News & Neighbors* 3, no. 3, November 1962, Local History Collection, Shaker Heights Public Library.

66 **"If you're honest, you know":** *When Ludlow Stopped Running*, documentary produced by local TV station WKYC-TV, part of a series called "Montage," 1966, Shaker Heights Public Library.

66 **Beverly Mason said in an interview for a book:** Molyneaux and Sackman, *75 Years*, 83.

67 **"We didn't want to just keep flooding":** Thomasine Mason, interview with author, November 12, 2021, Lyndhurst, OH. Other sources for Erv and Thomasine Mason's story include interviews with their children, Hilary Carrington Mason King and Ervin Proctor Mason Jr., as well as correspondence and newspaper clippings provided by Hilary King.

67 **The Grenells believed in integration:** Joan Cole, "The Grenell Housing Case," August 1962, container 51, folder 1, MS 3520, National Association for the Advancement of Colored People, Cleveland Branch Records, Western Reserve Historical Society, Cleveland, OH.

68 **Charles R. Bechtel:** According to newspaper coverage, in 1964 Bechtel pleaded guilty to three counts of sending obscene material through the mail. He admitted corresponding with a sailor he'd met in a bar and receiving obscene film footage from him, according to one account. This injects a certain irony into his role in the Mason case: he was perhaps subject to discrimination even as he was inflicting it on others. See "Insurance Man Pleads Guilty," *Plain Dealer*, April 18, 1964, and "Insurance Man Admits Obscene Mail Charges," no date or publication, personal files of Thomasine Mason.

68 **Around this time, word was getting out:** "Ex-Neighbor Tells of Role in Home Feud," *Cleveland Press*, March 4, 1964, files of Thomasine Mason.

68 **It was one of many times that Mintz would use:** Several Klain interviews detail Mintz's role, including his attempts to keep Black buyers out of Shaker. See container 10, folder 501; container 8, folder 374; container 13, folder 670; and container 4, folder 180, MS 4219, Maurice Klain Research Papers: Cleveland Area Leadership Studies, series I, Western Reserve Historical Society, Cleveland, OH. One of these interviews was with A. M. Pennybacker, April 29, 1964.

69 **The case was assigned:** Tom Brady, "Judge Rules for Negro in Home Fight," 1957, publication and date not noted on clip, Thomasine Mason files.

69 **But the court case dragged on:** Julian Krawcheck, "Negro in Home Fight Says Foes Jumped on Bandwagon," *Cleveland Press*, no date noted on clip, Thomasine Mason files.

69 **He said in an interview that neighbors:** Tom Brady, "Says Negro Wants Crusade More Than Home," no publication or date noted on clip, Thomasine Mason files.

71 **A newspaper headline in February 1962:** "24 White Families Move into Ludlow in 10 Months," February 22, 1962, Local History Collection, Shaker Heights Public Library. Story carries no byline and clip does not note the newspaper name.

71 **And Mintz, the Savings and Loan banker:** Mintz agreed that his bank would write first mortgages in Ludlow, working with the Ludlow Company, which offered secondary mortgages, on a program to encourage white families to move into the neighborhood. According to Joanne Finley, William Burton persuaded him to do so. See Klain interviews with Joanne Finley and William Burton, container 4, folder 194, and container 209, folder 71, MS 4219, Maurice Klain Research Papers: Cleveland Area Leadership Studies, series I, Western Reserve Historical Society, Cleveland, OH.

71 *Look* **magazine devoted:** Julius Horwitz, "New Neighbors," *Look*, January 14, 1964.

72 **Hawaii governor John A. Burns:** Julian Krawcheck, "Hawaii Head Praises Integrated Living," *Cleveland Press*, June 8, 1964, Local History Collection, Shaker Heights Public Library.

72 **In late 1962 or early 1963:** Emilie Barnett, "Crossing the Road."

72 **who had been denied service:** Renee Romano, "No Diplomatic Immunity: African Diplomats, the State Department, and Civil Rights, 1961–1964," *Journal of American History* 87, no. 2 (September 2000). In the early 1960s, African diplomats and their staffs and families were regularly thrown out of restaurants along Route 40, the highway that connected New York and Washington, D.C.

72 **Ludlow hosted ambassadors:** *Ludlow Notes, News & Neighbors* 6, no. 5, June 30, 1965, Local History Collection, Shaker Heights Public Library.

73 **a fundraising concert:** Kathleen O'Brien, "Ella Fitzgerald's Concert at Severance Hall Is a Huge Success," *Plain Dealer*, April 25, 1966; Ethel Boros, "Ella Fitzgerald Wins Standing Ovation Here," *Plain Dealer*, April 25, 1966; Winsor French, "Magic Is the Word for Ella," *Cleveland Press*, April 28, 1966; and "Ella at Severance" concert program, Local History Collection, Shaker Heights Public Library.

73 **the first jazz concert:** John S. Diekhoff, "My Fair Ludlow," *Educational Forum* 33, no. 3 (1969): 284. Andria Hoy, archivist for the Cleveland Orchestra, confirmed that records show no jazz performance prior to the Fitzgerald concert at Severance Hall; email to author, August 9, 2022.

73 **By November 1963:** Enrollment data included on series of charts created by the Shaker Heights City School District tracking total enrollment and "Negro enroll[ment]" by school, by year, District archives.

74 **The Fitzgerald concert was followed:** "Fantastic!," *Ludlow News* 9, no. 6, July 24, 1968, Local History Collection, Shaker Heights Public Library.

Chapter 5: The Reverend Albert M. Pennybacker Jr.

77 **Appearing on the stage, Pennybacker was stunned:** Klain interview with A. M. Pennybacker was conducted on April 29, 1964.

77 **and was a founding member:** "Interracial Organization Is Perfected," *Chattanooga Daily Times*, September 22, 1927, 5.

79 **Others responded in writing:** Letters to and from Pennybacker from container 1, folder 1, MS 3743, Albert M. Pennybacker Papers, Western Reserve Historical Society, Cleveland, OH.

79 **forty-eight people met:** "Minutes, Proposed Citizens' Commission," September 30, 1963, container 1, folder 3, MS 3743, Albert M. Pennybacker Papers, Western Reserve Historical Society, Cleveland, OH.

80 **He held what was at the time:** Container 4, folder 180, MS 4219, Maurice Klain Research Papers: Cleveland Area Leadership Studies, series I, Western Reserve Historical Society, Cleveland, OH.

80 **Emery wrote a memo:** Container 4, folder 180, MS 4219, Maurice Klain Research Papers.

81 **East View Village:** Virginia Dawson, "Moreland and the Development of the South Side of Shaker Heights," March 30, 2017, https://shakerlibrary.org/wp-content/uploads/A-Short-History-of-the-Moreland-Area-of-Shaker-Heights.pdf; Richard Raponi, "Building Porches, Doubles, and Bungalows in the Moreland Neighborhood," *Cleveland Historical*, https://clevelandhistorical.org/items/show/837.

81 **featuring the types of houses:** Michael Fleenor and Sena Kayasu, "An Architectural Guide to Southern Moreland," Cleveland Restoration Society, July 2017, https://shakerlibrary .org/wp-content/uploads/Architectural-Guide-to-Southern-Moreland.pdf.

81 **In the 1940s and '50s:** Richard Raponi, "Shaker-Lee Synagogue," *Cleveland Historical*, https://clevelandhistorical.org/items/show/839.

81 **Kinsman Jewish Center:** "Kinsman Jewish Center," *Encyclopedia of Cleveland History*, Case Western Reserve University, https://case.edu/ech/articles/k/kinsman-jewish-center.

81 **A 1958 study estimated the Moreland school:** Dawson, "Moreland and the Development of the South Side of Shaker." Dawson cites "Report of the Self-Study Conducted by the Planning Committee" (Shaker Heights: East View Congregational Church, 1958), Shaker Historical Society.

82 **"There were [real estate] agents out on the street":** Cleveland Voices, Moreland History Project, interview with Steven A. Minter, December 12, 2017, https://clevelandvoices.org /items/show/3117. See also Dolly Minter, commencement address, Hiram College, June 13, 1992, provided by her daughter, Robyn Minter Smyers.

82 **Jerry Greenberg:** Interview with author, April 11, 2021.

83 **The group had examined 4,350 homes:** "Shaker Heights Property Values Study," container 1, folder 3, MS 3743, Albert M. Pennybacker Papers, Western Reserve Historical Society, Cleveland, OH.

83 **"There has been no panic selling":** "Study Report—Intercongregational Group * Fairmont Temple, April 22, 1964, by A.M.P," speech prepared for delivery, container 1, folder 3, MS 3743, Albert M. Pennybacker Papers, Western Reserve Historical Society, Cleveland, OH.

83 **The study had its flaws:** Kent Weeks and Karen Weeks, "A Suburb Faces Its Future" (unpublished, circa 1968), Local History Collection, Shaker Heights Public Library, 147–49.

83 **and Lomond followed in 1963:** Weeks and Weeks, "A Suburb Faces," 119.

84 **what happened on a Sunday in August 1961:** Kenneth Jay Suid, "Housing and Employment Opportunities for Negroes in Cleveland" (unpublished Princeton University senior thesis, April 19, 1962), available from Princeton University on request, 49–50.

84 **The March 1964 *Lomond Newsletter*:** "Selling Season Begins," *Lomond Newsletter*, March 1964, 1, MS 3598, Lomond Association Records, Western Reserve Historical Society, Cleveland, OH.

84 **Both neighborhoods also established housing programs:** Formation of Lomond Association described in Weeks and Weeks, "A Suburb Faces," 127.

84 **The Lomond Association's message to the neighborhood:** Weeks and Weeks, "A Suburb Faces," 128.

85 **The April 1965 *Lomond Newsletter* addressed the point:** "An Editorial," *Lomond Newsletter*, April 1965, 1, MS 3598, Lomond Association Records, Western Reserve Historical Society, Cleveland, OH.

85 **by the summer of 1965:** Weeks and Weeks, "A Suburb Faces," 132–33.

85 **In 1961, the City Council passed an antiblockbusting ordinance:** H. L. Samford, "Integration Works, White Families Moving In," *Sun Press*, July 20, 1961, 1.

86 **Black brokers (known then as Realtists):** W. Dennis Keating, *The Suburban Racial Dilemma: Housing and Neighborhoods* (Philadelphia: Temple University Press, 1994), 100.

86 **"orderly and constructive process":** David G. Molyneaux and Sue Sackman, eds., *75 Years: An Informal History of Shaker Heights* (Shaker Heights, OH: Shaker Heights Public Library, 1987), 82.

86 **the mayor and the City Council needed a shove:** Weeks and Weeks, "A Suburb Faces," 152.

86 **Alan Gressel:** Carolyn Milter, "Ludlow Community Association: Striving for Integration in a Divided America" (unpublished paper, December 8, 1972), 17.

87 **in what may have been a first:** Milter, "Ludlow Community Association," 18.

87 **In 1973, *Money* magazine cited Shaker:** Avery Comarow, "It Pays to Stay When Blacks Move In," *Money*, November 1973, Local History Collection, Shaker Heights Public Library.

87   **In 1977, officials from Southfield:** Ken Fireman, "Integration: It Works in This Suburb," *Detroit Free Press*, June 26, 1977, Local History Collection, Shaker Heights Public Library.

87   **Other communities that came calling for advice:** "The Shaker Heights Housing Office: A History" (undated), District archives.

87   **In 1979, *U.S. News & World Report* wrote about Shaker:** Lowell McKirgan, "We Feel Good About Ourselves," *U.S. News & World Report*, May 28, 1979, Local History Collection, Shaker Heights Public Library.

88   **Isabel Ann Lewis:** Interview with author, April 10, 2021.

88   **Another Shaker Heights Housing Office employee:** Cynthia Mills Richter, "Integrating the Suburban Dream: Shaker Heights, Ohio" (dissertation submitted to the University of Minnesota, December 1999), 247.

88   **When the three community associations asked:** Weeks and Weeks, "A Suburb Faces," 165–66.

89   **On the morning of:** Joan Campbell, interview with author, August 29, 2021. In 2017, after Pennybacker's first wife died and Campbell divorced, the pair married.

90   **"I still have faith in the future":** "History," Heights Christian Church website, with video of King speech, https://www.heightschristianchurch.org/history/.

90   **It sat on the edge of an urban corridor:** Virginia Dawson, "Moreland and the Development of the South Side of Shaker Heights," 11–12, citing *Moreland News* 4, no. 6 (November 1965), container 46, folder 1148, MS 4092, Cleveland Foundation Records, series II, Western Reserve Historical Society, Cleveland, OH.

90   **"Unfortunately, these homes are not attractive":** Letter from Alan Gressel to Paul Jones, August 24, 1965, container 2, folder 88, MS 4167, Ludlow Community Association Records, series II, Western Reserve Historical Society, Cleveland, OH.

91   **In 1966, the city hatched an urban renewal plan:** "Shaker Heights Shapes Master Program for Affluent Society," *Sun Press*, February 23, 1967, 1. See also Dawson, "Moreland and the Development of the South Side of Shaker Heights," 12–14; and Richter, "Integrating the Suburban Dream," 166–69.

91   **"Where can we go for open housing in Shaker?":** "Yes and No Is Response to Shaker Moreland Plan," *Sun Press*, May 4, 1967.

91   **In response to these critics:** "Civic Center Erased from Moreland Plan," *Sun Press*, May 11, 1967, 1.

91   **Alan Gressel called the proposal:** Milter, "Ludlow Community Association," 18.

92   **The city retaliated:** "Dismissals Disturb Ludlow Unit Head," *Sun Press*, November 11, 1968; "Rehiring of Housing Aides Asked" (publication unclear), December 3, 1968; "Shaker's Mayor Mum on Firings," *Plain Dealer*, December 4, 1968, 8-D; William Insull Jr., "Ludlow Assn. Protests Firings of Shaker Housing Employees," letter to the editor, *Sun Press*, December 5, 1968, Local History Collection, Shaker Heights Public Library, and online *Plain Dealer* archives.

93   **After one emotional meeting:** Milter, "Ludlow Community Association," 21.

93   **"There were people who carried feelings":** Carolyn Milter, interview with author, January 5, 2022.

93   **In an address:** "Address by J. J. Berner," January 27, 1971; MS 3662, Ludlow Community Association Records, Western Reserve Historical Society, Cleveland, OH.

93   **Hard work toward racial balance had moved the percentage:** Enrollment data by school in series of memos and charts in District archives, several of which were marked "confidential."

Chapter 6: Jack Lawson

95   **"Negro children suffer serious harm":** "Racial Isolation in the Public Schools," U.S. Commission on Civil Rights, 1967, https://books.google.com/books?id=ADG7AAAAIAAJ.

95   **John H. Lawson was getting ready:** Thoughts and views of Jack Lawson, unless otherwise noted, from his memoir, "Jack Lawson's Memoirs: Part VI—Spending over a Decade in Shaker Heights" (unpublished, 2000), provided by his son, John Lawson.

96   **In 1965, his first year:** "Negro Enrollments for the Shaker Schools in the Current School Year," memo to Board of Education members from John H. Lawson, October 20, 1966, District archives.

97   **The school board considered his positive attitude:** Gardner P. Dunnan, "Escalation of School Board Action in an Integrating Suburb: EA 400 Project Proposal," (Harvard University Graduate School of Education thesis, November 1967), 26.

97   **a Lawson aide reported that the number of Black teachers:** "Shakerites to Discuss Busing of Some Moreland Students," *Sun Press*, February 12, 1970, District archives.

97   **Complaints came from parents and real estate agents:** Email from Gardner P. Dunnan to author, January 19, 2022.

97   **he addressed the district's teachers:** A copy of Lawson's address to teachers included in letter to Herbert J. Hansell from John H. Lawson, September 25, 1967, District archives.

98   **a census of students was recorded:** Enrollment figures on October 1, 1967, cited in memo from Gardner P. Dunnan to John H. Lawson, "A Proposal," March 20, 1968, 4, District archives.

98   **Lawson and his staff consulted:** Dunnan, "Escalation of School Board" (proposal), 40–41.

99   **The school board discussed the proposal:** Gardner P. Dunnan, "Escalating School Board Action in a Racially Integrating Suburb: A Final Report Presented to the Faculty of the Graduate School of Education of Harvard University in Partial Fulfillment of the Requirements of the Degree of Doctor of Education," May 13, 1968, 21–25.

99   **Lawson applied to the Ford Foundation:** Application for grant, February 13, 1969, District archives.

99   **the foundation responded:** A letter from Lawson to the Ford Foundation thanking the foundation indicates the grant was for $165,547; District archives. Other documents, including the *School Review* and some newspaper coverage, indicate grant was for $150,000. See Peggy Gokay, "Community Meetings Weigh Staff Proposal," *School Review*, March 1970, 4.

99   **That fall, he returned with a developed plan:** Lawson, "Memoirs," 50.

99   **On November 20, four months after winning the grant:** John H. Lawson, "Meeting with 'Concerned Citizens for an Integrated Moreland School,'" memo to Board of Education members, November 20, 1969, District archives.

100   **The Moreland group's seven-page proposal:** "Proposal to the Shaker Heights School Board, Prepared by Concerned Citizens for an Integrated Moreland School," undated, District archives.

100   **A few days before Lawson would announce:** "Integration in Shaker Schools Discussed," *Cleveland Press*, February 6, 1970, District archives.

100   **Before an official announcement:** Lawson, "Memoirs," 55.

101   **In February 1970, another group:** Letter to members of the Shaker Heights Board of Education from the Moreland Parents Committee, February 8, 1970, Local History Collection, Shaker Heights Public Library.

101   **Lawson announced his plan:** John H. Lawson, "Educational Report: 'Staff Study of Racial Imbalance in Moreland,'" February 10, 1970, District archives.

102   **a subsequent session:** Leslie Kay, "Integration Plan Winning Support," *Plain Dealer*, March 4, 1970, District archives.

102   **its own unscientific reader survey:** "71% in Poll Oppose Shaker Busing Plan," *Sun Press*, May 7, 1970. Readers had to send in responses to the poll by mail; the paper received 397 votes.

102   **Nervousness was evident:** Percy C. O'Rourk, "Sussex Scoop," March 1970, Local History Collection, Shaker Heights Public Library.

102   **the Moreland Community Association formally came out:** Letter to John H. Lawson, February 24, 1970, Local History Collection, Shaker Heights Public Library.

102   **The *Plain Dealer* reported:** "Moreland Busing Draws Opposition of Black Parents," *Plain Dealer*, February 24, 1970.

103   **He recalled being booed:** Lawson, "Memoirs," 54.

103   **The Western Reserve Women's Republican Club:** Postcard from the Western Reserve Women's Republican Club of Shaker Heights, Local History Collection, Shaker Heights Public Library.

103   **a newly formed Shaker Taxpayers Association:** "Lawson Pleased with Bus Response," *Sun Press*, May 14, 1970, Local History Collection, Shaker Heights Public Library.

103   **At one of the public meetings:** Leslie Kay, "Shaker Hts. Busing Poses Knotty Issue," *Plain Dealer*, March 8, 1970, Local History Collection, Shaker Heights Public Library.

103   **Hundreds of calls and letters:** Letters and memos recording calls on file in the Local History Collection, Shaker Heights Public Library.

106   **the Committee for Voluntary Cross-Enrollment:** "Preliminary Proposal of Committee for Voluntary Cross Enrollment," and letter to John H. Lawson from Oliver N. Edwards and John W. Horner, co-chairmen, March 16, 1970, District archives. Proposal is marked with notes by Lawson. Memos to Lawson from Mildred McFarland, March 23, 1970; W. Roger Snead, March 20, 1970; and Fredrick A. David, March 23, 1970, District archives.

108   **Thousands of Black teachers:** Greg Toppo, "Thousands of Black Teachers Lost Job," *USA Today*, April 28, 2004. In the eleven years immediately following *Brown*, more than 38,000 Black teachers and administrators in seventeen Southern and border states lost their jobs.

109   **A year after the plan began:** Letter to Dr. Edward McMillan from Mrs. Dorothy M. Uhlig, Center for Education Policy Research, Graduate School of Education, Harvard University, July 9, 1971; Memo to John H. Lawson from Edward L. McMillan Jr., July 14, 1971, including Lawson's handwritten response; Letter to Uhlig from McMillan, July 19, 1971, District archives.

111   **Participating in the plan:** Katherine and Doug McWilliams, interview with author, May 14, 2021.

111   **In September 1970, the school year began:** Peter Almond, "Shaker Schools Bus Plan Starts Smoothly," *Cleveland Press*, September 10, 1970.

112   **The district vigorously studied the plan's implementation:** "An Interim Evaluation of the Shaker Schools Plan," February 1972, District archives.

113   **Lawson and his aides were nervous:** School board president Herbert J. Hansell suggested postponing a parent survey about the busing plan until after the levy vote for fear of "reopening wounds." Letter from Herbert J. Hansell to Edward L. McMillan Jr., February 4, 1971, District archives.

114   **Since 1933, the schools had gone to the voters:** "History of School Issues for Shaker Heights City Schools," Local History Collection, Shaker Heights Public Library.

114   **In an interview decades later:** Larry Selhorst, interview with author, June 22, 2021.

114   **"integration is more of a cocktail party discussion topic":** Leslie Kay, "Shaker Hts. Integrates Via Busing and Housing," *Plain Dealer*, December 19, 1970.

114   **"I attended the School Board Meeting":** Letter to Lawson from Mrs. Robert Rich, May 8, 1970, Local History Collection, Shaker Heights Public Library.

114   **In 1975, the *New York Times*:** William K. Stevens, "An Integrated Suburb Thrives in Ohio," *New York Times*, October 18, 1975, 1.

115   **all the head custodians:** Lawson, "Memoirs," 133–34.

116   **a group of Black Moreland parents:** Lawson, "Memoirs," 142–43.

116   **Similarly, he told the story:** Lawson, "Memoirs," 148–49.

Chapter 7: Herlinda Bradley

117   **the racial balance almost perfectly reflected:** "Racial/Ethnic Report: 1964–1978–79, with Supporting Data," Shaker Heights City School District, submitted by Mark Freeman, November 1978, District archives. Charts showed the district overall was 37.7 percent minority; Sussex School was 37 percent.

118 **Shaker schools first offered Advanced Placement classes:** Anne Galletta, "Under One Roof, Through Many Doors: Understanding Racial Equality in an Unequal World" (dissertation submitted to the City University of New York, 2003), 165–66.

118 **In 1955, the district bragged:** "From the Superintendent's Desk: Editor Interviews Superintendent on Work for Gifted Children," *School Review*, December 1955, Local History Collection, Shaker Heights Public Library.

118 **a new and sweeping Levels of Instruction system:** "Levels of Instruction Inaugurated in Shaker," *School Review*, November 1964, Local History Collection, Shaker Heights Public Library.

119 **Byron created three levels for English:** "Woodbury Inaugurates Individual Pupil-Scheduling," *School Review*, October 1966, 3. Byron's new leveling is described in "September: The Year's at the Morn," *School Review*, September 1966, 3, Local History Collection, Shaker Heights Public Library.

121 **Alan Geismer:** Interview with author, July 27, 2021.

125 **Arthur J. Lelyveld:** Lawrence Van Gelder, "Rabbi Arthur L Lelyveld, 83, Rights Crusader," *New York Times*, April 16, 1996, https://www.nytimes.com/1996/04/16/us/rabbi-arthur-j-lelyveld-83-rights-crusader.html.

126 **informal concerns about the scant Black participation:** Galletta, "Under One Roof," 203–5.

126 **In the 1976–77 school year:** Galletta, "Under One Roof." Data cited by Galletta is from *Cleveland Press*, March 28, 1977, "Teachers Told to Increase Enrichment of Minorities."

126 **"These statistics are":** "Dear Colleagues," dictated and read by Dr. Freeman, February 17, 1977, District archives. The two-and-a-half-page letter, or perhaps speech text, is on file in the archives but there is no notation as to when or where this message was delivered.

126 **The district added programs:** "Selected Initiatives to Improve Student Achievement in Shaker Heights City Schools," Shaker Heights City School District, January 15, 1997, District archives.

127 **In 1978, PUSH Excel established an office:** "The PUSH for Excellence Concept Shaker Heights, OH; December, 1978–December, 1980," District archives.

127 **"What I was seeing":** Mary Lynne McGovern interview with author, November 28, 2017.

128 **In February 1980:** Letter to Curmie Price, education director of the Urban League of Cleveland, from Mark Freeman, February 22, 1980, District archives.

128 **The Urban League issued its report:** "Educational Tracking: The System's Response to Black Migration," Urban League of Greater Cleveland, District archives. Undated, but other documents and press coverage indicate it was released in the summer of 1980.

129 **Writing in the May 1980 *School Review*:** Jack P. Taylor, "The Leveling System: A Commitment to Excellence," *School Review*, May 1980, 1.

130 **In a position paper:** Galletta, "Under One Roof," 236. The district's position paper examined 1979–80 enrollment in order to refute the Urban League's claims that there were no Black students in level 5 classes. It found 26 Black students in level 5 English, 13 in level 5 science, 8 in level 5 social studies, and 12 in level 5 math.

Chapter 8: Winston Richie

133 **Winston Richie was back:** *Shaker Life, May 1987*, Shaker Life cable access television show, Local History Collection, Shaker Heights Public Library, https://youtu.be/7RlEWUxtcmM?t=1323.

135 **as the only Black player:** Jodie Valade, "Dad's Wisdom Helped WNBA Boss Blaze Her Own Trail," *Plain Dealer*, June 19, 2011, C1.

135 **He told the story of another Black man:** Cynthia Mills Richter, "Integrating the Suburban Dream: Shaker Heights, Ohio" (dissertation submitted to the University of Minnesota, December 1999), 78.

135 **When he married Beatrice Jourdain:** "Dr. Winston Richie Back with New England Bride," *Call & Post*, September 26, 1953, 1-B.

136 **"I strongly believed":** David G. Molyneaux and Sue Sackman, eds., *75 Years: An Informal History of Shaker Heights* (Shaker Heights, OH: Shaker Heights Public Library, 1987), 83.

137 **in June 1964, the company would not approve the sale:** Letter to James J. Dougherty from James B. Lewis, president of the Van Sweringen Company, June 4, 1964, Shaker Law Department, Box 153.

137 **One of the first neighbors he approached:** Molyneaux and Sackman, *75 Years*, 84; Virginia P. Dawson, "Protection from Undesirable Neighbors: The Use Deed Restrictions in Shaker Heights, Ohio," *Journal of Planning History* 18, no. 2 (May 2019): 23–24.

138 **Two years after the Van Sweringen Company forced:** Letter to Lewis from Winston Richie, May 26, 1966, Shaker Law Department, Box 153.

138 **In May 1967, he published:** *Ludlow Notes, News & Neighbors*, May 29, 1967, container 3, folder 4, MS 3662 Ludlow Community Association Records, Western Reserve Historical Society, Cleveland, OH.

138 **The move to Mercer made a dramatic impact:** Interview by author with Winston, Beth, Laurel, and Anne Richie, February 13, 2022.

138 **Records for the previous school year:** Untitled chart showing total enrollment and Black enrollment by school, District archives.

140 **In 1971, St. Ann's Church:** "Blacks, Whites Being 'Steered' in Housing Here, Audit Shows," *Sun Press*, September 7, 1972.

141 **The study was circulated widely:** Jean McCann, "A Congregation Divided: Some at St. Ann Unhappy About Housing Study," *Plain Dealer*, January 13, 1973.

141 **formed in 1962 by activists in Ludlow:** "Equal Rights Realty Sales Office Set," *Plain Dealer*, May 1, 1962, 7; Marcus Gleisser, "Realty Firm Plans Sales to Minorities," *Plain Dealer*, October 15, 1963, 1.

141 **"We've got to urge Negroes":** "Checkerboard Communities—Pattern for Living," *Newsweek*, April 25, 1966, 89.

142 **"too militant":** Molyneaux and Sackman, *75 Years*, 84.

142 **"I think by that time":** Molyneaux and Sackman, *75 Years*, 84.

142 **He told the *Call & Post*:** "IN SHAKER HGTS.: Winston Richie to Run for City Council Seat," *Call & Post*, July 24, 1971, 13-B.

144 **An early flare went up in 1972:** Richter, "Integrating the Suburban Dream," 91.

144 **They interpreted the city's response:** Elizabeth Quigley, "Why Did the Barricades Cross the Road? Integration Maintenance and Race Relations in Shaker Heights, Ohio," History 480, Davidson College, December 6, 2020, Shaker Heights Public Library Local History collection. Public letter from the employees read in part: "It was the growing ambiguity of whether the housing office was about integration or containment which caused us to ask for a clarification of policy. It was the clarification in favor of containment which forced us to resign en masse April 9."

145 **In April 1979:** Arnie Rosenberg, "Shaker Drafts New Housing Office Policy," *Sun Press*, April 19, 1979.

145 **A few months later, the controversy:** Stephen Alfred, "Promoting Integration Results in Inequality," letter to the editor, *Sun Press*, October 7, 1979.

145 **Tom Webb, a city councilman:** "SPECIAL MEETING, June 19, 1980, LCA Board and members of Shaker Housing Office Governing Committee," District archives. Webb defended Anderson during a meeting between the Ludlow Community Association and city officials, according to the minutes, though details were not recorded.

145 **That month, the Ludlow Community Association board:** "SPECIAL MEETING, June 19, 1980."

147 **"The more traffic on a street":** Quigley, "Why Did the Barricades," 15.

147 **"I think that if we could solve the race problems":** Richter, "Integrating the Suburban Dream," 107.

148 **In March, the City Council:** Description of the March 13, 1982, meeting, its agenda, atten-

dance, and background, are included in memo and attachments sent to the school board, City Council, Mayor Walter Kelley, and school superintendent Jack Taylor, March 5, 1982, from the Housing Office Governing Board. District archives.

148 **Members left the session convinced:** Memo to Housing Office Governing Board from Tom Webb, reporting on the March 13 meeting, March 22, 1982, District archives.

148 **soon after, Anderson was forced to resign:** Judy Ernest, "Community Services Head Is Dedicated to Integration," *Sun Press*, September 30, 1982. Anderson had support from Mayor Kelley but was forced out by City Council and the school board.

148 **Interviewed thirteen years later:** Richter, "Integrating the Suburban Dream," 97.

149 **"will serve all areas of the City":** "Housing Governing Board: Reorganization Plan," April 1982, District archives.

149 **In May 1983, the Justice Department opened:** Department of Justice, "Remarks of Wm. Bradford Reynolds" before the National Bar Association, August 9, 1983, District archives.

149 **"Mr. Reynolds' approach":** Letter to Congressman Louis Stokes from Donald L. DeMarco, August 30, 1984, with notation that same letter was sent to Senators John Glenn and Howard Metzenbaum, District archives.

150 **Shaker hired Don DeMarco:** Judy Ernest, "Community Services Head Is Dedicated to Integration," *Sun Press*, September 9, 1982, Local History Collection, Shaker Heights Public Library.

150 **"I am dedicated to integration":** Ernest, "Community Services Head Is Dedicated to Integration."

150 **Many years later, DeMarco recalled:** Don DeMarco, interview with author, December 27, 2021.

150 **In an interview with the *Sun Press*:** Ernest, "Community Services Head Is Dedicated to Integration."

150 **A few months later, he told the *Sun Press*:** Judy Ernest, "Shaker to Encourage Other Suburbs to Foster Integration," *Sun Press*, December 16, 1982, Local History Collection, Shaker Heights Public Library.

150 **In July 1983, Shaker Heights:** Mike Marcellino, "Group to Promote Area's Racial Mix," *Sun Press*, July 7, 1983, Local History Collection, Shaker Heights Public Library.

151 **"I have support in all of the city's neighborhoods":** "Black Gains in Shaker Linked to Winston Richie," *Call & Post*, November 3, 1983, 1-A.

151 **Nonetheless, the *Call & Post* endorsed Stephen Alfred:** "Alfred for Shaker Heights Mayor," *Call & Post*, November 3, 1983, 8-A.

152 **Richie threw himself into this new line of work:** Terri Doyle, "Area Group Hears of Efforts Toward Peaceful Integration," *Sun Press*, October 18, 1984; and Megan Harding, "Hillcrest Office Set for ESCOC," *Sun Press*, December 27, 1984, Local History Collection, Shaker Heights Public Library.

152 **Working with Black agents:** *Shaker Life, May 1987* video.

153 **Local officials were not particularly excited:** Richter, "Integrating the Suburban Dream," 104, citing Madeleine Fletcher and Karen Wilbourn, "Integration: Hillcrest Defensive About Planning for It," *Sun Press*, February 28, 1980, 1-A.

154 **In 1985, the City of Shaker Heights added a fresh strategy:** W. Dennis Keating, *The Suburban Racial Dilemma: Housing and Neighborhoods* (Philadelphia: Temple University Press, 1994),105–6.

154 **(The Fund for the Future continued until 2012):** Jane Wood, "Fund for the Future of SH Goes out of Business," *This Week in Shaker*, April 30, 2012. The leftover money was donated to the nonprofit Shaker Heights Development Corporation.

154 **This program helped Shaker:** The prize was awarded by the Innovations in State and Local Government Awards Program at Harvard University's John F. Kennedy School of Government, https://ash.harvard.edu/news/racial-integration-incentives.

154 **Richmond Heights schools:** "Innovations in Government Awards," January 1, 1988, https://ash.harvard.edu/news/racial-integration-incentives.

154   **Richie resigned:** Benjamin Marrison, "ESCOC Director Quits 'Frustrated' by Segregation," *Plain Dealer*, October 26, 1990.

155   **In 1997, he sold more than $3 million worth:** Grant Segall, "Dr. Winston Richie, Shaker Heights Councilman, Integration Pioneer, Dies at 90," *Plain Dealer*, February 16, 2016.

Chapter 9: Emily Hooper

156   **John Gray didn't mind offending people:** The request for an event like this is laid out in a letter to Superintendent Peter Horoschak from Kaffie Weaver, coordinator of Woodbury Concerned Parents, December 7, 1982, District archives. Documents indicate there was extensive planning ahead of this event, with Horoschak watching Ted Paynther's presentation at a neighboring district ahead of time and a plan for follow-up conversations involving parents, students, and faculty.

159   **"It hurt her an awful lot":** Cynthia Mills Richter, "Integrating the Suburban Dream: Shaker Heights, Ohio" (dissertation submitted to the University of Minnesota, December 1999), 195.

165   **In an essay for *Shaker Life* magazine:** Terry Pollack, essay in "A History of Looking Ahead: The Shaker Schools Celebrate 100 Years," https://www.shaker.org/Downloads/Schools%20Celebrate%20100%20Years.pdf.

166   **government teacher Jerry Graham:** Letter from Jerry Graham to Dr. Horoschak, October 9, 1984, District archives.

166   **Another memo around this time:** "Supt's Professional Advisory Council Loose End," Memo to Dr. Horoschak from Bill Newby, November 27, 1984, District archives.

166   **One "concept strategy" proposal:** "Concept of a Strategy to Improve Academic Achievement in the Shaker Heights City School District," Prepared by John Addison, October 1984, District archives.

167   **they submitted a formal proposal:** "Student Group Report to the Principals Concerning the Improvement of Race Relations in the Shaker Heights School System," July 14, 1983, District archives. The proposal was signed by Brad Albert, Ken Danford, Ruth Diener, Herman Graham, James Hexter, Emily Hooper, Tia Melton, Darleen Pope, Marleen Pope, BerRonica Steele, Michele Thomas, Darrin Thorton, Robert Ware, Alan Weiss, and Robert Weissman.

Chapter 10: Carolyn Milter

170   **The schools were facing a huge budget shortfall:** "Shaker to Limit School Spending," *Plain Dealer*, February 9, 1983, 8-E.

170   **but some Shaker residents:** David Beard, "Battle of Levies Comes to Shaker," *Plain Dealer*, May 29, 1983, 1-A.

170   **Within weeks of the levy's defeat:** "School Facilities Utilization Study Committee: Report to the Shaker Heights Board of Education," June 12, 1984, Local History Collection, Shaker Heights Public Library.

172   **(In fact, whites would rapidly depart):** W. Dennis Keating, *The Suburban Racial Dilemma: Housing and Neighborhoods* (Philadelphia: Temple University Press, 1994), 77.

172   **"They really didn't have to sell me on it":** Cynthia Mills Richter, "Integrating the Suburban Dream: Shaker Heights, Ohio" (dissertation submitted to the University of Minnesota, December 1999), 235.

173   **The Shaker Schools Plan:** Lois Cooper, "Asks Integration Plan," *Sun Press*, November 25, 1976, 1-A.

173   **In 1974, the Supreme Court had set a high bar:** Milliken v. Bradley, *Oyez*, www.oyez.org/cases/1973/73-434. The Court held that courts could not order regional desegregation plans if they did not find intentional discrimination on the part of the outlying, or suburban, districts.

173   **the NAACP asked the court:** Anne Galletta, "Under One Roof, Through Many Doors: Understanding Racial Equality in an Unequal World" (dissertation submitted to the City University of New York, 2003), 178.

173   **some thought Battisti might go along:** Channel 5 news report, February 11, 1976, archived in the Cleveland Memory Project, Reed v. Rhodes collection, http://flash.ulib.csuohio.edu /cmp/jcu/jcu008.html. In the news report, an analyst said, "Now you don't have to be a geographer to know the Black neighborhoods are a lot closer to some eastern suburbs than to the city of Cleveland's far west side, so busing to suburbs might seem to make some sense."

173   **Superintendent Jack Taylor:** Jack P. Taylor, "The Battisti Decision . . ." Intra-Staff Communication, September 1976, District archives.

174   **Later that month, Taylor spoke:** Cooper, "Asks Integration Plan."

174   **In June 1977:** "Hearings Before the Subcommittee on Elementary, Secondary, and Vocational Education of the Committee on Education and Labor, House of Representatives, on H.R. 15," June 14–16, 1977 (Washington, D.C.: U.S. Government Printing Office, 1977), https://books.google.ca/books?id=0S_RAAAAMAAJ e.

174   **In June 1978:** Ohio State Board of Education and the Kirwan Institute for the Student of Race and Ethnicity at Ohio State University, "Diversity Strategies for Successful Schools: Recommendations," September 12, 2011, https://education.ohio.gov/getattachment /State-Board/State-Board-Reports-and-Policies/Diversity-Strategies-Policy/Diversity -Strategies-Report-Final-Recommendations-9–12–11.pdf.aspx.

175   **the Black population in the schools continued to climb:** Jack P. Taylor, "State Guidelines for Desegregation," memo to school board, January 5, 1981, District archives.

175   **The voluntary busing and magnet programs:** "A Review of School and Housing Integration Data in Shaker Heights and Strategies to Improve School Integration Through Housing Policy and a Special Report on Data and Data Needs Related to School and Housing Integration," Shaker Heights City School District, table 1, p. 19, Local History Collection, Shaker Heights Public Library.

175   **Nonetheless, concerns were voiced:** Galletta, "Under One Roof," 255.

175   **"Virtually no other district":** Art Steller, "Progress of Desegregation," memo to Board of Education members, approved by Jack Taylor, June 28, 1982, District archives.

175   **This was driven home:** Carolyn Milter, "Growing Up White in a (Largely) Black Elementary School," *Plain Dealer*, April 11, 1977.

177   **At a community meeting about the committee's work:** "Shaker Heights School Closings Meetings Tape 1 of 2," Shaker Heights Cable Access Television, Local History Collection, Shaker Heights Public Library, https://youtu.be/BciTiLhmjbQ.

179   **The school board mostly punted:** George E. Jordan, "Shaker Hts. Board Ends Classes at Woodbury Next Fall," *Plain Dealer*, September 26, 1984.

181   **Sears also wrote a letter to the editor:** Kathy Sears, "Keep Moreland Open," *Plain Dealer*, February 6, 1987, 12-B.

181   **"If we had known they were going to close the school":** Tom Breckenridge, "Shaker Heights Agonizing over Closing of Four Schools," *Plain Dealer*, March 8, 1987, 1-B.

182   **Leiken received about thirty phone calls:** Breckenridge, "Shaker Heights Agonizing over Closing of Four Schools."

183   **Some 250 people crowded into the high school auditorium:** Tom Breckenridge, "Shaker to Close 4 Grade Schools," *Plain Dealer*, March 11, 1987, 1-A.

183   **In the years that followed:** Gary Orfield and Danielle Jarvie, "Black Segregation Matters," Civil Rights Project, December 2020, https://www.civilrightsproject.ucla.edu/research/k -12-education/integration-and-diversity/black-segregation-matters-school-resegregation -and-black-educational-opportunity/BLACK-SEGREGATION-MATTERS-final-121820 .pdf.

185   **In 1967, Ernie and Jackie Tinsley:** Interview with Carolyn Milter by author, January 5, 2022; see also Sue Starrett, "The Straw Buy," *Shaker Life*, August/September 2012, 43–44 and 61, https://shaker.life/wp-content/uploads/2017/04/Aug-Sep_2012_Shaker -Life.pdf.

185   **with a pro bono attorney:** The pro bono attorney who handled the case was Byron Krantz, according to Carolyn Milter.

Chapter 11: Reuben Harris Jr.

189   **settled on his replacement without a search:** "Shaker Schools Chief," *Plain Dealer*, June 2, 1988, 7-B.

190   **the *Shakerite* reported familiar statistics:** "Imbalance Reaches High Level," *Shakerite*, April 14, 1988.

190   **By 1988, the Student Group on Race Relations had grown:** Steve Lee, "SGORR Prides Itself on Increased Membership, Student Interest," *Shakerite*, December 15, 1988.

191   **she recalled years later:** Interview with Mary Lynne McGovern, November 28, 2017, Shaker Heights High School.

192   **In January 1997, Freeman wrote the committee:** Letter to Project Achieve participants from Mark Freeman, January 22, 1997, Reuben Harris files, Local History Collection, Shaker Heights Public Library.

194   **The story was published on a Thursday:** Jeff Sikorovsky, "The Power of the Pen: Shakerite Article Offends Blacks," *Sun Press*, March 6, 1997, 1-A, District archives.

194   **Principal Jack Rumbaugh sent a letter:** A. Jack Rumbaugh, letter to High School Parents and Guardians, February 28, 1997, Reuben Harris files, Local History Collection, Shaker Heights Public Library.

195   **addressed the school over the PA system:** Sikorovsky, "The Power of the Pen."

195   **a conversation that stretched two and a half hours:** Carole McElrath, "Shakerite Omitted Positives, Stressed Negatives of Blacks," *Cleveland Jewish News*, March 14, 1997, District archives.

195   **One Black girl:** *Shaker Heights: The Struggle for Integration*, directed and produced by Stuart Math (Independent Television Service, 1997), 1:30 to 5:33.

197   **The investigation was not prompted by a complaint:** Felicity Hill, "Government Studies AP Class Make-Up," *Sun Press*, May 29, 1997, Reuben Harris files, Local History Collection, Shaker Heights Public Library.

197   **In a follow-up letter:** Letter from David Millstone of Squire, Sanders & Dempsey, January 7, 1997, Local History Collection, Shaker Heights Public Library.

198   **The Reverend Marvin McMickle:** Jesse Tinsley, "Grim Numbers; Shaker Residents Unite for Task of Bridging the Gap Between Black and White Students," *Plain Dealer*, March 16, 1997, 1-A, Reuben Harris files, Local History Collection, Shaker Heights Public Library.

199   **who had gained prominence:** Felicia R. Lee, "Why Are Black Students Lagging?" *New York Times*, November 30, 2002, B-9, https://www.nytimes.com/2002/11/30/arts/why-are-black-students-lagging.html.

200   **The district would spend $14,000:** Rosa Maria Santana, "Shaker's Academic Gap Gets Close Look; Author's Conclusions on Black, White Pupils Bring Intense Debate," *Plain Dealer*, January 5, 2003, 1-A, Reuben Harris files, Local History Collection, Shaker Heights Public Library.

200   **Ogbu was excited about the opportunity:** Susan Goldsmith, "Rich, Black, Flunking: Cal Professor John Ogbu Thinks He Knows Why Rich Black Kids Are Failing in School. Nobody Wants to Hear It," *East Bay Express*, May 21, 2003, https://eastbayexpress.com/rich-black-flunking-1/.

200   **In a meeting with counselors:** Transcript of Ogbu interview with school counselors, circa May 30, 1997, Reuben Harris files, Local History Collection, Shaker Heights Public Library.

200   **In one discussion with students:** Transcript of Ogbu interview.

202   **Ogbu's book drew national attention:** Santana, "Shaker's Academic Gap Gets Close Look."

203   **Ferguson's findings:** Michael Winerip, "Closing the Achievement Gap Without Widening a

Racial One," *New York Times*, February 14, 2011; "Facts on Achievement Gaps," Achievement Gap Initiative at Harvard University.

206   **In a speech at a local church:** Draft of remarks, Reuben Harris files, Local History Collection, Shaker Heights Public Library.

208   **In a letter to colleagues:** Steven Fox, "To my colleagues," April 7, 1997, Reuben Harris files, Local History Collection, Shaker Heights Public Library.

209   **Fox said she did not:** Carol Fox, interview with author, July 21, 2022.

Chapter 12: Gregory Hutchings Jr.

213   **In September 2012, Freeman read the room:** "Longtime Shaker Heights Superintendent to Step Down," *Plain Dealer*, September 5, 2012, 2-B.

213   **Hutchings, who is Black, had been in a hurry:** StoryCorps interview with Gregory Hutchings Jr., May 20, 2013, https://youtu.be/ll_sOV6vXxQ.

213   **Greg's grades and test scores were middling:** Gregory C. Hutchings Jr. and Douglas S. Reed, *Getting into Good Trouble at School: A Guide to Building an Antiracist School System* (Thousand, Oaks, CA: Corwin, 2022), 2; and StoryCorps interview with Gregory Hutchings Jr.

214   **(where he dropped his premed plans):** Dr. Gregory C. Hutchings Jr.'s farewell interview with Leon Bibb, May 10, 2018, https://youtu.be/NLDMb_8G6rM.

214   **As he read the leadership profile:** StoryCorps interview.

214   **was invited to a public interview:** "Dr. Gregory C. Hutchings, Community Superintendent Candidate Session," March 14, 2013, https://youtu.be/MBY5W3gUCXE.

219   **Between 2000 and 2010, census data shows:** "Demographic Trends 2000 to 2018," provided by Kamla Lewis, former director of Neighborhood Revitalization, Shaker Heights, OH.

220   **In 1989, the first year for which census data:** "1990 Census of Population: Social and Economic Characteristics: Ohio," 1990 CP-2–37. Data on median income: Table 186, p. 895; Data on poverty: Table 187, p. 913. In unadjusted dollars, the median white household income was $60,855; the median Black household income was $37,755.

221   **For years, younger students had traveled:** Jennifer Proe, "In Shaker Schools, Science Is Elementary," *Shaker Life*, October/November 2013, https://www.shaker.org/Downloads/K-4%20Science%20Feature.pdf?fbclid=IwAR2pkrLR-bgxY8GcFqQD4scGbBo6kL8wbusF_uLq6zlFKLexDFFl4zR-UHk.

221   **In April 2017, the administration announced:** Gregory C. Hutchings Jr., Board of Education Memorandum, "Woodbury Science Lab (Pre-K through 6)," April 21, 2017, https://www.boarddocs.com/oh/shaker/Board.nsf/files/ALMSZZ6807C8.

221   **The response from many in the community was sharply negative:** For example, a post about the decision on the Living in Shaker Heights Facebook group drew 246 comments, the vast majority critical.

221   **helped launch an online petition:** "Shaker Heights K-4 Science Lab Coordinator and Field Trips," Lisa Cremer, petition author, https://www.change.org/p/sh-shaker-heights-k-4-science-lab-coordinator-and-field-trips.

224   **An incident in January 2015:** Editorial Board, "'Rite Idea: District Let Down Lomond Students," *Shakerite*, March 4, 2015, https://shakerite.com/opinion/district-let-down-lomond-students/04/2015.

228   **In April 2015, Griffith announced:** Abby White, "After Griffith Announces Resignation, Sorrow, Respect Hang Heavy," *Shakerite*, April 13, 2015, https://shakerite.com/campus-and-city/after-griffith-announces-resignation-sorrow-respect-hang-heavy/13/2015/.

228   **A February 2015 survey of 137 teachers:** Tony Cuda, "Faculty Senate Survey," conducted February 3–6, 2017.

229   **In May 2015:** High School Members of the Shaker Heights Teachers' Association, "An Open Letter to the Shaker Heights City School Board, Central Administration, and Community," May 13, 2015; *SHTA News*, May 19, 2015, 27, http://www.shtaweb.org/media/1121/may%20newsletter,%202015.pdf.

229 **Lara Mullen, a white mom of two:** Laura Meckler, "This Trail-Blazing Suburb Has Tried for 60 Years to Tackle Race. What If Trying Isn't Enough?" *Washington Post*, October 11, 2019, https://www.washingtonpost.com/education/2019/10/11/this-trail-blazing -suburb-has-tried-years-tackle-race-what-if-trying-isnt-enough/.

231 **Both candidates were also endorsed:** Editorial Board, "'Rite Idea: Cremer, Hardaway and Weingart for Board of Education," *Shakerite*, October 28, 2017. The second woman backed by the parent group was Heather Weingart.

233 **During a public farewell interview:** Hutchings interview with Bibb.

233 **A check of seven other diverse Ohio districts:** Archived state report card data available at https://reportcard.education.ohio.gov/archives. Other diverse districts looked at were Cleveland Heights–University Heights, South Euclid–Lyndhurst, Princeton City, Finney-town, Columbus City, Whitehall, and Reynoldsburg.

234 **The policy was approved by the board:** "Minutes of the February 12, 2019, Regular Board of Education Meeting," https://www.shaker.org/Downloads/RegMtg%2021219%20 final%20jh2.pdf.

Chapter 13: Olivia McDowell and Jody Podl

235 **"We need people in power who listen":** Editorial Board, "'Rite Idea: The Stakes Have Never Been Higher," *Shakerite*, December 21, 2018, https://shakerite.com/top-stories /stakes-have-never-been-higher/21/2018/.

235 **Olivia McDowell was feeling sleepy:** Olivia McDowell's version of events based on her statement to the school district, October 9, 2018, and several interviews with author. Jody Podl's version of events from memo from Podl to Marla Robinson, October 22, 2018, and several interviews with author. The text notes where their recollections differ; otherwise, their versions were identical or very similar.

240 **which lasted about nine minutes:** Email from Sara Chengelis to Marla Robinson, October 11, 2018, with time stamps of Olivia McDowell and Jody Podl's movements that afternoon.

242 **District officials took the complaint seriously:** "Investigative Report," which includes details of the district's investigation.

242 **On October 9, more than two weeks after the incident:** "List Timeline of Actions" and Olivia McDowell statement, investigation report, Shaker Heights City School District.

243 **(there had recently been a case):** Adam Ferrise, "Disgraced Shaker Heights Teacher Gets Prison Time for Having Sex with Student 22 Years Ago," Cleveland.com, October 12, 2017, https://www.cleveland.com/metro/2017/10/beloved_ex-shaker_heights_teac .html.

245 **Just the previous spring:** Email from parent to Gregory C. Hutchings, May 29, 2018, included in investigation report.

245 **Soon after this, Kuehnle himself was reassigned:** Jane Kaufman, "Shaker Heights Prin-cipal Reassigned Following Complaint," *Cleveland Jewish News*, March 20, 2019, https:// www.clevelandjewishnews.com/news/local_news/shaker-heights-principal-reassigned -following-complaint/article_f2e97e0c-4b67-11e9-bb9b-2f070030447f.html#1.

246 **As soon as she sat down:** "In the Matter of Arbitration Between Shaker Heights Teachers Association and Shaker Heights City School District," transcript of arbitration hearing held on February 12, 2019; John Morris, "SHTA HS Communication: Jody Podl," email to SHTA members, November 7, 2018.

248 **The meeting started badly:** Quotes from and description of the meeting come from video posted on Facebook by Fox 8 News and a transcript created and posted by the *Shakerite*, https://www.facebook.com/Fox8NewsCleveland/videos/1936671206420915/ and https:// shakerite.com/campus-and-city/nov-8–2018-meeting/12/2018/.

256 **An arbitration hearing:** Arbitration transcript.

261 **Bradley insisted, in fact:** Interview with author, April 15, 2019.

Chapter 14: David Glasner

263   **"It's an opportunity to do things":** Rahm Emanuel interview, "Never Let a Good Crisis Go to Waste," *Wall Street Journal*, CEO Council, 2008, https://youtu.be/Pb-YuhFWCr4.

266   **For his dissertation, Glasner studied math education:** David P. Glasner, "The Impact of Tracking Students in Mathematics on Middle School Student Achievement Outcomes," (unpublished dissertation, Cleveland State University, 2018), https://engagedscholarship .csuohio.edu/cgi/viewcontent.cgi?article=2112&context=etdarchive.

269   **Academic tracking was introduced in America:** Maureen T. Hallinan, "The Detracking Movement," *Education Next* 4, no. 4 (June 30, 2006), https://www.educationnext.org/the -detracking-movement/.

269   **school districts began experimenting:** Laura Meckler, "Can Honors and Regular Students Learn Math Together? A New Approach Argues Yes," *Washington Post*, June 4, 2021, https://www.washingtonpost.com/education/2021/06/04/california-math-class-detrack -race-equity/.

269   **Federal data shows:** Tom Loveless, "Does Detracking Promote Educational Equity?" *Brown Center Chalkboard*, October 4, 2021. Data from the 2019 "12th Grade National Assessment of Educational Progress Mathematics Assessment," https://www.brookings.edu/blog /brown-center-chalkboard/2021/10/04/does-detracking-promote-educational-equity/.

270   **Research published in 2019:** Allison Attebury et al., "Opening the Gates: Detracking and the International Baccalaureate," *Teachers College Record*, September 2019, https://www .colorado.edu/education/sites/default/files/attached-files/openingthegates_tcr_2019 _1008.pdf.

270   **Ron Ferguson, the Harvard professor:** Interview with author, April 9, 2022.

272   **Data from Ohio's 2021–22 state report cards:** Ohio School Report Cards, https:// reportcard.education.ohio.gov/home. Shaker demographics and test results were compared with those of seventeen other racially diverse Ohio districts.

274   **(One parent featured in the district's own video):** Shaker Rising Video Project, Video #5: Sangeeta Prakash, https://www.shaker.org/ShakerRisingVideoProject.aspx.

Chapter 15: Eric Juli

292   **In Evanston, Illinois, students from marginalized groups:** Douglas Belkin and Lee Hawkins, "Can School Be 'Antiracist'? A New Superintendent in Evanston, Ill., Has a Plan," *Wall Street Journal*, October 6, 2020, https://www.wsj.com/articles/can-school-be -antiracist-a-new-superintendent-in-evanston-ill-has-a-plan-11601982001.

292   **Changes to how grades were administered:** Valerie Strauss and Donna St. George, "Teachers Second-Guess Letter Grades as They Search for a Better Way," *Washington Post*, February 28, 2022, https://www.washingtonpost.com/education/2022/02/28/letter-grades -grading-a-f/.

292   **Los Angeles and San Diego Unified:** Paloma Esquivel, "Faced with Soaring Ds and Fs, Schools Are Ditching the Old Way of Grading," *Los Angeles Times*, November 8, 2021, https://www.latimes.com/california/story/2021-11-08/as-ds-and-fs-soar-schools-ditch -inequitable-grade-systems.

293   **One of the people driving the change nationally:** Joe Feldman, *Grading for Equity: What It Is, Why It Matters, and How It Can Transform Schools and Classrooms* (Thousand Oaks, CA: Corwin, 2018), xxi–xxii.

Chapter 16: Kathleen FitzSimons

305   **(he'd been sentenced to ten years):** "Man Sentenced to 10 Years for Killing Friend with Survival Tool," 19 News, September 27, 2005. Andre Smith, the son of former Cleveland Cavalier Bobby "Bingo" Smith, was sentenced to ten years in prison.

https://www.cleveland19.com/story/3904808/man-sentenced-to-10-years-for-killing-friend-with-survival-tool/.

Chapter 17: Kim Harris

310   **an accident caused during work on the roof:** Thomas Jewell, "Shaker Heights Rules Fernway School Fire Cause as Accidental, Equipment-Related," Cleveland.com, September 14, 2018, https://www.cleveland.com/shaker-heights/2018/09/shaker_rules_fernway_school_fi.html#:~:text=%22The%20ignition%20source%20for%20this,14.

311   **In an article about Fernway:** Scott Stephens, "The Rebirth of Fernway," *Shaker Life*, Fall 2020, https://shaker.life/schools/the-rebirth-of-fernway/.

313   **Black students were more likely to qualify for busing:** "Bussing Data," a district-produced spreadsheet, showed that in 2021–22, 68 percent of those eligible for busing—meaning they lived a certain distance from their assigned school—were Black or multiracial, while just 54 percent of all Shaker students were Black or multiracial. That 14 percentage point gap was halved when Fernway Elementary School, which had the biggest gap, was taken out of the equation.

323   **Hooker's journey to Shaker Heights:** Interview with Tasha Hooker, August 13, 2022, Cleveland, OH.

Chapter 18: Dream Town Revisited

336   **"We are responsible for our own ignorance":** Isabel Wilkerson, *Caste: The Origins of Our Discontents* (New York: Random House, 2020), 388.

SELECTED BIBLIOGRAPHY

Dawson, Virginia P. "Protection from Undesirable Neighbors: The Use Deed Restrictions in Shaker Heights, Ohio." *Journal of Planning History* 18, no. 2 (May 2019).

Frankenberg, Erica, and Gary Orfield (editors). *The Resegregation of Suburban Schools: A Hidden Crisis in American Education*. Cambridge, MA: Harvard Education Press, 2012.

Haberman, Ian S. *The Van Sweringens of Cleveland: The Biography of an Empire*. Cleveland, OH: Western Reserve Historical Society, 1979.

Harwood, Herbert H., Jr. *Invisible Giants: The Empires of Cleveland's Van Sweringen Brothers*. Bloomington: Indiana University Press, 2003.

Hutchings, Gregory C., Jr., and Douglas S. Reed. *Getting into Good Trouble at School: A Guide to Building an Antiracist School System*. Thousand, Oaks, CA: Corwin, 2022.

Jackson, Kenneth T. *Crabgrass Frontier: The Suburbanization of the United States*. New York: Oxford University Press, 1985.

Johnson, Rucker C. *Children of the Dream: Why School Integration Works*. New York: Hachette Book Group, 2019.

Kaeser, Susan. *Resisting Segregation: Cleveland Heights Activists Shape Their Community, 1964–1976.* University Heights, OH: Cleveland Landmarks Press, 2020.

Keating, W. Dennis. *The Suburban Racial Dilemma: Housing and Neighborhoods.* Philadelphia: Temple University Press, 1994.

Kusmer, Kenneth L. *A Ghetto Takes Shape: Black Cleveland, 1870–1930.* Champaign: University of Illinois Press, 1976.

Lawson, John H. "Jack Lawson's Memoirs." Unpublished, 2000. Provided to author by Lawson's son, John Lawson.

Lewis, Amanda E., and John B. Diamond. *Despite the Best Intentions: How Racial Inequality Thrives in Good Schools.* New York: Oxford University Press, 2015.

Marshall, Bruce T. *Images of America: Shaker Heights.* Arcadia Publishing, 2006.

Michney, Todd M. *Surrogate Suburbs: Black Upward Mobility and Neighborhood Change in Cleveland, 1900–1980.* Chapel Hill: University of North Carolina Press, 2017.

Molyneaux, David G., and Sue Sackman, eds. *75 Years: An Informal History of Shaker Heights.* Shaker Heights, OH: Shaker Heights Public Library, 1987.

Ogbu, John U. *Black American Students in an Affluent Suburb: A Study of Academic Disengagement.* Hillsdale, NJ: Lawrence Erlbaum Associates, 2003.

Rothstein, Richard. *The Color of Law: A Forgotten History of How Our Government Segregated America.* New York: Liveright Publishing, 2017.

Weeks, Kent, and Karen Weeks. "A Suburb Faces Its Future." Unpublished, ca. 1968. Local History collection, Shaker Heights Public Library.

Wiese, Andrew. *Places of Their Own: African American Suburbanization in the Twentieth Century.* Chicago: University of Chicago Press, 2004.

Wilkerson, Isabel. *The Warmth of Other Suns: The Epic Story of America's Great Migration.* New York: Vintage Books, 2010.

ACKNOWLEDGMENTS

My gratitude begins with the people who helped me bring alive the past, in particular the children of those featured here who are no longer living. That includes Bill and Laura Barnett; John Lawson; and Winston, Beth, Laurel, and Anne Richie, who helped me tell the stories of their remarkable parents.

Among this group is Paul Mason, to whom I owe a special thanks. In addition to sharing his parents' story, he helped me more broadly as I reported and wrote this book, understanding what I was trying to do, offering encouragement when I really needed it, along with wise counsel and countless big and small suggestions that improved the final product.

My profound thanks as well go to the book's central characters who are living today and allowed me into their work and lives, sometimes in deeply personal ways. Thank you to Herlinda Bradley, Emily Hooper Lansana (and also Earline, Sam, and Paula Hooper), Carolyn Milter, Reuben Harris Jr., Gregory Hutchings Jr., Jody Podl, Olivia McDowell, David Glasner, Eric Juli, Kathleen FitzSimons, and Kim Harris. So many others helped me as well, though I owe a special thanks to Mark Freeman and John Morris, who answered countless questions with good cheer.

Two sources for this book died while I was working on the project. I am eternally grateful that I had the chance to talk with the Rev. Albert M. Pennybacker Jr., an inspiring leader. And my deepest values and earliest memories were shaped by another extraordinary person, Diane Lardie, my next-door neighbor when I was a child.

My thanks also to Mark Joseph, another source for the book, who offered insightful perspective, advice, and encouragement.

Shaker Heights had been studied and written about many times before I came along, and my work stands on the shoulders of previous researchers. I relied on the academic dissertations of Cynthia Richter and Anne Galletta, as well as the work of Virginia Dawson, who did groundbreaking research on the original housing restrictions in Shaker Heights and from whom I learned of the Klain papers, an important primary source.

Scott Stephens, the school district's communications director, proved time and again that while he may be a spokesman now, he retains the heart of the journalist he was for many years. Over five years of my reporting on the schools, he facilitated access to countless officials and troves of documents, and I am forever grateful for his help. My thanks also to Laurie Brem, whose title is senior administrative assistant at Shaker Heights High School but whose knowledge and skills go well beyond that. She helped make every one of my visits to the high school more pleasant and productive.

If you read the acknowledgments section of any work regarding Shaker Heights, you are bound to spot the name Meghan Hays, the supremely talented and helpful local history librarian at the Shaker Heights Public Library. She has built and nourished the library's significant collection of documents (on paper and online) and is a true treasure for this community. She's also just a really nice person.

My thanks to Ann Sindelar at the Western Reserve Historical Society, which holds a vast and fascinating collection of material on Shaker Heights and the greater Cleveland area. Ann helped me find my way through the collections with good cheer. Thanks as well to Brianna Treleven at the Shaker Historical Society, who helped me with early Shaker history. And thank you to Joe Blake, who wrote his senior thesis on the Van Sweringen brothers back in 1968 and has developed a true expertise on their lives, which he generously shared with me.

I had expert help from Tom Shroder, Sean Lavery, and Sydney Trent. Two recently graduated Shaker students, Chethan Chandra and Madeline Price, ably assisted with the research for this book.

Junior high school was one of the more traumatic periods of my life, but one good thing that came out of it was my friendship with Amy Berger Zlotnik. When I moved back to Shaker in the summer of 2021 with a mission to read through countless boxes of documents, Amy asked if I needed any help. As it turns out, she actually meant that, and she spent weeks with me in the Shaker library, the historical society, the basement of the high school, and the Western

Reserve Historical Society, over two summers. Her work with Cleveland's adoption network, helping adoptees find their birth parents, also paid benefits for me as she helped me track down countless people whose names we came upon in documents and their children. She also is a great lunch date and a joy to be around, and I'll be forever grateful for her help. When you write your book, Amy, I'll be your first reader.

The first person I met on my first day as a professional journalist was Susan Glaser, an excellent journalist and another Shaker alum who became a lifelong friend. She helped me think through countless reporting questions and gave me invaluable feedback on the manuscript.

I'm grateful to Serena Jones at Holt, who saw potential in this project and nurtured it to fruition, and to Anita Sheih, who made many helpful suggestions and kept the train moving. And I don't know if this book would ever have gotten off the ground without the encouragement, wisdom, and support of my agent, Gail Ross. Howard Yoon and Dara Kaye at Ross Yoon also provided much good advice along the way.

A warm thank-you to Jerry Seib, who changed my life when he hired me at the *Wall Street Journal* and who is one of the finest leaders and journalists I know, and to Aaron Zitner, who supported my early reporting on Shaker at the *Journal*. A heaping bowl of thanks goes, too, to Stephen Smith, my excellent first editor at the *Washington Post*, who immediately embraced the Shaker story, shepherded it into the newspaper, and was the first person to suggest that it might be a book. My sincere thanks also to Mike Semel, Valerie Strauss, and numerous other *Post* colleagues who make it such a terrific place to work.

I am so grateful to friends who were kind enough to read portions or the entirety of this manuscript and offer constructive feedback that helped me make this book better. My thanks to Anjetta McQueen Thackery, Renee Romano, Naftali Bendavid, Jesse Holland, Mimi Laver, Joe Tone, Adam Kushner, Jonathan Ringel, and Eun Kim. My friend Catherine Pages also gave me excellent guidance. Michelle Buzgon and Barbara Kancelbaum, wonderful friends with the sharpest of eyes, were the dream team who looked at every sentence and made lots of them better. I'm also grateful for early encouragement and helpful advice from Stefan Fatsis, Michael Kranish, Amy Goldstein, and Karen Tumulty. I'm lucky to have close friends from every phase of my life, who cheered me on as I worked through this project. My love and thanks to dear friends who listened to me talk about this project on repeat, including Tanya Charlick-Paley, Donna Lawrence, Sue Peschin, Julie Becker, Alan Silverleib, Jennifer and Glenn Leon, Ani and Scott Alprin, and Diane Keaggy.

A shout-out also to my book club, still going strong more than twenty years after it was formed! Thank you for occasionally agreeing to read nonfiction.

My mother, Marsha Meckler, died while I was working on this book, but I know how proud she was of me and this endeavor. My mom lived her values every day, providing a model for me and my sister. I remember, as a kid, her telling me that she spoke in a meeting in favor of the original busing plan in Shaker, but until I did the research for this book, I didn't realize how controversial a stand that was at the time. I wish she were here to see this published.

My father, Bill Meckler, most happily, is here, and I am grateful not just for the encouragement he's given me on this project but for the love, support, humor, and cheerleading he has provided me at every single turn of my life. He's the only one I know who would have suggested, when I was applying for jobs, that I send prospective employers every single story I had ever written rather than just the best of the lot. I think he actually thought they were all fabulous. I have never doubted that my dad was in my corner, and that's a gift I don't take for granted.

My stepmother, Jeanne Van Atta—a feminist, antiracist, and health food aficionada before any of those things were cool—spent countless evenings with me as I puzzled through how to organize and structure this book, offering good advice and helping me see the path forward. If not already obvious, the dedication includes Jeanne.

I'm grateful, too, for my sister, Amy Meckler, who is an excellent poet and writer and who works tirelessly to stop the improper use of "quotation marks" and other sins of our time. She has thought deeply about issues of race, and she talked through this project with me in depth as I was shaping it. I am better for her wise counsel on this and many other topics.

As I finished this book, one of my kids asked if he was going to be thanked. Well, the answer is yes! Luke and Zander, you are super kids and I love you both buckets. Thank you for understanding when on weekends and vacations I had to spend time working on my book.

Finally, there aren't enough words of thanks for my husband, Paul Brodsky, who was my final reader and who made sure our home continued to function as I spent the vast majority of my free time on this book. You have enabled me to have both a family and a career that I love. I was late for our first date because of a late-breaking story and told you it would probably happen again. Thank you for not leaving right then and there. I love you and the life we have built together. Your support, encouragement, and valiant service in our war on clutter and chaos are treasured beyond measure.

INDEX

Page numbers in *italics* refer to the map.

PHOTOGRAPH CREDITS

1. Cleveland Public Library/Photograph Collection

2. Cleveland Public Library/Photograph Collection

3. Caydie Heller

4. Maddie McGarvey for *The Washington Post*

5. Courtesy of Hearst Magazine Media Inc. Cover photo © Bob Willoughby/ptvimages.com/Cosmopolitan

6. Maddie McGarvey for *The Washington Post*

7. Photo from the Cleveland Press Collections, courtesy of the Michael Schwartz Library Special Collections, Cleveland State University

8. Photo from the Cleveland Press Collections, courtesy of the Michael Schwartz Library Special Collections, Cleveland State University

9. Local History Collection, Shaker Heights Public Library

10. Photo from the Cleveland Press Collections, courtesy of the Michael Schwartz Library Special Collections, Cleveland State University

11. Local History Collection, Shaker Heights Public Library

12. Local History Collection, Shaker Heights Public Library

13. Maddie McGarvey for *The Washington Post*

14. Courtesy of the Richie family

15. Michael A. Hobbs/*The Plain Dealer*

16. Courtesy of Carolyn Milter

17. Maddie McGarvey for *The Washington Post*

18. Local History Collection, Shaker Heights Public Library

19. Courtesy of the Shaker Heights City School District

20a. Maddie McGarvey for *The Washington Post*

20b. Maddie McGarvey for *The Washington Post*

21. David Vahey/*The Shakerite*

22. David Vahey/*The Shakerite*

23. Maddie McGarvey for *The Washington Post*

24. David Vahey/*The Shakerite*

25. Jeanne Van Atta

26. Courtesy of the author

27. Courtesy of the author

28. Maddie McGarvey for *The Washington Post*

ABOUT THE AUTHOR

Laura Meckler is national education writer for the *Washington Post*, where she covers the news, politics, and people shaping American schools. She previously reported on the White House, presidential politics, changing American demographics, immigration, and health care for the *Wall Street Journal*, as well as on health and social policy for the Associated Press. Her honors include a Nieman Fellowship and a Livingston Award for National Reporting, and she was part of a team that won the George Polk Award for Justice Reporting. Meckler graduated from Washington University in St. Louis. She lives in Washington, D.C., with her husband and two sons.

www.laurameckler.com